INTRODUCTION TO
MODULA-2

Prentice Hall International
Series in Computer Science

C. A. R. Hoare, Series Editor

BACKHOUSE, R. C., *Program Construction and Verification*
BACKHOUSE, R. C., *Syntax of Programming Languages, Theory and Practice*
de BAKKER, J. W., *Mathematical Theory of Program Correctness*
BJÖRNER, D., and JONES, C. B., *Formal Specification and Software Developm*
BORNAT, R., *Programming from First Principles*
CLARK, K. L., and McCABE, F. G., *micro-PROLOG: Programming in Logic*
DROMEY, R. G., *How to Solve it by Computer*
DUNCAN, F., *Microprocessor Programming and Software Development*
ELDER, J., *Construction of Data Processing Software*
GOLDSCHLAGER, L., and LISTER, A., *Computer Science: A Modern Introdu*
HAYES, I. (Editor), *Specification Case Studies*
HEHNER, E. C. R., *The Logic of Programming*
HENDERSON, P., *Functional Programming: Application and Implementation*
HOARE, C. A. R., *Communicating Sequential Processes*
HOARE, C. A. R., and SHEPHERDSON, J. C. (Editors), *Mathematical Logic an*
   Programming Languages
INMOS LTD, *Occam Programming Manual*
JACKSON, M. A., *System Development*
JOHNSTON, H., *Learning to Program*
JONES, C. B., *Systematic Software Development Using VDM*
JONES, G., *Programming in Occam*
JOSEPH, M., PRASAD, V. R., and NATARAJAN, N., *A Multiprocessor Operati*
   System
LEW, A., *Computer Science: A Mathematical Introduction*
MacCALLUM, I., *Pascal for the Apple*
MacCALLUM, I., *UCSD Pascal for the IBM PC*
MARTIN, J. J., *Data Types and Data Structures*
POMBERGER, G., *Software Engineering and Modula-2*
REYNOLDS, J. C., *The Craft of Programming*
SLOMAN, M., and KRAMER, J., *Distributed Systems and Computer Networks*
TENNENT, R. D., *Principles of Programming Languages*
WELSH, J., and ELDER, J., *Introduction to Modula-2*
WELSH, J., and ELDER, J., *Introduction to Pascal, 2nd Edition*
WELSH, J., ELDER, J., and BUSTARD, D., *Sequential Program Structures*
WELSH, J., and HAY, A., *A Model Implementation of Standard Pascal*
WELSH, J., and McKEAG, M., *Structured System Programming*

INTRODUCTION TO MODULA-2

JIM WELSH

University of Queensland,
Australia

JOHN ELDER

Queen's University of Belfast,
Northern Ireland

PRENTICE HALL
New York   London   Sydney   Tokyo

Library of Congress Cataloging-in-Publication Data

Welsh, Jim, 1943—
  Introduction to Modula-2.

  (Prentice Hall International Series in Computer
Science)
  Includes index.
    1. Modula-2 (Computer program language) I. Elder,
John, 1949— . II. Title. III. Title: Introduction
to Modula-Two. IV. Series.
QA76.73.M63W45 1987   005.13'3   87-11521
ISBN 0-13-488610-0 (pbk.)

British Library Cataloguing in Publication Data

Welsh, Jim
  Introduction to Modula-2.—(Prentice
  Hall International Series in Computer
  Science).
  1. Modula-2 (Computer program language)
  I. Title   II. Elder, John, *1949-*
  005.13'3   QA76.73.M63

  ISBN 0-13-488610-0

© 1987 Prentice Hall International (UK) Ltd

Prentice Hall is an imprint of the Simon & Schuster
International Group.

Printed and bound in Great Britain for
Simon & Schuster International Group,
66 Wood Lane End, Hemel Hempstead,
Hertfordshire, HP2 4RG
by A. Wheaton and Company Limited, Exeter

2 3 4 5   91 90 89 88 87

0-13-488610-0

Contents

PREFACE, XI

CHAPTER 1   **COMPUTERS AND PROGRAMMING, 1**

- The computer, 1
- Writing a computer program, 3
- Running a computer program, 4
- Language implementations, 6
- Programming objectives, 6
  - Correctness, 6
  - Clarity, 7
  - Efficiency, 8

CHAPTER 2   **NOTATIONS AND BASIC CONCEPTS, 9**

- Which Modula-2?, 9
- Extended Backus–Naur form, 10
- The vocabulary of Modula-2, 12
- Numbers, 13
- Identifiers, 14
- Strings, 16
- Comments, 17
- Basic program structure, 18
- Exercises, 21

CHAPTER 3   **DATA TYPES AND DECLARATIONS, 22**

- Data types, 22
  - The type INTEGER, 23
  - The type CARDINAL, 25
  - The type LONGINT, 25
  - The type REAL, 26
  - The type CHAR, 27
  - The type BOOLEAN, 29
  - Enumerated types, 31

• Subrange types, 32
• Data declarations, 34
    • Constants and constant declarations, 34
    • Type declarations, 35
    • Variable declarations, 37
• Uniqueness and order of declarations, 38
• Exercises, 39

CHAPTER 4   STATEMENTS, EXPRESSIONS
                 AND ASSIGNMENTS, 41

• Statements, 41
• Expressions, 42
• The assignment statement, 46
• Exercises, 49

CHAPTER 5   INPUT AND OUTPUT OF DATA, 51

• Transferring data to and from the program, 51
• Output from Modula-2 programs, 52
• Input to Modula-2 programs, 55
• Import-lists, 58
• Case study 1, 59
• Alternative input and output streams, 63
• Exercises, 65

CHAPTER 6   BASIC CONTROL STRUCTURES, 66

• Statement sequences, 66
• Conditional statements, 68
    • The *if-statement*, 68
• Case study 2, 72
    • The *case-statement*, 74
• Case study 3, 77
• Repetitive statements, 80
    • The *while-statement*, 81
    • The *repeat-statement*, 83
    • The *for-statement*, 84
    • Nested loops, 88
• Case study 4, 89
    • The *loop-statement*, 93
• Exercises, 97

CHAPTER 7   **PROCEDURES AND FUNCTIONS, 99**

- The procedure concept, 99
  - The *return-statement*, 105
- Block structure and scope, 107
- Parameters, 112
  - Variable parameters, 114
  - Value parameters, 116
- Case study 5, 118
- Function procedures, 122
  - Side effects of functions, 126
- Case study 6, 128
- Procedures and functions as parameters, 131
- Recursion, 135
- Case study 7, 139
- Exercises, 142

CHAPTER 8   **ARRAYS, 144**

- The array concept, 144
- Two-dimensional arrays, 150
- Whole array operations, 152
- Case study 8, 154
- Strings, 159
- Case study 9, 161
- Open array parameters, 169
- Data validation, 173
- Other structured types, 177
- Exercises, 178

CHAPTER 9   **RECORDS, 179**

- The record concept, 179
  - The *with-statement*, 182
- Mixed structures, 185
- Case study 10, 186
- Variant records, 195
- Case study 11, 200
- Exercises, 207

CHAPTER 10   **SETS, 208**

- The set concept, 208
- Manipulating sets, 210
  - Construction, 210
    - Membership testing, 211
  - Set arithmetic, 213
- Case study 12, 214
- Case study 13, 221
- The type BITSET, 226
- Exercises, 227

CHAPTER 11   **POINTERS, 229**

- The pointer concept, 229
- Programming a stack, 235
- Case study 14, 237
- Non-linear structures, 250
- Exercises, 255

CHAPTER 12   **MODULES, 257**

- The module concept, 257
- Local modules, 261
  - A module for word input, 261
  - A word list module, 263
  - A list of occurrences module, 265
  - The overall modular program, 266
  - Qualified export, 268
  - Implicit import and export, 270
- Separately compiled modules, 271
  - The program module, 273
  - The definition modules, 274
  - The implementation modules, 276
  - Compiling and recompiling modules, 281
- Opaque types and interface security, 282
- Scope rules and semantics of modules, 285
- Module flexibility and utility programming, 289
  - Utility modules, 291
  - Abstract objects, 293
  - Abstract data types, 298
- Exercises, 303

CHAPTER 13 **LOW-LEVEL PROGRAMMING, 306**

- Bypassing strict type-checking, 308
- Coroutines 310,
- Case study 15, 311
- Low-level I/O facilities, 316
  - Direct I/O device control, 317
  - I/O under multi-user operating systems, 320
- Exercises, 322

CHAPTER 14 **CONCURRENT PROGRAMMING, 323**

- Concurrent processes, 323
- The module *Processes*, 325
- An implementation of *Processes*, 334

APPENDIX 1 **MODULA-2 SYNTAX DIAGRAMS, 342**

APPENDIX 2 **RESERVED WORDS AND STANDARD IDENTIFIERS, 351**

- Reserved words, 351
- Standard identifiers, 351

APPENDIX 3 **LIBRARY MODULE DEFINITIONS, 353**

- MathLib0, 353
- InOut, 354
- RealInOut, 356
- SYSTEM, 356
- Storage, 357

APPENDIX 4 **THE ASCII CHARACTER SET, 358**

APPENDIX 5 **SOLUTIONS TO SELECTED EXERCISES, 359**

INDEX, 383

Preface

The programming language Modula-2 is a worthy successor to Pascal in both the teaching and application of computer programming. Like Pascal, Modula-2 provides those fundamental programming concepts that are essential to the initial teaching of programming as a logical and systematic discipline. In addition, however, it provides for the construction of large-scale programs in a modular form, and also provides a basic capacity for system programming at the level required in imbedded control systems and similar applications. For these reasons its range of application in practical software development far exceeds that of Pascal.

This book provides a comprehensive introduction to Modula-2, and is suitable for use by novice programmers and by those with a knowledge of other programming languages. The primary purpose of the book is to present the features of Modula-2, but more general principles of programming are illustrated implicitly in the text. The style of programming used throughout is consistent with the basic programming methods of stepwise refinement and modular decomposition.

The sequence of material presented in the book is suitable for a reader learning Modula-2, or indeed learning to program, for the first time. Aspects of computers and computer organization, of which a first-time programmer must be aware, are not covered in detail, but chapter 1 presents a summary of the knowledge and terminology on which subsequent chapters depend. Chapters 2–6 then introduce the basic data types, statements, procedures and functions of Modula-2 which support the stepwise refinement of computer algorithms. In chapters 8–11 the refinement of significant data structures is introduced, using Modula-2's data-structuring facilities—arrays, records, sets and pointers. Chapter 12 then introduces modular program construction as a means of controlling program complexity, and demonstrates the potential of flexible general-purpose modules as a basis for program assembly. In Chapter 13 Modula-2's facilities for system programming are outlined, and in Chapter 14 its capacity to support concurrent programming is explored.

A full treatment of the programming topics addressed in Chapters 12—14, namely modular programming, system programming and concurrency, is clearly beyond the scope of an introductory text of this nature. The chapters in question are intended to do no more than demonstrate Modula-2's potential in these areas, and to define the language features concerned.

A distinctive feature of the book is the inclusion in each chapter of one or more complete case-study programs. In all, the book contains 15 such case studies illustrating the use of Modula-2 features and basic computing algorithms in an appropriate practical context. For each case study the design of the program is derived by tracing its stepwise refinement, and a final version of the program is shown together with samples of the results it produces.

Most chapters end with a set of programming exercises which involve further use of the language features described in the chapter. These exercises require modifications or extensions to be made to earlier case-study programs as well as the construction of new programs. Solutions to a selection of these exercises are given as Appendix 5.

The book is also suitable for use in reference mode. To facilitate its use the book includes a number of appendices and a comprehensive index. The appendices include syntax diagrams of Modula-2 which provide a concise summary of the language features, lists of reserved words and standard identifiers, and definitions of a set of library modules made available by many implementations of Modula-2. The index lists all formal and informal terms used in the text showing the defining occurrence of each, together with other occurrences which may help to clarify its significance.

We wish to thank Professor Niklaus Wirth for providing us with yet another excellent programming language, Professor Tony Hoare for encouraging us to write about it, and all those who read drafts of the manuscript, pointed out our mistakes and made constructive suggestions. The discrepancies that remain are entirely our responsibility. The final camera-ready copy for the book's production was prepared using facilities in the Department of Computer Science at the University of Queensland, for which we are also grateful.

Jim Welsh and John Elder

1

Computers and Programming

Computer programming requires an understanding of the nature of computers, of computer programs and of the programming languages in which programs may be expressed. Subsequent chapters of this book explain how computer programs may be written in the programming language Modula-2. This first chapter summarizes the general concepts of computers and their programming on which the subsequent chapters depend.

For those readers who have already programmed computers in other languages the chapter may provide a summary of the terminology, and perhaps a hint of the programming philosophy, used in the following chapters.

For those learning to program for the first time this chapter provides a very brief summary of the facts and concepts which they must come to appreciate while programming in Modula-2 or any other language. A course instructor may provide a more detailed treatment of these topics before or during study of the material covered in the following chapters.

THE COMPUTER

A *computer* is a machine which can carry out long, complex and repetitive sequences of operations at very high speed. These operations are applied to *information* or *data* supplied by the user to produce further information or *results* which the user requires. The sequence of operations required to produce the desired results in any particular computing task is specified as a *computer program* prepared for that task.

The essential components of a computer are a *processor*, a *memory* and some *input and output devices*.

The *processor* is the work horse which carries out the sequence of operations specified by the program. The individual operations provided by the processor are very simple but are carried out at very high speed—perhaps one million or more operations per second.

The *memory* is used to store the information to which the processor's operations are applied. Memory is of two kinds—*primary* or *main store*, and *secondary* or *backing store.* The main store enables the processor to fetch and store units of information at a speed which is comparable to its speed of operation, in fact each operation normally involves at least one store access. To enable the processor to proceed from one operation to the next without delay the sequence of program instructions which specifies these operations is also held in the main store. The main store thus holds both *instructions* and *data,* on which the processor operates. The logical organization of a computer is shown in Figure 1.1.

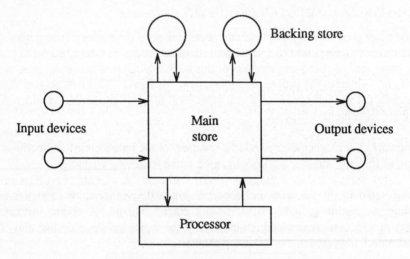

Figure 1.1 Organization of a computer

The amount of main store available to the processor is limited, and is used to hold only the programs and data on which the processor is operating at that time. It is not used for any permanent storage of data. In some cases the main store may not even be large enough to hold all the instructions or data involved in the execution of one program. For these reasons computers are also equipped with secondary storage devices such as magnetic disks or tapes. The essential characteristics of these devices are:

(a) their capacity is normally much greater than that of the main store;
(b) information can be held by them permanently, e.g., from one program execution to another.

However, the speed at which information can be transferred to and from secondary storage is much lower than for main store.

The information held in this backing store is usually organized in units known as *files,* and for this reason the backing store is often referred to as the *file store.*

Input and output devices are used to transfer information from the outside world to the computer's main store *(input)* and from the main store to the outside world *(output)*. Familiar input devices are terminal keyboards, which transfer the characters indicated by key depressions into the computer store. Familiar output devices are printers or typewriters which print information on paper, and visual displays which display textual or graphic information on the screen of a cathode ray tube.

WRITING A COMPUTER PROGRAM

The use of a computer for a particular task involves three essential steps:

(a) specifying the task the computer is to carry out, in terms of the input data to be supplied and the output data or results to be produced;

(b) devising an *algorithm* or sequence of steps, by which the computer can produce the required output from the available input;

(c) expressing this algorithm as a computer program in a programming language such as Modula-2.

Step (a), the specification, is not normally considered as part of the programming process but a precise specification is an essential prerequisite for a successful program.

It has been common practice in the past to separate steps (b) and (c), first defining the algorithm in a notation convenient for its design, and then translating or encoding this design into the chosen programming language. However, the language Modula-2 provides a notation which may be used both for the design and for the final coding of the program required. With Modula-2, therefore, steps (b) and (c) are not usually separated, but are merged as a continuous design/programming process. This approach is well illustrated by the case-study programs considered in the following chapters of this book.

In principle, once the computer program has been written, the programmer's task is complete, since execution of this program by the computer should produce the required results. In practice, because the task to be carried out by the computer is complex, and the human programmer's ability is limited, the first program written may not produce the required results. The programmer, therefore, engages in a cycle of checking and correcting the program until he or she is satisfied that it meets its specification completely. This process of detecting and correcting errors in a program is known as *debugging*. Debugging is commonly accomplished by running the program on a computer with suitable test data.

RUNNING A COMPUTER PROGRAM

In a "high-level" language such as Modula-2 the program is expressed as a sequence of elementary steps which are convenient to the programmer. Likewise the program is prepared in a form which is convenient for the programmer to generate—as a piece of text written or printed on paper, or typed at a computer-terminal keyboard. This preparation of the program text is usually accomplished using an *editor* program, which enables the user to input and alter the program text in a convenient manner. In some cases the editor may be designed specifically for input of programs in a particular programming language—a so-called *language-based* or *language-oriented* editor. More commonly it is a general-purpose text editor which can be used for the preparation of any information in textual form—programs, data, or other documents.

The textual form of the program is convenient for the programmer to read and understand. However, the program which the computer's processor executes must be expressed as a sequence of the much simpler "low-level" operations available to the processor, and must be held in the computer store as a sequence of encoded instructions each of which is immediately executable by the processor. Preparation of a program in this form would be an extremely tedious and painstaking task for a human programmer.

Fortunately, however, the translation of a program text expressed in a high-level language into an equivalent sequence of processor-executable instructions within the computer store is itself a routine task which can be carried out by a computer program. Such a program is provided for each high-level language which may be used on a computer, and is known as the *compiler* for that language.

Thus a program written in a high-level language in text form is first input to the computer's file-store via an editor program. When the programmer believes it is complete, it is then compiled using the compiler program for the language concerned. The compiler produces an equivalent executable program, which may then be executed or *run* to produce the desired effect. Figure 1.2 shows this three-stage process in schematic form.

When the executable program is running, the data which it is required to process may be supplied by the user of the program through a terminal keyboard (*interactive* or *on-line* input) or may be obtained from a data file held in the computer's file-store (*off-line* input). Likewise, the results of the program execution may be output directly to the screen or typewriter of the user's terminal or to a line printer, or else to a file-store file (possibly for subsequent input to another program).

In translating a high-level language program the compiler may detect many of the simple mistakes which the programmer has made in expressing the program in that language. The compiler reports these errors to the programmer by outputting some form of *error listing*. This may consist of some or all of the

Stage 1: Editing

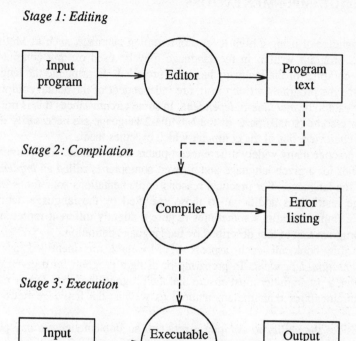

Figure 1.2 Stages in running a program

program text with interleaved messages identifying any errors detected, or simply a list of error messages to be read in conjunction with the original program text. Program errors detected in this way are known as *compile-time errors*.

In running the executable program produced by the compiler, further situations, which are not permitted by the language rules, may be detected—such errors are known as *run-time errors* or *exceptions*.

A program which produces no compile-time errors during its compilation, and no exceptions during its execution, may still not produce the correct results, due to some flaw in the chosen algorithm or its expression in the program. Such errors are known as *logical errors*.

Debugging therefore requires the elimination of all compile-time, run-time and logical errors from the program. To do so the programmer must have an understanding of the language, and of the *implementation* which he or she is using.

LANGUAGE IMPLEMENTATIONS

One advantage of using a high-level programming language, such as Modula-2, is that a program written in the language may be used on any computer for which a compiler of the language has been provided. In principle the language, and hence the programs written in it, are independent of the actual computer—they are said to be *machine-independent*. In some circumstances this is not quite true, since some (small) parts of the Modula-2 language are necessarily dependent on characteristics of the computer which executes them.

In practice many widely different computers are available. The provision of a compiler for a given language and a given computer is called an *implementation* of the language. For practical reasons implementations sometimes impose language restrictions additional to those specified by the language definition. Likewise implementations sometimes require a slightly different representation of the program text to that described by the language definition.

In this book all such aspects of Modula-2 are identified as being *implementation-dependent*. In preparing or using a program for a given implementation, a programmer must ensure that the program conforms to any particular requirements of that implementation, as well as the language rules themselves.

Besides the ability to compile a program an implementation may provide other aids to the programmer. For example, the detection of a run-time or logical error does not necessarily identify its cause. Implementations may provide specific *debugging aids* to help the programmer in doing so. As such features are wholly dependent on the implementation, they are not discussed in this book, but again a programmer should establish what additional features the available implementation provides.

PROGRAMMING OBJECTIVES

In preparing a program a programmer may have to choose between alternative solutions at many points. Each choice must be made to meet the objectives and constraints of the particular programming task. In this book the following are assumed to be objectives appropriate to every programming task.

Correctness

An obvious objective in writing any computer program is that it should meet its specification exactly. All too often, however, because of the complexity of the program's task, and inadequate understanding or care on the part of the programmer, a program fails to meet some part of its specification. A programmer must be mindful at all times of the correctness or adequacy of the program for its specified purpose.

A key factor in achieving correctness is *simplicity*. By choosing the simplest algorithm or technique available a programmer is more likely to see whether or not it meets the requirements of the program specification, and is less likely to describe it incorrectly in the program. Unnecessary complexity serves no purpose in computer programming.

Some programs are, of course, inherently complex. For such programs the programmer must adopt a systematic approach which controls and limits the complexity dealt with at each stage. Such an approach is illustrated by the case-study programs in this book.

Clarity

A program is necessarily as complex as the algorithm which it describes. However, it is important that the way in which the algorithm is described by the program text be no more complicated than is necessary. Program clarity is an important aid to the programmer himself, in the design and debugging of the program; and to others who may have to read and amend the program at some later stage.

Program clarity is achieved in much the same way as for any written text, such as an essay or a book. It requires

(a) a logical separation of the text into meaningful parts (chapters, sections, etc.) which reflect the distinction between the subjects they describe, and their presentation in a logical sequence which reflects the relationships between them;

(b) a careful choice of the language features used within each part to express its intended meaning as precisely as possible;

(c) a further careful choice of the words used to denote the objects and concepts involved;

(d) the inclusion of additional comments and preambles to clarify the main text when necessary;

(e) an exploitation of text-layout devices, such as blank lines and indentation, to emphasize the relationship between the text's component parts.

A programmer should be as assiduous in the use of these techniques for achieving clarity as the author of any text. In many cases the usefulness of a program is as much determined by the clarity of its text, as by the qualities of the algorithm which it describes.

Efficiency

The cost of executing a computer program is normally measured in terms of

(a) the *time* taken by the computer to carry out the sequence of operations involved;

(b) the amount of computer *store* used in doing so.

For some programs, or parts of programs, the efficient use of time or storage may be critical, for others less so. Clearly the programmer must be aware of any such efficiency requirements when writing the program. Even where specific requirements are not defined, due consideration of efficiency issues is still good programming practice. In many environments the program will compete with other programs for the use of these computer resources, and it is therefore prudent to minimize the program's requirements of each.

The time taken to execute the program is directly proportional to the number of operations which the processor has to carry out in doing so. The programmer should therefore choose an algorithm which minimizes the operations involved, and take care to avoid any redundant operations in expressing the algorithm as a computer program.

The store used by the program during its execution is determined by the amount of data which must be held and by the number of processor operations required to define the program, since these too must be held in store. To minimize the storage used by a program the programmer must therefore consider both the data manipulated, and the number of operations specified by the program.

2

Notations and Basic Concepts

WHICH MODULA-2?

The main purpose of this chapter is to introduce the basic concepts and notations which are used in describing Modula-2 in subsequent chapters. Before doing so, however, it is appropriate to say a few words about the precise version of Modula-2 which the book describes.

At the time of writing this book, the universally accepted definition of Modula-2 is that given by its designer, Professor Niklaus Wirth, in his book *Programming in Modula-2*. In practice, three editions of the book have been published, and there are minor differences between the definition of some language features in these editions. The changes made reflect refinements of the language itself which Professor Wirth recognized as desirable. Unfortunately, this has led to the existence of implementations of Modula-2, some of which conform to the definition given in one edition and some to another.

For this and other reasons, the British Standards Institute (BSI) established a working party in 1985, to draft a potential standard definition of Modula-2 and submit it to the International Standards Organization (ISO) for ratification. The BSI working party hoped to complete its draft by the end of 1986, but given the technical, administrative and political procedures involved in achieving international ratification thereafter, it is likely to be some time before a ratified standard exists, and implementations conforming to it are widely available.

The variations between successive editions of Professor Wirth's definition and the draft standard likely to be produced by the BSI working party are not major, and have limited significance for someone learning or using Modula-2 on any given implementation. By default the language we describe in this text is that defined in the third edition of Professor Wirth's book. However, in describing its individual features, we will try to note each point at which significant variations may be encountered.

EXTENDED BACKUS–NAUR FORM

A computer program is first constructed as a sequence of symbols or characters which form the program "text". The following is a simple program written in the programming language Modula-2.

```
MODULE AddTwoNumbers;
  FROM InOut IMPORT ReadInt, WriteInt, WriteString, WriteLn;
  VAR First, Second, Sum: INTEGER;
  BEGIN
    WriteString("First Number  = "); ReadInt(First); WriteLn;
    WriteString("Second Number = "); ReadInt(Second); WriteLn;
    Sum := First + Second;
    WriteString("Sum = "); WriteInt(Sum, 6); WriteLn
  END AddTwoNumbers.
```

As with natural languages, every programming language has a strictly defined set of rules associated with it which describes how a valid program may be constructed in the language. These rules are necessary firstly so that the programmer may be sure of the correctness and effect of the program he writes and, secondly, so that his program may be understood both by the computer system and anyone who reads the program.

The language rules are made up of two parts, known as the *syntax* and *semantics* of the language. The syntax rules define how the words (or *vocabulary*) of the language may be put together to form "sentences". The semantic rules ascribe meaning and significance to these combinations of words. These semantic rules are usually stated less formally than the syntax rules which, for the language Modula-2, may be described by means of a formalism known as *Extended Backus–Naur Form*, or simply *EBNF*.

For example, the form of a Modula-2 program is defined by the following EBNF rule

program = program-heading block identifier ".".

This rule is read as "A *program* is defined as a *program-heading* followed by a *block* followed by an *identifier* followed by a period ".""". Further EBNF rules then define the allowable forms for a *program-heading*, a *block* and an *identifier*. In the example program given above, the first two lines of symbols form the *program-heading*. The following symbols from VAR to END form a *block*. AddTwoNumbers is an acceptable *identifier*. In an EBNF rule the appearance of a language symbol within quote marks, e.g., ".", denotes the symbol itself. Each rule is terminated by a period.

Sometimes a syntactic category may have several alternative forms. For example, the rule

$$digit = "0" \mid "1" \mid "2" \mid "3" \mid "4" \mid "5" \mid "6" \mid "7" \mid "8" \mid "9".$$

defines a *digit* in Modula-2 as one of the ten characters 0, 1, ..., 9 by means of a list of alternatives. The above rule is read as "A *digit* is defined as either a "0" or a "1" or a "2" or ...".

Enclosure of a syntax construct by the brackets { } is used to denote repetition of the enclosed construct zero or more times. For example, the rule

$$unsigned\text{-}digit\text{-}sequence = digit\ \{digit\}.$$

defines an *unsigned-digit-sequence* as a sequence of one or more of the digits defined above. Thus the following are examples of unsigned-digit-sequences:

1   27   97300

Enclosure of a syntax construct by the brackets [ ] denotes that the enclosed construct is optional, e.g., the rules

$$digit\text{-}sequence = [sign]\ unsigned\text{-}digit\text{-}sequence.$$
$$sign = "+" \mid "-".$$

define a *digit-sequence* as an *unsigned-digit-sequence* preceded, optionally, by either a "+" or "−" symbol.

Parentheses ( ) may be used, where necessary, to group syntactic categories together, e.g., the rules for *digit-sequence* above may be re-expressed as

$$digit\text{-}sequence = signed\text{-}digit\text{-}sequence \mid unsigned\text{-}digit\text{-}sequence.$$
$$signed\text{-}digit\text{-}sequence = ("+" \mid "-")\ unsigned\text{-}digit\text{-}sequence.$$

In general the syntactic categories defined by EBNF rules are denoted by single (possibly hyphenated) words giving suitable English descriptions.

Throughout this book we shall introduce, along with new features of the language, their EBNF definitions. These define concisely the full range of constructions for each syntactic category. Some constructions may include other syntactic categories not yet fully defined at the point of introduction. A student learning the language may ignore these undefined categories at that point as they will be dealt with in due course. The index of syntax definitions given at the end of the book enables the definition and explanation of all syntactic categories to be located.

The syntax of Modula-2 is sometimes defined by means of *syntax diagrams*. These give a concise graphic specification of the sequences of symbols allowed in each of the major constructs of Modula-2 and are useful to those familiar with the language for checking the validity or allowable form of particular constructs. Appendix 1 summarizes the syntax of Modula-2 in this form.

THE VOCABULARY OF MODULA-2

Every language, whether it is a spoken language or a computer programming
language, makes use of a *vocabulary*. English, for instance, in its written form,
consists of words, numbers, and punctuation symbols. The vocabulary of the
programming language Modula-2 consists of letters, digits and special symbols.
Sentences of the language are then constructed out of this vocabulary according
to the syntax of Modula-2.

According to the definition of Modula-2, a letter may be any of the 26
letters in the Roman alphabet in either upper-case or lower-case form, i.e., there
are 52 alternatives in the syntactic category *letter:*

> *letter =*
>   *"A" | "B" | "C" | "D" | "E" | "F" | "G" | "H" | "I" | "J" | "K" | "L" | "M" |*
>   *"N" | "O" | "P" | "Q" | "R" | "S" | "T" | "U" | "V" | "W" | "X" | "Y" | "Z" |*
>   *"a" | "b" | "c" | "d" | "e" | "f" | "g" | "h" | "i" | "j" | "k" | "l" | "m" |*
>   *"n" | "o" | "p" | "q" | "r" | "s" | "t" | "u" | "v" | "w" | "x" | "y" | "z".*

A *digit* in Modula-2 is any one of the ten Arabic digits, i.e.,

> *digit = "0" | "1" | "2" | "3" | "4" | "5" | "6" | "7" | "8" | "9".*

Note that the letter "O" and the digit "0" are two quite distinct characters.

The number of special symbols required by Modula-2 for punctuation and
various other purposes is quite high. Many of these special symbols are
represented as words rather than special characters, thus:

> *special-symbol =*
>   *"+" | "−" | "*" | "/" | "=" | "#" | "<>" | "<" | "<=" |*
>   *">" | ">=" | "&" | "~" | "(" | ")" | "[" | "]" | "{" | "}" |*
>   *":=" | "." | "," | ":" | ";" | "|" | ".." | "^" | "(*" | "*)" |*
>   *"AND" | "ARRAY" | "BEGIN" | "BY" | "CASE" | "CONST" |*
>   *"DEFINITION" | "DIV" | "DO" | "ELSE" | "ELSIF" |*
>   *"END" | "EXIT" | "EXPORT" | "FOR" | "FROM" | "IF" |*
>   *"IMPLEMENTATION" | "IMPORT" | "IN" | "LOOP" |*
>   *"MOD" | "MODULE" | "NOT" | "OF" | "OR" | "POINTER" |*
>   *"PROCEDURE" | "QUALIFIED" | "RECORD" | "REPEAT" |*
>   *"RETURN" | "SET" | "THEN" | "TO" | "TYPE" | "UNTIL" |*
>   *"VAR" | "WHILE" | "WITH".*

The definition of Modula-2 states that the words used to represent special symbols are reserved words which may not be used for any other purpose, and can
thus be written without underlining or any other distinguishing marks. Note,
however, that these reserved words must be written in upper case; an equivalent
sequence of letters, some of which are lower case, is an *identifier* by the rules
given in a later section.

NUMBERS

Numbers in Modula-2 may be represented in either of two forms—integers or real numbers.

number = integer-number / real-number.

An *integer-number* is a whole number which may be positive or zero. The number is written as a sequence of digits of any length.

In everyday life we denote whole numbers as decimal numbers, i.e., to base 10, but in computing it is sometimes convenient to denote them as *octal numbers*, i.e., to base 8, or as *hexadecimal numbers*, i.e., to base 16. Modula-2 permits all three notations. If an integer-number has a letter B at its end it is taken as being an octal number, if it has an H at the end it is taken to be a hexadecimal number, otherwise it is a decimal number. Hence the complete EBNF definition of an *integer-number* is

> *integer-number =*
> *decimal-digit {decimal-digit} /*
> *octal-digit {octal-digit} "B" /*
> *decimal-digit {hexadecimal-digit} "H".*
> *octal-digit = "0" / "1" / "2" / "3" / "4" / "5" / "6" / "7".*
> *decimal-digit = octal-digit / "8" / "9".*
> *hexadecimal-digit = decimal-digit / "A" / "B" / "C" / "D" / "E" / "F".*

Examples of valid integer numbers:

> 6
> 0
> 7000000
> 123B   (i.e., decimal 83)
> 7BH   (i.e., decimal 123)
> 0AAH   (i.e., decimal 170)

Note that to avoid confusion with identifiers, which are described later, a hexadecimal number must begin with a decimal digit (possibly 0).

The following are invalid integer numbers for the reasons specified:

> 6,437,271   (an integer must not contain commas)
> 6.0   (an integer must not contain a decimal point)
> 79B   (9 is not an octal digit)
> FFH   (an integer must begin with a digit)

Although the above definition allows integers of any size, in practice each implementation of Modula-2 will define a limited range of integers that it permits. This is necessary because the maximum number of digits that can be used in an integer depends on the size of the memory location in the computer that will store the integer. For instance, in many 16-bit microcomputer implementations of Modula-2 the largest integer number permitted is 65535 (2 to the power 16, minus 1).

Numbers outside the permitted range of integers, or numbers with fractional parts, may be represented as *real* numbers. A real number can be written in two different forms. In the first form the number is written with a decimal point which, however, must be preceded by at least one digit.

Examples of valid real numbers:

$$0.0 \quad 0.873 \quad 73.36789$$

The following are invalid real numbers for the reasons indicated:

.736   (no digit before the decimal point)
2,736.45   (comma not allowed)

In the second form of representation the real number is expressed as a decimal number multiplied by an integral power of 10 (this is known as the *scientific* or *exponential* form). The decimal number is followed immediately by the letter E (in upper case, meaning "ten to the power of") and a decimal integer number (known as the *exponent* or *scale-factor*).

Examples of valid real numbers:

$$0.0E0 \quad 8.73E+02 \quad 741.0E{-}1 \quad 0.7336789E2$$

The following are all acceptable ways of writing the real number 253.0:

$$253. \quad 253.0 \quad 2.53E2 \quad 25.3E+01 \quad 253.0E0 \quad 2530.0E{-}1$$

The syntactic definition of a real number is thus:

real-number = digit-sequence "." [digit-sequence] [scale-factor].
scale-factor = "E" ["+" | "−"] digit-sequence.
digit-sequence = decimal-digit {decimal-digit}.

The range of real numbers permitted by implementations is also restricted, but is usually very much greater than that of integers. However, the representation of real numbers on a computer is only an approximation whereas integers are represented exactly. Thus, whenever possible, a number should be represented as an integer to gain maximum accuracy in operations involving the number. A fuller discussion of real numbers follows in Chapter 3.

IDENTIFIERS

Modula-2 requires that various quantities used in a program, such as data items and pieces of program text, be given names by which they can be identified. These names are known as *identifiers*, and are created by the programmer.

Modula-2 provides a large degree of flexibility in the choice of identifiers by the programmer. An identifier consists of a letter followed by any number of letters and digits, i.e.,

$$identifier = letter \; \{letter \mid digit\}.$$

Thus, in theory, an identifier may be of any length (and we shall encourage the use of meaningful and hence, possibly, long identifiers) but, in practice, some implementations of Modula-2 impose a restriction on the length of each line of program text, and hence on the length of identifiers.

Examples of valid identifiers:

    i   Modula2   AVeryLongNameIndeed   Australia   UFO

The following are illegal identifiers for the reasons indicated:

3abc	(an identifier must begin with a letter)
Modula-2	(an identifier must not contain a hyphen)
$100	(an identifier must begin with a letter)

Note that Modula-2 identifiers may contain both upper-case and lower-case letters, and that upper-case and lower-case letters are considered distinct. Hence the following identifiers are considered distinct:

    somename   SOMENAME   SomeName

However, the practice of using identifiers which differ only in the case of some of their letters should be avoided, as it detracts from the clarity of the program for a human reader.

Note also that some of the *special symbols* of Modula-2 are upper-case reserved words which cannot be used for other purposes. Thus words such as ARRAY and BEGIN cannot be used as identifiers.

Although the programmer has an otherwise unlimited choice of possible identifier names at his disposal, it is accepted practice to choose identifiers whose meaning in the program is suggested by their names. If a program makes use of values describing temperatures and pressures then it is much more meaningful to the reader of the program if these values are represented by identifiers such as Temperature and Pressure, rather than the shorter, but less obvious, T and P.

Some implementations of Modula-2 permit the use of the underscore character within identifiers, which enables the structure of a multiword identifier to be made explicit, thus: Some_Name. It is possible that this facility will be included in the BSI draft standard definition of Modula-2.

However meaningfully its name has been chosen, an identifier does not by itself determine the quantity which it identifies, as far as the language rules are concerned. This information must be given in the form of a *declaration*. The allowable forms of identifier declaration will be explained as we describe the various quantities which an identifier may denote in Modula-2.

Certain upper-case identifiers, known as *standard identifiers*, are predeclared in every implementation of Modula-2. These describe standard quantities and facilities provided by the language such as data types and functions. Table 2.1 gives a full list of standard identifiers, as defined by the third edition of *Programming in Modula-2*. The variations from this list which occur in earlier editions are summarized in Appendix 2.

ABS	FLOAT	NIL
BITSET	HALT	ODD
BOOLEAN	HIGH	ORD
CAP	INC	PROC
CARDINAL	INCL	REAL
CHAR	INTEGER	SIZE
CHR	LONGINT	TRUE
DEC	LONGREAL	TRUNC
EXCL	MAX	VAL
FALSE	MIN	

Table 2.1   Standard identifiers

In contrast with the reserved words which may not be used at all as identifiers, the programmer may re-use any of the standard identifiers to denote a quantity which is introduced within the program. However, doing so removes the capability to use the standard Modula-2 facility named by that identifier, and creates a potential confusion for any subsequent reader of the program. The practice is not recommended.

We shall see later that in Modula-2 an identifier sometimes has to be *qualified* by another identifier, e.g., an identifier I may be prefixed with another identifier J and a period, viz., J.I. This composite identifier is called a *qualified-identifier*.

$$qualified\text{-}identifier = \{identifier \; "."\} \; identifier.$$

However, for the present, we shall encounter only identifiers which are unqualified in the programs that we consider.

STRINGS

A sequence of characters enclosed by quotes forms what is known as a *string*. It is used within a program to denote the sequence of characters themselves. However, if the string of characters is to include a quote then the string should be enclosed instead in apostrophes (in which case the string must not contain any apostrophes). Thus the syntactic definition of a *string* is

> *string =*
> *""" {any-string-character-except-quote} """ /*
> *"" " {any-string-character-except-apostrophe} "" ".*

Some examples of strings are

> "This is an example of a string"
> "?"
>
> "His name is O'Brien"
> 'He said "May I?" and came in'
> ""

The last example is a string of length zero, known as an *empty* string.

In principle, the set of characters which can be manipulated on an implementation of Modula-2 is implementation-dependent, though almost all implementations support the American Standard character set (ASCII). Such character sets include some so-called *control characters*, which cannot be printed but which are used to convey control information from and to input and output devices. For most implementations the term *string-character* as used above excludes control characters, i.e., such characters cannot be represented within strings.

In Modula-2 programs which manipulate character data, strings of length one, such as "?" above, are used to denote particular character values. To allow control characters to be denoted, an alternative notation is also provided in which the character is denoted by its octal-numeric representation followed by the upper-case letter C:

> *octal-char = octal-digit {octal-digit} "C".*

For example, in the ASCII character set the printer form-feed control character has numeric representation 14B, and thus may be denoted in a Modula-2 program by the octal-char notation 14C.

It is possible that this octal-char notation will be eliminated from the BSI's draft standard definition of Modula-2, since a proposed relaxation of the rules for *constant-expressions* (discussed in Chapter 4) will provide an equivalent effect.

COMMENTS

A Modula-2 program is expressed as a sequence of identifiers, numbers, strings and special symbols, as described in the preceding sections. In preparing a program text the programmer has considerable freedom in how these identifiers, numbers and symbols are positioned within and across lines of text.

In general an arbitrary number of blank characters or tabs or ends of line may occur between the identifiers, numbers, and symbols. However, blanks, tabs or ends of line may not occur within any identifier, number or special symbol, and at least one blank, tab or end of line must occur between those identifiers, numbers and reserved word symbols which would otherwise be indistinguishable.

We shall attempt to show in the program examples in this book that a considered layout of the program text and a careful choice of identifiers help to make a Modula-2 program largely self-explanatory. However, it is still necessary or desirable that the programmer should provide additional explanatory text, or *commentary*, to explain some of the actions carried out within his program to a subsequent reader.

In Modula-2 any sequence of characters enclosed by the double character symbols (* and *) form what is known as a *comment*. Comments may appear anywhere that a blank or end of line may appear, but have absolutely no significance as far as the execution of the program is concerned. They serve solely as a means whereby the programmer can make the meaning of his program clearer by the inclusion of explanatory remarks in natural language.

Example:

(* This is a comment written in ordinary English *)

There is no limit on the length of a comment—it may range from a few characters to many hundreds of lines of the program text.

Comments may be *nested,* i.e., a comment may contain another comment within it, as in the following example:

(* This is a comment (* with another comment inside *) *)

A comment is therefore defined as a sequence which extends from an initial (* to the first *) such that an equal number of (* and *) are included in the sequence.

BASIC PROGRAM STRUCTURE

The special symbols, reserved words, identifiers, numbers, strings and comments described in preceding sections are the building blocks out of which all Modula-2 programs are composed. To define the context in which they are used, and to provide a framework for the various aspects of Modula-2 described in subsequent chapters, we finish this chapter with a brief look at the overall structure of Modula-2 programs.

In Modula-2 an executable program is formally defined as a *program-module,* as follows:

program-module = program-heading block identifier ".".
program-heading = "MODULE" identifier [priority] ";" {import-list ";"}.
import-list = ["FROM" identifier] "IMPORT" identifier-list.
identifier-list = identifier {"," identifier}.

That is, a *program* consists of a *program-heading* followed by a *block* followed by an *identifier* and terminated by a period.

A computer program must describe the nature of the *data* to be manipulated, and the *actions* to be performed upon those data. These two aspects of a program are reflected in the syntax of a *block,* which is defined as follows:

block = declaration-part statement-part "END".
declaration-part = {declaration} .
declaration =
  constant-declaration-part |
  type-declaration-part |
  variable-declaration-part |
  procedure-declaration ";" |
  module-declaration ";".
statement-part = ["BEGIN" statement-sequence].

Thus, a *block* consists of a *declaration-part* followed by a *statement-part* followed by END. In its simplest form, the *declaration-part* defines the data-items on which the *block* operates, while the *statement-part* defines the actions to be carried out on these items.

To illustrate the role played by these component parts of a program-module, together with the concepts and notations introduced in preceding sections, consider a slightly augmented version of the program text given at the start of this chapter, with line numbers appended for ease of reference:

```
MODULE AddTwoNumbers;                                              (1)
   FROM InOut IMPORT ReadInt, WriteInt, WriteString, WriteLn;      (2)
                                                                   (3)
   (* a trivial example of program structure *)                   (4)
                                                                   (5)
   VAR First, Second, Sum: INTEGER;                                (6)
                                                                   (7)
BEGIN                                                              (8)
   WriteString("First Number  = "); ReadInt(First); WriteLn;       (9)
   WriteString("Second Number = "); ReadInt(Second); WriteLn;     (10)
   Sum := First + Second;                                         (11)
   WriteString("Sum = "); WriteInt(Sum, 6); WriteLn              (12)
END AddTwoNumbers.                                                (13)
```

The program is composed of

six *reserved-words:*	MODULE FROM IMPORT VAR BEGIN END
seven *special-symbols:*	; , : ( ) := .
ten *identifiers:*	AddTwoNumbers InOut ReadInt WriteInt WriteString WriteLn First Second Sum INTEGER
three *strings:*	"First Number = " "Second Number = " "Sum = "
one *integer-number:*	6
one *comment:*	(* a trivial example of program structure *)

The program conforms to the syntax rules given in this section as follows. The symbols on lines 1 and 2 form the *program-heading,* with those on line 2 forming an *import-list.* The symbols from the start of line 6 to the END on line 13 form a *block,* in which those on line 6 form the *declaration-part,* and those on lines 8 to 12 form the *statement-part.*

Note that the comment on line 4, and the blank lines 3, 5, and 7, play no part in the syntactic structure of the program. Syntactically, this version of the program is identical to that given at the start of the chapter.

Finally, as an introduction to the contents of subsequent chapters, we outline the *meaning* of the program illustrated here, whose overall purpose is to read in two numbers input by a terminal user and print out their sum.

The first line of the program-heading gives this particular *program-module* the name AddTwoNumbers. This name might be used to refer to the program in general, and to request its execution when required, though the way in which execution of Modula-2 programs is activated is *implementation-defined,* and not part of the language itself. Note that the final period of the program text is preceded by the same identifier, a convention which is also imposed elsewhere in Modula-2.

To achieve its purpose the program needs to read in values from the user and to transmit results back to the user. To this end the import-list on line 2 indicates that this program-module uses operations ReadInt, WriteInt, WriteString and WriteLn, which are defined by another (server) module called InOut. The range and use of operations defined by InOut is explained in Chapter 5, with general consideration of the definition and use of server modules being given in Chapter 12.

The declaration-part on line 6 names the three data items used in the program and states that they will be whole numbers. Simple data declarations of this sort are discussed in Chapter 3, with more advanced data declarations being considered in Chapters 8 to 11.

The overall action to be carried out by the program is defined by the statement-part, which in this case comprises a sequence of ten component actions defined on lines 9 to 12. Firstly two whole numbers are prompted for by suitable messages, and their values are read in and recorded as the data items First and Second. These two values are then added and their sum recorded as the data item Sum. Finally, the sum is written out, preceded by a suitable message. The range of *statements* used to express these simple actions is discussed in Chapters 4 and 5, with more elaborate statement forms being introduced in Chapters 6 and 7.

EXERCISES

2.1 Consider the following numbers:

127	3,475	7.4	.1475	6000
6E3	275.0	0.001	27365982	0
10E–4	0.074E3	0.1E999	275.	0.0620

Which are valid integer numbers in Modula-2?
Which are valid real numbers in Modula-2?
Which denote the same values in Modula-2?
Which of those valid in Modula-2 are also acceptable on the implementation to which you have access?

2.2 Write down the decimal integers 9 to 19 in the alternative octal and hexadecimal forms permitted in Modula-2.

2.3 Which of the following are valid identifiers in Modula-2?

H2SO4	X–RAY	alphabetic	ALPHABETIC
ALPHA	McDougall	BEGIN	ALPHABETICAL
omega	X99999	trunc	NEW

2.4 Which of the following lines are valid strings in Modula-2?

"JACK SPRATT"
"six + one = ninety seven"
"SPRATT'S WIFE"
'HIS WIFE'S DOG'
"″″″″″″

2.5 The following is a valid sequence of Modula-2 symbols:

```
IF P^ # X THEN Get(P)
ELSE P^ := P^ + 1 ; Y := ~Y & Z
END
```

Can it be written in this form on your implementation?
If not, what changes are necessary?

3

Data Types and Declarations

DATA TYPES

A computer program manipulates information, or *data*, to obtain some desired effect or result. The data operated upon by a program are ultimately represented as a sequence of electrical signals within the hardware of the computer. However, high-level programming languages such as Modula-2 enable the programmer to ignore the actual machine representation and express the nature of data in terms of *data types*.

A data type defines a set of values. Modula-2, in common with most other high-level languages, requires that every data item in a program must have a *type* associated with it, based on the following assumptions:

(a) the type of a data item determines the *range of values* which it may take, and the *range of operations* which may be applied to it;
(b) each data item has a single type;
(c) the type of a data item in a program can be deduced solely from its form or context, without any knowledge of the particular values which it may take during execution of the program;
(d) each *operator* in the language requires *operands* of specified types and produces a result of specified type.

The significance and effect of these rules will be described and illustrated throughout the next two chapters.

By providing a range of readily available types, together with appropriate operators, the language enables the programmer to describe the manipulation of his data in terms natural to the data, rather than the underlying machine representation. Also, by enforcing the above four constraints, the language protects the programmer from forming illogical combinations of data and operators, a protection which is not available at the machine level.

It will be seen in later chapters that Modula-2 allows the definition of highly structured and complex data types. This is one of the features of Modula-

2 (together with Pascal and other programming languages whose designs have been based on Pascal) that sets it apart from earlier languages. Ultimately, however, all data types are structured out of *unstructured types*. In Modula-2 an unstructured type is either defined by the programmer or else it is one of the standard predefined types (sometimes known as the *primitive* types of the language) which are denoted by the identifiers INTEGER, LONGINT, CARDINAL, REAL, LONGREAL, CHAR, BOOLEAN and PROC.

We begin our treatment of unstructured data types by looking at the properties of each of the first seven of these primitive types.

The Type INTEGER

This type represents the set of (positive and negative) whole numbers and any value of this type is therefore a whole number. However, as was mentioned in Chapter 2, all computers have a limit to the size of the largest whole number which they can store conveniently, and so each implementation of Modula-2 restricts integer values to a subset of the whole numbers. Thus the type INTEGER in practice is the set of whole numbers defined by a given implementation. A value of the type INTEGER is one of the whole numbers in this implementation-defined subset. The various representations of integer numbers (in decimal, octal, or hexadecimal form) were described in the previous chapter.

Modula-2 defines a number of arithmetic operators which take integer operands and return integer results, i.e.,

+	add
–	subtract
*	multiply
DIV	division with truncation
MOD	modulo (remainder of division)

These are *dyadic infix operators*, i.e., they are used with two operands written one on each side of the operator, thus A + B. However, + and – may also be used as *monadic prefix operators*, +A and –A, to denote sign identity and sign inversion (negation). Some examples of integer operations are given in Table 3.1.

When the operands A and B have the same sign the operation A DIV B gives familiar integer division results, e.g.,

$$7 \text{ DIV } 3 = 2$$
$$(-7) \text{ DIV } (-3) = 2$$

When the operands differ in sign, and therefore the true quotient is negative, "truncation" means towards zero, so that

$$(-7) \text{ DIV } 3 = -2$$
$$7 \text{ DIV } (-3) = -2$$

Operation	Result
7 + 3	10
7 − 3	4
7 * 3	21
7 DIV 3	2
7 MOD 3	1
−3	−3
+3	3

Table 3.1   Some examples of integer operations

The modulo operation A MOD B is defined only for positive B. The value of A MOD B is defined to be the remainder of the integer division A DIV B. Thus

$$6 \text{ MOD } 3 = 0$$
$$7 \text{ MOD } 3 = 1$$

Care must be taken to ensure that the result of adding, subtracting or multiplying two values does not produce a result outside the integer range defined by the implementation. If it does then an *overflow* exception is said to occur. Likewise division by zero is an exception, as is a modulo operation whose second operand is zero or negative. Most implementations of Modula-2 provide some means whereby the occurrence of these exceptions during the execution of a program may be detected.

Besides the infix and prefix operators listed above, Modula-2 provides some *standard functions* which may be applied to integer values. One of these is

ABS(X)   *if* X *is an integer value then the standard function* ABS(X) *denotes the absolute integer value of* X

Thus

ABS(7)	gives	7
ABS (−6)	gives	6

A number of other standard functions which relate to integers and other data types are introduced in the following sections.

In common with other unstructured types (other than REAL) in Modula-2 the type INTEGER defines an ordered succession of values—from a least value to a greatest value, both of which are defined by the particular implementation of the language. Each value except the least has a *predecessor*, and each value except the greatest has a *successor*. Such types are called *ordinal* types. For integers the successor of any value can be obtained by adding 1, and the predecessor by subtracting 1.

The Type CARDINAL

This type represents the set of non-negative whole numbers, i.e., 0, 1, 2, ...
However, each implementation of Modula-2 restricts cardinal values to a subset
of the non-negative whole numbers. In practice the upper limit of the
implementation-defined subset forming the type CARDINAL is usually greater
than the upper limit of the subset forming the type INTEGER.

The operators and functions applicable to values of the type CARDINAL are
exactly the same as for the type INTEGER, except that sign inversion using − is
not allowed, and the ABS function obviously has no effect.

If an arithmetic operation involves operands of type INTEGER and CARDI-
NAL then one of the operands must be converted to a value of the other type.
This is achieved by use of the type names INTEGER and CARDINAL as *type
transfer functions* (i.e., functions which convert a value of one type into a value
of another type). Hence, if I is an integer data item and C is a cardinal data item,
then I+C is illegal in Modula-2 (since + requires both operands to be of the same
type), but

<pre>
       I + INTEGER(C)   is of type INTEGER, and
       CARDINAL(I) + C   is of type CARDINAL.
</pre>

These type transfers are consistent in numerical terms (i.e. the INTEGER value N
transfers to the CARDINAL value N, and vice versa) only if the value C in the
first case, or I in the second, lies within the overlapping range of values of the
CARDINAL and INTEGER types (i.e., 0 to the maximum INTEGER value).
Strictly speaking, even this consistency is implementation-dependent, as we
shall see in Chapter 13, but for all normal implementations the property holds.

The Type LONGINT

The standard type LONGINT provides an extended INTEGER type with a larger
range of values. However, not all Modula-2 implementations make such an
extended range available.

The operations applicable to values of the type LONGINT are the same as
those applicable to values of type INTEGER. Just as INTEGER and CARDINAL
are not compatible types for use with arithmetic operators, so LONGINT and
INTEGER are not compatible with one another. For example, if I is of type
INTEGER and LI is of type LONGINT, then we can write

<pre>
       I + INTEGER(LI)   or   LONGINT(I) + LI
</pre>

which are of types INTEGER and LONGINT respectively. However, as we shall
see in Chapter 13, the arithmetic consistency of the results produced by such
expressions is implementation-dependent, and as such they must be used with
caution.

The Type REAL

The values of this type are the set of real numbers. However, once again, there is a limit to the size of such numbers that a computer can conveniently represent and so, in each implementation of Modula-2, the type REAL consists of the real values in some implementation-defined range. The representation of real numbers was described in the previous chapter.

Modula-2 provides a number of arithmetic operators which take real operands and produce real-valued results, i.e.,

+   add
−   subtract
*   multiply
/   divide

As with the integer operators these are dyadic infix operators but + and − may also be used as monadic prefix operators to denote sign identity and inversion. Some examples of real operations are given in Table 3.2.

Operation	Result
2.1 + 1.4	3.5
2.1 − 1.4	0.7
2.1 * 1.4	2.94
2.1 / 1.4	1.5

Table 3.2   Some examples of real operations

Although the range of real values is much greater than that allowed for integers, it must also be remembered that limits still apply and *overflow*, i.e., an attempt to calculate a real value outside this range, may still occur. Implementations usually provide some means of detecting such overflow during execution of real operations.

It should be noted that the representation of real numbers within a computer is not exact and the execution of operations upon these approximate values may produce consequent and greater inaccuracies. The study of the estimation and effect of such inaccuracies belongs to numerical mathematics and will not be discussed further here. However, the reader is warned that, for instance, for real values X and Y the relation

$$(X/Y)*Y = X$$

may not always hold in computer arithmetic.

The standard function ABS which was introduced previously for integer arguments, may also be used with real arguments to give real results.

ABS(X)   *if* X *is a real value then the standard function* ABS(X) *denotes the absolute real value of* X

Thus

$$ABS(-6.4) \quad \text{gives} \quad 6.4$$

If it is required to use real and cardinal operands in an operation, e.g., X+C, where X is real and C is cardinal, then one of the operands must be converted to a value of the other type. Two standard functions are provided in Modula-2 for converting real values to cardinal values, and vice versa. Conversion from a cardinal value to a real value is achieved by use of the FLOAT function, defined as follows:

FLOAT(C)   *takes a cardinal value C as its argument and produces as its result the equivalent real value.*

Thus,

$$FLOAT(7) \quad \text{gives} \quad 7.0$$

Conversion from a real value to a cardinal value requires the use of the *truncation* function, defined as follows:

TRUNC(R)   *takes a real value as its argument and produces as its result the whole part of the value.*

Thus,

$$TRUNC(7.1) \quad \text{gives} \quad 7$$

In using the function TRUNC care must be taken that the desired result does not lie outside the allowed range of cardinals—if it does an exception occurs.

The standard type LONGREAL provides an extended real type which may represent real values to a higher precision and possibly over a greater range. As with LONGINT this extended range and precision may not be provided in all Modula-2 implementations. We shall not make further use of these types in this book.

The Type CHAR

Every computer system has an associated set of characters by means of which it communicates with its environment, i.e., these characters are available on the input and output devices (such as keyboards and printers) which are used to transfer readable character information to and from the computer. As noted in Chapter 2, the set of characters available on any implementation of Modula-2 is necessarily implementation-dependent, though most implementations support the ASCII character set, as listed in Appendix 4.

In Modula-2 the type CHAR is defined as the set of characters available on the computer system which executes the program. The documents defining a particular Modula-2 implementation will normally specify the available character set.

As noted in Chapter 2, a value of type CHAR is denoted either by a string of length one, or by the *octal-char* notation:

$$\text{"A"} \quad \text{"4"} \quad \text{'?'} \quad \text{' '} \quad \text{"+"} \quad 014C$$

The following standard function is defined for manipulation of values of type CHAR:

CAP(C)   *is a standard function which maps a lower-case letter* C *onto the corresponding upper-case letter; if* C *is an upper-case letter then the application of* CAP *has no effect, but if the argument is a non-letter character then an exception occurs.*

Thus,

$$\begin{array}{ll}
\text{CAP("x")} & \text{gives "X"} \\
\text{CAP("X")} & \text{gives "X"} \\
\text{CAP("+")} & \text{is undefined}
\end{array}$$

Two standard transfer functions are provided in Modula-2 to map the character set onto a consecutive set of cardinal values starting at zero (called the *ordinal numbers* of the character set), and vice versa. In practice the numbers used are the underlying numeric representation of characters on the computer system. Appendix 4 also shows the numeric representation defined for the ASCII character set, as used on most computer systems.

ORD(C)   *is the ordinal number of the character* C *in the character set.*

CHR(N)   *is the character value whose ordinal number equals the cardinal value* N, *if one exists; if no character value with ordinal number* N *exists, an exception occurs.*

Obviously ORD and CHR are inverse functions, and

$$\text{CHR(ORD(C))} = C \qquad \text{ORD(CHR(I))} = I$$

will always hold.

In most character sets (including ASCII) the characters denoting decimal digits are given an ordered coherent set of ordinal numbers, so that

$$\text{ORD("0")} = \text{ORD("1")} - 1$$
$$\text{ORD("1")} = \text{ORD("2")} - 1$$

.

.

$$\text{ORD("8")} = \text{ORD("9")} - 1$$

In many character sets (including ASCII) the upper-case and lower-case letters of the alphabet also have coherent ordered sets of ordinal numbers, so that

$$ORD("A") = ORD("B") - 1 \qquad ORD("a") = ORD("b") - 1$$
$$ORD("B") = ORD("C") - 1 \qquad ORD("b") = ORD("c") - 1$$

.   .

.   .

$$ORD("Y") = ORD("Z") - 1 \qquad ORD("y") = ORD("z") - 1$$

However, the definition of Modula-2 does not require that this is so, and users should check that it is for their implementation before writing any program that depends upon it. In general the ordinal values of letters in the character set are always ordered, i.e.,

$$ORD("A") < ORD("B") \qquad ORD("a") < ORD("b")$$
$$ORD("B") < ORD("C") \qquad ORD("b") < ORD("c")$$

.   .

.   .

$$ORD("Y") < ORD("Z") \qquad ORD("y") < ORD("z")$$

This condition is sufficient to explain the ordered comparison of letter characters as defined in the next section.

The mapping of the values of type CHAR onto a set of consecutive cardinal values enables it to be designated an ordinal type.

The Type BOOLEAN

A Boolean value is one of the logical truth values represented by the standard Modula-2 identifiers TRUE and FALSE.

Modula-2 provides standard operators which take Boolean values as operands and produce a Boolean result. These operators include

AND   logical and (also denoted by &)
OR   logical inclusive or
NOT   logical negation (also denoted by ~)

Table 3.3 shows the results of applying these operators to Boolean arguments P and Q. In fact we shall see in the next chapter that the Modula-2 evaluation rules are slightly different, although the results are identical.

P	Q	P AND Q	P OR Q	NOT P
FALSE	FALSE	FALSE	FALSE	TRUE
FALSE	TRUE	FALSE	TRUE	TRUE
TRUE	FALSE	FALSE	TRUE	FALSE
TRUE	TRUE	TRUE	TRUE	FALSE

Table 3.3   Action of AND, OR and NOT operators

Boolean values may also be produced by applying *relational operators* to operands of other types. Modula-2 provides the six relational operators of mathematics, which are as follows:

=	equal to
<>	not equal to (also denoted by #)
<	less than
<=	less than or equal to
>	greater than
>=	greater than or equal to

A *relation* consists of two operands separated by a relational operator. If the relation is satisfied then it has the value TRUE, otherwise the value FALSE, i.e., the result of a relation is a Boolean value. The above operators may be applied to any two operands of the same unstructured type. (Their use with operands of other types is discussed further in this and later chapters.)

For integer, cardinal and real operands the relational operators have their usual meanings. Thus

7 = 11	gives	FALSE
7 < 11	gives	TRUE
3.4 <= 5.9	gives	TRUE

For operands of type CHAR the result is determined by applying the mathematical relation to the ordinal numbers corresponding to the operands. Thus for any relational operator R and operands C1, C2 of type CHAR

$$C1 \ R \ C2$$

is equivalent to

$$ORD(C1) \ R \ ORD(C2)$$

Note that in most character sets the ordinal numbers of the values of type CHAR ensure that the following character relations are true:

"0" < "1"	"A" < "B"	"a" < "b"
"1" < "2"	"B" < "C"	"b" < "c"
.	.	.
.	.	.

A similar ordering convention is adopted for the type BOOLEAN itself, which is defined to be an ordinal type such that

$$ORD(FALSE) = 0 \qquad ORD(TRUE) = 1$$

With this convention other Boolean operators can be expressed in terms of the relational operators, e.g.,

the *implication* operator is expressed by the <= operator;
the *equivalence* operator is expressed by the = operator;
the *exclusive or* operator is expressed by the <> operator.

Table 3.4 confirms that these relational operators correspond to the named logical operators.

P	Q	$P <= Q$	$P = Q$	$P <> Q$
FALSE	FALSE	TRUE	TRUE	FALSE
FALSE	TRUE	TRUE	FALSE	TRUE
TRUE	FALSE	FALSE	FALSE	TRUE
TRUE	TRUE	TRUE	TRUE	FALSE

Table 3.4   Further Boolean operators

Modula-2 provides one standard function which yields a Boolean result—such a function is known as a *predicate*. It is defined as follows:

ODD(C)   *for a cardinal argument* C, ODD(C) *gives the result* TRUE *if* C *is odd,* FALSE *otherwise.*

Enumerated Types

We have now considered the standard, or primitive, data types provided by Modula-2. These data types can be used primarily for the description of numerical, character and logical data. However, the programmer may find that none of these types provides values suitable for the description of the data which are to be manipulated by a particular program. For instance, the data items may be the four suits of a pack of cards (clubs, diamonds, hearts and spades) or the seven days of the week (Sunday to Saturday). Neither of these is naturally describable in terms of the standard types of Modula-2. Fortunately, Modula-2 allows the programmer to define additional data types in a form suitable to the particular application.

An *enumerated-type* is defined simply by listing the identifiers by which the values of the type are to be denoted. The identifiers are enclosed in parentheses and separated by commas, thus:

enumerated-type = "(" identifier-list ")".
identifier-list = identifier {"," identifier}.

The suits in a pack of cards could thus be defined as an enumerated-type

(Club, Diamond, Heart, Spade)

Items of this type can take only the values denoted by the identifiers Club, Diamond, Heart and Spade.

The days of the week could be defined as an enumerated-type

(Sunday, Monday, Tuesday, Wednesday, Thursday, Friday, Saturday)

The order in which the values of the type are enumerated also defines their ordering for the purposes of applying relational operators, thus

Club < Diamond	gives	TRUE
Monday >= Friday	gives	FALSE

All six relational operators described previously can be applied to values of enumerated types producing, as always, Boolean-valued results.

All enumerated-types are defined to be ordinal types. The successor of an enumerated-type value is the next value in the enumeration (if that value exists), while the predecessor is the preceding value in the enumeration (if that value exists).

The standard function ORD (previously defined for the types CHAR and BOOLEAN) is also applicable to arguments which are values of an enumerated-type. This function maps the values of the enumerated-type, in order, onto the integers 0 to $N-1$ (where N is the number of values, or *cardinality*, of the enumerated-type). Thus,

ORD(Club)	gives the result	0
ORD(Diamond)	gives the result	1
ORD(Heart)	gives the result	2
ORD(Spade)	gives the result	3

Note that the standard type BOOLEAN is equivalent to an enumerated-type of the form (FALSE, TRUE).

Subrange Types

When a data item takes a range of values which is a subrange of the values described by some existing ordinal type, its type may be defined as a *subrange* of that *host* type. The subrange type is defined by indicating the lower and upper *bounds* of the values in the subrange, separated by the symbol "..", and enclosed within square brackets "[" and "]".

subrange-type = [host-type-identifier] "[" lower-bound ".." upper-bound "]".
host-type-identifier = type-identifier.
lower-bound = constant-expression.
upper-bound = constant-expression.

The value of the *lower-bound* must not be greater than that of the *upper-bound*. The full range of possible forms of a *constant-expression* is defined in the next chapter. Thus,

["A" .. "Z"]	is a subrange of the type CHAR;
[Monday .. Friday]	is a subrange of the enumeration in the previous sub-section;
[–9 .. +9]	is a subrange of the type INTEGER;
[1900 .. 1999]	is a subrange of the type CARDINAL.

In fact the Modula-2 types INTEGER and CARDINAL are themselves really subranges—the implementation-defined subsets of the infinite range of whole numbers.

Note that

(a) it is not permitted to define a subrange of the type REAL since it is not an ordinal type;

(b) on most implementations the subrange ["A" .. "Z"] defines the twenty-six upper-case letters of the alphabet as its only values, but for the reasons explained earlier, this is not necessarily so. On some implementations this subrange may define more than twenty-six values, and include non-alphabetic characters;

(c) the syntax of *subrange-type* allows the host-type to be identified explicitly. Hence we might write

CHAR ["A".."Z"]

INTEGER [–9 .. +9]

However, in practice, the *host-type-identifier* can usually be omitted, since the host-type can be determined from the type of the constant-expressions (which must be of the same type). The exception is when the host-type might be either INTEGER or CARDINAL, as in

[1900 .. 1999]

above, in which case the host-type is assumed to be CARDINAL, unless otherwise explicitly indicated, thus:

INTEGER [1900 ..1999]

A subrange-type is a means of indicating that the values taken by specific data items lie in a certain subrange. However, each value taken is regarded as being of the host-type, and thus the operators and functions defined for the host-type are applicable to (the value of) a data item of the subrange-type. For example, the integer arithmetic operators may be applied to operands of integer subrange-types. In general, however, the value produced by applying an operation to operands of a subrange-type does not necessarily lie within the same subrange. The result of such an operation is always considered to be of the parent host-type.

DATA DECLARATIONS

The data items which a program manipulates may be divided into *two* classes—those whose values remain fixed during execution of a program, and those whose values are changed by the execution. The former are known as *constants*, the latter are known as *variables*. Items of either class share the properties of type as described in the previous section. However, the way in which the items are introduced in a Modula-2 program depends on their class, as the following sub-sections explain.

Constants and Constant Declarations

In previous subsections we have seen how particular values of unstructured data types may be denoted. For example,

123   denotes a particular value of type CARDINAL (or INTEGER);
−123   denotes a particular value of type INTEGER;
12.75   denotes a particular value of type REAL;
"A"   denotes a particular value of type CHAR;
Heart   denotes a particular value of an enumerated-type.

A constant data item of an unstructured type may thus be denoted by explicitly writing its value at each point in the program which refers to it. However, this is not always the most satisfactory solution, as the following example will show:

A mathematical program may make frequent use of the real value 3.1415926, which is an approximation to the value of the mathematical constant π. Writing this value at each point has the following disadvantages:

(a) the actual sequence of digits is less meaningful than the symbol π;
(b) writing out this digit sequence repeatedly is tedious, and prone to error—one may write 3.1415926 or 3.1415962 or 3.1451926 without the discrepancies being detected;
(c) a decision to change, say, the precision of the value used for π involves changing each occurrence of the digit sequence.

An ideal solution for the programmer is to use the symbol π itself, defining the value which it denotes at one point only in the program. Given that Greek letters such as π are not provided on computer systems, the use of a meaningful identifier, such as Pi, is an acceptable substitute—a solution permitted by Modula-2.

In Modula-2 an identifier may be defined to denote a particular constant value, by means of a *constant-declaration*. Thereafter each occurrence of the identifier is equivalent to an explicit occurrence of the value itself at that point. Constant-declarations are grouped together into a *constant-declaration-part* which has the following form:

> *constant-declaration-part = "CONST" {constant-declaration ";"}.*
> *constant-declaration = identifier "=" constant-expression.*

A *constant-expression* is one in which all the operands of all the operators used are themselves constants—expressions are dealt with more fully in the next chapter.

The following is an example *constant-declaration-part*:

```
CONST Pi = 3.1415926;
      Asterisk = "*";
      FormFeed = 014C;
      MyAddress = "10 Cotswold Court, Bangor";
      WordLength = 16;
      MostSignificantBit = WordLength − 1;
      DayOff = Thursday;
      MatrixSize = 10;
      NumberOfElements = MatrixSize * MatrixSize;
```

Given this constant-declaration-part, the constant values concerned may be denoted by the corresponding identifiers. Modula-2 provides three standard identifiers which may be used without prior declaration and which denote standard constant values—these are FALSE and TRUE which denote the only values of the standard type BOOLEAN, and a pointer constant NIL which is used in pointer manipulation (see Chapter 11).

Throughout this book the term *constant-identifier* is used to mean one of the following:

(a) an identifier declared in a constant-declaration;
(b) an identifier introduced as one of the values of an enumerated-type; or
(c) one of the standard identifiers FALSE, TRUE, NIL.

The syntax category

> *constant-identifier = qualified-identifier.*

is introduced simply to denote the class of all identifiers so defined.

Type Declarations

The primitive types of Modula-2 described so far may be used in a program without prior definition—each reference to one of them being indicated by the corresponding identifier INTEGER, LONGINT, CARDINAL, REAL, LONGREAL, CHAR or BOOLEAN. It is often necessary, or convenient, that types defined in the program itself are also denoted by identifiers, so-called *type-identifiers*.

Each type-identifier is introduced by means of a *type-declaration*. Type declarations are grouped together in a *type-declaration-part*, which has the following form:

type-declaration-part = "TYPE" {type-declaration ";"}.
type-declaration = identifier "=" type.
type = simple-type | structured-type | pointer-type | procedure-type.
simple-type = type-identifier | subrange-type | enumerated-type.

The possible forms of *structured-*, *pointer-* and *procedure-types* are explained in later chapters. The following is an example of a type-declaration-part involving only simple types.

```
TYPE DayOfWeek =
        (Sunday, Monday, Tuesday, Wednesday, Thursday, Friday, Saturday);
     BitRange = [0 .. WordLength – 1];
     DayOfMonth = [1 .. 31];
     Year = [1900 .. 1999];
     WorkDay = [Monday .. Friday];
     UpperCaseLetter = ["A" .. "Z"];
```

Thereafter the types involved may be denoted by the identifiers DayOfWeek, BitRange, DayOfMonth, Year, WorkDay and UpperCaseLetter in the same way as the standard types are denoted by INTEGER, CARDINAL, REAL, etc.

Throughout this book the term *type-identifier* is used to mean either

(a) an identifier introduced by a type-declaration, or
(b) one of the standard identifiers provided in Modula-2 to denote standard types, viz., INTEGER, LONGINT, CARDINAL, REAL, LONGREAL, CHAR, BOOLEAN, PROC and BITSET. (The type PROC is explained in Chapter 7 and BITSET is explained in Chapter 10.)

The syntax category

type-identifier = qualified-identifier.

is used to denote the class of identifiers so defined.

The syntax of a type-declaration allows one type-identifier to be defined in terms of another defined elsewhere, thus

```
TYPE T1 = ... ;
     .
     .
     TYPE T2 = T1 ;
```

With such a declaration the type-identifier T2 is said to denote the *same* type as that denoted by T1.

Modula-2 provides three standard functions which can be used in conjunction with any ordinal type identifier.

VAL(T, N)   *If* T *is the type-identifier of an ordinal type, and* N *is a* CARDINAL *value, then* VAL(T, N) *gives the value of type* T *whose ordinal number is* N, *if one exists. If no such value exists, an exception occurs.*

MIN(T)   *gives the least value of the ordinal type* T,

MAX(T)   *gives the greatest value of the ordinal type* T.

Hence, for the type definitions given to date

VAL(DayOfWeek, 3)	gives	Wednesday
VAL(CARDINAL, 1)	gives	1

and, in general, for any value X of an ordinal type T

$$VAL(T, ORD(X)) = X \quad \text{and} \quad ORD(VAL (T, N)) = N$$

always hold.

Likewise, for the type definitions given to date,

MIN(CARDINAL)	gives	0
MAX(BOOLEAN)	gives	TRUE
MIN(DayOfWeek)	gives	Sunday
MAX(WorkDay)	gives	Friday

The function calls MAX(CARDINAL), MAX(INTEGER) and MIN(INTEGER) can be used to denote the maximum and minimum values for the types CARDINAL and INTEGER as fixed by the implementation concerned. However, the functions MIN and MAX were added to the language by the third edition of *Programming in Modula-2* and are not supported by all implementations. On such implementations, standard constants MAXCARD, MAXINT and MININT are sometimes available for import from the module SYSTEM, which is described in Chapter 13.

Variable Declarations

Variables, those data items whose values are changed by execution of the program, are always denoted by identifiers. Each *variable-identifier* is introduced by a *variable-declaration*, which also specifies the type of the values which the variable may take. Variable-declarations are grouped in one or more *variable-declaration-parts*, which have the following form:

variable-declaration-part = "VAR" {variable-declaration ";"}.
variable-declaration = identifier-list ":" type.

Given the type declarations of the preceding subsection, the following is an example of a variable-declaration-part:

```
VAR Today: DayOfWeek;
    ThisYear, NextYear: Year;
    DaysWorked: [0 .. 5];
    OnLeave: BOOLEAN;
```

Thereafter the identifier Today denotes a variable data item which at any moment may take one of the seven values Sunday, Monday, ..., Saturday;

ThisYear and NextYear denote distinct data items which may take cardinal values in the range 1900 ... 1999;

DaysWorked denotes a variable data item which may take any cardinal value in the range 0 ... 5;

OnLeave denotes a variable data item which may take a Boolean value TRUE or FALSE.

Note that

(a) several variables may be declared by the same declaration, provided that they are to share the same type;

(b) the type of the variables declared may be defined explicitly in the variable-declaration itself—if this is the only point in the program where the type is to be used then it is superfluous to introduce an identifier naming the type in a type-declaration;

(c) two variables are said to have the same type if they are declared in the same variable-declaration, or if they are declared (in different variable-declarations) using the same type-identifier, or using different type-identifiers that denote the same type.

Hereafter the syntax category

variable-identifier = qualified-identifier.

is used to denote the class of identifiers introduced by variable-declarations.

UNIQUENESS AND ORDER OF DECLARATIONS

Constant-declarations, enumerated-types, type-declarations and variable-declarations all have the effect of associating identifiers with the constants, types or variables which they are used to denote. (Further means of associating identifiers with other program quantities are described in following chapters.)

Modula-2 requires that the association of each identifier with the quantity which it denotes must be unique throughout its *scope*, or range of use within the program. The concept of identifier scope is discussed fully in Chapters 7 and 12. For the moment it may be assumed that the association of each identifier must be unique throughout the program. Thus the declarations:

```
TYPE Range = [1 .. 100];
VAR  X, Y: Range; Y, Z, Range: REAL;
```

are invalid, since the identifiers Range and Y are each declared twice (in the same scope).

The definition of Modula-2 imposes a declaration-before-use requirement on identifiers which are used in other declarations. Thus, it requires that constant-identifiers are declared before they are used in defining other constant-identifiers, or in defining types; and that type-identifiers are declared before they are used in defining other types or in declaring variables. Thus the following declarations are not allowed:

```
CONST  XMin = –XMax – 1; XMax = 100;
TYPE   YRange = XRange; XRange = [XMin .. XMax];
```

since XMax and XRange are each used before they are declared, whereas the following equivalent declarations are acceptable:

```
CONST  XMax = 100; XMin = –XMax – 1;
TYPE   XRange = [XMin .. XMax]; YRange = XRange;
```

This property of each identifier being declared before it is used in the program text adds considerably to program clarity, and is recommended programming practice even in those situations where the language rules do not require it. As we shall see in Chapter 10, there is a specific exception to the Modula-2 rules for declaring *pointer-types*, where such a rule would be impossible to observe.

EXERCISES

3.1 Which of the following combinations of operators and operands are valid in Modula-2 ?

67 DIV 8	12*2.75	67 MOD 8	(–3) DIV 8
ABS(–2.5)	"A" < "Z"	67 / 8	6.7 DIV 8
1001*1001	67 MOD (–8)	CAP("a")	10.0E4*10.0E4
CHR(62)	ORD("A")	47.1 + 1	FLOAT(–7)

Write down the result of each valid combination. Are all the results defined on your implementation ?

3.2 Study the following sequence of Modula-2 declarations:

CONST LineMax = 64;
      PrintWanted = TRUE;

TYPE LinePosition = [1 .. LineMax];
     Spacing = (Single, Double, Treble);

VAR ThisChar, LastChar: CHAR;
    ThisPosition: LinePosition;
    SpacingNow: Spacing;

List all the *constant-identifiers*,
   all the *type-identifiers*,
   all the *variable-identifiers*, which occur.

3.3 Write a *constant-declaration-part* which defines the following constant-identifiers with appropriate values:

InchesPerMeter   CurrencySymbol
DegreesPerRadian   SpeedLimit

3.4 Write a *type-declaration-part* which defines types suitable for the values of the age, sex, height, weight and marital status of a person.

3.5 A typical estate agent's description of a house reads

"Three bedrooms, two reception rooms, oil-fired central heating, garage, ...".

Write a *variable-declaration-part* which declares the variables involved, with an appropriate type for each.

4

Statements, Expressions and Assignments

STATEMENTS

In Chapters 2 and 3 the concepts of data and data types were introduced, together with the means of defining constant and variable data items in Modula-2 programs—the *declaration-part*. The manipulation which the program performs on its data items is defined by its *statement-part*.

The *statement-part* defines the actions to be carried out as a sequence of statements, where each statement specifies one corresponding action.

statement-part = ["BEGIN" statement-sequence].

Modula-2 is a *sequential* programming language in that the statements of the statement-part are executed sequentially in time, one after the other, and never simultaneously. This sequential execution of statements is reflected in the structure of a *statement-sequence*, which is as follows:

statement-sequence = statement {";" statement}.

The semicolon symbol acts as a statement separator.

Chapter 2 introduced an example program which included a simple example of a statement-sequence, consisting of ten statements to be executed in the order given, as shown below:

```
WriteString("First Number  = "); ReadInt(First); WriteLn;
WriteString("Second Number = "); ReadInt(Second); WriteLn;
Sum := First + Second;
WriteString("Sum = "); WriteInt(Sum, 6); WriteLn
```

Modula-2 provides a variety of statement forms, both simple and structured, by which program actions may be specified:

statement = simple-statement / structured-statement.

Structured-statements are used to describe composite actions in terms of other component statements, and are discussed first in Chapter 6. For the moment we concentrate on the *simple-statement*, of which five possible forms are provided

simple-statement =
[assignment-statement / exit-statement /
procedure-statement / return-statement].

Note that one of these five forms is a statement which consists of no symbols at all—this is known as an *empty-statement*. As we shall see, it is used at certain points in a program to denote that no action is to be taken. *Exit-statements* are discussed in Chapter 6, and *procedure-* and *return-statements* in Chapter 7.

An *assignment-statement* is used to assign a particular value to a variable. The value is specified by means of an *expression*, whose form we first consider.

EXPRESSIONS

An *expression* is a rule for computing a value. It consists of one or more operands combined by means of the operators already defined in Chapter 3. An operand may be any of the following:

a constant value;
the current value of a variable;
the result of a function call.

For the present the only function calls we consider are those involving the standard functions defined in Chapter 3.

As with normal mathematical expressions a Modula-2 expression is evaluated according to the notion of *operator precedence*. Each of the operators is assigned a *precedence*. The precedence of the Modula-2 operators is given in Table 4.1.

Precedence	Operators
4	NOT ~
3	* / DIV MOD AND &
2	+ – OR
1	= <> # < <= > >=

Table 4.1 Operator precedences

The rules of evaluation of an expression are then:

(1) if all the operators in an expression have the same precedence the evaluation of the operations proceeds strictly from left to right;

(2) when operators of different precedences are present then the highest precedence operations are evaluated first (on a left-to-right basis), then the next highest precedence operations are evaluated, and so on;

(3) rules (1) and (2) can be overridden by the inclusion of parentheses in an expression—in this case those operations within the parentheses are evaluated first, with the same precedence rules being applied within the parentheses;

(4) the order of evaluation of the operands of a dyadic operator, i.e., one with two operands, other than AND and OR, is implementation-dependent—as we shall see in Chapter 7, this must be remembered when using some functions.

The effect of these rules of evaluation is best described by means of some examples.

(a) 6 * 2 + 4 * 3

Since the * operators are of highest precedence, this expression is equivalent to (6 * 2) + (4 * 3), which gives a result of 24.

(b) If one wishes to add 4 and 2, and multiply the result by 3, then the following expression

(4 + 2) * 3

may be used. Note that

4 + 2 * 3

does not produce the correct result since the * operation, being of higher precedence, would be performed first.

(c) 10 MOD 3 * 4

Here the two operators MOD and * are of equal precedence and so are evaluated from left to right, to give the result 4.

Some Boolean operations involving AND and OR can be evaluated without evaluating both the operands. For example

FALSE AND B   TRUE OR B

give the values FALSE and TRUE respectively, regardless of the value of B. In Modula-2 programs the second operand of an AND or an OR operator is not evaluated in the case when the result is already known after evaluation of the first operand.

The rules given in Chapter 3 determine the type of the result of each operator within an expression, from the type of its operands. The type of a complete expression is determined by applying these rules to each operator and its operands in the order in which the operations are to be carried out. For example

(d) 2.1 + FLOAT((3 + 1) + 11 * 5)

The contents of the outer parentheses are evaluated first. Within these parentheses (3 + 1) is first evaluated to give a cardinal result, then 11*5 again giving a cardinal result, and these two results are added to give a cardinal result of 59. Then FLOAT(59) is evaluated to give a real result 59.0 and, finally, 2.1 is added to 59.0 to give a real result of 61.1.

(e) In some cases the omission of parentheses leads not to incorrect values but in fact produces illegal expressions, e.g.,

(3 > 0) AND (3 < 10)

gives the value TRUE. However, if the parentheses are omitted, i.e.,

3 > 0 AND 3 < 10

then we have an ill-formed expression. Precedence requires that the AND operation be performed first, but 0 AND 3 is an illegal operation since AND requires Boolean-valued operands.

Readers should study the expressions in Table 4.2 and convince themselves, by applying the rules for evaluation of expressions, that they produce the indicated values.

Expression	Value
3 * 17 – 193 MOD 19	48
193 MOD 19 DIV 3 * 127	127
(–4 + 23 * 2) DIV 3	14
(7 + 3) <= 10	TRUE
((3 > 7) OR (3 <= 7)) AND (7 <> 10)	TRUE
FLOAT(37 + 15 MOD 4) / 5.0	8.0
TRUNC(3.2 * 4) DIV 3	4

Table 4.2   Some expressions and their values

The Modula-2 notation for expressions is less flexible than that used in mathematics, and care must be taken in translating mathematical expressions into Modula-2. In Table 4.3 we give some mathematical expressions and show how they are expressed in Modula-2.

The following points should also be noted concerning expressions in Modula-2:

Mathematical expression	Modula-2 expression
$\dfrac{x+2}{y+4}$	(x+2)/(y+4)
$x(y+w(3-v))$	x*(y+w*(3-v))
$\dfrac{xy}{w+2}$	x*y/(w+2)
$a + \dfrac{b}{c}$	a+b/c

Table 4.3   Mathematical expressions and their Modula-2 counterparts

(a) every variable used in evaluating an expression must already have been given a value in some way, otherwise an exception will occur;

(b) two arithmetic operators must never be written side by side, e.g., A*–B is an illegal expression and must be written A*(–B);

(c) the multiplication sign should never be omitted when a multiplication operation is required;

(d) there is no harm in using possibly redundant parentheses. Therefore, when in doubt about the precedence rules, use parentheses to construct expressions.

The method of construction of expressions and the operator precedence rules governing their evaluation are defined by the following syntax rules (these syntax definitions merely summarize the rules we have given and are presented here only for reference purposes).

> *expression = simple-expression [relational-operator simple-expression].*
> *simple-expression = ["+" | "–"] term {addition-operator term}.*
> *term = factor {multiplication-operator factor}.*
> *factor =*
> *variable | constant-literal | constant-identifier |*
> *procedure-identifier | function-identifier | function-call | set |*
> *"(" expression ")" | ("NOT" | "~") factor.*
> *constant-literal = number | string | octal-char.*
> *relational-operator = "=" | "<>" | "#" | "<" | "<=" | ">" | ">=" | "IN".*
> *addition-operator = "+" | "-" | "OR".*
> *multiplication-operator = "*" | "/" | "DIV" | "MOD" | "AND" | "&".*

The occurrence of a variable in an expression indicates that the current value of the variable is to be used as an operand in evaluating the expression. As we saw in Chapter 3, a variable is denoted by an identifier introduced in a variable-declaration. The identifiers that are introduced by declarations of variables of the data types considered in Chapter 3 denote what are known as *entire-variables*. The full syntactic definition of a *variable* as denoted within the statement-part is

> *variable* = *entire-variable* / *component-variable* / *referenced-variable*.
> *entire-variable* = *variable-identifier* / *field-identifier*.

In Chapters 8 and 9 we see that variables sometimes consist of a number of components, each of which may be considered as a variable in its own right with a corresponding *component-variable* notation. *Referenced-variables* are described in Chapter 11, and the use of *field-identifiers* as *entire-variables* is explained in Chapter 9.

The allowable forms for *constant-expressions*, which were introduced in Chapter 3, are a subset of those for *expressions*, and the evaluation rules by which the value of a constant-expression is determined are equivalent to those given above for expressions. The basic requirement is that the value of a constant-expression can be determined without execution of the program in which it occurs. The obvious restriction is therefore that variables may not appear in constant-expressions, but, in practice, implementations also exclude the use of procedure- or function-identifiers in constant-expressions, and either exclude or restrict the inclusion of function-calls. At most, each operand in a constant-expression may be one of the following:

(a) a constant-literal or constant-identifier;
(b) a set (see Chapter 10) whose elements if present are constant-expressions;
(c) a call of a standard function with an argument which is a constant-expression (or a type-identifier);
(d) a type transfer of the form *type-identifier(constant-expression)*.

Users of individual implementations of Modula-2 should check the precise restrictions imposed on constant-expressions by the implementation concerned.

THE ASSIGNMENT STATEMENT

An *assignment-statement* has the following form:

> *assignment-statement* = *variable* ":=" *expression*.

The two-character symbol ":=" is known as the *assignment operator* and is usually read as "becomes".

The effect of executing an assignment-statement is to evaluate the expression on the right of the assignment operator and to assign the resultant value to the variable on the left.

For example,

$$I := 3$$

means replace the current value of the variable I by the value 3;

$$I := J$$

means replace the current value of the variable I by the current value of the variable J.

Variables of any of the types we have introduced so far, be they of the primitive types, an enumerated type, or a subrange type, may be assigned new values. However, a variable may only be assigned a value of an appropriate type. Thus, the variable on the left-hand side of the assignment operator and the value of the expression on the right-hand side must be of identical type, with the following qualifications:

(a) an expression consisting solely of a variable of a subrange-type is considered to be of the corresponding host type;
(b) a variable of a subrange-type may be assigned a value of the corresponding host type, provided the value lies within the required subrange;
(c) the variable and the expression value may be any combination of CARDINAL, INTEGER, or subranges of any of these, provided that the expression value lies within the permitted range of values of the variable.

A value meeting these conditions is said to be *assignment compatible* with the type of the variable to be assigned. Assignment compatibility for string and set types is discussed in Chapters 8 and 10 respectively.

The result of assigning a value which is outside the required subrange to a variable of a subrange-type is an exception. Most implementations provide some means of detecting such *range exceptions* during execution of the program.

Consider the following sequence of assignment-statements:

```
A := 3.52;
A := B * B * B;
J := J + 1;
P := (J > 0) OR (C <> " ");
C := ".".
```

For these to be legal assignment-statements the variable A must be of type REAL, B must also be REAL, J may be of type INTEGER or CARDINAL (or subranges thereof), P must be BOOLEAN, and C must be of type CHAR (or a subrange of CHAR that includes the character ".").

As an exercise the reader should confirm that the following sequence of assignment-statements applied to INTEGER variables X, Y and W leaves all three variables with the final value 100:

```
X := 27;
Y := 343;
W := X + Y - 300;
X := W DIV 10 + 23;
Y := (X + W) DIV 10 * 10;
X := X + 70 + Y MOD 10;
W := W + X - 70
```

Assignment-statements which increment or decrement the value of a variable by a constant amount, e.g.,

```
X := X + 1 ;
Y := Y - 1
```

occur very frequently in programs, and hence Modula-2 provides some special statements to express such operations. These statements are applicable to variables of any ordinal type and are defined as follows:

INC(X)   *assigns to the variable* X *the immediate successor of its current value, if it exists;*

INC(X, N)   *assigns to the variable* X *the* N*th successor of its current value, if it exists;*

DEC(X)   *assigns to the variable* X *the immediate predecessor of its current value, if it exists;*

DEC(X, N)   *assigns to the variable* X *the* N*th predecessor of its current value, if it exists;*

When present, the second argument N must be an expression yielding a CARDINAL value.

For a variable I of type INTEGER, or CARDINAL,

INC(I)	is equivalent to the assignment-statement	I := I + 1
INC(I, N)	is equivalent to the assignment-statement	I := I + N
DEC(I)	is equivalent to the assignment-statement	I := I - 1
DEC(I, N)	is equivalent to the assignment-statement	I := I - N

Since REAL is not an ordinal type, INC and DEC may not be used with variables of type REAL. For a variable C of type CHAR,

INC(C)	is equivalent to	C := CHR(ORD(C) + 1)
INC(C, N)	is equivalent to	C := CHR(ORD(C) + N)
DEC(C)	is equivalent to	C := CHR(ORD(C) - 1)
DEC(C, N)	is equivalent to	C := CHR(ORD(C) - N)

Given a variable D of the enumerated-type DayOfWeek defined earlier, and assuming that the current value of D is Tuesday,

    INC(D)   assigns Wednesday as the new value of D,
    DEC(D)   assigns Monday as the new value of D.

In general, for a variable V of an enumerated-type T,

INC(V)	is equivalent to	V := VAL(T, ORD(V) + 1)
INC(V, N)	is equivalent to	V := VAL(T, ORD(V) + N)
DEC(V)	is equivalent to	V := VAL(T, ORD(V) − 1)
DEC(V, N)	is equivalent to	V := VAL(T, ORD(V) − N)

In the case of a variable whose value is the greatest value of an enumerated-type, the use of INC produces an exception—likewise the use of DEC with a variable whose value is the minimum of the type. Thus, if D has the value Saturday then INC(D) produces an exception, and if D has the value Sunday then DEC(D) also produces an exception.

    INC and DEC are examples of the use of *procedures* (see Chapter 7), in this case *standard procedures* provided as standard facilities in all Modula-2 implementations.

EXERCISES

4.1 Insert parentheses to clarify the meanings of the following expressions, and then calculate the value of each:

```
6.75 − 12.3 / 3.0
6 * 11 − 42 DIV 5
175 MOD 15 DIV 3 * 65
13 + 7 * 5 − 4 * 5 DIV 2
11 MOD 4 DIV 2 <> 0
("A" >= "Z") OR ("9" >= "8") AND ("A" < "I")
```

4.2 Assuming X, Y and Z are INTEGER variables, what values will they have after execution of the following sequence of statements?

```
X := 50;
Y := 340;
Z := X + Y − 190;
X := 17;
Y := X + Z;
Z := X + 200;
INC(Z)
```

4.3 Write down Boolean expressions which determine whether

(a) the value of an INTEGER variable I lies in the range 1 to 100 inclusive;
(b) either of the values of two CARDINAL variables J and K is a multiple of the other;
(c) the year Y in the twentieth century is a leap year.

4.4 Using any additional variables necessary, write a sequence of assignment-statements which exchanges the values of two REAL variables X and Y.

4.5 X, Y and Z are INTEGER variables. Write down assignment-statements to assign their sum, product and average to variables named Sum, Product and Average. What types have you assumed for the variables Sum, Product, and Average?

4.6 H, T and U are variables declared as follows:

VAR H, T, U: ["0".."9"];

i.e., they take character values *h*, *t* and *u* which are decimal digits. Write down an assignment-statement which will assign to a CARDINAL variable I the decimal number denoted by the characters *htu* in that order.

5

Input and Output of Data

TRANSFERRING DATA TO AND FROM THE PROGRAM

It is the purpose of every program to manipulate data—a payroll program operates on data describing the employees and the hours they have worked; a program for solving systems of linear equations needs to know the coefficients of each of the equations. These data could actually be built into the program but then, in order to compute the next week's payroll or solve another system of equations, it would be necessary to alter the program. What is really required is some means of informing the program of the data to be manipulated on this particular occasion, i.e., a means of entering the data into the program during its execution, from some device outside the computer. Then the same programs can be used to carry out each week's payroll calculation, or to solve many sets of linear equations.

Many such external devices exist—card readers read information punched on cards, disk drives read information encoded on magnetic disk surfaces, terminal keyboards act as a means of presenting the information typed to the computer. These, and many others, are means of *inputting* data to a program.

Similarly, we wish to see the results produced by a program—a payroll program must print pay slips for the employees to inspect, and checks for them to cash; it will be necessary to examine the solution to a set of linear equations. Therefore a means is required of communicating the results of a program to the outside world. Once again devices exist, such as printers and video screens, on which information can be printed or displayed. These devices are means of *outputting* data from a program.

In this chapter we restrict ourselves to considering only input and output of information in character form. Our Modula-2 programs are, for the time being, considered to be processes which obtain information from an *input stream* and deliver information to an *output stream*, via external devices with the ability to handle character information organized as a sequence of lines.

In the first part of this chapter we consider the input of information from, and output of information to, a program user at a terminal consisting of a keyboard and a video screen. We shall refer to the keyboard and screen as the *standard* input/output streams. Such input and output is said to be *interactive* or *online*, in that the user at the terminal supplies information on demand by the program, and observes the results produced directly.

An alternative means of communication with a program is to prepare a file of data on disk, say, and have the program read information from this file as it is required. Likewise, the output from a program can be sent to a disk file rather than to the terminal. This file might be inspected via a video screen at some later stage, printed using a printing device, or used as input to a subsequent execution of the same or another program. Such input and output is said to be *offline*, since the user does not participate directly in the input and output concerned. The final section of this chapter outlines how such offline input/output may be programmed in Modula-2.

In Modula-2, unlike many other languages, the basic operations necessary to manipulate the input and output character streams can be programmed in Modula-2 itself. This property means that the language does not have to define a comprehensive range of input/output facilities as special language features. Instead the language design assumes that a set of operations for controlling the input and output streams will be made available by each implementation of Modula-2, in the form of one or more *library modules*, i.e., as pre-programmed modules which are available for use without further effort by individual programmers.

While this approach to the provision of input/output facilities simplifies the language itself, it means that the facilities actually available are implementation-dependent, and in practice significant variations do exist between implementations. In this chapter we describe the facilities provided by the library modules InOut and RealInOut, defined in Professor Wirth's *Programming in Modula-2*. These are the facilities most commonly provided by current implementations, and typify the way in which such facilities can be provided by library modules. Users of a particular implementation must familiarize themselves with whatever facilities are provided by that implementation.

OUTPUT FROM MODULA-2 PROGRAMS

The basic output statements provided by Wirth's InOut and RealInOut modules include the following:

WriteLn	WriteInt(I, FW)
Write(Ch)	WriteCard(C, FW)
WriteString(S)	WriteReal(R, FW)

The expressions Ch, S, I, C and R determine the values to be output, while the expression FW, known as the *field-width*, controls the number of output character positions used. The effect of these statements is defined as follows.

Write(Ch)   *outputs the character value Ch at the next available position on the current line.*

WriteLn   *causes the current output line to be terminated; the next available output position is then the first character position of the next line.*

WriteString(S) *outputs the characters of the string S at the next available positions on the current output line.*

Consider the sequence of statements

```
Write("A"); Write("B"); WriteLn;
Write("C"); Write("D"); WriteLn;
WriteLn;
Write("E"); WriteLn
```

The output resulting from execution of this sequence would be as follows

```
AB
CD

E
```

Execution of the statement sequence

```
WriteString("Hello");
WriteLn;
WriteString("Today is Tuesday")
```

produces output

```
Hello
Today is Tuesday
```

WriteCard(C, FW) *outputs the CARDINAL value C as an appropriate sequence of decimal digits, at the next available positions on the current output line.*

WriteInt(I, FW)   *outputs the INTEGER value I as an appropriate sequence of decimal digits, and preceding minus sign if necessary, at the next available positions on the current output line.*

WriteReal(R, FW) *outputs the REAL value R as an appropriate sequence of sign, decimal digits, decimal point, exponent, etc. at the next available positions on the current output line.*

IM-C

The exact number of characters output for each value, which is called the *field-width*, is determined by the value of the second expression FW in the WriteInt, WriteCard and WriteReal statements. If the actual value to be output requires less than the number of characters specified by the value FW, an appropriate number of blank characters is output before the value itself. If the actual value to be output requires more than the number of characters specified as the field width, the minimum increased field width required to represent the value is used.

Table 5.1 compares the output produced by several WriteInt statements, assuming the INTEGER variable I has the value 999 in each case. For the sake of clarity, a tilde ~ is used to represent each output blank.

Statement	Output	Comments
WriteInt(I, 6)	~~~999	3 leading blanks output
WriteInt(I+1, 6)	~~1000	2 leading blanks output
WriteInt(−(I+1), 6)	~−1000	1 leading blank output
WriteInt(I, 3)	999	no leading blanks needed
WriteInt(I+1, 3)	1000	field-width extended to 4

Table 5.1   Some output statements showing field-width control

The advantages of using character strings and appropriate field width specifications can be seen from Table 5.2, which compares various sequences of output statements and the output they produce.

Statement(s)	Output
WriteReal(A, 16)	−0.357000000E+02
WriteReal(A, 10)	−0.357E+02
WriteString("A = "); WriteReal(A, 10)	A = −0.357E+02

Table 5.2   Some output statements showing layout control

The library modules defined in Professor Wirth's book provide no facilities for output of Boolean values, of values of enumerated types, or of real values in "fixed-point" format (i.e., without an exponent), though some implementations of WriteReal choose between fixed and floating-point formats according to the magnitude of the real value to be output. The module InOut, however, does provide additional facilities for output of integer and real values in octal and hexadecimal form. The complete range of the facilities provided by Wirth's definition is summarized in Appendix 3. Individual implementations of Modula-2 may include additional facilities in the InOut and RealInOut modules they provide, or may provide equivalent facilities in a different form. Modula-2 users must therefore take care to find out the exact input/output facilities provided by each implementation that they use.

INPUT TO MODULA-2 PROGRAMS

If a program requires input from a user at a terminal keyboard, then some sort of dialogue between the program and the user must be performed in order that the required input data may be obtained. Hence, when the input device is the standard terminal keyboard, a program requiring some input data should first send a *prompt* message to the terminal screen informing the user as to the nature of the information required. Suppose a program executes the statement

WriteString ("Enter your age : ")

If we use an underscore _ to denote the input cursor position on the screen, this would cause the following display:

```
Enter your age :  _
```

If the next statement executed by the program is then

ReadInt(Age)

where Age is a variable of type INTEGER, this attempts to read the characters typed in response, and form a valid integer value. Suppose the user types in a "7", thus:

```
Enter your age : 7_
```

(Note that the input character "7" appears on the screen at this stage, not through any action by the program, but as a result of the *automatic echo* facility provided for keyboard input by most computer systems.)

Having read the "7", the program still cannot continue as it has no indication as yet that the user has finished typing in the integer value (for instance, the user's age may be 71). Hence the ReadInt statement needs to know that typing of the number is complete before allowing execution to continue at the next statement. This is achieved by typing a character which cannot be part of an integer number, e.g., a space or the RETURN key. By convention in this book we shall assume that the RETURN key is always typed to indicate termination of any data input in response to a prompt output by a program.

Suppose that a "1" and RETURN are now typed. The screen will look like this:

```
Enter your age : 71

_
```

Note that the new position of the cursor implies that RETURN has been typed. On detecting the RETURN, ReadInt will assign the value 71 to the variable Age, and the program will continue execution at the statement following the ReadInt statement.

The ReadInt statement illustrated is just one of a range of statements made available by InOut and ReallnOut for inputting values from the standard input stream to a Modula-2 program. These include

Read(Ch)   ReadInt(I)
ReadCard(C)   ReadReal(R)

Direct input of values of an enumerated-type, or the type BOOLEAN, is not provided. Input of strings is provided, but we do not consider it until Chapter 8.

As illustrated for ReadInt above, the action on execution of any of these statements is to obtain from the standard input data stream the required data value, and to assign it to the variable concerned. Thus

Read(Ch)   *obtains the next character from the input stream and assigns its value to the* CHAR *variable* Ch.

ReadInt(I)   *obtains an integer value from the input stream and assigns its value to the* INTEGER *variable* I.

ReadCard(C)   *obtains a cardinal value from the input stream and assigns its value to the* CARDINAL *variable* C.

ReadReal(R)   *obtains a real value from the input stream and assigns its value to the* REAL *variable* R.

Each of the above input statements may be thought of as an assignment-statement which obtains the value to be assigned to the named variable from the input stream rather than from an expression. Therefore, the value obtained must be assignment compatible with the type of the variable to which it is to be assigned. How the value is represented in the input stream depends on the input statement concerned.

A character value in the input stream is represented simply by the single character to be assigned. For character input, blank characters are significant and are not ignored. Likewise ends of line are significant during character input—an end of line is input by typing RETURN, and the resultant value assigned to the character variable concerned is that denoted by a constant-identifier EOL declared within the InOut module.

Each INTEGER value in the input stream is represented by a sequence of decimal digits and may be immediately preceded by a plus or minus sign. However, a CARDINAL value must be an unsigned integer number. Likewise a REAL value may be represented as a sequence of characters in any of the forms allowed for a real number or an integer number (see Chapter 2), and it may be immediately preceded by a plus or minus sign. Each integer, cardinal or real value may be preceded by any number of blank characters, but there must be no characters between the sign (if present) and the number.

The characters input to a program are treated as a continuous stream. Each input statement executed begins to obtain values from the point in the input stream immediately following the last value obtained by the previously executed input statement. No character in the input stream can be read more than once.

Reading a numeric value from the input data stream causes the program to read one character beyond the end of the number. In some cases the program needs to inspect that terminating character and so the InOut module provides a variable

VAR termCH: CHAR;

whose value is set by the ReadCard and ReadInt statements to the value of the first character following the number read. For example, if the program executes the statement

ReadInt(Age)

and the next characters in the input stream are "7", "1" and RETURN, then 71 will be assigned to Age, and termCH will be assigned the value denoted by the constant-identifier EOL.

In most implementations, the ReadReal statement also sets termCH, though this is not strictly required by Professor Wirth's definition.

A read operation may fail to obtain the value requested from the input stream, either because the stream is exhausted, or because the characters read do not form a valid sequence for the required input type, e.g., if ReadCard finds an input character sequence which is not a valid representation of a cardinal number. To enable programs to detect such an event, InOut provides a Boolean variable

VAR Done: BOOLEAN;

Each execution of Read, ReadInt or ReadCard that obtains a valid value of the required type assigns the value TRUE to Done, while each execution that fails assigns the value FALSE to Done. The use of Done to control the input of a sequence of values is illustrated in Chapter 6.

For input from a keyboard the user indicates that no further input data is available, i.e., that the end of the input data stream has been reached, by typing a special implementation-defined key. The ESCAPE key is used in many Modula-2 systems for this purpose, but some systems use other keys. Reading of this character by an input statement in a program will cause FALSE to be assigned to Done.

As an example of the possible forms of the input data and the effect of execution of the various input statements, consider the following sequence of input statements:

ReadReal(R);
Read(Ch);
Read(Ch);
Read(Ch);

```
ReadCard(C);
ReadInt(I);
Read(Ch)
```

Table 5.3 shows the values normally assigned to R, Ch, C, I, Done and termCH
as a result of inputting the character sequence

     640.0<*RETURN*>XYZ104<*SPACE*>-12<*RETURN*><*ESCAPE*>

where <*RETURN*>, <*SPACE*> and <*ESCAPE*> denote the RETURN, blank and
ESCAPE keys on the keyboard, and <*ESCAPE*> is assumed to denote the end of
the input data stream.

	R	*Ch*	*C*	*I*	*termCH*	*Done*
ReadReal(R)	640.0				EOL	TRUE
Read(Ch)		"X"				TRUE
Read(Ch)		"Y"				TRUE
Read(Ch)		"Z"				TRUE
ReadCard(C)			104		" "	TRUE
ReadInt(I)				-12	EOL	TRUE
Read(Ch)						FALSE

Table 5.3 Some input statements and their effects

IMPORT-LISTS

Each program which uses any of the input and output facilities described in this
chapter must contain appropriate *import-lists* to specify which of the data items
and statements provided by InOut and RealInOut it intends to use. Table 5.4
shows to which of these two modules each of the various data items and statements described in this book belongs.

	InOut		*RealInOut*
Write	Read	OpenInput	WriteReal
WriteInt	ReadInt	CloseInput	ReadReal
WriteCard	ReadCard	OpenOutput	(variable) Done
WriteString	ReadString	CloseOutput	
WriteLn	(constant) EOL		
	(variable) Done		

Table 5.4 Exported facilities of InOut and RealInOut

Of the facilities listed, OpenInput, CloseInput, OpenOutput and CloseOutput are
discussed later in this chapter, while ReadString is discussed in Chapter 8.

Depending on the nature of the input and output actions performed by a program, it must specify each of the actual facilities of InOut and RealInOut it uses in import-lists in the program-heading. Hence a program which uses EOL, Read, Write, WriteLn and ReadReal, say, normally contains the import-lists:

FROM InOut IMPORT EOL, Read, Write, WriteLn;
FROM RealInOut IMPORT ReadReal;

Note, however, that RealInOut also provides a Boolean variable Done which may be used to determine whether an attempt to input a real value via ReadReal has been successful. If Done is imported from both InOut and RealInOut a name clash occurs. In programs which need to use the Done variables of both modules, *qualified import* (as explained in Chapter 11) must be used. Thus a program which uses both ReadInt and ReadReal, and needs to use the appropriate Done variable in each case, might use the following import list

IMPORT InOut, RealInOut

and refer to each of the facilities used in qualified form, thus:

InOut.ReadInt   InOut.Done   RealInOut.ReadReal   RealInOut.Done

The use of the input and output facilities provided by InOut and RealInOut is illustrated in the following case study, and in most of the example and case study programs of this book. Appendix 3 contains a detailed definition of the various facilities provided by the InOut and RealInOut modules.

CASE STUDY 1

A program is required which will read in from the terminal three integers representing the blast-off time of a rocket expressed in hours, minutes and seconds on the 24-hour clock, then read in another integer giving the rocket's flight time in seconds, and finally use these data values to calculate the time of day at which the rocket will return to Earth, with this time displayed in a readable format.

The method used in designing the program for this and all other case studies in this book is to break the specified problem down into a number of sub-problems expressed in concise, ordinary English. This same approach is then used to break down each sub-problem into further sub-problems. The method is repeatedly applied until each of the sub-problems can be readily and easily expressed in Modula-2. This technique is often referred to as "programming by stepwise refinement".

Noting that it is good practice to write out any data read in by a program (so that any errors in the preparation of the input data may be detected) the solution to the problem may be stated informally as:

obtain and confirm data;
calculate time of arrival;
print out time of arrival

The first action, *obtain and confirm data*, consists of two actions:

obtain and confirm blast-off time;
obtain and confirm flight time

The introduction of three positive integer (i.e., CARDINAL) variables Hours, Minutes and Seconds allows the first of these two actions to be expressed as a combination of various input and output statements provided by the InOut module. The input statements required are simply

ReadCard(Hours); ReadCard(Minutes); ReadCard(Seconds);

preceded by a suitable prompt message specifying the format in which the time should be supplied

WriteString("Give blast-off time as hh mm ss <RETURN> : ");

The output statements must print a string "Blast-off time is" and the blast-off time in the format *hh:mm:ss*. This is to appear on a line by itself, and we leave a blank line between each of the lines of significant output produced by the program. Thus, we use the following statements:

WriteString("Blast-off time is ");
WriteCard(Hours, 2); Write(":");
WriteCard(Minutes, 2); Write(":");
WriteCard(Seconds, 2);
WriteLn; WriteLn

Note that the cardinal values have been output with a field width of 2 to obtain the required format.

Similarly, *obtain and confirm flight time* can be programmed as a simple series of input and output statements involving a CARDINAL variable FlightTime:

WriteString("Give flight time in seconds, followed by <RETURN> : ");
ReadCard(FlightTime);
WriteString("Flight time = ");
WriteCard(FlightTime, 7); WriteString(" seconds");
WriteLn; WriteLn

Next we deal with the sub-problem *calculate time of arrival*. The problem requires the time of day at which the rocket returns to Earth to be found. This is computed by means of the six assignment-statements listed below. Note that the order of the assignments is critical and another order might produce erroneous results.

```
Seconds := Seconds + FlightTime;
Minutes := Minutes + Seconds DIV 60;
Seconds := Seconds MOD 60;
Hours := Hours + Minutes DIV 60;
Minutes := Minutes MOD 60;
Hours := Hours MOD 24
```

Finally, *print out time of arrival* consists of outputting a suitable caption followed by the values of the variables Hours, Minutes and Seconds, suitably formatted. The required output statements are

```
WriteString ("Expected time of arrival = ") ;
WriteCard (Hours, 2) ; Write (":") ;
WriteCard (Minutes, 2) ; Write (":") ;
WriteCard (Seconds, 2) ;
WriteLn
```

The final program Rocket can now be put together. It consists of a program-heading, with an import-list naming the input and output statements from InOut that are used, the variable declarations and the statement part. The variables are all of type CARDINAL. The statement-part contains the statements we have developed above, enclosed by BEGIN and END and followed by the program-identifier Rocket and a period to denote the end of the program.

```
MODULE Rocket;
    (* This program reads in three numbers representing the blast-off time of
       a rocket expressed in hours, minutes and seconds on the 24-hour clock.
       It then reads a fourth number giving the flight time in seconds, and
       prints out the estimated time of arrival.                           *)

    FROM InOut IMPORT ReadCard, Write, WriteString, WriteCard, WriteLn;

    VAR Hours, Minutes, Seconds, FlightTime: CARDINAL;

    BEGIN
        (* read in and print out data: *)
        WriteString("Give blast-off time as hh mm ss <RETURN> : ");
        ReadCard(Hours); ReadCard(Minutes); ReadCard(Seconds);
        WriteLn;
        WriteString("Blast-off time is ");
        WriteCard(Hours, 2); Write(":");
        WriteCard(Minutes, 2); Write(":");
        WriteCard(Seconds, 2);
        WriteLn; WriteLn;
```

```
WriteString("Give flight time in seconds, followed by <RETURN> : ");
ReadCard(FlightTime);
WriteLn;
WriteString("Flight time = ");
WriteCard(FlightTime, 7); WriteString(" seconds");
WriteLn; WriteLn;

(* calculate time of arrival: *)
Seconds := Seconds + FlightTime;
Minutes := Minutes + Seconds DIV 60;
Seconds := Seconds MOD 60;
Hours := Hours + Minutes DIV 60;
Minutes := Minutes MOD 60;
Hours := Hours MOD 24;

(* print out time of arrival: *)
WriteString("Expected time of arrival = ");
WriteCard(Hours, 2); Write(":");
WriteCard(Minutes, 2); Write(":");
WriteCard(Seconds, 2);
WriteLn
END Rocket.
```

A sample of the information displayed on the terminal screen by an execution of
the program follows:

```
Give blast-off time as hh mm ss <RETURN> : 3 47 32

Blast-off time is  3:47:32

Give flight time in seconds, followed by <RETURN> : 45678

Flight time =   45678 seconds

Expected time of arrival = 16:28:50
```

This program is somewhat unsatisfactory in the way in which it handles the
input from the terminal. Should the user enter erroneous data values, e.g., an
invalid blast-off time, then the program will produce unpredictable results. A
better, more *robust*, program would examine the input data and, if it is not satisfactory, inform the user and request input of a correct value until acceptable
input has been obtained. We are not yet in a position to program the actions
required to do so but will consider them in Chapter 8. In the meantime, our
example programs will assume that the user supplies valid input data.

ALTERNATIVE INPUT AND OUTPUT STREAMS

In some situations it is not appropriate to provide input from a keyboard. For example, there may be a large volume of information to be input, in which case it may be preferable to prepare in advance a disk file containing the information to be processed.

Likewise, it may not always be desirable to send the output from a program to a terminal screen, e.g., because there is a large volume of data that we wish to inspect at our leisure, because we wish to print it using a special printer, or because we may wish to have some subsequent program read this output as its input data. In this case we may wish to send the output in character form to a disk file for subsequent printing or input to another program.

As we have already explained, the InOut module, assumes that every program has an input data stream and an output data stream which are both sequences of characters. By default, the various input and output statements provided by InOut assume that these two streams are allocated to the terminal keyboard and screen, respectively.

These default allocations may be changed by means of four further statements provided by the InOut module

OpenInput(S)   OpenOutput(S)

CloseInput   CloseOutput

where S is a string.

Execution of the statement

OpenInput(S)

causes an implementation-defined dialogue to take place between the program and the user—this dialogue usually involves the user entering (through the keyboard) the name of the file which contains the input data. The program then determines if such a file exists (by searching the "directory" of files accessible to the user). If the file exists then the file is "opened" for reading, and Done is assigned TRUE. Subsequent input statements then obtain their input from the sequence of characters in this file. If no file of the given name exists then Done is assigned FALSE, and subsequent input statements will continue to access the standard input stream, i.e., the terminal keyboard.

To cease taking input from a file opened in this way, the statement

CloseInput

must be executed by the program. This causes the current input file to be "closed", and input to revert to the standard input stream.

To create a file containing output generated by a program, the statement

OpenOutput(S)

is executed. Again an implementation-defined dialogue takes place, which usually requires the user to input (via the keyboard) the name of the output file. If an empty file with this name can be created in the user's file directory it is, the file is opened for output, and Done is assigned TRUE. All subsequent output from the program is then directed to the named file. If, for some reason, an empty file with the required name cannot be created, then Done is assigned FALSE, and subsequent output will continue to be directed to the standard output stream, e.g., the user's terminal screen.

Execution of

CloseOutput

causes the current output file to be closed, and subsequent output reverts back to the standard output stream.

The string S required by OpenInput and OpenOutput usually contains some information that relates to the conventions used by the particular computer system for naming files. Since these conventions vary widely, for simplicity in this book we shall assume that the string S is always the empty string, and that all information relating to the file name is entered during the dialogue invoked by OpenInput and OpenOutput. For instance, suppose we wish to use a file called PAYROLL as our input file and send output to a file called CHECKS, the program concerned would contain statements such as

OpenInput (""); OpenOutput ("")

Execution of the OpenInput statement might cause a message of the following form to appear on the screen

```
Enter Input File Name: _
```

and the program user at the terminal would respond with

```
Enter Input File Name: PAYROLL

_
```

Likewise, execution of OpenOutput would have a similar effect, e.g.,

```
Enter Output File Name: _
```

and the user's response would have the effect

```
Enter Output File Name: CHECKS

_
```

All subsequent input and output statements of the program would then use PAYROLL and CHECKS, respectively, until these files are closed by the statements CloseInput and CloseOutput.

In principle, all files opened by a program must be closed, though in practice the implementation or its surrounding environment may make provision for doing so if the program does not. In general, however, it is good programming practice to close all files that are opened within the program itself. In particular, the definition of the InOut module does not specify what happens if a program tries to open a second file as its input (or output) stream without closing the first, and an exception may occur in this case. Likewise an exception may occur if the program tries to close a file as its input (or output) stream when none is open for this purpose.

EXERCISES

5.1 Given the following input data

```
    24.7      -33E10   0.075<RETURN>
```

and variables declared as follows

VAR X, Y, Z: REAL; I, J, K: INTEGER; C: CHAR;

what effect would you expect on executing each of the following sequences of input statements?

(a) ReadReal(X); ReadReal(Y); ReadReal(Z)

(b) ReadInt(I); Read(C); ReadInt(J); ReadInt(K)

Indicate the value of termCH following execution of each statement. Check your predictions against an available implementation of InOut and ReallnOut, if available. The actual effects may not be those you anticipated!

5.2 Given CARDINAL variables Count, Min and Max, and a REAL variable Mean, write a sequence of statements to print their values as follows:

```
    NUMBER         RANGE        MEAN
    xxx            xx..xx       xx.x
```

5.3 Write a program which reads a sum of money written in the form *ddd.dd*, increases it by 8 per cent, and prints out the original and increased sums. Would your program work if the input was in the form *ddd:dd*? If not, how would you modify your program to make it work?

5.4 Write a program which reads in the cost of an item sold, and the amount of money tendered by the customer, and prints out the following:

```
    AMOUNT DUE          $xxx.xx
    AMOUNT TENDERED     $xxx.xx
    CHANGE DUE          $xxx.xx
```

6

Basic Control Structures

The basic power of a computer lies in its ability to carry out sequential, selective, and repetitive actions at great speed. Modula-2 provides for the expression of such actions by a variety of *structured-statements*:

> *structured-statement =*
> *conditional-statement | repetitive-statement | with-statement.*

The *with-statement* is a special-purpose construct whose use we consider in Chapter 9, but the remaining structured-statements are all explained in this chapter.

STATEMENT SEQUENCES

A *statement-sequence* has the form

> *statement-sequence = statement {";" statement}.*

i.e., it consists of a sequence of *statements* separated by semicolons. Execution of a statement-sequence simply involves the execution of its component statements in the order in which they are written.

For example,

> A := B; B := C; C := A

is a statement-sequence consisting of three assignment-statements. We have already seen examples of statement-sequences in the programs considered in previous chapters—the *statement-part* of each Modula-2 program itself contains a statement-sequence.

Figure 6.1 shows the sequence of actions resulting from a statement-sequence s1; s2; s3 in the form of a flow diagram. Although we use flow diagrams in this chapter to show the flow of control that Modula-2's structured statements imply, we do not recommend their use as a tool for program design as they permit an undisciplined approach to program construction.

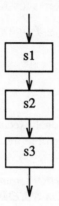

Figure 6.1   Flow of control in a statement sequence

The significant role of a statement-sequence is to place a sequence of one or more statements under the control of one of Modula-2's structured statements, as we shall see in the following sections.

Within the statement-sequence the semicolon acts as a statement separator. As we saw in Chapter 4, an *empty-statement* is a statement consisting of no symbols and having no effect. Thus

$$A := B; ; B := C; C := A;$$

is a valid statement-sequence consisting of an assignment-statement, an empty-statement, two more assignment-statements, and a final empty-statement. Within a statement-sequence such empty-statements have no effect, so in the above example omission of the second and last semicolons would not alter the effect of the sequence in any way. Note, however, that a statement-sequence can itself consist of a single statement, and hence of a single empty-statement, i.e., of no symbols.

Thus the sequence of symbols

MODULE null; BEGIN END null.

is a valid if unexciting Modula-2 program, which does nothing! However, we see later that an empty statement-sequence is useful in expressing some program actions.

CONDITIONAL STATEMENTS

It is often necessary to make the execution of a statement or statement sequence dependent upon some condition, or else at some point to choose to execute one of a number of possible statement sequences depending upon some condition. Modula-2 provides two statement forms for this purpose

conditional-statement = if-statement / case-statement.

which we consider in turn.

The If-statement

The *if-statement* allows the conditional execution of one statement-sequence, or the choice between execution of two or more statement sequences.

if-statement =
"IF" expression "THEN" statement-sequence
{ "ELSIF" expression "THEN" statement-sequence }
["ELSE" statement-sequence]
"END".

Each of the expressions which follows the IF or ELSIF keywords must produce a Boolean result.
    Thus, an *if-statement* has the general form

```
IF e1 THEN ss1
ELSIF e2 THEN ss2
ELSIF e3 THEN ss3
...
ELSE ssn
END
```

where the ELSIF and ELSE clauses are optional.
    In its shortest form, i.e., without ELSIF and ELSE clauses, thus

```
IF e1 THEN ss1 END
```

the action of the if-statement is to evaluate the expression e1 and, if and only if its value is TRUE, to execute the statement-sequence ss1. In either case execution then continues at the statement following the if-statement.
    If an ELSE clause is present but no ELSIF clauses are used, e.g.,

```
IF e1 THEN ss1 ELSE ss2 END
```

the Boolean expression e1 is evaluated and if its value is TRUE then the statement-sequence following THEN (i.e., ss1) is executed, otherwise the statement-sequence following ELSE (i.e., ss2) is executed. Once again, in either case execution continues at the statement following the if-statement.

If ELSIF clauses are present then the expressions following the IF and ELSIF clauses are evaluated in order of appearance until one yields the value TRUE, in which case the associated statement-sequence is executed. If none of the expressions is TRUE and an ELSE clause is present, then the statement-sequence following ELSE is executed.

The control structures for the simplest if-statements are illustrated in Figure 6.2.

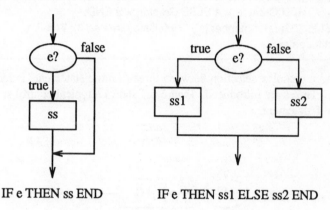

IF e THEN ss END   IF e THEN ss1 ELSE ss2 END

Figure 6.2 Flow of control in simple if-statements

Some examples of such if-statements are:

```
IF Ch = EOL THEN EndOfLine := TRUE END
```

```
IF Done THEN Write(Ch)
ELSE WriteString("Data all read")
END
```

```
IF ThisMonth = December THEN
  ThisMonth := January; ThisYear := ThisYear + 1
ELSE INC(ThisMonth)
END
```

```
IF B*B < 4.0*A*C THEN
  WriteString("Quadratic has complex roots")
ELSE
  D := sqrt(B*B - 4.0*A*C);
  WriteReal((-B+D)/(2.0*A), 12);
  WriteReal((-B-D)/(2.0*A), 12)
END
```

The program FindGreater reads in two positive integers and determines the greater of their values.

```
MODULE FindGreater;
  FROM InOut IMPORT ReadCard, WriteCard, WriteString, WriteLn;
  VAR A, B, Greater: CARDINAL;
  BEGIN
    WriteString("Type in first number: "); ReadCard(A); WriteLn;
    WriteString("Type in second number: "); ReadCard(B); WriteLn;
    IF A > B THEN Greater := A ELSE Greater := B END;
    WriteString("Greater number is"); WriteCard(Greater, 8); WriteLn
  END FindGreater.
```

If a more complex selection between three or more statements is required, then ELSIF clauses are introduced. Figure 6.3 shows a typical control structure for such an if-statement.

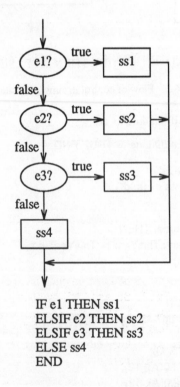

```
IF e1 THEN ss1
ELSIF e2 THEN ss2
ELSIF e3 THEN ss3
ELSE ss4
END
```

Figure 6.3   Flow of control using ELSIF

Some examples of such if-statements are:

```
IF X < 0 THEN Sign := TRUE
ELSIF X > 0 THEN Sign := FALSE
ELSE WriteString("Value is zero")
END

IF Ch = "I" THEN n := 1
ELSIF Ch = "V" THEN n := 5
ELSIF Ch = "X" THEN n := 10
ELSIF Ch = "L" THEN n := 50
END
```

The program BuzzBuzz1 reads an integer value (assumed to be positive and less than 100) and outputs one of the following messages:

(a) the word "buzz" if the value contains the digit 7, otherwise
(b) the word "buzz-buzz" if the value is a multiple of 7, otherwise
(c) the value itself.

```
MODULE BuzzBuzz1;
  FROM InOut IMPORT ReadCard, WriteCard, WriteString, WriteLn;
  VAR I: CARDINAL;
  BEGIN
    WriteString("Input number in range [1..99]: "); ReadCard(I); WriteLn;
    IF (I DIV 10 = 7) OR (I MOD 10 = 7) THEN WriteString("buzz")
    ELSIF I MOD 7 = 0 THEN WriteString("buzz-buzz")
    ELSE WriteCard(I, 3)
    END;
    WriteLn
  END BuzzBuzz1.
```

Note that in setting out if-statements we will consistently use one of two formats:

(a) if the entire if-statement can be fitted on one line, it is;
(b) otherwise the IF, ELSIF, ELSE and END symbols are aligned to the same left margin; in this case each statement-sequence within the if-statement is placed on the same line as the THEN or ELSE preceding it if the entire sequence fits on the same line, otherwise it is set out on the following line(s) with an indented left margin.

These conventions are not required by Modula-2, but systematic use of them significantly increases the readability of programs.

CASE STUDY 2

A program is required which reads in three positive integers, in ascending order, which are assumed to represent the lengths of the sides of a triangle, and prints out these input data, together with one of the following descriptions of the nature of the triangle so defined:

> *not a triangle*
> *an equilateral triangle*
> *an isosceles triangle*
> *a scalene triangle*

and the area of the triangle (when appropriate).

In outline the required program can be broken down into two steps:

read and print the lengths of the sides;
determine and print details of the triangle

The step *read and print the lengths of the sides* is immediately expressible as input and output statements using three CARDINAL variables A, B, C to represent the lengths of the three sides in ascending order.

The step *determine and print details of the triangle* can first be broken down as

IF *it is a triangle* THEN
 determine and print its nature and area
ELSE WriteString ("not a triangle")
END

Three lines form a triangle if and only if the length of the longest line is less than the sum of the lengths of the two shorter lines. Since A, B, C represent the sides in ascending order of length the condition *it is a triangle* is immediately expressible as

$$A + B > C$$

Determining the nature of the triangle is also readily expressible in terms of these ordered lengths, thus:

IF A = C THEN *triangle is equilateral*
ELSIF (A =B) OR (B = C) THEN *triangle is isosceles*
ELSE *triangle is scalene*
END

The area of a triangle of sides *a, b, c* is given by the formula

$$Area = \sqrt{s(s-a)(s-b)(s-c)}$$

where *s* is half the sum of the sides *a, b, c,* so this too is easily programmed using real values for *s* and the area to allow for the possible fractional parts. Modula-2 itself does not provide a square root function but we assume here that one is provided in a library module named MathLib0. Like InOut and RealInOut, the library module MathLib0 is defined in Wirth's *Programming in Modula-2* and is supported by most implementations. Its recommended facilities are summarized in Appendix 3.

We can now construct the final program Triangles, as shown:

```
MODULE Triangles;
    FROM InOut IMPORT ReadCard, WriteCard, WriteString, WriteLn;
    FROM RealInOut IMPORT WriteReal;
    FROM MathLib0 IMPORT sqrt;

    (* This program inputs three cardinal values which are presumed
       to be the lengths of the sides of a triangle,  determines if
       they define a possible triangle, and if so determines its
       class (scalene, isosceles or equilateral) and its area.       *)

    VAR   A, B, C: CARDINAL; S, Area: REAL;

    BEGIN
        (* read and print sides in ascending order *)
        WriteString("Input lengths of sides, separated by <SPACE>: ");
        ReadCard(A); ReadCard(B); ReadCard(C);
        WriteLn;
        WriteCard(A, 3); WriteCard(B, 3); WriteCard(C, 3); WriteString(" ... ");

        (* determine and print details *)
        IF A + B > C THEN

            (* determine and print nature of triangle *)
            IF A = C THEN WriteString("an equilateral triangle")
            ELSIF (A = B) OR (B = C) THEN WriteString("an isosceles triangle")
            ELSE WriteString("a scalene triangle")
            END;

            (* determine and print area *)
            S := 0.5 * FLOAT(A+B+C);
            Area := sqrt( S * (S–FLOAT(A)) * (S–FLOAT(B)) * (S–FLOAT(C)) );
            WriteString(" of area "); WriteReal(Area, 11)

        ELSE WriteString("not a triangle")
        END;
        WriteLn
    END Triangles.
```

The Case-statement

One pattern which we have seen already and which occurs frequently in programming, and so deserves special consideration, is the *selection* of one of a set of actions according to the value of some expression. This can be expressed using an if-statement, as in the Roman numeral example given earlier:

```
IF Ch = "I" THEN n := 1
ELSIF Ch = "V" THEN n := 5
ELSIF Ch = "X" THEN n := 10
ELSIF Ch = "L" THEN n := 50
END
```

A more elegant way of expressing such an action in Modula-2 is to use the *case-statement*, which has the following syntax:

> *case-statement* =
>   *"CASE" expression "OF"*
>   *case-limb {"|" case-limb}*
>   *["ELSE" statement-sequence]*
>   *"END".*
> *case-limb = [case-label-list ":" statement-sequence].*
> *case-label-list = case-labels {"," case-labels}.*
> *case-labels = constant-expression [".." constant-expression].*

The *expression* following CASE is known as the *selector*, and must yield a value of an ordinal type. The *constant-expressions* which prefix the *statement-sequence* in each *case-limb* are known as *case-labels*, and must yield values of the same type as the selector.

The action of a case-statement is to evaluate the selector *expression* and then execute the statement-sequence labeled by the resulting value. After this, execution proceeds to the statement which follows the case-statement. If there is no case label corresponding to the selector value and an ELSE clause is present then the statement-sequence following ELSE is selected, otherwise an exception occurs.

Figure 6.4 shows a typical form of case-statement and the resultant control structure.

The statement at the start of this subsection can now be rewritten as

```
CASE Ch OF
  "I": n := 1 |
  "V": n := 5 |
  "X": n := 10 |
  "L": n := 50
END
```

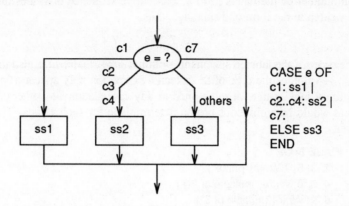

Figure 6.4 Flow of control in a case-statement

The program PocketCalculator1 simulates the action of a very simple pocket calculator. It reads in two real values separated by an arithmetic operator +, −, * or /, and calculates the result of the operation. Thus, input of 7.1+5.3 produces output of 12.4 in floating-point form.

```
MODULE PocketCalculator1;
  FROM InOut IMPORT Read, WriteString, WriteLn;
  FROM RealInOut IMPORT ReadReal, WriteReal;

  VAR Value1, Value2: REAL; Operator: CHAR;
  BEGIN
    WriteString("Input number operator number <RETURN>: ");
    ReadReal(Value1); Read(Operator); ReadReal(Value2);
    WriteLn;
    CASE Operator OF
      "+": WriteReal(Value1 + Value2, 10) |
      "−": WriteReal(Value1 − Value2, 10) |
      "*": WriteReal(Value1 * Value2, 10) |
      "/": WriteReal(Value1 / Value2, 10)
    END;
    WriteLn
  END PocketCalculator1.
```

In a case-statement, two or more case-labels may be associated with the same statement-sequence, in which case they are separated by commas (and need not be written in any particular order), e.g.,

$$3, 7, 2, 1, 15: X := Y + 2$$

If a number of the labels form a consecutive sequence of values then they may be written in the form of a subrange, thus

$$1..3, 7, 15: X := Y + 2$$

The order of the labeled statements within a *case-statement* is also irrelevant.

A value of the type of the selector expression may appear as a label, or lie within a label range, at most once in any case-statement—otherwise the statement would be ambiguous or non-deterministic for such values. Thus the statement

```
CASE N OF
  1..3, 5, 7:Write("prime") |
  4, 6, 8: Write("multiple of 2") |
  6, 9: Write("multiple of 3")
END
```

is illegal since it is ambiguous for N = 6.

When no ELSE clause is included in a case-statement, each value to be taken by the selector expression must appear as a label, or lie within a label range, in exactly one of the case-limbs. Thus the statement

```
CASE N OF
  1: N := 2 |
  3: N := 4 |
  5..7: N := 8
END
```

is inadequate for adjusting a variable N (with value in the range 1 to 8) to the smallest power of 2 greater than or equal to its original value, since it does not specify an action when N is 2, 4 or 8. If no action is to be taken for certain values of the selector expression then those values must be associated with an empty-statement, either in a case-limb or by the ELSE clause, thus:

```
CASE N OF                    CASE N OF
  1: N := 2 |                  1: N := 2 |
  3: N := 4 |                  3: N := 4 |
  5..7: N := 8 |               5..7: N := 8 |
  2, 4, 8:                     ELSE
END                          END
```

Note, however, that if N takes an unexpected value outside the range 1 to 8, execution of the first statement causes an exception to occur, while execution of the second does not. In this sense the first statement is more precise, in that it enumerates all cases envisaged by the programmer, and enables unexpected data cases to be detected as exceptions. Before using an ELSE clause in a case-statement, a programmer must be certain that all possible values of the selector expression are properly handled by doing so.

The pocket calculator program given earlier is unsatisfactory in that if the user types an operator character other than +, –, * or / an exception occurs. To make the program more robust we might use an ELSE clause, as in the program PocketCalculator2.

```
MODULE PocketCalculator2;
  FROM InOut IMPORT Read, Write, WriteString, WriteLn;
  FROM RealInOut IMPORT ReadReal, WriteReal;

  CONST BELL = 07C; (* Terminal Bell Character *)

  VAR Value1, Value2: REAL; Operator: CHAR;

  BEGIN
    WriteString("Input number operator number <RETURN>: ");
    ReadReal(Value1); Read(Operator); ReadReal(Value2);
    WriteLn;
    CASE Operator OF
      "+": WriteReal(Value1 + Value2, 10) |
      "–": WriteReal(Value1 – Value2, 10) |
      "*": WriteReal(Value1 * Value2, 10) |
      "/": WriteReal(Value1 / Value2, 10)
    ELSE
        Write (BELL);
        WriteString("Illegal operator symbol")
    END;
    WriteLn
  END PocketCalculator2.
```

CASE STUDY 3

Here we construct a program which, given three integers whose values represent a day between 1 January 1900 and 31 December 1999, will output the values representing the day following.

The input data consist of three integers representing the month, day of month, and year of date, e.g., 12 2 1985 represents the 2nd of December 1985. The outline structure of the program is thus:

read date; confirm date;
update date to following day;
output date

The date can be represented by three variables

> Month   a variable of the subrange-type [1 .. 12];
> Day   a variable of the subrange-type [1 .. 31];
> Year   a variable of the subrange-type [1900 .. 2000].

The *read date* operation is programmed as

```
WriteString("Input date as mm  dd  yyyy: ");
ReadCard(C); Month := C;
ReadCard(C); Day := C;
ReadCard(C); Year := C;
WriteLn;
```

where the auxiliary variable

```
VAR C: CARDINAL;
```

is introduced because ReadCard will only input and assign a value to a variable of type CARDINAL and not to a variable of a CARDINAL subrange type.

Confirming the date input is best achieved as a preamble to the output of the new date, thus:

```
WriteString("The day following "); WriteCard(Month, 2); Write("/");
WriteCard(Day, 2); Write("/"); WriteCard(Year, 4); WriteString(" is ")
```

Expressing the updating operation abstractly as

```
IF last day of month THEN first day of next month
ELSE next day of this month
END
```

we need, first of all, to find the number of days in the month denoted by the value of Month. Introducing a variable DaysInMonth this can be computed using a case-statement:

```
CASE Month OF
  1, 3, 5, 7, 8, 10, 12: DaysInMonth := 31 |
  4, 6, 9, 11: DaysInMonth := 30 |
  2: IF (Year MOD 4 = 0) AND (Year <> 1900)
     THEN DaysInMonth := 29
     ELSE DaysInMonth := 28
     END
END
```

In determining the next month, the step *first day of next month* must also distinguish the case when the current month is December, thus:

```
IF last month of year THEN first month of next year
ELSE next month of this year
END
```

Hence, the updating operation becomes

```
IF Day = DaysInMonth THEN
  Day := 1;
  IF Month = 12 THEN Month := 1; Year := Year + 1
  ELSE Month := Month + 1
  END
ELSE Day := Day + 1
END
```

The output of the new date is obviously similar to that of the input date.

The resultant program NextDay is as shown.

```
MODULE NextDay;
  FROM InOut IMPORT ReadCard, WriteString, WriteCard, Write, WriteLn;
  (* This program determines the date following an input date *)
  VAR
    Day: [1 .. 31]; Month: [1 .. 12]; Year: [1900 .. 2000];
    DaysInMonth: [28 .. 31]; C: CARDINAL;
  BEGIN
    (* read date *)
    WriteString("Input date as mm  dd  yyyy: ");
    ReadCard(C); Month := C;
    ReadCard(C); Day := C;
    ReadCard(C); Year := C;
    WriteLn;
    (* confirm date input *)
    WriteString("The day following "); WriteCard(Month, 2); Write("/");
    WriteCard(Day, 2); Write("/"); WriteCard(Year, 4); WriteString(" is ");
    (* find number of days in month *)
    CASE Month OF
      1, 3, 5, 7, 8, 10, 12: DaysInMonth := 31 |
```

```
    4, 6, 9, 11: DaysInMonth := 30 |
    2: IF (Year MOD 4 = 0) AND (Year <> 1900) THEN DaysInMonth := 29
       ELSE DaysInMonth := 28
       END
  END;

  (* update date to next day *)
  IF Day = DaysInMonth THEN
    Day := 1;
    IF Month = 12 THEN Month := 1; Year := Year + 1
    ELSE Month := Month + 1
    END
  ELSE Day := Day + 1
  END;

  (* output date *)
  WriteCard(Month, 2); Write("/"); WriteCard(Day, 2); Write("/");
  WriteCard(Year, 4); WriteLn
END NextDay.
```

The output produced by a typical input date is as follows:

```
Input date as mm dd yyyy: 12 31 1985

The day following 12/31/1985 is  1/ 1/1986
```

REPETITIVE STATEMENTS

An important class of actions in computer programs is the *loop*, which enables the repetition of some statement, or group of statements, subject normally to some terminating condition.

Modula-2 provides four repetition constructs which reflect the needs of loop construction in most programming situations, viz.,

> *repetitive-statement* =
> *while-statement* | *repeat-statement* |
> *for-statement* | *loop-statement*.

The form and effect of each of these four constructs is defined and illustrated in the following subsections.

The While-statement

This has the syntactic form

while-statement = "WHILE" expression "DO" statement-sequence "END".

The *expression* must produce a value of type BOOLEAN. The action upon execution of a *while-statement* is as follows. The *expression* is repeatedly evaluated and, while it remains true, the *statement-sequence* is executed following each expression evaluation. The repetition terminates as soon as the value of the *expression* becomes false. The flow of control produced by a statement

WHILE e DO SS END

is thus as shown in Figure 6.5.

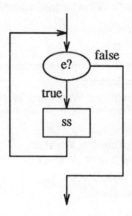

Figure 6.5   Flow of control in a while-statement

Note that, if the expression is initially false, the statement-sequence is not executed at all.

Some examples of while-statements are as follows:

WHILE Ch <> EOL DO Read(Ch) END

WHILE ABS(X-A/X) > 1.0E-6 DO X := 0.5*(X+A/X) END

WHILE Ch = Space DO
  SpaceCount := SpaceCount + 1; Read(Ch)
END

The program Division reads in two positive integers and divides the first integer by the second, using only subtraction and addition operations.

The program GreatestCommonDivisor reads in two positive integers and calculates their greatest common divisor.

```
MODULE Division;
  FROM InOut IMPORT ReadCard, WriteCard, WriteString, WriteLn;
  VAR X, Y, Quotient, Remainder: CARDINAL;
  BEGIN
    WriteString("x = "); ReadCard(X); WriteLn;
    WriteString("y = "); ReadCard(Y); WriteLn;
    Remainder := X; Quotient := 0;
    WHILE Remainder >= Y DO
      Quotient := Quotient + 1; Remainder := Remainder – Y
    END;
    WriteCard(X, 1); WriteString(" divided by "); WriteCard(Y, 1);
    WriteString(" gives "); WriteCard(Quotient, 1);
    WriteString(", remainder "); WriteCard(Remainder, 1);
    WriteLn
  END Division.
```

```
MODULE GreatestCommonDivisor;
  FROM InOut IMPORT ReadCard, WriteCard, WriteString, WriteLn;
  VAR A, B: CARDINAL;
  BEGIN
    WriteString("a = "); ReadCard(A); WriteLn;
    WriteString("b = "); ReadCard(B); WriteLn;
    WriteString("GCD of "); WriteCard(A, 1);
    WriteString(" and "); WriteCard(B, 1);
    WHILE A <> B DO
      IF A > B THEN A := A – B ELSE B := B – A END
    END;
    WriteString(" is "); WriteCard(A, 1); WriteLn
  END GreatestCommonDivisor.
```

While-statements are often used in programming the reading of data items from the input stream. The structure of a program which processes a stream (of indeterminate length) of items of some arbitrary type is expressible as

```
read an item;
WHILE Done DO
  process an item;
  read an item
END
```

where Done is the variable defined by the InOut (or RealInOut) module whose value indicates whether an item was indeed read by the previous input statement.

For the data types we have seen so far, the action *read an item* may be expressed directly using Read, ReadCard, ReadInt, or ReadReal. In Chapters 9–12 we shall describe data items of *structured-types* and see that *read an item* may be expressed in an equivalent form. Irrespective of the actual nature of the data, however, we shall see that the reading of the overall input sequence is still expressible in terms of the above basic while-loop structure.

The Repeat-statement

A *repeat-statement* has the form

repeat-statement = "REPEAT" statement-sequence "UNTIL" expression.

Once again the *expression* must produce a value of type BOOLEAN. The action upon execution of a *repeat-statement* is as follows. The sequence of statements between REPEAT and UNTIL is executed and the Boolean *expression* is then evaluated. If its value is TRUE then the *repeat-statement* is terminated and execution continues at the next statement of the program, otherwise execution of the *statement-sequence* is repeated until the *expression* becomes true. The flow of control resulting from a statement

REPEAT ss UNTIL e

is thus as shown in Figure 6.6.

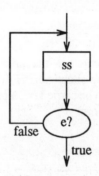

Figure 6.6　Flow of control in a repeat-statement

Some examples of repeat-statements are as follows:

```
REPEAT X := 0.5*(X+A/X) UNTIL ABS(X-A/X) <= 1.0E-6
REPEAT
  SpaceCount := SpaceCount + 1; Read(Ch)
UNTIL Ch <> SPACE
```

The essential difference between repeat- and while-statements is that in the repeat-statement the loop body (i.e., sequence of statements to be repeatedly executed) is performed at least once, before the first evaluation of the terminating condition, whereas in the while-statement the terminating condition is evaluated first and so the loop body may not be executed at all. It is sometimes argued that this difference is insufficient to justify two distinct loop constructs and that one, the while-statement, is adequate for both situations. However, besides making explicit the fact that the loop body is executed once, the repeat-statement plays a useful role in avoiding potential programming errors. In repeat loop situations it is often the case that the values of variables contributing to the terminating condition are either indeterminate or positively misleading before the first execution of a loop body. To express the loop using a while-statement the programmer must first arrange some artificial setting of these variables such that the terminating condition is false, a task which is too often done wrongly, or not at all. For example

REPEAT Read (Ch) UNTIL Ch = "?"

would have to be expressed as, e.g.,

Ch := ";";
WHILE Ch <> "?" DO Read (Ch) END

where Ch is initially set to some value other than "?" to force the initial Boolean expression evaluation to yield false.

The For-statement

The while- and repeat-statements are the primary constructs for expressing repetitions in most programming situations. However, the *for-statement* may be used for operations which are to be carried out a predetermined number of times.
    A *for-statement* takes the form

for-statement =
    "FOR" variable-identifier ":="
    initial-expression "TO" final-expression ["BY" increment-expression]
    "DO" statement-sequence "END".
initial-expression = expression.
final-expression = expression.
increment-expression = constant-expression.

The *variable-identifier* must denote an entire-variable of some ordinal type, and is known as the *control variable*. This variable must not be a parameter of a procedure (see Chapter 7) or have been imported from another module (see Chapter 12).

The *initial-expression* and *final-expression* must yield values of the same ordinal type as the control variable. If an *increment-expression* is specified it must yield a value of CARDINAL or INTEGER type.

The general form of a for-statement is thus

FOR v := i TO f BY c DO ss END

where i, f and c are the values of the initial-expression, final-expression, and increment-expression, respectively. Together, these values determine a sequence of values to be taken by the control variable as the statement-sequence ss is executed repeatedly.

If no increment-expression is specified then the succession of values is the ascending sequence from i to f each of which must be assignment-compatible with the type of the control variable v. The action of the for-statement is to assign each of these values to the control variable in turn, and execute the statement-sequence ss after each assignment. If the initial value i is greater than the final value f, ss is not executed at all.

Thus, the statement

FOR J := 1 TO 10 DO WriteCard(J*J*J, 4) END

writes the first ten cubes, 1, 8, 27, ..., 1000, to the current output stream.

If LinesWritten is the number of lines written so far, the statement

FOR I := LinesWritten+1 TO PageSize DO WriteLn END

writes the number of blank lines required to make the total number of lines written equal to PageSize. If LinesWritten is already equal to (or greater than) PageSize no blank lines are written.

The statement

```
FOR Day := Monday TO Friday DO
ReadCard(HoursWorked);
TotalHours := TotalHours + HoursWorked
END
```

reads a cardinal value representing the hours worked on each of the days Monday to Friday in turn, and adds this to the variable TotalHours.

If an increment-expression c is specified in a for-statement it determines the *step* by which each value in the sequence is determined from its predecessor. (By default this step is 1 when the increment-expression is omitted.)

Thus, the statement

FOR J := 1 TO 9 BY 2 DO WriteCard(J, 4) END

writes the odd numbers, 1, 3, 5, 7, 9, to the current output stream, while the statement

FOR Day := Friday TO Monday BY -1 DO ... END

executes the statement-sequence following DO five times with Day taking the values Friday, Thursday, Wednesday, Tuesday, Monday, in that order.

In general the sequence of values assigned to the control variable v by the for-statement

FOR v := i TO f BY c DO ... END

when v is of an integer or cardinal type is

$$i, i + c, i + 2c, ..., i + nc$$

where $i + nc$ is the last such value not greater than f if c is positive, or not less than f if c is negative.

When v is of an ordinal type other than INTEGER or CARDINAL, the sequence is defined as

$$i, VAL(T, ORD(i)+c), VAL(T, ORD(i)+2c), ..., VAL(T, ORD(i)+nc)$$

where the final value is again the last such value not greater than f if c is positive, or not less than f if c is negative.

In interpreting the definition of a for-statement the following points should be noted:

(a)   The initial and final values determined by the initial-expression and final-expression are evaluated once only, on entry to the for-statement. They are not re-evaluated on each cycle, and changes during the repetitive execution in the values of any variables involved in these expressions do not in any way affect the sequence of values assigned to the control variable.

(b)   The value of the control variable is changed implicitly by each cycle of the repetition and no action to change its value should appear within the body of the for-statement, or within any procedure or function (see Chapter 7) that is called from the body.

(c)   After completion of a for-statement the value of the control variable is not defined, and programs should not make any assumptions as to its value.

The four programs Sum1, Sum2, Sum3 and Sum4 which follow perform similar actions in that each reads in a series of positive integers and computes their sum, but, due to the slightly different conditions in each case, a different repetitive structure is used.

(a)   For Sum1, the length of the sequence is unknown but the last positive integer is followed by a negative integer. It is possible that there are no integers in the positive sequence.

(b)   For Sum2 the same conditions hold as for Sum1, except that it is guaranteed that there is at least one positive integer in the sequence.

```
MODULE Sum1;
  FROM InOut IMPORT ReadInt, WriteCard, WriteString, WriteLn;
  VAR X: INTEGER; Sum: CARDINAL;
  BEGIN
    Sum := 0;
    WriteString("Input integer (negative value terminates input): ");
    ReadInt(X); WriteLn;
    WHILE X > 0 DO
      Sum := Sum + CARDINAL(X);
      WriteString("Input integer (negative value terminates input): ");
      ReadInt(X); WriteLn
    END;
    WriteString("Sum of input positive values = ");
    WriteCard(Sum, 8); WriteLn
  END Sum1.
```

```
MODULE Sum2;
  FROM InOut IMPORT ReadInt, WriteCard, WriteString, WriteLn;
  VAR X: INTEGER; Sum: CARDINAL;
  BEGIN
    Sum := 0;
    WriteString("Input first positive integer: "); ReadInt(X); WriteLn;
    REPEAT
      Sum := Sum + CARDINAL(X);
      WriteString("Input next integer (negative value terminates input): ");
      ReadInt(X); WriteLn;
    UNTIL X < 0;
    WriteString("Sum of input positive values = ");
    WriteCard(Sum, 8); WriteLn
  END Sum2.
```

(c) For Sum3, the sequence is preceded by an integer value specifying the number of integers in the sequence. This number may be greater than or equal to zero.

(d) For Sum4, the input stream consists only of the positive integer sequence to be summed, with no preceding or following data. The end of the input sequence is therefore detected by the exhaustion of the input stream itself, as signaled by InOut.

```
MODULE Sum3;
  FROM InOut IMPORT ReadCard, WriteCard, WriteString, WriteLn;
  VAR Length, K, X, Sum: CARDINAL;
  BEGIN
    WriteString("Input length of sequence: "); ReadCard(Length); WriteLn;
    Sum := 0;
    FOR K := 1 TO Length DO
      WriteString("Input integer: "); ReadCard(X); WriteLn;
      Sum := Sum + X
    END;
    WriteString("Sum of input values = "); WriteCard(Sum, 8); WriteLn
  END Sum3.
```

```
MODULE Sum4;
  FROM InOut IMPORT Done, ReadCard, WriteCard, WriteString, WriteLn;
  VAR X, Sum: CARDINAL;
  BEGIN
    Sum := 0;
    WriteString("Input integer: "); ReadCard(X); WriteLn;
    WHILE Done DO
      Sum := Sum + X;
      WriteString("Input integer: "); ReadCard(X); WriteLn
    END;
    WriteString("Sum of input values = "); WriteCard(Sum, 8); WriteLn
  END Sum4.
```

Nested Loops

The statement(s) controlled by a repetitive statement may be any of the allowable statement forms defined at the start of this chapter. In particular, the body
of the repetitive statement may itself contain another repetitive statement, in
which case the repetitive statements are said to be *nested*. This nesting of repetitive statements is illustrated in the program SumNtoNth, which reads a positive
integer N and calculates the sum of the series

$$1^1 + 2^2 + 3^3 + ... + N^N$$

```
MODULE SumNtoNth;
  FROM InOut IMPORT ReadCard, WriteCard, WriteString, WriteLn;
  VAR N, X, Power, I, Sum: CARDINAL;
  BEGIN
    WriteString("N = "); ReadCard(N); WriteLn;
    Sum := 0;
    FOR X := 1 TO N DO
      Power := 1;
      FOR I := 1 to X DO Power := Power * X END;
      Sum := Sum + Power
    END;
    WriteString("Sum of powers = "); WriteCard(Sum, 8); WriteLn
  END SumNtoNth.
```

CASE STUDY 4

A class consists of 50 students, each of whom studies five subjects. The grades obtained by each student in each subject are input to a computer, as one line per student of a text file *GRADES*. Each line consists of the student's name, which is not more than 30 characters long and terminated by a period, followed by five grade numbers in the range 0 to 10, separated by spaces; e.g.,

```
MARY SMITH. 7 7 10 6 4
HOWARD BLACKBURN. 4 7 5 4 5
```

A program is required to read this input file and tabulate the students' overall performance in a table which shows each student's name, his or her overall total grade in a vertically aligned column, and a horizontal bar measure of this overall performance. For example, the above inputs might produce outputs:

```
MARY SMITH.                  34 **************
HOWARD BLACKBURN.            25 **********
```

The program clearly has an overall structure of a loop which is executed once for each student

```
open the input file;
FOR Student := 1 TO MaxStudents DO
  read and print data on one student
END
```

where the constant MaxStudents has the value 50 in this program.

The process *read and print data on one student* can be broken down into a sequence of simpler steps, thus:

read and print name;
read and print grades;
align input, output for next student

The action *read and print name* is apparently a simple character-by-character read and print loop which terminates on a period:

```
REPEAT Read(NameChar); Write(NameChar) UNTIL NameChar = "."
```

The action *read and print grades* can be broken into the sequence:

read and total grades;
print total grade;
print bar measure

Then *read and total grades* can be written as:

```
Total := 0;
FOR Subject := 1 TO MaxSubjects DO
  ReadCard(C); Grade := C; Total:= Total + Grade
END
```

where MaxSubjects is declared as a constant with value 5.

However, to print the grade total at an aligned column position we must know how many print positions have been used by the student's name. We therefore amend the *read and print name* loop to print sufficient spaces to bring the total number of characters up to 30, as shown below. The constant Max-NameLength is declared to have the value 30.

```
NameLength := 0;
REPEAT
  Read(NameChar); Write(NameChar); NameLength := NameLength + 1
UNTIL NameChar = ".";
WHILE NameLength < MaxNameLength DO
  Write(" "); NameLength := NameLength + 1
END;
```

Thus, to print the total with its final digit in the fortieth print position we write

```
WriteCard(Total, 10)
```

To print a bar measure of the student's performance simply involves printing a sequence of identical characters, "*", say, where the length of the sequence is proportional to the grade total achieved. Since the raw grade total may vary from 0 to 50 (MaxGrade) we scale this down by a factor of 2/5 (Scale) to give a more convenient printed line length. For visual clarity the first "*" of the bar is separated from the preceding grade total by two blank characters. Printing the bar measure can therefore be programmed as

```
WriteString(" ");
FOR Star := 1 TO TRUNC(Scale*FLOAT(Total)+0.5) DO Write("*") END;
```

Finally, re-aligning the input and output positions for the next student involves:

```
FollowingChar := termCH;
WHILE FollowingChar <> EOL DO Read(FollowingChar) END;
WriteLn
```

We can now assemble the various program fragments into a final program, with suitable import-lists, constant declarations and variable declarations. The resultant program Grades1, and a sample of the output it produces, is shown.

```
MODULE Grades1;
  FROM InOut IMPORT
    EOL, termCH, OpenInput, CloseInput, Done, Read, ReadCard,
    Write, WriteString, WriteCard, WriteLn;

(* This program inputs a sequence of lines from a user-specified file.
   Each line contains a student name and the grades obtained by that
   student in each of five subjects, in the form:
        name. grade grade grade grade grade
   each grade being in the range 0 to 10.
   A corresponding line is output for each student, showing their name
   and grade total, both as a number and as a horizontal bar measure. *)
CONST
  MaxStudents = 50; MaxSubjects = 5; MaxNameLength = 30;
  MaxGrade = 10; MaxTotal = MaxSubjects * MaxGrade; Scale = 0.4;
VAR
  Student: [1 .. MaxStudents];
  NameLength: [0 .. MaxNameLength]; NameChar: CHAR;
  Subject: [1 .. MaxSubjects]; Grade: [0 .. MaxGrade]; Total: [0 .. MaxTotal];
  C, Star: CARDINAL; FollowingChar: CHAR;
BEGIN
  OpenInput(""); WriteLn;
  IF Done THEN
    FOR Student := 1 TO MaxStudents DO
      (* read and print name: *)
      NameLength := 0;
      REPEAT
        Read(NameChar); Write(NameChar); NameLength := NameLength + 1
      UNTIL NameChar = ".";
```

```
    WHILE NameLength < MaxNameLength DO
      Write(" "); NameLength := NameLength + 1
    END;
    (* read and total grades: *)
    Total := 0;
    FOR Subject := 1 TO MaxSubjects DO
      ReadCard(C); Grade := C; Total := Total + Grade
    END;
    (* print total in aligned position: *)
    WriteCard(Total, 10);
    (* print bar measure: *)
    WriteString(" ");
    FOR Star := 1 TO TRUNC(Scale*FLOAT(Total)+0.5) DO Write("*") END;
    (* align input and output: *)
    FollowingChar := termCH;
    WHILE FollowingChar <> EOL DO Read(FollowingChar) END;
    WriteLn
  END;
  CloseInput
 END
END Grades1.
```

```
Enter Input File Name: GRADES

ALAN LEWIN.                          22  ********
BETTY CALLAGHAN.                     19  *******
CHRIS FARMER.                        17  *******
DEBORAH HIBBETT.                     20  *******
ERNEST ATKINS.                       28  **********
FRANCES WEST.                        30  ***********
GRAHAM BARTLETT.                     17  *******
DAVID ANDERSON.                      29  ***********
BRIAN REITH.                         31  ***********
JACQUELINE HARRISON.                 27  **********
KENNETH LAMB.                        17  *******
CRAIG RICHARDS.                      19  ********
JOHN BANKS.                          18  *******
STEPHEN STEWART.                     25  *********
WILLIAM JONES.                       27  **********
ANNE SMITH.                          29  ***********
ELAINE PASCOE.                       18  *******
STEPHANIE OLD.                       22  ********
```

The Loop-statement

While-, repeat- and for-statements provide a natural expression of most repetition patterns, and indeed a single construct such as the while-statement can be used to express all such patterns. There are, however, some situations in which none of these statements provide the neatest expression of the repetition required. Consider, for example, the loop required in the program Sum1.

```
Sum := 0;
WriteString("Input integer (negative value terminates input): ");
ReadInt(I); WriteLn;
WHILE I > 0 DO
  Sum := Sum + CARDINAL(I);
  WriteString("Input integer (negative value terminates input): ");
  ReadInt(I); WriteLn
END;
```

To achieve the required effect using a while-statement, the statements which obtain each input value, viz.

```
WriteString("Input integer (negative value terminates input): ");
ReadInt(I); WriteLn;
```

are duplicated inside and outside the loop. This duplication can be avoided by using an if-statement inside a repeat-statement, thus:

```
Sum := 0;
REPEAT
  WriteString("Input integer (negative value terminates input): ");
  ReadInt(I); WriteLn;
  IF I >= 0 THEN
    Sum := Sum + CARDINAL(I)
  END;
UNTIL I < 0
```

but this seems inefficient since the terminating condition is evaluated twice per iteration.

The basic problem with the repetition required is that the statements to input the next value must be executed one time more than the statement which increments Sum. None of the repetition statements considered so far enable this to be expressed directly.

Such a repetition is enabled by the *loop-statement*, which is a generalization of the while- and repeat-statements in that the termination condition may be specified and tested at any point within the loop body.

loop-statement = "LOOP" statement-sequence "END".

Repeated execution of the statement-sequence is terminated by the execution of an exit-statement within the sequence:

exit-statement = "EXIT".

Execution of an exit-statement causes the immediately enclosing loop-statement to be terminated, and execution continues at the statement following that loop-statement.

In normal circumstances, at least one of the statements in the body of a loop-statement involves evaluation of a terminating condition and, if the condition is true, execution of an exit-statement.

Thus the loop from program Sum1 can now be written as

```
Sum := 0;
LOOP
  WriteString("Input integer (negative value terminates input): ");
  ReadInt(I); WriteLn;
  IF I < 0 THEN EXIT END;
  Sum := Sum + CARDINAL(I)
END
```

A similar construction can be used in program Sum4, to handle termination of the loop when ReadCard fails to obtain another value from the exhausted input stream:

```
Sum := 0;
LOOP
  WriteString("Input integer: "); ReadCard(I); WriteLn;
  IF NOT Done THEN EXIT END;
  Sum := Sum + I
END
```

In general the loop-statement is well-suited to programming input loops which terminate on input stream exhaustion, as signaled by InOut, since $n+1$ read operations are required to process a stream of n items, i.e., the general pattern required is

```
LOOP
  attempt to read next item;
  IF NOT Done THEN EXIT END;
  process item read
END
```

Our examples so far have used a single EXIT statement in each loop-statement, but in general a loop-statement may contain two or more separate exit-statements if required. This possibility is sometimes useful in expressing abnormal termination of a loop, due to the detection of an error in the data processed, say. Consider an augmented version of the program Sum4 which checks for possible overflow in computing the sum of the integer sequence, and terminates with a diagnostic message when this is about to occur. Using a loop-statement with two exit-statements this can be programmed as in SafeSum4.

```
MODULE SafeSum4;
  FROM InOut IMPORT Done, ReadCard, WriteCard, WriteString, WriteLn;
  VAR X, Sum: CARDINAL;
  BEGIN
    Sum := 0;
    LOOP
      WriteString("Input integer: "); ReadCard(X); WriteLn;
      IF NOT Done THEN EXIT END;
      IF X > MAX(CARDINAL) – Sum THEN
        (* overflow is about to occur! *)
        WriteString("Aborted due to imminent overflow of sum");
        EXIT
      END;
      Sum := Sum + X
    END;
    WriteString("Sum of input values = "); WriteCard(Sum, 8); WriteLn
  END SafeSum4.
```

In the examples so far the exit statements used have been directly contained by if-statements which are direct constituents of the statement-sequence repeatedly executed by the loop-statement. In general, however, an exit-statement may occur in any context contained by that statement-sequence. As an example, consider the program SafeSumXtoNth, which computes the sum of a given power of the input integer sequence, while guarding against overflow as before.

In this case a third exit-statement is needed to terminate the loop when overflow is about to occur in computing the required power of an individual input number. The exit-statement required occurs within an if-statement which is within a for-loop which is itself within an if-statement within the loop-statement to be terminated. Regardless of such intervening structure, an exit-statement terminates the execution of the *immediately enclosing loop-statement*. Identification of the loop-statement to be terminated is unaffected by the presence of intervening conditional or repetitive statements of other forms.

As noted earlier, while- and repeat-statements may be expressed as loop-statements containing a single exit-statement. In the case of a while-statement the termination test and exit-statement occur at the beginning of the corresponding loop-statement body, while in the case of a repeat-statement the termination test and exit-statement occur at the end of the corresponding loop-statement body. In principle the loop-statement can be used to realize all the repetition

```
MODULE SafeSumXtoNth;
  FROM InOut IMPORT Done, ReadCard, WriteCard, WriteString, WriteLn;
  VAR N, X, XtoNth, K, Sum: CARDINAL;
  BEGIN
    WriteString("Input power required: "); ReadCard(N); WriteLn;
    Sum := 0;
    LOOP
      ReadCard(X);
      IF NOT Done THEN EXIT END;
      IF X <> 0 THEN

        (* compute X to power N *)
        XtoNth := 1;
        FOR K := 1 TO N DO
          IF XtoNth > MAX(CARDINAL) DIV X THEN
            (* overflow is about to occur in computing power! *)
            WriteString("Aborted due to imminent overflow in term");
            EXIT
          END;
          XtoNth := XtoNth * X
        END;

        (* add to sum *)
        IF XtoNth > MAX(CARDINAL) - Sum THEN
          (* overflow is about to occur in computing sum! *)
          WriteString("Aborted due to imminent overflow in sum");
          EXIT
        END;
        Sum := Sum + XtoNth
      END
    END;
    WriteString("Sum of input values to power "); WriteCard(N, 1);
    WriteString(" = "); WriteCard(Sum, 1); WriteLn
  END SafeSumXtoNth.
```

constructs described previously. The result of doing so, however, is that the
intended structure is less obvious, and an error in realizing that structure may go
undetected. This tendency to obscure useful structure is a significant disadvantage of the loop- and exit-statements. For this reason, Modula-2's other repetition constructs are preferred in all situations where they do not imply significant duplication of program code or loss of run-time efficiency.

EXERCISES

6.1 Modify the program Rocket in Case Study 1 so that, if the expected time of arrival is not on the same day as the blast-off, the output takes the following form:

> Expected time of arrival = *hh*/*mm*/*ss* on day plus *d*

If the arrival is on the same day as the blast-off the output should be as before.

Make a further modification such that, if the arrival is on the day following blast-off, the output has the form:

> Expected time of arrival = *hh*/*mm*/*ss* next day

6.2 Some letters are drawn with straight lines only, e.g., A,E,F,H,... while others require curves, e.g., B,C,D,G,... . Write a program which reads and prints a line of text, replacing all letters requiring curves with an asterisk. Write the program using

(a) an *if-statement*;
(b) a *case-statement*.

6.3 Write a program which reads a positive integer N and tabulates the factorials of the numbers from 1 to N in the form

I	1	2	3	4	...	N
FACTORIAL(I)	1	2	6	24	...	

$$\{ factorial(i) = 1*2*3*...*(i-1)*i \}$$

Rewrite your program to tabulate all the factorials less than the maximum cardinal value allowed by your implementation of Modula-2.

6.4 A building society lends money to house purchasers subject to a monthly payment of 1 percent of the amount borrowed. This payment covers both capital repayment and interest due, interest being charged at a rate of 8 percent per annum, calculated monthly. Write a program which reads in the amount of a loan, and tabulates the series of payments required, as a four column table showing the payment number, the interest due that month, the capital repayment that month, and the outstanding capital balance. The table should also show the final non-standard payment required to complete the repayment.

6.5 Write a program to print out the digit pyramid in Figure 6.7.

```
                1
               121
              12321
             1234321
            123454321
           12345654321
          1234567654321
         123456787654321
        12345678987654321
```

Figure 6.7

6.6 Write a program to read and print an input text, and determine the number of lines, sentences, and words involved. You may assume

(a)   that each sentence ends with a period, and that the period character is not used for any other purpose;

(b)   words consist solely of letters.

7

Procedures and Functions

THE PROCEDURE CONCEPT

The method used in the construction of case study programs in this book is to take the initial problem and break it down into a series of simpler problems. This break-down of the problem is expressed using a combination of Modula-2 structured statements and natural English. For instance, at an early stage of its development the grades program in Case Study 4 was expressed as:

```
FOR Student := 1 TO MaxStudents DO
    read and print data on one student
END
```

with the process *read and print data on one student* subsequently being refined as a statement-sequence of simpler steps.

```
FOR Student := 1 TO MaxStudents DO
    read and print name;
    read and print grades;
    align input, output for next student
END
```

Each of the three sub-problems in the above statement-sequence was then refined in terms of further sub-problems or, if possible, expressed directly in Modula-2 itself. Eventually this stepwise refinement process led to a situation in which all parts of the program design were expressed fully in Modula-2.

When we design larger and more complex programs this approach is of even greater value. However, the actions isolated in the early levels of the refinement process may themselves go through many further levels of refinement before developing into large and complicated sequences of Modula-2, each of which covers many lines, or even pages, of program text. When one comes to read the program, the sheer length of the text makes the structure of the program difficult to appreciate—using the Modula-2 facilities described so far the only method of incorporating the levels of refinement explicitly within the final program is by the use of comments. What we need is a means of textually dividing the program into units corresponding to the significant sub-problems identified during the construction, and expressing the program's overall action by a short sequence of text which refers to these units. This would help the reader to perceive the design of the program more clearly, and thus would make the program easier to understand and to change if required.

Modula-2, in common with most programming languages, provides a facility for the description of programs in this way. The programmer may define an action or group of actions in the form of a *procedure*, to which a name, or *procedure-identifier*, is given. This procedure may then be invoked from another point in the program by means of a *procedure-statement* which cites the *procedure-identifier*.

The syntax of a *procedure-statement* is

procedure-statement = procedure-designator ["(" actual-parameter-list ")"].
procedure-designator = procedure-identifier | variable.
procedure-identifier = qualified-identifier.

A *variable* that is used in a *procedure-designator* must be a procedure variable—such variables are introduced later in this chapter, as are actual parameter lists. For the moment we deal only with the simplest form of procedure-statement, i.e., a *procedure-identifier*. A procedure-statement is said to *call* the procedure named by the identifier. Its effect is to execute the actions defined by that procedure (with execution then continuing at the statement immediately following the procedure-statement).

A procedure-statement is one of the allowed forms of a *simple-statement* defined in Chapter 4 and can be used anywhere that it is legal to use a *statement*. We can thus retain the above refinement as an active part of the final program itself by writing it as shown below, where ReadAndPrintName, ReadAndPrintGrades and AlignInputAndOutput are now procedure-statements and the procedures defining the required actions are declared elsewhere in the program.

```
FOR Student := 1 TO MaxStudents DO
  ReadAndPrintName;
  ReadAndPrintGrades;
  AlignInputAndOutput
END
```

The declaration of a procedure is defined as follows:

procedure-declaration =
statement-procedure-declaration | function-procedure-declaration.
statement-procedure-declaration =
procedure-heading ";" procedure-body identifier.
procedure-heading =
"PROCEDURE" identifier ["(" formal-parameter-list ")"].
procedure-body = block.

Function-procedure-declarations are discussed later in this chapter. For the present we concentrate upon *statement-procedure-declarations*.

A *statement-procedure-declaration* consists of a *procedure-heading* and a *procedure-body*, separated by a semicolon and followed by an identifier. The essential role of the *procedure-heading* is to associate a name or identifier with the procedure being declared. The identifier following the *procedure-body* must be the same as the identifier of the *procedure-heading*. The syntax category

procedure-identifier = qualified-identifier.

is introduced simply to denote the class of identifiers defined by means of statement-procedure-declarations. The purpose and use of *formal-parameter-lists* are discussed later in this chapter.

The action of the procedure is defined by the procedure-body, which takes the form of a *block*. As we saw in Chapter 2 a block begins with a *declaration-part* which may or may not be empty, but its essential component is a *statement-part*.

block = declaration-part statement-part "END".

Just as the statement-part of the program block defines the action of the program, the statement-part of a procedure block defines the actions of that procedure, i.e., the action to be carried out each time the procedure is called. Thus we declare the procedure ReadAndPrintName as shown below.

```
PROCEDURE ReadAndPrintName;
  VAR NameLength: [0 .. MaxNameLength]; NameChar: CHAR;
  BEGIN
    NameLength := 0;
    REPEAT
      Read(NameChar); Write(NameChar); NameLength := NameLength + 1
    UNTIL NameChar = ".";
    WHILE NameLength < MaxNameLength DO
      Write(" "); NameLength := NameLength + 1
    END;
  END ReadAndPrintName
```

The other two procedures required for our revised grades program can be declared in a similar manner.

A *procedure-declaration* in Modula-2 is, as we saw in Chapter 2, one of the possible components of the declaration-part. Thus, in re-writing the grades program with procedures, the three procedures are declared after the constant and variable declarations and before the revised statement-part, as shown in the program Grades2. The repositioning of some of the variable declarations is discussed in the next section.

```
MODULE Grades2;
  FROM InOut IMPORT
    EOL, termCH, OpenInput, CloseInput, Done, Read, ReadCard,
    Write, WriteString, WriteCard, WriteLn;
  CONST
    MaxStudents = 50; MaxSubjects = 5; MaxGrade = 10;
    MaxTotal = MaxSubjects * MaxGrade; MaxNameLength = 30;
    Scale = 0.4;
  VAR  Student: [1 .. MaxStudents];
  PROCEDURE ReadAndPrintName;
    VAR NameLength: [0 .. MaxNameLength]; NameChar: CHAR;
    BEGIN
      NameLength := 0;
      REPEAT
        Read(NameChar); Write(NameChar); NameLength := NameLength + 1
      UNTIL NameChar = ".";
      WHILE NameLength < MaxNameLength DO
        Write(" "); NameLength := NameLength + 1
      END;
    END ReadAndPrintName;
  PROCEDURE ReadAndPrintGrades;
    VAR
      Subject: [1 .. MaxSubjects]; Grade: [0 .. MaxGrade];
      Total: [0 .. MaxTotal]; Star, C: CARDINAL;
    BEGIN
      (* read and total grades: *)
      Total := 0;
      FOR Subject := 1 TO MaxSubjects DO
        ReadCard(C); Grade := C; Total := Total + Grade
      END;
```

```
      (* print total in aligned position: *)
      WriteCard(Total, 10);
      (* print bar measure: *)
      WriteString(" ");
      FOR Star := 1 TO TRUNC(Scale*FLOAT(Total)+0.5) DO Write("*") END;
    END ReadAndPrintGrades;
  PROCEDURE AlignInputAndOutput;
    VAR FollowingChar: CHAR;
    BEGIN
      FollowingChar := termCH;
      WHILE FollowingChar <> EOL DO Read(FollowingChar) END;
      WriteLn
    END AlignInputAndOutput;
  BEGIN
    OpenInput(""); WriteLn;
    IF Done THEN
      FOR Student := 1 TO MaxStudents DO
        ReadAndPrintName;
        ReadAndPrintGrades;
        AlignInputAndOutput
      END;
      CloseInput
    END
  END Grades2.
```

In this revised program the statement-part shows explicitly the overall structure conceived for the program—that of a loop whose body involves a sequence of three subsidiary actions—while the procedure declarations give the details of how each of these actions is to be carried out. In this example some of these actions are trivial and their expression as procedures may seem extravagant. However, the example shows clearly how, in a larger and more complex program, the significant levels of refinement of the program's actions may be expressed as short sequences of statements involving procedure calls. The further refinements of the actions which these statements invoke are textually separated from the statements themselves, and from each other, as an appropriate set of procedure-declarations.

The declaration of a procedure does not cause its body or statement-part to be executed—this is only caused by the execution of a corresponding *procedure-statement*, or *call*. In our example above, each procedure had exactly one calling statement but this is not necessarily so—two or more independent statements calling the same procedure may be used in a program. To illustrate this let us reconsider the program BuzzBuzz given in Chapter 6. Let us amend the program so that it will read in an integer value n ($0<n<100$) and produce as output the sequence of integers $n, n+1, n+2,...$ interspersed with the words buzz and buzz-buzz, as before. On reaching 100 the sequence should continue cyclically at 1 and on reaching $n-1$ the program should stop. This can be achieved quite simply by the use of a procedure, as in program BuzzBuzz2.

```
MODULE BuzzBuzz2;
  FROM InOut IMPORT ReadCard, WriteCard, WriteString, WriteLn;
  VAR I, n: CARDINAL;
  PROCEDURE WriteBuzz;
    BEGIN
      IF (I DIV 10 = 7) OR (I MOD 10 = 7) THEN WriteString("buzz")
      ELSIF I MOD 7 = 0 THEN WriteString("buzz-buzz")
      ELSE WriteCard(I, 3)
      END;
      WriteLn
    END WriteBuzz;
  BEGIN
    WriteString("Input your start number (in range 1..99): ");
    ReadCard(n); WriteLn;
    FOR I := n TO 99 DO WriteBuzz END;
    FOR I := 1 TO n-1 DO WriteBuzz END
  END BuzzBuzz2.
```

In this case the use of two for-statements expresses, simply and clearly, the control required to generate the appropriate sequences of values for I. Each loop body applies the same action to the current value of I and is therefore expressed as a call to the common procedure WriteBuzz.

To use the same control structure without a procedure in this case would involve writing two copies of the procedure body—one for each for-statement. Using a procedure thus reduces the overall length of the final program text. In general, when a procedure is called from two or more distinct points within a program there is a net reduction in the length of the program text compared with the same program written without procedures. This reduction in the textual length of the program is normally reflected by a corresponding reduction in the size of the executable program held within the computer. Use of a procedure which is called from two or more points in the program has a threefold economic advantage in that it reduces

(a) the programming task, as measured by the length of the program;
(b) the area for potential programming error;
(c) the size of the resultant executable program.

These savings have been the primary motivation for the inclusion of procedures in many languages.

Conversely it may be argued that the use of a procedure which is only called at one point in a program increases the length of the program text—by the overhead of the extra symbols involved in the procedure-declaration and procedure-statement. It is also true that a corresponding overhead is normally introduced into the resultant executable program—both in its size and the time which it takes to execute its task. These overheads must be balanced against the increased clarity, and the consequent decreased probability of programming errors, which the introduction of a procedure brings about. In most programming situations the latter advantages far outweigh the overheads involved. In the remainder of this book procedures are used freely, both to emphasize the perceived program structure, and to share a common action between two or more program points, where appropriate.

The Return-statement

Termination of execution of a procedure normally occurs as a result of executing the final statement of the statement-part of the procedure-body. However, it is possible to terminate execution at any point in the statement-part, by means of a *return-statement*:

$$return\text{-}statement = "RETURN" \ [expression].$$

When used in statement-procedures, a return-statement does not include an *expression* but consists solely of the symbol RETURN. Execution of a return-statement causes immediate termination of the procedure execution and control returns to the statement following the call of the procedure. Hence, a return-statement is implied at the end of every procedure-body.

The program SafePowers computes the specified power of each of a sequence of input numbers, but guards against overflow in computing each power.

As this program shows, the return-statement within a statement-procedure has an analogous effect to that of an exit-statement within a loop—it forces termination of the procedure execution from whatever context it occupies in the procedure body. Return-statements are often used in statement-procedures to deal with exceptional data values which prevent the end of the procedure being reached in the normal way.

Modula-2 also provides a standard procedure HALT which may be used to terminate execution of the entire program from any point. If the above program is not required to continue computation of powers once an overflowing power occurs, a call of the standard procedure HALT could replace the return-statement in the procedure WriteXtoNth.

```
MODULE SafePowers;
  FROM InOut IMPORT Done, ReadCard, WriteCard, WriteString, WriteLn;
  VAR N, X: CARDINAL;
  PROCEDURE WriteXtoNth;
    VAR XtoNth, K: CARDINAL;
    BEGIN
      XtoNth := 1;
      FOR K := 1 TO N DO
        IF XtoNth > MAX(CARDINAL) DIV X THEN
          (* overflow is about to occur in computing power! *)
          WriteString("too large to compute");
          RETURN
        END;
        XtoNth := XtoNth * X
      END;
      WriteCard(XtoNth, 1)
    END WriteXtoNth;

  BEGIN
    WriteString("Input power required: "); ReadCard(N); WriteLn;
    LOOP
      WriteString("Input next number: "); ReadCard(X); WriteLn;
      IF NOT Done THEN EXIT END;
      WriteCard(X, 1); WriteString(" to the power "); WriteCard(N, 1);
      WriteString(" is "); WriteXtoNth; WriteLn
    END
  END SafePowers.
```

Both the return-statement and the standard procedure HALT share the disad-vantage noted for the exit-statement in Chapter 6, namely that their use tends to reduce program clarity. A procedure that always terminates by reaching the end of its body is easier to understand than one which may terminate at any of several alternative points within its body. Likewise a program that always ter-minates by reaching its final END is easier to understand than one which may terminate at any of several alternative points within its body or those of the pro-cedures it calls. For this reason it is good programming practice to use the return-statement and the HALT procedure with caution, and avoid multiple termi-nation points as far as possible.

As we shall see later in this Chapter, however, return-statements have an additional and essential role to play in function-procedures.

BLOCK STRUCTURE AND SCOPE

In rewriting the grades program in the previous section, the declarations of variables used in each procedure have been located in that procedure—in general the syntactic definition of a *procedure-body* as a *block* allows us to declare data inside a procedure. Indeed, not only can we declare constants, types and variables, but also further procedures.

Any identifiers introduced within the *declaration-part* of a block to represent constants, types, variables and procedures are said to be *local* to the block. The block is the only part of the program in which these identifiers may be referenced and is known as the *scope* of the identifiers. For instance, suppose we declare a variable A within a procedure P, viz.,

```
PROCEDURE P;
  VAR A: INTEGER;
  BEGIN
    ...
  END P;
```

Then the variable A may only be referenced in the body of the procedure P—A is said to be a *local variable* of the procedure P, and is unknown outside the procedure.

However, identifiers declared outside a block, i.e., in the declaration-part of the enclosing block, are known and may be referenced inside the enclosed block. Such identifiers are said to be *non-local*, or *global*, to the enclosed block. For example, in the program segment below, the variable B may be referenced inside the procedure P, and is said to be a *non-local* or *global variable* of the procedure P.

```
VAR B: INTEGER;
PROCEDURE P;
  BEGIN
    ...
  END P;
```

Consider again the program Grades2. The variables NameChar and NameLength are used only within the procedure ReadAndPrintName and are therefore declared local to that procedure. Likewise the variables Total, Subject, Grade and Star are declared local to procedure ReadAndPrintGrades. The variable Student is used by the statement-part of the program itself and must therefore be declared in the program block. This means that Student could be referenced as a global variable by any of the procedures, although none in fact does so. This use of local declarations has three significant advantages:

(a) it makes explicitly clear that the variables NameChar, NameLength, Total, Subject, Grade, FollowingChar, C and Star are significant only within the

procedures in which they are declared, a considerable simplification for a
reader of the program;

(b)   it ensures that certain errors involving inadvertent use of these variables by
      other parts of the program are immediately detected by the compiler;

(c)   as we shall see, it helps the implementation to minimize the storage used.

In the examples which we have used so far, we have only used procedures
declared in the declaration-part of the program block itself. In principle, however, each procedure-body is itself a block, whose declaration-part may contain
further procedure declarations and hence further blocks. A procedure declared
within another procedure is said to be *nested*. For example, in refining the procedure ReadAndPrintGrades in our revised grades program we might have introduced further procedures as follows.

```
PROCEDURE ReadAndPrintGrades;
  VAR Total: [0 .. MaxTotal];

  PROCEDURE ReadAndTotalGrades;
    VAR Subject: [1 .. MaxSubjects]; Grade: [0 .. GradeMax]; C: CARDINAL;
    BEGIN
      Total := 0;
      FOR Subject := 1 TO MaxSubjects DO
        ReadCard(C); Grade := C;
        Total := Total + Grade
      END
    END ReadAndTotalGrades;

  PROCEDURE PrintTotalGrade;
    BEGIN
      WriteCard(Total, 10);
    END PrintTotalGrade;

  PROCEDURE PrintBarMeasure;
    VAR Star: CARDINAL;
    BEGIN
      WriteString(" ");
      FOR Star := 1 TO TRUNC(Scale*FLOAT(Total)+0.5) DO Write("*") END;
    END PrintBarMeasure;

  BEGIN
    ReadAndTotalGrades;
    PrintTotalGrade;
    PrintBarMeasure
  END ReadAndPrintGrades;
```

The overall structure of a Modula-2 program is thus a set of blocks, some
of which are nested within others to an arbitrary level of nesting. Any of these

blocks may introduce new identifiers in its declaration-part, and the *rules of scope* must determine the accessibility of all these identifiers throughout the nested block structure.

In the examples used so far the identifiers used have all been unique throughout the program. In Chapter 3 we said that the association of each identifier must be unique within its range of use—this range of use, or scope, has now been defined as the block in which the identifier is declared. Clearly an identifier must not be declared for two distinct purposes in the same block. However, there is no reason why the same identifier may not be declared for distinct purposes in different blocks provided the rules of scope make clear which declaration, if any, applies at all points in the resultant program.

The rules of identifier scope for Modula-2 programs composed from procedures may be stated as follows:

(1) The scope of an identifier declaration is the block in which the declaration occurs, and all procedure blocks enclosed by that block, subject to rule (2).
(2) When an identifier declared in a block A is redeclared in some block B enclosed by A, then block B and all blocks enclosed by B are excluded from the scope of the identifier's declaration in A.

A more precise set of scope rules for programs which include *modules* is given in Chapter 12.

In terms of the above rules, the standard identifiers of Modula-2 may be considered to be declared in an imaginary block enclosing the entire program.

The rule introduced in Chapter 3, that a constant or type identifier must be declared before it is used in another declaration, is now stated more precisely as follows:

(3) If an identifier I is used in the declaration of another identifier J, then the declaration of I must precede the declaration of J in the program text.

Since constant and type identifiers are the only identifiers normally used in declarations, this rule is effectively equivalent to that given in Chapter 3. However, note that scope rule (2) means that if an identifier I is redeclared in block B it cannot be used in the part of B preceding its redeclaration with some non-local meaning from an enclosing block A, since all of block B is excluded from the scope of I's declaration in A.

An identifier is said to be *visible* within the scope of its declaration in any program. The skeleton program Scopes illustrates the application of the scope rules to determine which identifiers are visible in the statement-parts of the various procedures and the main program shown. Readers should ensure, before continuing, that they understand how the scope rules lead to the visible identifiers listed by the comments in each statement-part.

Note that procedure-identifiers are subject to the same rules of scope as other identifiers, and hence a procedure can only be used within the block in

```
MODULE Scopes;

    VAR I, J: INTEGER;
    PROCEDURE Q;

        CONST I = 16;
        VAR K: CHAR;
        PROCEDURE R;

            VAR J: REAL;
            BEGIN
                (* this statement-part may use
                    local variable J: REAL;
                    non-local constant I = 16;
                    non-local variable K: CHAR;
                    non-local procedures R, Q;
                    and all standard identifiers  *)
            END R;

        BEGIN
            (* this statement-part may use
                local constant I = 16;
                local variable K: CHAR;
                local procedure R;
                non-local variable J: INTEGER;
                non-local procedure Q;
                and all standard identifiers *)
        END Q;

    BEGIN
        (* this statement-part may use
            local variables I, J: INTEGER;
            local procedure Q;
            and all standard identifiers *)
    END Scopes.
```

which its declaration appears (and any blocks enclosed by that block). The ability of a procedure to refer to, and hence call, itself (known as *recursion*) is discussed later in this chapter.

Note also the use of indentation to indicate the nesting of procedures blocks within the program text. This is good programming practice which enables a reader of the program to appreciate the procedural structure of the program.

The scope rules determine the textual limits on the use of identifiers within a particular program. The same rules are used to determine the lifetime, or *existence*, of variables. Modula-2 decrees that variables declared local to a procedure exist only during execution of the procedure, being created upon entry to the procedure and destroyed upon exit. It follows that

(a) a variable declared local to a procedure cannot be referenced by the program sequence which called the procedure since the variable is created only on entry to the procedure and ceases to exist before control returns to the calling sequence; and

(b) there is no necessary relationship between the values of variables created by successive executions of the same procedure. The value of a local variable is always undefined upon entry to a procedure (and so the first action of a procedure will generally be to initialize its local variables) since a new set of variables is created each time a procedure is called.

This limit on the existence or lifetime of variables enables implementations to control the storage used in representing them within the computer. The storage used to represent the local variables of a procedure is acquired only when the procedure is entered, and becomes available for reuse when execution of the procedure is complete. Thus two procedures called in sequence may use the same storage for their local variables. By localizing variables wherever possible, the programmer helps the implementation to minimize the storage required.

Initially the rules of identifier scope and lifetime may seem complex to a user who is unfamiliar with any block-structured programming language. However, he will quickly find these rules a positive aid to the construction of programs which are clear, free from error, and economical in data storage. The proper positioning of declarations to obtain these benefits usually follows quite naturally from a stepwise refinement in which procedures are freely used to express the program structure developed. Within this structural framework the following guiding principles should be observed:

(a) Declare an identifier in the block in which it is used, wherever possible. Doing so increases program clarity, minimizes the likelihood of errors through inadvertent use of the identifier elsewhere, and minimizes the storage requirements produced by variable data.

(b) When an identifier must be used in two or more blocks to denote the same object, declare it in the block which immediately encloses all the uses of the identifier.

(c) When a variable used by a procedure must hold its value from one call of the procedure to the next, declare it in the first enclosing block which ensures that its lifetime embraces all of the dependent procedure calls.

Localizing identifiers wherever possible also increases the programmer's free-dom in choosing the identifiers to be used. The identifiers local to two pro-cedures which are completely separate from each other (i.e., one does not enclose the other) may be chosen quite independently. Thus the following is a valid Modula-2 representation of two procedures occurring in the same program.

```
PROCEDURE P;
  CONST C = "?";
  VAR D, E: CHAR;
  BEGIN
    ...
  END P;
PROCEDURE Q;
  TYPE E = [1 .. 100];
  VAR C: BOOLEAN; D: CHAR;
  BEGIN
    ...
  END Q;
```

The items denoted by the identifiers used in one procedure bear absolutely no relation to those of the same name used in the other.

PARAMETERS

As we have seen, a procedure may be used to define an action, or sequence of actions, which is required at two or more distinct points in a program. For exam-ple suppose that, at various points in a program, we wish to order the values of two global integer variables X and Y so that the value of X is not greater than the value of Y, by exchanging their values if necessary. Instead of writing

```
IF X > Y THEN T := X; X := Y; Y := T END
```

at each point where the ordering operation is required, we might declare a pro-cedure

```
PROCEDURE Order;
  VAR T: INTEGER;
  BEGIN
    IF X > Y THEN T := X; X := Y; Y := T END
  END Order;
```

and call the procedure by means of the procedure-statement

```
Order
```

at the relevant points in the program.

This procedure orders the values of the two integer variables X and Y. In practice it is often more convenient to declare a procedure which orders the values of any two integer variables, not just X and Y. Then, if at some point in the program we wish to order the values of X and Y, we may write

Order(X, Y)

At another point, if we wish to order the values of Y and another integer variable Z, we may write

Order(Y, Z)

This is possible in Modula-2 by the declaration of a procedure which includes a *formal-parameter-list* in its heading, thus:

PROCEDURE *identifier* (*formal-parameter-list*);
...
...

The *formal-parameter-list* defines a set of dummy quantities, called *formal-parameters*, in terms of which the procedure body is expressed. When the procedure is called, these formal parameters are replaced by corresponding *actual parameters* specified in the *procedure-statement*, thus

procedure-identifier (*actual-parameter-list*)

For the procedure Order an appropriate declaration would be

```
PROCEDURE Order(VAR A, B: INTEGER);
  VAR T: INTEGER;
  BEGIN
    IF A > B THEN T := A; A := B; B := T END
  END Order;
```

Here A and B are the *formal parameters* in terms of which procedure Order is defined. To order the values of variables X and Y the procedure-statement required is

Order(X, Y)

where X and Y are the *actual parameters* which replace A and B in this particular execution of the procedure.

In detail a *formal-parameter-list* consists of one or more sections, separated by semicolons and enclosed by parentheses, thus

formal-parameter-list =
    formal-parameter-section {";" formal-parameter-section}.

Each section introduces one or more formal parameters of the same class. There are two *classes* of formal parameter in Modula-2, viz., *value* parameters, and *variable* parameters.

The class of each formal parameter is determined by the form of the *formal-parameter-section* in which it occurs:

> *formal-parameter-section =*
>   *value-parameter-section | variable-parameter-section.*
> *value-parameter-section = identifier-list ":" formal-type.*
> *variable-parameter-section = "VAR" identifier-list ":" formal-type.*
> *formal-type = type-identifier | open-array-schema.*

Within each section one or more identifiers are declared to denote the formal parameters required and the corresponding type is specified. Note that a *formal-type* (other than an *open-array-schema* which we discuss in Chapter 8) can only be specified by a type-identifier which has already been defined.

Each *actual-parameter-list* used in a procedure-statement takes a form corresponding to the procedure's *formal-parameter-list*. It consists of an appropriate number of actual parameters separated by commas, thus

> *actual-parameter-list = actual-parameter {"," actual-parameter}.*

The form of each actual-parameter is determined by the class of the corresponding formal-parameter.

> *actual-parameter = actual-value | actual-variable.*
> *actual-value = expression.*
> *actual-variable = variable.*

The correspondence between the actual and formal parameter lists of a *procedure-statement* and the *procedure-declaration* must be as follows:

(a)   the number of parameters in the two lists must be the same;
(b)   each actual parameter corresponds to the formal parameter occupying the same position in the formal-parameter-list;
(c)   corresponding actual and formal parameters must agree as detailed for each class in the next two sub-sections.

Variable Parameters

A *variable* formal parameter is used to denote an actual parameter whose value may be altered by execution of the procedure. Each corresponding actual parameter must therefore be a variable of the type specified for the formal parameter. Execution of a particular procedure-statement determines the actual parameter involved and, throughout the resultant execution of the procedure-body, each operation involving the formal parameter is applied directly to this actual variable.

In some cases the procedure may use the existing value of an actual variable parameter before changing it. For example, the procedure Order which we defined as

```
PROCEDURE Order(VAR A, B: INTEGER);
VAR T: INTEGER;
BEGIN
  IF A > B THEN T := A; A := B; B := T END
END Order;
```

examines and, if necessary, exchanges the values of its two parameters.

The formal parameters A and B must be declared as *variable* parameters—hence the prefix VAR on their declaration. In a corresponding procedure-statement

```
Order(X, Y)
```

the actual parameters X and Y must be INTEGER *variables*. Furthermore, they must have already been assigned values since the procedure first examines these values to determine its subsequent action.

In other cases the existing values of variable parameters may be irrelevant. For example, the procedure

```
PROCEDURE ReadAsMeters(VAR Feet, Inches: CARDINAL);
  VAR Meters: REAL; LengthInInches: CARDINAL;
BEGIN
  ReadReal(Meters);
  LengthInInches := TRUNC(Meters*39.39 + 0.5);
  Feet := LengthInInches DIV 12;
  Inches := LengthInInches MOD 12
END ReadAsMeters;
```

reads a real number representing a distance in meters and converts it to feet and inches (to the nearest inch). In a corresponding calling statement, e.g.,

```
ReadAsMeters(Ft, Ins)
```

the actual parameters Ft and Ins must be CARDINAL variables, but their existing values are irrelevant since the procedure makes no attempt to use them before assigning new values to them.

Parameters, such as those of ReadAsMeters, which are used to carry values out of a procedure are sometimes known as *output* parameters. Parameters, such as those of Order, which are used to carry values into and out of a procedure, are known as *transput* parameters. In either case they must be declared as variable parameters in Modula-2.

Value Parameters

A *value* parameter is used when the parameter's only role is to carry a value into a procedure—a so-called *input* parameter. The formal parameter simply denotes a value which is supplied by the calling statement, and the corresponding actual parameter may therefore be any expression which produces a value that is assignment compatible with the formal parameter type.

For example, the following procedure

```
PROCEDURE WriteAsMeters(Feet, Inches: CARDINAL);
  VAR Meters: REAL; LengthInInches: CARDINAL;
  BEGIN
    LengthInInches := 12*Feet + Inches;
    Meters := FLOAT(LengthInInches) / 39.39;
    WriteReal(Meters, 12)
  END WriteAsMeters;
```

accepts two CARDINAL values representing a distance in feet and inches and writes it out as meters. In this case Feet and Inches are *value* parameters, which is indicated by the absence of the prefix VAR in their declaration. The corresponding actual parameters in statements calling the procedure may be any expressions producing CARDINAL values. For example

```
WriteAsMeters(6, 4)
WriteAsMeters(Ft, Ins)
WriteAsMeters(Ft + 1, 0)
```

are all acceptable calling statements for this procedure, assuming Ft and Ins are CARDINAL variables as before.

In Modula-2 the expression forming an actual value parameter is evaluated when the procedure-statement is executed and assigned to the corresponding formal parameter as if the latter were a local variable of the procedure. During its execution the procedure-body may examine the formal parameter and may assign further values to it, again as if it were a local variable. However, such assignments have no effect on the actual parameter in the procedure-statement.

For example, we might have programmed the procedure WriteAsMeters without the local variable LengthInInches, as

```
PROCEDURE WriteAsMeters(Feet, Inches: CARDINAL);
  VAR Meters: REAL;
  BEGIN
    Inches := 12*Feet + Inches;
    Meters := FLOAT(Inches) / 39.39;
    WriteReal(Meters, 12)
  END WriteAsMeters;
```

The outward effect of this procedure is exactly as before. In particular, a call of the form

    WriteAsMeters(Ft, Ins)

will not make any change to the variable Ins which supplied the input value for Inches. In practice of course the procedure-body could be written without any local variables—simply as a single WriteReal statement

    WriteReal(FLOAT(12*Feet + Inches) / 39.39, 12).

The ability to reuse value parameters as local variables is a convenient one in some cases. However, in consequence, a programmer must be very careful to ensure that all intended variable parameters are declared as such. Omission of the VAR symbol in the formal parameter list simply means that the formal parameters are taken as value parameters. Assignments to them within the procedure body remain valid but produce no effect on the corresponding actual variables supplied by calling statements. The result is a program which seems correct but does not produce the desired effect. The actual mistake—the omission of one VAR symbol—is often difficult to discern.

Many procedures involve a mixture of variable and value parameters. Their declarations require formal parameter lists with two or more sections to distinguish the classes of the formal parameters involved. For example, we might define procedures for internal conversion between meters and feet and inches as shown below.

```
PROCEDURE ConvertToMeters(Feet, Inches: CARDINAL;
                          VAR Meters: REAL);
BEGIN
  Meters := FLOAT(12*Feet + Inches) / 39.39
END ConvertToMeters;

PROCEDURE ConvertFromMeters(Meters: REAL;
                            VAR Feet, Inches: CARDINAL);
VAR LengthInInches: CARDINAL;
BEGIN
  LengthInInches:= TRUNC (Meters*39.39 + 0.5);
  Feet := LengthInInches DIV 12;
  Inches := LengthInInches MOD 12
END ConvertFromMeters;
```

The procedure SolveQuadratic accepts the real coefficients of a quadratic equation

$$Ax^2 + Bx + C = 0$$

and computes its real roots if they exist, setting a Boolean flag to indicate whether or not they do:

IM-E

```
PROCEDURE SolveQuadratic(A, B, C: REAL;
                         VAR Root1, Root2: REAL;
                         VAR RootsExist: BOOLEAN);
  VAR D: REAL;
  BEGIN
    D := B*B – 4.0*A*C;
    IF D < 0.0 THEN RootsExist := FALSE
    ELSE
      RootsExist := TRUE; D := sqrt(D);
      Root1 := – (B–D)/(2.0*A); Root2 := – (B+D)/(2.0*A)
    END
  END SolveQuadratic;
```

Note that
(a) although the first five parameters are all of type REAL, two formal parameter sections are required to distinguish the value and variable parameters;
(b) the symbol VAR must be repeated for each section of variable parameters of distinct type.

CASE STUDY 5

A program is to accept as input a number of sums of money less than $1000 represented as two integers separated by a space, and should output both the numeric form and its alphabetic equivalent for each sum. For example, input of

    42 99

should produce the output

    42 99   forty two dollars and ninety nine cents

Execution of the program is to terminate when the user indicates that there is to be no further input—hence the program is to repeatedly enquire as to whether the user wishes to continue inputting further amounts. An actual application of a program of this kind would be the printing of computerized bank checks.

The overall structure of the program might be seen, after one or more refinement steps, as

```
REPEAT
  obtain next amount from user;
  WriteCard(Dollars, 4); WriteCard(Cents, 3);
  IF both dollars and cents are zero THEN WriteString("nil")
  ELSE
    IF Dollars > 0 THEN
      convert dollars into words;
      WriteString(" dollars");
```

```
        IF Cents > 0 THEN WriteString(" and") END
      END;
      IF Cents > 0 THEN
        convert cents into words;
        WriteString(" cents")
      END
    END;
    WriteLn;
    determine if user is finished
UNTIL user is finished
```

The steps *convert dollars into words* and *convert cents into words* involve similar actions and are suitable for expression as calls of a procedure ConvertInto-Words with appropriate parameters, e.g.,

ConvertIntoWords(Dollars)

The procedure ConvertIntoWords has the heading

PROCEDURE ConvertIntoWords(X: Range)

where the type Range is defined in the main program as the subrange [0..999]. The action of the procedure is to write out the alphabetic form of its value parameter X. The outline of this procedure is

```
split X into its hundreds, tens and units digits;
IF the hundreds digit > 0 THEN
  convert the hundreds digit;
  WriteString(" hundred");
  IF the sum of the tens and units digits > 0 THEN
    WriteString(" and")
  END
END;
IF the tens digit = 1 THEN
  convert a number between 10 and 19
ELSE
  convert the tens digit;
  convert the units digit
END
```

The actions *convert the hundreds digit* and *convert the units digit* can both be expressed as calls of a procedure, say,

PROCEDURE Units(I: Digit)

where the type Digit of the value parameter I is declared non-locally as the subrange [0..9]. This procedure will be a local procedure of ConvertIntoWords and the type Digit will be declared within ConvertIntoWords.

Writing the procedure Units and expanding the abstract actions within ConvertIntoWords and the main program we arrive at the program NumbersToWords, and sample output, as shown.

```
MODULE NumbersToWords;

 (* This program accepts as input a sequence of numbers representing
    sums of money less than $1000 and prints their alphabetic equivalent. *)

FROM InOut IMPORT WriteString, WriteLn, WriteCard, Read, ReadCard;

TYPE Range = [0..999];

VAR Dollars: Range; Cents: [0..99]; C: CARDINAL;
    Reply: CHAR; UserIsFinished: BOOLEAN;

PROCEDURE ConvertIntoWords(X: Range);

  (* This procedure writes the number X as a sequence of words. For X = 0
     no words are written. Each word written is preceded by a blank.      *)

  TYPE Digit = [0..9];
  VAR  H, T, U: Digit;
  PROCEDURE Units(I: Digit);
   BEGIN
     CASE I OF
       0: |
       1: WriteString(" one") |
       2: WriteString(" two") |
       3: WriteString(" three") |
       4: WriteString(" four") |
       5: WriteString(" five") |
       6: WriteString(" six") |
       7: WriteString(" seven") |
       8: WriteString(" eight") |
       9: WriteString(" nine")
     END
   END Units;
  BEGIN
    H := X DIV 100; T := X MOD 100 DIV 10; U := X MOD 10;
    IF H > 0 THEN
      Units(H); WriteString(" hundred");
      IF T + U > 0 THEN WriteString(" and") END
    END;
    IF T = 1 THEN
      CASE U OF
```

```
          0: WriteString(" ten") |
          1: WriteString(" eleven") |
          2: WriteString(" twelve") |
          3: WriteString(" thirteen" ) |
          4: WriteString(" fourteen" ) |
          5: WriteString(" fifteen") |
          6: WriteString(" sixteen") |
          7: WriteString(" seventeen") |
          8: WriteString(" eighteen") |
          9: WriteString(" nineteen")
        END
      ELSE
        CASE T OF
          0: |
          2: WriteString(" twenty") |
          3: WriteString(" thirty") |
          4: WriteString(" forty") |
          5: WriteString(" fifty") |
          6: WriteString(" sixty") |
          7: WriteString(" seventy") |
          8: WriteString(" eighty") |
          9: WriteString(" ninety")
        END;
        Units(U)
      END
    END ConvertIntoWords;
  BEGIN
    REPEAT
      WriteString("Input amount: ");
      ReadCard(C); Dollars := C; ReadCard(C); Cents := C; WriteLn;
      WriteCard(Dollars, 4); WriteCard(Cents, 3); WriteString("     ");
      IF (Dollars = 0) AND (Cents = 0) THEN WriteString(" nil")
      ELSE
        IF Dollars > 0 THEN
          ConvertIntoWords(Dollars); WriteString(" dollars");
          IF Cents > 0 THEN WriteString(" and") END
        END;
        IF Cents > 0 THEN
          ConvertIntoWords(Cents); WriteString(" cents")
        END
      END;
```

```
    WriteLn; WriteLn;
    WriteString("Are you finished ? "); Read(Reply); WriteLn;
    UserIsFinished := (Reply = "Y") OR (Reply = "y")
  UNTIL UserIsFinished
END NumbersToWords.
```

```
Input amount:  0 00

   0  0       nil

Are you finished ? n
Input amount:  0 07

   0  7       seven cents

Are you finished ? n
Input amount:  0 83

   0 83       eighty three cents

Are you finished ? n
Input amount:  250 00

 250  0       two hundred and fifty dollars

Are you finished ? n
Input amount:  16 27

  16 27       sixteen dollars and twenty seven cents

Are you finished ? y
```

FUNCTION PROCEDURES

In previous chapters we have described the standard functions of Modula-2 (e.g., ABS, ORD, TRUNC) and discussed how they may be used in the construction of programs. For example, in the expression

$$I \text{ DIV } ABS(J) + 3$$

ABS(J) is a *function call* which has the effect of producing a result whose value is the absolute value of J, where J is an actual parameter of the function call. The value produced by the computation is substituted into the above expression and the expression then evaluated.

Modula-2 not only provides these standard functions (which do not require any declaration in the program) but also a means whereby the programmer can declare *function procedures* and have them evaluated, with appropriate parameters, as components of expressions. A function procedure (which we shall refer to simply as a *function*) is a special form of procedure which describes a computation that produces a single value as its result. However, whereas a procedure is activated by a procedure-statement, a function is activated from within an expression to whose value the result of the function evaluation contributes.

The declaration of a function is similar to that of a procedure and takes the following form:

function-procedure-declaration =
    function-heading ";" *function-body identifier.*
function-heading =
    "*PROCEDURE*" *identifier* "(" *[formal-parameter-list]* ")" ":" *result-type.*
result-type = *type-identifier.*
function-body = *block.*

A *function-declaration* appears, with any other declarations, in the *declaration-part* of a block. A *function-heading* is similar to a procedure-heading except that it contains an indication of the type of the result computed by the function—the *result-type*. The type identified may be any previously defined type although most Modula-2 implementations require that it must be an unstructured-type or pointer-type (see Chapter 11).

The *identifier* and *formal-parameter-list*, if any, in the function-heading play the same role as those in a procedure-heading, i.e., they determine how the function may be called. The syntax category

function-identifier = *qualified-identifier.*

is used hereafter to denote the class of identifiers introduced by function-procedure-declarations.

Note that a function, even if it has no formal parameters, must still include parentheses "(" and ")" in its heading, e.g.,

PROCEDURE NoParameters ( ): SomeType

The *function-body* is a *block*, and may therefore include declarations of further local constants, types, variables, procedures and functions. The same rules of identifier scope apply to blocks arising from function-declarations as to those from proper procedures. However, within the function-body there must appear at least one *return-statement*, and each return-statement must contain an expression which determines the result of the function, as a value which is assignment-compatible with the result-type. In each execution of the function the first value so determined gives the result of the function evaluation. If no return-statement is executed during an execution of a function the result of that function evaluation is an exception.

The following is an example of a function-declaration defining a function Max which yields as its result the larger of the values of its two real value parameters.

```
PROCEDURE Max(X, Y: REAL): REAL;
BEGIN
  IF X > Y THEN RETURN X ELSE RETURN Y END
END Max
```

The heading of the function specifies the identifier Max by which the function is known, its formal parameters, and the type REAL of the result of the computation performed by the function. The function-body defines this computation such that the result returned will be the larger of its two value parameters.

A function is called (invoked, or *designated*) simply by the occurrence of its identifier and *actual-parameter-list* within an expression, as we have already seen in the case of standard function calls. Recalling the syntactic definition of an *expression* given in Chapter 4:

> *factor =*
> *variable | constant-literal | constant-identifier |*
> *procedure-identifier | function-identifier | function-call | set |*
> *"(" expression ")" | ("NOT" | "~") factor .*

we now define a *function-call* as

> *function-call = function-designator "(" [actual-parameter-list] ")".*
> *function-designator = function-identifier | variable.*

A *variable* used as a *function-designator* must be of a procedure-type—procedure variables are discussed later in this chapter. The *actual-parameter-list* of a function call must obey the same rules of correspondence with the *formal-parameter-list* of the function-declaration as have already been stated for statement-procedure calls. Note also that even if a function has no parameters, any call of the function must still include the parentheses symbols (and), e.g., if NoParameters is declared as a parameterless function, as suggested earlier, it must be called as

    NoParameters()

The effect of a function call is to execute the statement-part of the corresponding function-declaration with actual parameters being substituted for formal parameters (according to their class). Provided that a return-statement produces a value for the function during this execution, the function returns a single value of its result type and this value is then used in the evaluation of the expression containing the function call. If X, Y and Z are variables of type REAL, then

    X := Max(Y, Z)

will assign to X the larger of the values of the variables Y and Z;

X := 2 * Max(Y, 1.5)

will assign to X twice the value of the larger of Y and 1.5;

X := Max(X, Max(Y, Z))

will assign to X the largest of the values of X, Y and Z. Since the expressions in the actual-parameter-list of the function call must be evaluated before the function itself is evaluated, this last example is equivalent to

T := Max(Y, Z); X := Max(X, T)

where T is an auxiliary variable not used for any other purpose.

The following are further simple examples of function-declarations.

```
PROCEDURE Power(X: REAL; N: CARDINAL): REAL;
  (* Computes X raised to the power N *)
  VAR I: CARDINAL; Answer: REAL;
  BEGIN
    Answer := 1.0;
    FOR I := 1 TO N DO Answer := Answer*X END;
    RETURN Answer
  END Power;
```

```
PROCEDURE SumOfSquares(N: CARDINAL): CARDINAL;
  (* Computes the sum of the squares of the first N whole numbers   *)
  VAR I, Sum: CARDINAL;
  BEGIN
    Sum := 0;
    FOR I := 1 TO N DO Sum := Sum + I*I END;
    RETURN Sum
  END SumOfSquares;
```

```
PROCEDURE Multiple(I, J: CARDINAL): BOOLEAN;
  (* Determines whether I and J are multiples of each other,
     assuming neither I nor J is zero *)
  BEGIN
    RETURN (I MOD J = 0) OR (J MOD I = 0)
  END Multiple;
```

The following are examples of statements which call the above functions:

```
Y := Power(6.3, 5)
I := SumOfSquares(3) + SumOfSquares(N)
WHILE NOT Multiple(J, K) DO J := J+1; K := K+1 END
```

The program PerfectNumbers reads in two CARDINAL values N and M (where N is assumed to be less than M) and produces as output a list of all the perfect numbers between N and M, inclusive. A perfect number is one for which the sum of its factors equals the number itself, e.g., $6 = 1+2+3$. The function Perfect determines whether or not its CARDINAL value parameter is a perfect number.

```
MODULE PerfectNumbers;
  FROM InOut IMPORT ReadCard, WriteCard, WriteString, WriteLn;

  VAR I, N, M: CARDINAL;

  PROCEDURE Perfect(J: CARDINAL): BOOLEAN;
    VAR I, Sum: CARDINAL;
    BEGIN
      Sum := 1;
      FOR I := 2 TO J DIV 2 DO
        IF J MOD I = 0 THEN Sum := Sum + I END
      END;
      RETURN (Sum = J)
    END Perfect;

  BEGIN
    WriteString("Input lower bound of required range: ");
    ReadCard(N); WriteLn;
    WriteString("Input upper bound of required range: ");
    ReadCard(M); WriteLn;
    WriteString("List of all perfect numbers between");
    WriteCard(N, 6); WriteString(" and"); WriteCard(M, 6); WriteLn;
    FOR I := N TO M DO
      IF Perfect(I) THEN WriteCard(I, 6); WriteLn END
    END
  END PerfectNumbers.
```

Side Effects of Functions

When a statement executed during evaluation of a function alters the value of a variable which is known outside the function this is called a *side effect* of the function. Side effects represent a potential data interaction between the function and the program which calls it which is always dangerous, since it makes the program difficult to understand (the value of a variable may change during evaluation of an expression containing a function call), and can make the meaning of a program ambiguous.

Suppose we have a function F which, during its execution, alters the value of some non-local variable V,

```
PROCEDURE F(I: CARDINAL): CARDINAL;
BEGIN
  V := V*I;
  F := I*I + 1
END F
```

Now consider the evaluation of the expression

$$F(X) + V$$

The value of this expression depends upon the order of evaluation of its operands, i.e., on whether the value of V is taken before or after the value of F(X) is determined. If F(X) is evaluated first, then the value of V produced by the assignment in F is added to the result of F(X), otherwise the original value of V is added to the result. In Modula-2 the order of evaluation of the operands of an arithmetic dyadic operator such as + is implementation dependent, and so the expression value is implementation dependent. Even when the order of evaluation is known, the expression F(X)+V may produce a different result from V+F(X)!

In the interests of avoiding such ambiguous situations, functions with side effects should be avoided where possible. It follows that formal parameter lists of functions should not include variable parameters, and functions should refrain from assigning values to non-local variables and from calling procedures which perform such assignments.

The evaluation of a function may require the execution of a substantial piece of program and so one should take care to avoid unnecessary calls in a program. For instance, if F is a function with a real value parameter, the statement

```
X := F(Y/2.0) + (F(Y/2.0)–1.0) * ABS(F(Y/2.0))
```

calls the function F three times with the same actual parameter value and thus all three calls produce the same result (assuming that F has no side effects). It is more efficient to evaluate the function once and assign its result to a variable, thus:

```
T := F(Y/2.0);
X := T + (T–1.0) * ABS(T)
```

However, if the function F has side effects, then these two approaches may produce different effects since F is called three times in the first form but only once in the second.

CASE STUDY 6

We wish to write a program which allows the user to input a series of integer values, each greater than 1, and outputs the nearest prime number to each. In the case of two prime numbers being equidistant from an input integer both should be output.

The required program has an overall action which may be expressed as follows:

```
REPEAT
    obtain a cardinal value J from user;
    WriteString("Nearest prime to"); WriteCard(J, 4); WriteString(" is");
    output nearest prime to J;
    determine if user is finished
UNTIL user is finished
```

The action *output nearest prime to J* might first be refined as:

```
IF J is prime THEN output J
ELSE locate and output nearest prime(s)
END
```

The step *locate and output nearest prime(s)* involves looking at the odd numbers starting with the closest odd number to the input value and working away from the input value until a prime number is found. If the input value is an even number then the nearest odd numbers are one greater and one less than it, otherwise they are two greater and two less. It can thus be expressed as a loop which tests the odd numbers working away from the input value and terminates when it finds a prime number. Remembering that if two primes are found equidistant from the input value they are both to be output, this may be written as:

```
IF ODD(J) THEN K := 2 ELSE K := 1 END;
REPEAT
    IF J+K is prime THEN output J+K END;
    IF J–K is prime THEN output J–K END;
    K := K + 2
UNTIL prime found;
```

Since the loop must terminate if either of the output actions is executed, the terminating condition is best expressed as a Boolean variable Found, initially false, which is set true when either value is output.

We thus have three points at which we must test whether a particular value, J, J+K, J–K respectively, is prime. The appropriate step is to introduce a function Prime, which takes a positive integer value as parameter, and returns a Boolean result, TRUE or FALSE, according to whether the integer is prime or not, thus:

```
PROCEDURE Prime(P: CARDINAL): BOOLEAN;
...
```

Assuming such a function, the action *locate and output nearest prime(s)* may be expressed as:

```
Found := FALSE;
IF ODD(J) THEN K := 2 ELSE K := 1 END;
REPEAT
  IF Prime(J+K) THEN Found := TRUE; WriteCard(J+K, 6) END;
  IF Prime(J–K) THEN Found := TRUE; WriteCard(J-K, 6) END;
  K := K + 2
UNTIL Found
```

We must now program the required function Prime. We may assume 2 and 3 to be prime numbers and take advantage of the fact that an even number greater than 2 is never prime because it is always divisible by 2. Therefore only odd numbers greater than 3 are further tested to determine if they are prime. Thus the outline of the function is

```
IF P < 4 THEN RETURN (P > 1)
ELSIF NOT ODD(P) THEN RETURN FALSE
ELSE test if P is prime
END
```

Since factors of a number exist in pairs such that one factor is greater than or equal to the square root, it follows that no number has any factors greater than its square root if it does not have factors less than its square root. In the step *test if P is prime* we are guaranteed that P is an odd number and so, in order to test for the primeness of P, we need only test if any of the odd numbers from 3 up to the square root of P are factors of P. Then P is a prime number if, and only if, this process is unable to find a factor of P. We may thus write *test if P is prime* as a loop which divides P by the odd numbers starting from 3 until either a factor of P is found or all the odd numbers up to, and including if necessary, the square root of P, have been tested. If the square root of P is not a whole number then we test the odd numbers up to the whole number part of the square root. To compute this limit we might, at first, use the function sqrt supplied in the library module MathLib0 as

$$TRUNC(sqrt(FLOAT(P)))$$

However, if P is a square of the form $(q+1)^2$, say, inaccuracies in the sqrt function might give a square root of the form $q.999...$ and truncation would then give a limiting value q rather than $q+1$. To guard against such inaccuracies we instead write

$$TRUNC(sqrt(FLOAT(P)) + 0.5)$$

though this will sometimes give a limit one greater than necessary. The action *test if P is prime* is thus programmed as:

```
Root := TRUNC(sqrt(FLOAT(P)) + 0.5); Divisor := 3;
WHILE (Divisor <= Root) AND (P MOD Divisor <> 0) DO
  Divisor := Divisor + 2
END;
RETURN (Divisor > Root)
```

and our complete program FindNearestPrimes is as shown.

```
MODULE FindNearestPrimes;
  FROM InOut IMPORT ReadCard, Read, WriteCard, WriteString, WriteLn;
  FROM MathLib0 IMPORT sqrt;

  (* This program reads a series of positive integers (each > 1); it then
     outputs the nearest prime to each. In the case of two prime numbers
     being equidistant from an input integer, both primes are output. *)

  VAR J, K: CARDINAL; UserIsFinished, Found: BOOLEAN; Reply: CHAR;

  PROCEDURE Prime(P: CARDINAL): BOOLEAN;
    (* determines whether P is prime or not *)
    VAR  Root, Divisor: CARDINAL;
    BEGIN
      IF P < 4 THEN RETURN (P > 1)
      ELSIF NOT ODD(P) THEN RETURN FALSE
      ELSE
        Root := TRUNC(sqrt(FLOAT(P)) + 0.5); Divisor := 3;
        WHILE (Divisor <= Root) AND (P MOD Divisor <> 0) DO
          Divisor := Divisor + 2
        END;
        RETURN (Divisor > Root)
      END
    END Prime;
  BEGIN
    REPEAT
      WriteString("Input a number: "); ReadCard(J); WriteLn;
      IF J > 1 THEN
        WriteString("Nearest prime to "); WriteCard(J, 1); WriteString(" is");
        IF Prime(J) THEN WriteCard(J, 6)
        ELSE
          Found := FALSE;
```

```
          IF ODD(J) THEN K := 2 ELSE K := 1 END;
          REPEAT
            IF Prime(J+K) THEN Found := TRUE; WriteCard(J+K, 6) END;
            IF Prime(J–K) THEN Found := TRUE; WriteCard(J-K, 6) END;
            K := K + 2
          UNTIL Found
        END
        ELSE WriteString("Input number must be greater than 1")
        END;
        WriteLn; WriteLn;
        WriteString("Are you finished ? "); Read(Reply); WriteLn;
        UserIsFinished := (Reply = "Y") OR (Reply = "y")
      UNTIL UserIsFinished
    END FindNearestPrimes.
```

PROCEDURES AND FUNCTIONS AS PARAMETERS

In discussing parameters earlier in this chapter we explained the two classes of parameters, namely value and variable parameters, in detail. However, in some programs we may wish to pass procedures and functions as parameters.

Modula-2 considers procedures, like data values, as objects that may be assigned to variables and hence permits the declaration of types whose values are procedures and functions. A *procedure-type* was introduced in Chapter 3 as one of the possible forms of a type. A *procedure-type* declaration specifies the number and types of parameters of procedures and functions of that type and, in the case of functions, the type of the result.

procedure-type = "PROCEDURE" [formal-type-list [":" result-type]].
formal-type-list = "(" [formal-specification {"," formal-specification}] ")".
formal-specification = ["VAR"] formal-type.
formal-type = type-identifier | open-array-schema.
result-type = type-identifier.

For example, a procedure type with two CARDINAL value parameters and one REAL variable parameter might be declared as a type Proc1:

    TYPE Proc1 = PROCEDURE(CARDINAL, CARDINAL, VAR REAL);

and another type

    TYPE Func1 = PROCEDURE(REAL, REAL): REAL;

would describe the class of functions that take two REAL value parameters producing REAL results.

Any procedure with two CARDINAL value parameters and one REAL variable parameter, declared in that order, is of type Proc1 and, likewise, any function with two REAL value parameters and a REAL result is of type Func1.

Variables of these types may be declared, e.g.,

VAR P: Proc1; F: Func1;

and assignments made to these variables, such as

P := ConvertToMeters;
F := Max

where ConvertToMeters and Max are the procedure and function, respectively, declared earlier.

Procedure variables may be used anywhere that a procedure-identifier may be used, e.g., as a procedure-designator in a procedure-statement, or as a function-designator in a function call. Thus, assuming the above assignment-statements have previously been executed, a call

P(I+1, J, M)

is equivalent to the call

ConvertToMeters(I+1, J, M)

and the assignment-statement

X := F(X, F(Y, Z))

is equivalent to

X := Max(X, Max(Y, Z))

One of the principal uses of procedure-types is to enable the passing of procedures and functions as parameters. Suppose that a procedure P requires as parameter another procedure which itself takes no parameters. The Modula-2 standard type-identifier PROC denotes such a parameterless procedure type. Hence, the heading

PROCEDURE P(A: PROC)

declares P to have one formal parameter, a procedure A which itself takes no parameters. A is said to be a *formal-procedure*. Within the body of P the identifier A may be used like any other procedure-identifier, e.g., in a procedure-statement.

Suppose another procedure Q requires as parameter a function which takes two REAL parameters and produces a REAL result. The heading of this procedure would be

PROCEDURE Q(F: Func1)

where Func1 is the procedure-type declared above. Within the body of Q the identifier F is used like any other function-identifier of this kind, e.g., in a function-call.

Two procedure-types are considered to be the same type if they are *structurally compatible*, i.e., they have the same parameter requirements and the same result-type (if any). When a procedure or function which has a formal parameter of a certain procedure-type is called, the corresponding actual parameter must be the identifier of a procedure or function of the same type. As the called procedure or function is executed, each occurrence of the formal parameter implies a corresponding use of the actual procedure or function supplied as parameter.

Suppose a program declares a type

```
TYPE Func2 = PROCEDURE(REAL): REAL;
```

and a procedure

```
PROCEDURE Tabulate(F: Func2; Lower, Upper, Step: REAL);
VAR X: REAL; J: CARDINAL;
BEGIN
  X := Lower;
  FOR J := 0 TO TRUNC((Upper–Lower)/Step) DO
    WriteReal(X, 12); WriteString("   ");
    WriteReal(F(X), 12); WriteLn;
    X := X + Step
  END
END Tabulate
```

The procedure Tabulate takes a function parameter F of type Func2 (i.e., with a REAL value parameter and producing a REAL result), and three value parameters of type REAL. Its effect is to generate a succession of values for X, as determined by the value parameters Lower, Upper and Step, and to evaluate and output F(X) for each. Thus a procedure-statement

```
Tabulate(F1, 0.0, 1.0, 0.01)
```

would cause the values of X and F1(X) to be tabulated for values of X in the range 0 to 1 at intervals of 0.01, while the procedure-statement

```
Tabulate(F2, 0.0, 1.0, 0.01)
```

would produce a similar tabulation for the values of a function F2, where F1 and F2 are both functions of a type structurally compatible with Func2, i.e., that take one REAL parameter and produce a REAL result, and are declared elsewhere in the program.

As an example of a function taking a function as parameter we might declare a procedure-type

```
Func3 = PROCEDURE(INTEGER): INTEGER
```

and a function Sigma:

```
PROCEDURE Sigma(F: Func3; Lower, Upper: INTEGER): INTEGER;
  VAR I, Sum: INTEGER;
  BEGIN
    Sum := 0;
    FOR I := Lower TO Upper DO Sum := Sum + F(I) END;
    RETURN Sum
  END Sigma
```

which computes the sum

$$\sum_{Lower}^{Upper} F(i)$$

where F is an integer-valued function of one integer argument. If the program contains a function such as

```
PROCEDURE Square(X: INTEGER): INTEGER;
  BEGIN
    RETURN X*X
  END Square
```

then the assignment-statement

```
S := Sigma(Square, 1, 10)
```

would call the function Sigma to evaluate the sum

$$\sum_{1}^{10} i^2$$

and assign the result to the INTEGER variable S.

The formal function F in the heading of Sigma and the actual function Square are said to be *congruous*, in that they take the same number and type of parameters and produce results of the same type.

The ability to pass procedures and functions to other procedures and functions is a very useful one in some situations and may be used to construct very general-purpose procedures or functions, such as Tabulate and Sigma above. However, the facility should be used with caution, as the effect of executing a procedure which receives another procedure as parameter is not always obvious. Interaction through the non-local data which each procedure manipulates can produce complex and sometimes unexpected effects. Programs using procedures as parameters are often both difficult to understand and debug for this reason.

Modula-2 allows only global procedures and functions, i.e., those declared in the outermost block of a program, to be assigned as values to procedure variables, or to be passed as parameters. Furthermore, it is not permitted to assign standard Modula-2 procedures and functions, or to pass them as parameters. Thus calls such as

S := Sigma(ABS, -10, 40)

are invalid. If necessary, this restriction is easily overcome by declaring an equivalent global function whose sole action is simply to call the standard function, and then calling the procedure (or function) with this equivalent function as parameter, e.g.,

```
PROCEDURE AbsoluteValueOf(X: INTEGER): INTEGER;
BEGIN
  RETURN ABS(X)
END AbsoluteValueOf
```

and a valid use of Sigma then becomes

S := Sigma(AbsoluteValueOf, −10, 40)

RECURSION

In defining the structure of statements in Modula-2 we have seen various examples of a *recursive* description, i.e., one expressed in terms of the structure being described. For example, the syntactic definition of a Modula-2 *statement* can be expressed as

> *statement* =
>   ... /
> *"REPEAT" statement-sequence "UNTIL" expression* /
>   ... .
> *statement-sequence = statement {";" statement}.*

where the syntactic entity *statement* is defined in terms of itself. Such recursive definitions occur throughout the syntax of Modula-2 and permit the construction of nested expressions, statements and blocks, etc.

This same technique can be used in describing a process. Consider for example the process which accepts a non-negative integer value N and outputs the sequence of decimal digits representing the number in reverse order. This process might be described abstractly as

> *output last digit of N*;
> IF *digits remain* THEN
>   *reverse remaining digits*
> END

In Modula-2 a procedure or function is permitted not only to call another procedure or function but also to call itself. Such a call is said to be *recursive*. Thus the above process may be written in Modula-2 as a recursive procedure

```
PROCEDURE Reverse(N: CARDINAL);
BEGIN
  WriteCard(N MOD 10, 1);
  IF N DIV 10 <> 0 THEN Reverse(N DIV 10) END
END Reverse
```

where the number to be reversed at each stage is passed as a value parameter in a call to the recursive procedure Reverse. A CARDINAL value I may be output with its digits reversed by the procedure-statement

```
Reverse(I)
```

Consider what happens when Reverse is called with a particular parameter value, say 327. The effect of the call Reverse(327) is

```
WriteCard(7, 1);
IF TRUE THEN Reverse(32) END
```

since 327 MOD 10 = 7 and 327 DIV 10 = 32. The effect of the embedded recursive call Reverse(32) is

```
WriteCard(2, 1);
IF TRUE THEN Reverse(3) END
```

The effect of the embedded recursive call Reverse(3) is

```
WriteCard(3, 1);
IF FALSE THEN Reverse(0) END
```

and because 3 DIV 10 = 0 no further recursive call arises. At this point the call Reverse(3) is complete and so the call Reverse(32) continues. This too is complete so the call Reverse(327) continues, and is in turn complete. Thus the net effect of the original call is to output the digits 7, 2, 3 in that order, with one call being made for each digit output. The succession of recursive calls terminates because of the conditional statement which controls the recursive call within the body of Reverse, a necessary property of all useful recursive procedures.

The duration, or *lifetime*, of each recursive call of procedure Reverse is strictly nested within the lifetime of its parent call. This nesting brings additional advantages when data are declared local to the recursive procedure. As we have already seen, the call of a procedure creates a set of local variables which is entirely unrelated to the set used in the previous execution of the procedure. This is also true when a procedure calls itself but, as the previous execution of the procedure has not been completed before it is called again recursively, the previous local variables still exist. (They can not, however, be accessed until the recursive call has been completed.) Thus, for each variable V declared local to a recursive procedure R, a call of R which results in the generation of k recursive procedure calls will produce $k+1$ distinct instances of the variable V, the lifetime of each being strictly nested in that of its predecessor.

This property of the local variables of a recursive procedure can be used to advantage in many applications of recursion. Consider a variation of our first recursive process—one which reads a sequence of characters of arbitrary length terminated by some special character such as "." say, and prints out the sequence in reverse. This process can be programmed recursively as:

```
PROCEDURE ReverseInput;
  VAR C: CHAR;
  BEGIN
    Read(C);
    IF C <> "." THEN ReverseInput END;
    Write(C)
  END ReverseInput
```

When called to reverse an input sequence of length N, ReverseInput creates a total of N recursive procedure calls with N instances of the variable C. At the ith level of recursion the variable instance C holds the ith character input, and as the recursion unwinds (i.e., the recursive calls are completed) these instances of C have their values output in the order

$$C_N \ C_{N-1} \ ... \ C_1.$$

Thus, ReverseInput automatically generates the exact number of variable instances required to reverse the particular input sequence, and each instance exists only as long as it is required to do so.

Many simple processes can be expressed recursively, but can also be expressed as equally simple non-recursive processes involving repetition. For instance, the procedure Reverse for reversing the digits of a cardinal value may be expressed non-recursively as:

```
PROCEDURE Reverse(N: CARDINAL);
  BEGIN
    REPEAT
      WriteCard(N MOD 10, 1);
      N := N DIV 10
    UNTIL N = 0
  END Reverse
```

Many mathematical functions are defined recursively and it thus appears natural to write recursive functions to compute their values. The *factorial* function is a familiar example which may be defined as

$$factorial(0) = 1$$

$factorial(n) = n * factorial(n-1), \quad \text{for } n > 0$

and so a Modula-2 function may be declared to evaluate the factorial of a given value as:

```
PROCEDURE Factorial(N: CARDINAL): CARDINAL;
  BEGIN
    IF N = 0 THEN RETURN 1
    ELSE RETURN N * Factorial(N–1)
    END
  END Factorial
```

However, the function Factorial could also be written in a simple non-recursive form, as:

```
PROCEDURE Factorial(N: CARDINAL): CARDINAL;
  VAR X, I: CARDINAL;
  BEGIN
    X := 1;
    FOR I := 1 TO N DO X := X*I END;
    RETURN X
  END Factorial
```

For many implementations these non-recursive forms of Reverse and Factorial are more efficient in data storage and execution time than their recursive equivalents. Replacement of recursive formulations by equivalent repetition forms may therefore be appropriate for reasons of both simplicity and efficiency.

In general it is possible to re-express any recursive procedure as a non-recursive procedure using a suitable form of repetition, but the re-expression is often far from trivial. Therefore, there are significant advantages in using recursive procedures in many situations:

(a) In many cases they are the most natural and most transparent means of describing a process, as is illustrated by some of the case-study programs later in this book. In particular, they are the primary tool used in describing the processing of data which are themselves recursive in nature (see Chapter 11).

(b) They permit the generation of certain repetitive processes, and of the data items necessary to control and support them, without the introduction of an explicit data "structure" to contain the data items. Unlike the procedure Reverse, the effect of the recursive procedure ReverseInput cannot be generated non-recursively without the introduction of some means of holding the entire input sequence of characters simultaneously. The procedure ReverseInput generates exactly the required number of character variables to hold the input characters, by means of its local variable C.

CASE STUDY 7

The *Towers of Hanoi* is a legendary problem (sometimes marketed as a children's toy) which, although appearing at first to be difficult to solve, can be solved quite simply by the use of a recursive procedure.

You are given three wooden poles (call them the left pole, middle pole, and right pole). A stack of N disks of decreasing size (such that the disk of largest diameter is at the bottom) is held on the left pole which passes through a hole in the center of each disk. The initial layout of the poles and disks is illustrated in Figure 7.1 for the case $N=5$.

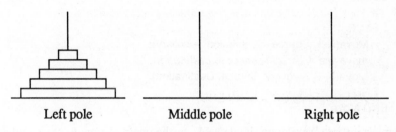

| Left pole | Middle pole | Right pole |

Figure 7.1   Towers of Hanoi

The problem is to move all the disks from the left pole to the right pole according to the following rules:

(a) only one disk may be moved at a time;
(b) a disk must never be placed on top of a smaller one;
(c) at any time each of the disks must be on one of the three poles.

We wish to construct a program which reads in an integer N and outputs the sequence of moves required to solve the problem for N disks.

The problem of moving N (>1) disks can be reduced to a problem of moving $N-1$ disks by considering the solution as involving three steps:

(a) move the topmost $N-1$ disks from the left pole to the middle pole using the right pole as an "auxiliary" pole;
(b) move the remaining disk from the left pole to the right pole;
(c) move the $N-1$ disks on the middle pole to the right pole, using the left pole as an "auxiliary" pole.

This method can be seen to obey the rules of the game.

Thus the problem of moving N disks has been reduced to a problem of moving $N-1$ disks. Expressed another way, the problem of moving N disks has been described recursively in terms of the same problem involving one disk fewer.

When $N=1$ the problem is solved simply by moving the disk from the left pole to the right pole.

We can thus attempt a recursive formulation of the problem of moving N disks from any pole to another. This procedure will require four parameters—the number of disks to be moved, the "source" pole from which the disks are to be moved, the "destination" pole to which the disks are to be moved, and the "auxiliary" pole which is to be used to hold disks during the intermediate moves.

By analogy with the previous recursive description of moving N disks from the left pole to the right pole we can write the procedure Move as:

```
PROCEDURE Move(N: DiskRange; Source, Auxiliary, Destination: Pole);
BEGIN
   IF N=1 THEN move one disk from source to destination
   ELSE
      Move(N-1, Source, Destination, Auxiliary);
      move one disk from source to destination;
      Move(N-1, Auxiliary, Source, Destination)
   END
END Move
```

where the type DiskRange is defined in the main program as a suitable subrange-type defining the number of possible disks, and the type Pole is an enumerated type:

```
TYPE Pole = (Left, Middle, Right);
```

The statement-part of the main program requires only to read the number of disks NumberOfDisks from the input stream and then call

```
Move(NumberOfDisks, Left, Middle, Right)
```

Since the output required is the sequence of moves which solve the problem, the action *move one disk from source to destination* is programmed as a procedure, each call of which prints out the corresponding move. It uses a local procedure PrintPole to output the identities of the poles involved in each move.

The complete program, and the output which it produces for $N=4$, is shown.

```
MODULE TowersOfHanoi;
  FROM InOut IMPORT ReadCard, WriteCard, WriteString, WriteLn;
  (* This program outputs the solution to the Towers of Hanoi problem,
     for a given number of disks.                                    *)
  CONST MaximumDisks = 10;
  TYPE Pole = (Left, Middle, Right); DiskRange = [1 .. MaximumDisks];
  VAR  NumberOfDisks: DiskRange; N: CARDINAL;
  PROCEDURE Move(N: DiskRange; Source, Auxiliary, Destination: Pole);
    PROCEDURE MoveADiskFromSourceToDestination;
      PROCEDURE PrintPole(P: Pole);
      BEGIN
        CASE P OF
          Left: WriteString("left") |
          Middle: WriteString("middle") |
          Right: WriteString("right")
        END
      END PrintPole;
    BEGIN
      WriteString("Move a disk from "); PrintPole(Source);
      WriteString(" to "); PrintPole(Destination); WriteLn
    END MoveADiskFromSourceToDestination;
  BEGIN
    IF N=1 THEN MoveADiskFromSourceToDestination
    ELSE
      Move(N-1, Source, Destination, Auxiliary);
      MoveADiskFromSourceToDestination;
      Move(N-1, Auxiliary, Source, Destination)
    END
  END Move;
BEGIN
  WriteString("Input number of disks: ");
  ReadCard(N); NumberOfDisks := N;
  WriteLn; WriteLn;
  WriteString("For "); WriteCard(NumberOfDisks, 1);
  WriteString(" disks the required moves are :");
  WriteLn; WriteLn;
  Move(NumberOfDisks, Left, Middle, Right)
END TowersOfHanoi.
```

```
Input number of disks: 4

For 4 disks the required moves are :

Move a disk from left to middle
Move a disk from left to right
Move a disk from middle to right
Move a disk from left to middle
Move a disk from right to left
Move a disk from right to middle
Move a disk from left to middle
Move a disk from left to right
Move a disk from middle to right
Move a disk from middle to left
Move a disk from right to left
Move a disk from middle to right
Move a disk from left to middle
Move a disk from left to right
Move a disk from middle to right
```

EXERCISES

7.1 Write a procedure Order3 which interchanges the values of its three integer parameters *A*, *B*, *C* if necessary, such that $A<=B<=C$. (Make use of the procedure Order given on p. 113). Use your procedure in rewriting the program Triangles so that the lengths of the sides of the triangle to be analyzed need not be input in ascending order.

7.2 Extend the procedure ConvertIntoWords in Case Study 5 to convert any number in the range 1 to 999999. Modify the program to accept sums of money less than one million dollars, and retest it with suitable data.

7.3 Using only the procedures Read and Write provided by the library module InOut, write

(a) a procedure ReadOctal which reads a sequence of octal digits and assigns the equivalent positive integer value to a parameter;

(b) a procedure WriteOctal which prints the sequence of octal digits denoting the value of its positive integer parameter.

Use these procedures in a program which reads a sequence of octal numbers, and prints out the numbers, followed by their octal sum.

7.4 The exponential e^x of a number *x* may be defined as

$$exp(x) = \sum_0^\infty \frac{x^i}{i!} = 1 + x + \frac{x^2}{2!} + \frac{x^3}{3!} \cdots$$

Write a function with heading

    PROCEDURE Exponential(x: REAL): REAL;

to compute this formula to an accuracy of four significant digits. Hint: stop adding new terms when the size of the new term is less than one ten-thousandth of the size of the sum so far. Incorporate this function in a program which tabulates the values of e^x for $x = 0.0, 0.1, 0.2, \ldots, 1.0$.

7.5 Write a function which accepts a positive integer and a decimal digit as parameters and determines whether the decimal representation of the integer contains the digit. Write a program which reads a digit D and tabulates all integer numbers from 1 to 100 such that the decimal representation of the number, its square and its cube all contain the digit D. For example, if $D = 1$, 13 is such a number, since 13, 169 and 2197 all contain the digit 1.

7.6 An arithmetic expression involving dyadic operators such as +, *, /, etc., can be written in *prefix* notation without the use of parentheses. Thus

a	is equivalent to	a
$+ab$	is equivalent to	$a+b$
$+a*bc$	is equivalent to	$a+b*c$
$*a+bc$	is equivalent to	$a*(b+c)$
$*+ab-cd$	is equivalent to	$(a+b)*(c-d)$

Write down an EBNF syntax which defines the allowable form of an expression in prefix notation, assuming that the only allowable operators are +, −, * and /, and that operands are single letters, a, b, c, ...

Write a recursive procedure which reads a valid expression in this prefix notation, and outputs an equivalent *fully parenthesized* infix expression, i.e.,

a	should produce	a
$+ab$	should produce	$(a+b)$
$+a*bc$	should produce	$(a+(b*c))$
$*a+bc$	should produce	$(a*(b+c))$
$*+ab-cd$	should produce	$((a+b)*(c-d))$

Test your procedure in a suitable program for interactive translation of prefix to infix notation.

8

Arrays

THE ARRAY CONCEPT

In Chapters 6 and 7 we saw how a composite program could be constructed out of elementary actions such as assignments and input and output statements, by means of statement-sequences, selection and repetition statements, and procedural abstraction. The data manipulated by such composite actions are themselves often composite, or structured, where the elementary components are values of the simple types introduced in Chapter 3. Describing the data in a structured way may both clarify the nature of the data and simplify their manipulation by the program.

Consider the following example. A firm employs a group of twenty salesmen (with reference numbers 1-20) who are paid commission on that portion of their sales which exceeds two-thirds of the average sales of the group. A program is required to read in the sales of each of the twenty salesmen and print out the reference number of those salesmen who qualify for commission, together with their sales.

There are two features of the problem which make it difficult to program using the Modula-2 facilities described so far. It appears that the program must carry out similar processing with each salesman's figures—read in each of the twenty sales figures; compute the average sales amount; compare each salesman's sales with two-thirds of the average to decide whether or not he has qualified for any commission. This similarity of processing suggests some form of repetition. Secondly, it is necessary to store the salesmen's amounts throughout the program—they are read in at the start and used to determine the commission level, but must also be available for the final part of the program when it is determined which salesmen will be receiving commission. Thus we require twenty variables to hold the twenty sales amounts. Twenty variables could be declared, of appropriate type, say Sales1, Sales2, Sales20. However, programming the problem now becomes extremely cumbersome—resulting in a program outline such as:

```
ReadReal(Sales1);
ReadReal(Sales2);
...
ReadReal(Sales20);
calculate CommissionLevel;
IF Sales1 > CommissionLevel THEN
    WriteCard(1, 6); WriteReal(Sales1, 16); WriteLn
END;
IF Sales2 > CommissionLevel THEN
    WriteCard(2, 6); WriteReal(Sales2, 16); WriteLn
END;
...
IF Sales20 > CommissionLevel THEN
    WriteCard(20, 6); WriteReal(Sales20, 16); WriteLn
END
```

Because the variables Sales1, Sales2, Sales20 are distinct we are forced to write the printout as a sequence of if-statements rather than the repetition of a single if-statement. Likewise, the potential repetition in reading the sales values, and in computing their sum, is precluded by the independence of these variables. Clearly this is a rather tedious program to write. Consider how much more tedious it would be if the firm had not 20, but 200, salesmen working for it.

A preferable solution is to consider these variables as components of a single data item Sales, and to denote the ith component by the mathematical convention of subscripting, thus $Sales_i$. The problem solution for any number N of salesmen can then be expressed as:

```
CONST CommissionRatio = 2.0/3.0;

Sum := 0.0;
FOR i := 1 TO N DO
    ReadReal(Sales_i);
    Sum := Sum + Sales_i;
END;
```

```
CommissionLevel := CommissionRatio * (Sum/FLOAT(N));
FOR i := 1 TO N DO
  IF Sales > CommissionLevel THEN
       i
    WriteCard(I, 6); WriteReal(Sales , 16); WriteLn
                                   i
  END
END
```

This solution assumes two language features not so far available:

(a)   the ability to denote a group of variables, or composite variable, by a single identifier Sales, and
(b)   the ability to distinguish a particular variable of the group, or *component*, by subscripting this identifier with a suitable value *i*.

In Modula-2 an array-type is defined as follows:

> *array-type = "ARRAY" index-type {"," index-type} "OF" element-type.*
> *index-type = simple-type.*
> *element-type = type.*

That is, an *array-type* consists of the symbol ARRAY followed by one or more *index-types* separated by commas followed by the symbol OF and an indication of the type of the individual elements of the array (the *element-type*). An *index-type* may be any enumerated-type, subrange-type, or one of the standard types BOOLEAN or CHAR, and the *element-type* may be any type. A variable of an array-type consists of one element for each value of the index-type, or one element for each combination of values of the index-types where two or more index-types are specified.

For example,

VAR Sales: ARRAY [1..20] OF REAL;

is an array variable-declaration which creates an array of 20 elements. In this case the *index-type* is the integer subrange [1..20] and the *element-type* is REAL.

The index-type of an array-type is often an integer subrange but need not necessarily be so. For example, an enumerated-type

TYPE Color = (Red, Blue, Yellow);

might be used in an array-type, thus

VAR FlowerCount: ARRAY Color OF CARDINAL;

to create an array of three integer elements, one for each of the index values Red, Blue, and Yellow.

An individual element of an array variable is denoted, as an *indexed-variable*, by writing the name of the array followed by the corresponding value (or values) of the index-type(s) enclosed in square brackets:

> *indexed-variable = array-variable "[" expression-list "]".*
> *array-variable = variable.*
> *expression-list = expression {"," expression}.*

The *expression(s)* enclosed in square brackets must yield value(s) that are assignment-compatible with the corresponding index-type(s).

For example,

Sales [14]

denotes the element of the array Sales corresponding to the index value 14, while

FlowerCount [Red]

denotes the element of array FlowerCount corresponding to index value Red.

This indexing operation is known as *subscripting* and the index value is referred to as the *subscript*, since it corresponds to the conventional mathematical notation $Sales_{14}$. However, in Modula-2 the subscript can only be written in square brackets immediately following the array name.

As the above definition shows, the index value within an indexed-variable need not be a constant—it may be any expression which produces a value belonging to the declared index-type of the array. Thus we may refer to any of the following:

```
Sales [I]
Sales [I+J]
Sales [TRUNC(X*4.2) + J]
```

provided that the expressions I, I+J, and TRUNC(X*4.2) + J all produce cardinal values which lie in the range 1 to 20. In general,

```
Sales [E]
```

is an acceptable indexed-variable provided E yields a cardinal value in the range 1 to 20. If the value of E lies outside this range then reference is being made to an array element which does not exist. This is known as an *array subscript error*. Most implementations provide means of detecting such exceptions during the execution of a program.

An array-type enables a (possibly large) number of variables of identical type to be declared and manipulated as (components of) a single array variable. When combined with the *for-statement* described in Chapter 6, arrays provide an extremely powerful and compact means of processing large numbers of variable data. For example, if a group of 500 real variables is represented as an array

```
VAR X: ARRAY [1..500] OF REAL;
```

then only one statement is required in order to set all 500 variables to zero, namely

```
FOR J := 1 TO 500 DO X[J] := 0.0 END
```

We are now in a position to present the complete program SalesCommission which solves the sales commission problem considered earlier. Should the number of salesmen in the group subsequently change, then the only modification required to this program is the alteration of the value of the constant NumberOfSalesmen.

```
MODULE SalesCommission;
  FROM InOut IMPORT WriteCard, WriteString, WriteLn;
  FROM RealInOut IMPORT ReadReal, WriteReal;
  (* This program reads the monthly sales figures for salesmen 1 to 20,
     and outputs those whose sales exceed the commission threshold of
     2/3 of the average sales per salesman *)
  CONST NumberOfSalesmen = 20; CommissionRatio = 2.0/3.0;
  TYPE SalesmenRange = [1 .. NumberOfSalesmen];
  VAR
    Sales: ARRAY SalesmenRange OF REAL;
    I: SalesmenRange; Sum, CommissionLevel: REAL;
  BEGIN
    (* input, store and sum sales figures *)
    WriteString("Input salesmen's totals: "); WriteLn;
    Sum := 0.0;
    FOR I := 1 TO NumberOfSalesmen DO
      WriteString("Salesman"); WriteCard(I, 3); WriteString(": ");
      ReadReal(Sales[I]); WriteLn; Sum := Sum + Sales[I]
    END;
    (* output those that exceed commission threshold *)
    CommissionLevel :=
      Sum * CommissionRatio / FLOAT(NumberOfSalesmen);
    FOR I := 1 TO NumberOfSalesmen DO
      IF Sales[I] > CommissionLevel THEN
        WriteCard(I, 6); WriteString('   '); WriteReal(Sales[I], 12); WriteLn
      END
    END
  END SalesCommission.
```

A *palindrome* is a sentence which (considering only the letters and ignoring all spaces, punctuation marks and case differences) reads the same both backwards and forwards. For example

Madam I'm Adam

The program Palindrome will read a sentence of up to 100 letters ending with a full stop and determine whether it is a palindrome or not.

```
MODULE Palindrome;
  FROM InOut IMPORT Read, Write, WriteString, WriteLn;
  (* This program tests whether the letters in an input sentence,
     terminated by a period, form a palindromic sequence *)
  CONST MaxLength = 100; Terminator = ".";
  TYPE LetterRange = [1 .. MaxLength];
  VAR
    Letter: ARRAY LetterRange OF CHAR;
    I: [0 .. MaxLength];  J: LetterRange; Ch: CHAR;
  BEGIN
    (* Read sentence, storing all letters in the array Letter *)
    WriteString('Input your sentence, terminated by "');
    Write(Terminator); WriteString('": ');
    I := 0; Read(Ch);
    REPEAT
      IF (Ch >= "A") AND (Ch <= "Z") OR (Ch >= "a") AND (Ch <= "z") THEN
        I := I + 1; Letter[I] := CAP(Ch)
      END;
      Read(Ch)
    UNTIL Ch = Terminator;
    (* Test if array contents form a palindrome *)
    J := 1;
    WHILE (J < I) AND (Letter[J] = Letter[I]) DO
      J := J + 1; I := I - 1
    END;
    IF J >= I THEN WriteString(" is") ELSE WriteString(" isn't") END;
    WriteString(" a palindrome"); WriteLn
  END Palindrome.
```

TWO-DIMENSIONAL ARRAYS

In our examples so far we have used only arrays with one index-type in their declared type, and which therefore require only one appropriately valued index to select a corresponding element. Such arrays are known as *one-dimensional arrays*. However, Modula-2 permits array-types with more than one index-type. For example, a printed page consisting of 66 lines each providing 120 character positions may be declared as an array variable

VAR Page: ARRAY [1..66], [1..120] OF CHAR;

The Jth character of line I of Page would then be the element denoted by

Page [I, J]

where I has a value in the range 1 to 66, and J a value in the range 1 to 120.

The following statement would set each of the 7920 character elements of the array Page to the blank character:

```
FOR I := 1 TO 66 DO
  FOR J := 1 TO 120 DO
    Page [I, J] := " "
  END
END
```

The array Page is said to be a *two-dimensional array*. Arrays may be specified with any number of indices—if an array has *n* indices then it is said to be an *n-dimensional array* and its elements are referenced using the array identifier followed by *n* indexing expressions.

A two-dimensional array is often used to represent the mathematical concept of a *matrix* (in the same way as a one-dimensional array may be used to represent a *vector*). The program Matrices reads a 6×8 matrix from the input stream into a two-dimensional array A, forms the row sums in a vector B and the column sums as a vector C, and outputs the three arrays in the form shown:

$$
\begin{array}{ll}
a\,a\,a\,a\,a\,a\,a\,a & b \\
a\,a\,a\,a\,a\,a\,a\,a & b \\
a\,a\,a\,a\,a\,a\,a\,a & b \\
a\,a\,a\,a\,a\,a\,a\,a & b \\
a\,a\,a\,a\,a\,a\,a\,a & b \\
a\,a\,a\,a\,a\,a\,a\,a & b \\
\\
c\,c\,c\,c\,c\,c\,c\,c &
\end{array}
$$

(In fact a very much shorter program with an equivalent effect can be written using only the vector C. This is left as an exercise for the reader.)

```
MODULE Matrices;
  FROM InOut IMPORT ReadInt, WriteInt, WriteString, WriteLn;
  (* This program reads in a 6 X 8 matrix of integer values, computes the
    row and column sums, and outputs these in a suitable format. *)
  CONST RowMax = 6; ColumnMax = 8;
  TYPE  Row = [1 .. RowMax]; Column = [1 .. ColumnMax];
  VAR
    A: ARRAY Row, Column OF INTEGER;
    B: ARRAY Row OF INTEGER;
    C: ARRAY Column OF INTEGER;
    R: Row; J: Column; Sum: INTEGER;
  BEGIN
    (* read matrix values into A *)
    WriteString('Input the array element values, row by row: '); WriteLn;
    FOR R := 1 TO RowMax DO
      FOR J := 1 TO ColumnMax DO ReadInt(A[R,J]) END
    END;
    (* form row sums in B *)
    FOR R := 1 TO RowMax DO
      Sum := 0;
      FOR J := 1 TO ColumnMax DO Sum := Sum + A[R,J] END;
      B[R] := Sum
    END;
    (* form column sums in C *)
    FOR J := 1 TO ColumnMax DO
      Sum := 0;
      FOR R := 1 TO RowMax DO Sum := Sum + A[R,J] END;
      C[J] := Sum
    END;
    (* output A, B, C in form required *)
    WriteLn; WriteLn;
    FOR R := 1 TO RowMax DO
      FOR J := 1 TO ColumnMax DO WriteInt(A[R,J], 5) END;
      WriteInt(B[R], 10); WriteLn
    END;
    WriteLn;
    FOR J := 1 TO ColumnMax DO WriteInt(C[J], 5) END;
    WriteLn
  END Matrices.
```

The elements of a Modula-2 array may be of any other type, in particular they may be of another array-type. This possibility enables the effect of a two-dimensional array to be created by a one-dimensional array whose elements are of another one-dimensional array-type. For example the array Page illustrated earlier could also be declared as

    VAR Page: ARRAY [1..66] OF ARRAY [1..120] OF CHAR;

The array again has a total of 7920 character elements, the Jth character of the Ith line being denoted by

    Page [I] [J]

In addition the identifier Page followed by only one subscript I thus

    Page [I]

denotes an element of type

    ARRAY [1..120] OF CHAR

i.e., the Ith line of the page represented. In fact the definition of Modula-2 states that this and the previous declaration of Page are completely equivalent, so that any of the indexed-variable forms

    Page [I, J]
    Page [I] [J]
    Page [I]

may be used with either declaration.

WHOLE ARRAY OPERATIONS

An array-type may be defined at the point of declaration of an array variable, as in the examples so far in this chapter, or it may be given a name in a type-declaration, e.g.,

    TYPE PunchCard = ARRAY [1..80] OF CHAR;
         Line = ARRAY [1..120] OF CHAR;
         PrintedPage = ARRAY [1..66] OF Line;
         MonthlyTotals = ARRAY [1980..1989], Month OF REAL;

These type names may then be used in variable-declarations such as

    VAR Card1, Card2: PunchCard;
        Page1: PrintedPage;
        L: Line;
        Rainfall, Sunshine: MonthlyTotals;

Where arrays of the same type have to be declared at different points in the program, such a type name must always be introduced, but even when used at one point only such a name often improves the clarity of a program.

If two array variables are of the same type, then it is possible to assign the values of each of the elements of one array to the corresponding elements of the other array in a single assignment-statement. For example, the assignment

    Card1 := Card2

is equivalent to the for-statement

    FOR I := 1 TO 80 DO Card1 [I] := Card2 [I] END

but is more efficient than the latter on most implementations.

Like other variables, a complete array may be passed as an actual parameter to a procedure or function. In this case the array-type must have been defined previously in a type-declaration in a block enclosing the procedure, since the type of the parameter in the formal parameter list can only be specified as an identifier. For instance, if we define an array-type

    TYPE SomeType = ARRAY [1..10] OF INTEGER;

and require a function to return as its result the sum of the values of the elements of an array of this type, the function could be declared as:

```
PROCEDURE Sum(A: SomeType): INTEGER;
VAR I: [1..10]; Total: INTEGER;
BEGIN
  Total := 0;
  FOR I := 1 TO 10 DO Total := Total + A [I] END;
  RETURN Total
END Sum;
```

If Array1 and Array2 are declared as variables of type SomeType, then the function may be called with them as parameters, e.g.,

    IF Sum(Array1) > Sum(Array2) THEN Array2 := Array1 END

The procedure MatrixMultiply will multiply two square matrices A and B and leave the result in a matrix C, where A, B and C are arrays of a type

    TYPE SquareMatrix = ARRAY [1 .. N], [1 .. N] OF REAL;

and N is a constant. Since the array C is altered by the procedure it must be declared as a variable parameter.

Each array assignment and each passing of an array as a value parameter involves the copying of the entire array, i.e., copying each of its element values. For large arrays this is a time-consuming operation, and the storage required by the value parameters is also large. A programmer should be mindful of this expense in manipulating whole arrays. It may be necessary in designing a program to minimize the array-copying operations which it involves.

```
PROCEDURE MatrixMultiply(A, B: SquareMatrix; VAR C: SquareMatrix);
  VAR I, J, K: [1 .. N]; Sum: REAL;
  BEGIN
    FOR J := 1 TO N DO
      FOR K := 1 TO N DO
        Sum := 0.0;
        FOR I := 1 TO N DO Sum := Sum + A[J,I] * B[I,K] END;
        C[J,K] := Sum
      END
    END
  END MatrixMultiply;
```

CASE STUDY 8

Each week the wages department of a firm must establish the number of notes and coins of the available denominations required from the bank in order to make up the staff pay packets. This is to be calculated by a program whose input is a file *WAGEFILE* consisting of a sequence of lines of data detailing the take-home pay of the staff. Each line contains the name of an employee (in character positions 1-20) followed by that employee's pay for the week.

The program is to calculate the way in which each pay packet can be made up using the least number of notes and coins. The available denominations are $10, $5 and $1 notes, and 25 cents, 10 cents, 5 cents and 1 cent coins ($1 = 100 cents). In order to assist the staff in the preparation of the pay packets the program must output, for each employee, the name and how the pay packet is to be made up. This should be followed by the total withdrawal required from the bank in terms of the required number of each denomination of note and coin. It is assumed that no employee takes home more than $200 per week.

The basic structure of the program is a loop which processes the data for each employee and accumulates the required totals:

```
FOR each employee DO
  read and write name and pay;
  calculate notes and coins required;
  update totals for pay, notes and coins
END;
output totals
```

At this stage the only significant problem arises in the expression of *calculate notes and coins required*. We shall express this as a procedure-statement

Change(WageInCents, NumberRequired)

where the first parameter is a value parameter giving the employee's wage in cents (in the range 0..20000) and the second parameter is a variable parameter of the type

TYPE MoneyArray = ARRAY Denominations OF CARDINAL;

The array NumberRequired will have its value set by the procedure Change to indicate the number of notes and coins of the various denominations required to make up the sum WageInCents in the most efficient manner. The type Denominations is an enumeration of the available kinds of notes and coins, i.e.,

Denominations =
(TenDollars, FiveDollars, OneDollar, TwentyFiveCents, TenCents,
FiveCents, OneCent);

We postpone further refinement of the procedure Change for the moment.

The main program keeps totals of the payroll and the number of notes and coins of each denomination required. Thus we introduce a variable

TotalPay: REAL;

(since we shall read in each employee's pay as a real number) and an array

TotalsRequired: MoneyArray;

which is initialized to zero and then used to keep running totals for the notes and coins of each denomination required.

The processing of the data for each employee involves reading a line of input and the overall processing terminates when the input data have all been read. Thus, the previous main program can now be extended to:

```
TotalPay := 0.0;
initialize array TotalsRequired to zero;
write heading;
WHILE data remains DO
    read and write next employee's name and wage;
    Change(WageInCents, NumberRequired);
    write out NumberRequired
    update TotalsRequired by NumberRequired;
    TotalPay := TotalPay + Wage
END;
print totals
```

Reading and writing each employee's name and wage is straightforward, but must include statements to read all remaining characters of the input line, so that the input for the next employee starts with the first character of the next line. The test *data remains* involves attempting to read the first character of each line.

Such an attempt fails whenever the end of the file has been reached, in which case a call of Read results in FALSE being assigned to Done.

The statement *initialize array TotalsRequired to zero* is obviously expressed as a for-statement:

FOR D := TenDollars TO OneCent DO TotalsRequired[D] := 0 END

Conceptually the steps *write out NumberRequired* and *update TotalsRequired by NumberRequired* each imply a similar for-statement, but in practice they can be amalgamated into a single loop as:

```
FOR D := TenDollars TO OneCent DO
  WriteCard(NumberRequired [D], 4);
  TotalsRequired[D] := TotalsRequired[D] + NumberRequired[D]
END
```

The procedure Change is now examined in detail. Its heading is

```
PROCEDURE Change(Amount: PayRange;
               VAR NumberOfEach: MoneyArray)
```

The strategy of expressing an amount in terms of the least number of notes and coins is clearly to use as many $10 notes as possible, then to make up the remainder with as many $5 notes as possible, then as many $1 notes, twenty five cent pieces, etc., i.e., the body of Change might be expressed informally as:

```
FOR each of the denominations taken in descending order of value DO
  calculate maximum number of that denomination that can be used;
  adjust the amount still to be considered
END
```

In fact we cannot express this, at present, as a for-statement, since the value associated with each denomination has to be introduced separately, e.g., we might write it as:

```
NumberRequired[TenDollars] := Amount DIV 1000;
Amount := Amount MOD 1000;
NumberRequired[FiveDollars] := Amount DIV 500;
Amount := Amount MOD 500;
  ...
NumberRequired[FiveCents] := Amount DIV 5;
Amount := Amount MOD 5;
NumberRequired[OneCent] := Amount DIV 1
```

However, we can express this sequence of statements as a simple for-statement by introducing an array, say,

VAR Value: ARRAY Denominations OF [1..1000];

to store the values (numbers of cents) associated with each denomination. Provided that this array is initialized properly, i.e.,

```
Value[TenDollars] := 1000;
Value[FiveDollars] := 500;
    ...
Value[OneCent] := 1
```

the for-statement required is

```
FOR D := TenDollars TO OneCent DO
  NumberOfEach[D] := Amount DIV Value[D];
  Amount := Amount MOD Value[D]
END
```

The complete program PayPackets, together with output from a sample execution, is shown. The procedure WriteAmount is used to output the value of an amount of money in the usual dollars and cents format using a given field width for the output. If an implementation provides a library procedure for outputting a real value in fixed-point format this procedure may be unnecessary.

```
MODULE PayPackets;
  FROM InOut IMPORT
    Done, EOL, termCH, OpenInput, CloseInput, Read,
    Write, WriteLn, WriteString, WriteCard;
  FROM RealInOut IMPORT ReadReal;
  (* This program reads a wages file consisting of lines of the form
        employee name(20 chars)   ddd.cc(wage due)
    and computes the make-up in notes and coins of each pay-packet,
    and the total bank withdrawal required.   *)
  CONST MaximumPayInCents = 20000; NameLength = 20;
  TYPE PayRange = [0 .. MaximumPayInCents];
       Denominations =
          (TenDollars, FiveDollars, OneDollar, TwentyFiveCents, TenCents,
          FiveCents, OneCent);
       MoneyArray = ARRAY Denominations OF CARDINAL;
  VAR Value: ARRAY Denominations OF [1 .. 1000];
      TotalsRequired, NumberRequired: MoneyArray;
      WageInCents: PayRange; ThisWage, TotalPay: REAL;
      D: Denominations; Ch: CHAR; I: [1 .. NameLength];
```

```
PROCEDURE Change(Amount: PayRange;
                          VAR NumberOfEach: MoneyArray);
  (* This procedure computes the number of each denomination of
     notes and coins required to make up the amount given (in cents) *)
  VAR D: Denominations;
  BEGIN
    FOR D := TenDollars TO OneCent DO
      NumberOfEach[D] := Amount DIV Value[D];
      Amount := Amount MOD Value[D]
    END
  END Change;
PROCEDURE WriteAmount(R: REAL; FieldWidth: CARDINAL);
  (* writes real value R in format ...ddd.dd in given fieldwidth *)
  VAR WholePart, FracPart: CARDINAL;
  BEGIN
    WholePart := TRUNC(R + 0.005);
    FracPart := TRUNC(100.0 * (R-FLOAT(WholePart))+0.5);
    WriteCard(WholePart, FieldWidth-3); Write(".");
    IF FracPart >= 10 THEN WriteCard(FracPart, 2)
    ELSE Write("0"); WriteCard(FracPart, 1)
    END
  END WriteAmount;
BEGIN
  OpenInput(""); WriteLn;
  IF Done THEN
    Value[TenDollars] := 1000; Value[FiveDollars] := 500;
    Value[OneDollar] := 100; Value[TwentyFiveCents] := 25;
    Value[TenCents] := 10; Value[FiveCents] := 5; Value[OneCent] := 1;
    TotalPay := 0.0;
    FOR D := TenDollars TO OneCent DO TotalsRequired[D] := 0 END;
    WriteString('Employee        Wage $10  $5  $1 25C ');
    WriteString('10C  5C  1C'); WriteLn;
    Read(Ch);
    WHILE Done DO
      FOR I := 1 TO NameLength DO Write(Ch); Read(Ch) END;
      ReadReal(ThisWage); WriteAmount(ThisWage, 6);
      Ch := termCH;
      WHILE Ch <> EOL DO Read(Ch) END;
```

```
          WageInCents := CARDINAL(TRUNC(ThisWage*100.0 + 0.5));
          Change(WageInCents, NumberRequired);
          FOR D := TenDollars TO OneCent DO
            WriteCard(NumberRequired[D], 4);
            TotalsRequired[D] := TotalsRequired[D] + NumberRequired[D]
          END;
          WriteLn;
          TotalPay := TotalPay + ThisWage;
          Read(Ch)
        END;
        CloseInput;
        WriteLn;
        WriteString("Total Withdrawal:");
        WriteAmount(TotalPay, NameLength-17+6);
        FOR D := TenDollars TO OneCent DO
          WriteCard(TotalsRequired[D], 4)
        END;
        WriteLn
      END
    END PayPackets.
```

```
Enter Input File Name: WAGEFILE

Employee              Wage  $10  $5  $1  25C  10C  5C  1C

GORDON QUIRK         58.74    5   1   3    2    2   0   4
JIMMY THOMPSON       86.76    8   1   1    3    0   0   1
VIRGINIA WELLS       97.58    9   1   2    2    0   1   3
BETTY COHEN          42.00    4   0   2    0    0   0   0
DAVID BERNARD        33.10    3   0   3    0    1   0   0
MURIEL HOYTE         42.50    4   0   2    2    0   0   0

Total Withdrawal:   360.68   33   3  13    9    3   1   8
```

STRINGS

There is one class of array which has a special status in Modula-2 and some special operations are associated with it. In Chapter 2 *strings* were introduced and defined as sequences of characters enclosed by quotes or apostrophes. A string of length N characters (excluding the enclosing quotes or apostrophes) is considered to be a constant of the type

    ARRAY [0..N-1] OF CHAR

For example,

"TODAY IS THURSDAY"

is a constant of the type

ARRAY [0..16] OF CHAR

Variables of a type ARRAY [0..N-1] OF CHAR are called *string variables* of length N and may be used to hold strings of length N.

We have already seen that the value of an array may be assigned to another array variable of the same type. If we define a type

TYPE Name = ARRAY [0..11] OF CHAR;

and declare

VAR Name1, Name2: Name;

as variables of type Name, then the assignment-statement

Name1 := Name2

is permitted, as it is for any two arrays of the same type. In addition, however, any string of length 12 characters or less may be used as the value to be assigned, e.g.,

Name1 := "JOHN F JONES"

If the assigned string has less than 12 characters, say,

Name2 := "JOHN JONES"

then the assignment copies the available characters to the first ten positions in the string variable, and inserts a *NUL* control character (i.e., 0C) in the eleventh position.

A string is thus assignment-compatible with any string variable of the same or greater length.

As we saw in Chapter 5, the procedure WriteString provided by the module InOut allows the output of strings of any length, as in

WriteString("The answer is ")

It is also permitted to output the value of a string variable in this way. For example the statements

WriteString("Name: "); WriteString(Name1)

will output two strings, to produce an output line of the form

Name: JOHN F JONES

In general, the effect of outputting a string containing a *NUL* character is implementation-dependent, but some implementations take the first *NUL* character encountered to indicate the end of the significant string.

The module InOut also provides a procedure ReadString which enables the input of a string of any length and its assignment to a string variable. A call

ReadString(S)

will read in from the input stream a sequence of characters terminated by a blank or any control character, and assign this sequence to the string variable S. Any leading blanks will be ignored by ReadString. The value of the character terminating the input is assigned by ReadString to the variable termCH provided by InOut. If the input sequence has fewer characters than the string variable S then in general the effect on the remaining character positions of S is implementation-defined, but some implementations again insert a *NUL* character after the last character read. If the input sequence has more characters than S the effect is also implementation-dependent, but usually the number of characters read is equal to the length of the string S.

For input from a keyboard via ReadString, the control character *DEL* has the effect of erasing the previous character input.

CASE STUDY 9

A program is required to examine a piece of text in a given file and produce a list, in alphabetical order, of all the distinct words which appear in the text, e.g., examination of the input

the black dog chased the black cat

should produce the corresponding output

> *black*
> *cat*
> *chased*
> *dog*
> *the*

It may be assumed that no words are longer than 16 letters long, that no words contain apostrophes or hyphens, that upper and lower case letters are equivalent, and the output may be produced in either upper case or lower case.

The program requires the construction of a list of all the distinct words which appear in the text. Defining the type WordSpelling as a string type of length 16

CONST MaxWordLength = 16;

TYPE WordSpelling = ARRAY [0..MaxWordLength−1] OF CHAR;

a suitable structure for the representation of this word list is an array

    CONST IndexMax = 200;

    TYPE IndexRange = [1 .. IndexMax];

    VAR   Index: ARRAY IndexRange OF WordSpelling;

together with a variable

    VAR Size: [0 .. IndexMax];

defining the length of the list, i.e., the number of significant entries held in the array Index.

The contents of the list, when the input has all been examined, are to be output in alphabetical order. We must therefore decide whether to construct the list in such a way that its contents are always in alphabetical order (i.e., by inserting new entries into the list so that the ordering is maintained), or to construct an unordered list and then sort it immediately before output of the list of occurring words. We shall choose the former method, since it is somewhat more efficient, i.e., we shall construct the list so that the contents of the array Index always satisfy the relation

$$\text{for all } i, j \text{ such that } i < j <= Size, \quad Index[i] < Index[j]$$

This relation assumes that values of the string type WordSpelling can be compared using the < operator—however, Modula-2 does not provide relational operators for use with strings and so we shall have to define our own ordering function. Introducing the type

    TYPE Relation = (LessThan, Equals, GreaterThan);

we define the following ordering function Compare with arguments of type WordSpelling:

```
PROCEDURE Compare(W1, W2: WordSpelling): Relation;
VAR I: [0..MaxWordLength-1];
BEGIN
  I := 0;
  LOOP
    IF W1[I] < W2[I] THEN RETURN LessThan
    ELSIF W1[I] > W2[I] THEN RETURN GreaterThan
    ELSIF I = MaxWordLength-1 THEN RETURN Equals
    ELSE I := I + 1
    END
  END
END Compare;
```

Given the ordering relationships for characters noted in Chapter 3, the relation *LessThan* is equivalent to conventional lexicographic or dictionary ordering, i.e., *Compare(w1, w2) = LessThan* implies that *w1* precedes *w2* in a dictionary.

Where one word is a stem or initial substring of another, e.g., *cat* and *cataract,* the ordering determined by *Compare* depends on the character used to pad out short word spellings. With the ASCII character set, if the blank character is used then the shorter word will precede the longer, since " " < *c* holds for every word character *c* in the ASCII character set.

The basic structure of the program is a loop which determines the next word in the input stream and, if necessary, inserts its spelling into the list. The loop terminates when the input file has been completely scanned.

```
EndOfWords := FALSE; GetNextWord;
WHILE NOT EndOfWords DO RecordWord; GetNextWord END;
PrintWords
```

The procedure GetNextWord scans through the text looking for the next word. If the input is exhausted then it sets the value of the global Boolean variable EndOfWords to TRUE, otherwise it stores the next word in a global variable

```
VAR Word: WordSpelling;
```

so that the procedure RecordWord can, if necessary, add this word to the list of words which have occurred in the text. The structure of the procedure GetNext-Word is therefore

scan through text until letter or end of text is found;
IF *letter found* THEN *scan and record word spelling*
ELSE EndOfWords := TRUE
END

Each execution of this procedure reads any non-letter characters preceding the next word, the letters making up the word, and one character following. The variable Done provided by the InOut module, which indicates when the input stream has been completely read, may become false during the non-letter scan, in which case EndOfWords must be set true, or on trying to read the character following the word, in which case EndOfWords must be set true by the *following* call of GetNextWord.

Introducing a character variable Ch, the above may be rewritten as

IF Done THEN
    REPEAT Read(Ch) UNTIL NOT Done OR *Ch is a letter*
END;
IF Done THEN *scan and record word spelling*
ELSE EndOfWords := TRUE
END

If we assume that the upper case and lower case letters each form a coherent subrange of the values of type CHAR, as they do in many Modula-2 implementations, the condition *Ch is a letter* can be written as

((Ch>='A') AND (Ch<='Z')) OR ((Ch>='a') AND (Ch<='z'))

If this is not so, a more complex test is required. To localize this implementation-dependence, and to avoid writing the above lengthy expression several times, we introduce a predicate, or Boolean function, which determines if a given character is a letter:

```
PROCEDURE Letter(Ch: CHAR): BOOLEAN;
  BEGIN
    RETURN ((Ch >= 'A') AND (Ch <= 'Z')) OR ((Ch >= 'a') AND (Ch <= 'z'))
  END Letter;
```

The step *scan and record word spelling* must scan the input text up to the first non-letter (or end of the input), record the letters scanned in the string variable Word and pad this string with blanks if less than 16 letters have been scanned. Introducing a variable Length to count the letters recorded, we may write the scanning process as

```
Length := 0;
REPEAT
  Word[Length] := CAP(Ch); Length := Length + 1; Read(Ch)
UNTIL NOT Done OR NOT Letter(Ch);
FOR I := Length TO MaxWordLength-1 DO Word[Length] := " " END
```

Note the use of the standard function CAP so that all word spellings are recorded in upper case form.

The procedure RecordWord takes the word recorded in Word and searches Index to determine whether or not that word has already occurred in the text. If not, the new word must be inserted in the index in such a way as to maintain the alphabetical ordering of the entries. The outline of RecordWord is thus

search list;
create a new entry in list if necessary

We shall perform a linear search of the list, i.e., noting that the entries in Index are in ascending alphabetic order, we begin the search at the first element of Index and inspect successive elements until either the required word is found, or the whole list has been inspected, or an alphabetically greater word is encountered. By introducing a local variable

```
I: [1 .. IndexMax+1]
```

the action *search list* may be expressed as

```
I := 1;
WHILE (I <= Size) AND (Compare(Index[I], Word) = LessThan) DO
  I := I + 1
END;
```

Note that the terminating condition in this while-statement relies on the fact that the definition of Modula-2 specifies that the second operand B in a Boolean expression A *AND* B is not evaluated if the first, A, is false. This ensures that when I reaches Size+1 an attempt to evaluate Index[I] will not occur, thus avoiding an access of an unassigned element of the array, or even an array subscript error (if Size = IndexMax). If the two components of the terminating condition were written in the opposite order, such exceptions would be possible.

There are faster methods of searching an unordered list, such as that held in the array Index, than the above *linear search*. In a *binary split search*, for example, the mid-point entry in the list is first examined to determine in which half of the list the required word may be. The mid-point entry of the appropriate half is then examined, and so on, until either the required word is found or it is established that the word is not in the list. If the list contains 2^N entries, then this technique requires at most N comparisons. The program given in this case study uses a linear search—it is left as an exercise for the reader to modify the program to perform the more efficient binary search.

The statement *create a new entry in list if necessary* is then expressible as

```
IF I <= Size THEN
  IF Compare(Index[I], Word) <> Equals THEN
    add a new entry (at position I)
  END
ELSE add a new entry (at end of list)
END
```

In either case the position of the new entry is indicated by the value of I on exit from the *search list* loop, so each addition process is expressible as a call to a local procedure InsertWord.

To add a new word to Index we increase Size by 1 and move all the words alphabetically greater than the new word down the list by one place to make room for the new word, which may then be inserted. To avoid over-writing the entries in the list, this repositioning must begin at the last entry currently in the list. Remembering that the position of the new word is given by the value of I on exit from the search loop, the procedure InsertWord becomes

```
PROCEDURE InsertWord;
  VAR J: IndexRange;
  BEGIN
    IF Size < IndexMax THEN
      Size := Size + 1;
      FOR J := Size TO I + 1 BY –1 DO Index[J] := Index[J–1] END;
      Index[I] := Word
    END
  END InsertWord;
```

Finally, the outputting of the index is performed by a simple loop which prints the significant elements of Index. Since these are represented as strings, each may be output directly, i.e.,

FOR I := 1 TO Size DO WriteString(Index[I]); WriteLn END

The complete program Concordance is shown, together with a sample index produced by execution of the program with the following input file contents:

```
THE PROFILE

    The Profile is an edited, automatically formatted,
listing of the source program which displays the frequency
of execution of each statement of the program.
```

```
MODULE Concordance;
  FROM InOut IMPORT
    OpenInput, CloseInput, WriteString, WriteLn, Done, Read;

  (* This program reads a specified text file and outputs
     a sorted concordance of the words occurring in it.   *)

  CONST MaxWordLength = 16; IndexMax = 200;

  TYPE WordSpelling = ARRAY [0..MaxWordLength–1] OF CHAR;
       IndexRange = [1 .. IndexMax];

  VAR Index: ARRAY IndexRange OF WordSpelling; Size: [0 .. IndexMax];
      Word: WordSpelling; EndOfWords: BOOLEAN;

  PROCEDURE Letter(Ch: CHAR): BOOLEAN;
    BEGIN
      RETURN ((Ch >= 'A') AND (Ch <= 'Z')) OR ((Ch >= 'a') AND (Ch <= 'z'))
    END Letter;

  PROCEDURE GetNextWord;

  (* This procedure puts the next word from the input in the global variable
     Word if one exists; otherwise it sets the global EndOfWords true. *)

    VAR Ch: CHAR; I, Length: [0..MaxWordLength];
    BEGIN
      IF Done THEN
        REPEAT Read(Ch) UNTIL NOT Done OR Letter(Ch);
      END;
```

```
      IF Done THEN
        Length := 0;
        REPEAT
          Word[Length] := CAP(Ch); Length := Length + 1; Read(Ch)
        UNTIL NOT Done OR NOT Letter(Ch);
        FOR I := Length TO MaxWordLength – 1 DO Word[I] := " " END
      ELSE EndOfWords := TRUE
      END
    END GetNextWord;

PROCEDURE RecordWord;

  (* This procedure adds the word in the global variable Word to the
     ordered list of words in the global array Index, if necessary.  *)

  VAR I: [1 .. IndexMax+1];

  PROCEDURE InsertWord;

    (* This procedure adds the word at position I *)
    VAR  J: IndexRange;
    BEGIN
      IF Size < IndexMax THEN
        Size := Size + 1;
        FOR J := Size TO I + 1 BY –1 DO Index[J] := Index[J-1] END;
        Index[I] := Word
      ELSE WriteString("Concordance too large"); WriteLn; HALT
      END
    END InsertWord;

  TYPE Relation = (LessThan, Equals, GreaterThan);

  PROCEDURE Compare(W1, W2: WordSpelling): Relation;
    VAR I: [0..MaxWordLength–1];
    BEGIN
      I := 0;
      LOOP
        IF W1[I] < W2[I] THEN RETURN LessThan
        ELSIF W1[I] > W2[I] THEN RETURN GreaterThan
        ELSIF I = MaxWordLength – 1 THEN RETURN Equals
        ELSE I := I + 1
        END
      END
    END Compare;
```

```
    BEGIN
      I := 1;
      WHILE (I <= Size) AND (Compare(Index[I], Word) = LessThan) DO
        I := I + 1
      END;
      IF I <= Size THEN
        IF Compare(Index[I], Word) <> Equals THEN InsertWord END
      ELSE InsertWord
      END
    END RecordWord;

  PROCEDURE PrintWords;
    VAR I: IndexRange;
    BEGIN
      WriteString('*** Index ***'); WriteLn; WriteLn;
      FOR I := 1 TO Size DO WriteString(Index[I]); WriteLn END
    END PrintWords;

  BEGIN
    OpenInput(""); WriteLn;
    IF Done THEN
      EndOfWords := FALSE; Size := 0; GetNextWord;
      WHILE NOT EndOfWords DO RecordWord; GetNextWord END;
      CloseInput; PrintWords
    END
  END Concordance.
```

```
Enter Input File Name: PROFILE

*** Index ***

AN
AUTOMATICALLY
DISPLAYS
EACH
EDITED
EXECUTION
FORMATTED
FREQUENCY
IS
LISTING
OF
PROFILE
. . .
```

OPEN ARRAY PARAMETERS

The facility for passing arrays as parameters described in the section *Whole Array Operations* is effective when the actual parameters corresponding to a given formal parameter in different calls of the procedure or function concerned are identical in type. In some cases, however, it is convenient to define a procedure or function whose actual array parameters vary in the number of elements they contain from one call to another. For example, we might envisage a function Sum similar to that defined on page 153 which might be used at one point to compute the sum of the ten elements of an array declared as follows:

```
VAR X: ARRAY [1..10] OF INTEGER;
```

and at another point to compute the sum of 100 elements of an array declared as follows:

```
VAR Y: ARRAY [100..199] OF INTEGER;
```

The essential form of the function required is similar to that given on page 153 and might be written as follows:

```
PROCEDURE Sum(... A: ... ?): INTEGER;
  VAR I, Total: INTEGER;
  BEGIN
    Total := 0;
    FOR I := First TO Last DO Total := Total + A[I] END;
    RETURN Total
  END Sum
```

where First and Last represent the initial and final index values for the actual array parameter. The problem is how these values are actually transmitted to the function, and how the array parameter is described in the formal parameter list of the function. To overcome this problem, Modula-2 allows parameters to be declared as *open array parameters*. Using the open array parameter mechanism, the above problem can be solved by use of a function of the following form:

```
PROCEDURE Sum(A: ARRAY OF INTEGER): INTEGER;
  VAR I: CARDINAL; Total: INTEGER;
  BEGIN
    Total := 0;
    FOR I := 0 TO HIGH(A) DO Total := Total + A[I] END;
    RETURN Total
  END Sum
```

In this form, the formal-parameter-list indicates that A is a one-dimensional array of integers but does not indicate the exact index-type involved. The parameter A is said to be an *open array parameter* and the corresponding actual parameter must be a one-dimensional array of integers. For each actual parameter passed, irrespective of its index-type, the index-type is assumed to be a CARDINAL subrange in which the lower bound of the subrange is assumed to be zero and the upper bound of the subrange is the CARDINAL value given by the standard function call

HIGH(A)

The elements of the actual array parameter must be type-compatible with those of the formal array parameter. Hence the actual parameter A is considered to be an array

ARRAY [0..M] OF INTEGER

where M = HIGH(A), and M+1 is the *cardinality*, or number of elements, in the actual array passed to the procedure.

For a call Sum(X), the evaluation of HIGH(A) within Sum will produce the value 9; whereas, for a call Sum(Y), the evaluation of HIGH(A) produces the value 99.

An open array parameter is introduced in a formal-parameter-list by a variable or value parameter section in which the formal-type is expressed as an *open-array-schema*, whose form is defined as follows:

open-array-schema = "ARRAY" "OF" type-identifier.

An *open-array-schema* defines the type of the elements of each open array parameter declared in the section. It does not, however, define the index-type. The procedure or function that manipulates the open array parameter considers it to have an index-type which is a CARDINAL subrange with lower bound zero and upper bound given by the result of the standard function call HIGH(A), as illustrated by the function Sum earlier.

The open array parameter mechanism allows procedures and functions that manipulate strings of varying lengths to be written. For example, the following procedure Encode can be used to write in coded form a string of any length, using a character encoding function of the procedure-type

TYPE CodeFunction = PROCEDURE (CHAR): CHAR;

as a second parameter:

```
PROCEDURE Encode(S: ARRAY OF CHAR; Code: CodeFunction);
  VAR I: CARDINAL;
  BEGIN
    FOR I := 0 TO HIGH(S) DO Write(Code(S[I])) END
  END Encode
```

The actual parameters passed to this procedure Encode may be of any array-type whose element-type is CHAR and whose index-type is an enumerated-type or a subrange-type. Within Encode the actual parameter is considered to be of the string type

ARRAY [0 .. HIGH(S)] OF CHAR

and so the parameter S above is considered to be a string within the procedure.

The procedures WriteString and ReadString provided by the InOut module are themselves examples of procedures with open array parameters. Their headings are as follows:

PROCEDURE WriteString(S: ARRAY OF CHAR)

PROCEDURE ReadString(VAR S: ARRAY OF CHAR)

The procedure WriteString could be expressed in terms of the Write procedure also provided by InOut, simply as:

```
PROCEDURE WriteString(S: ARRAY OF CHAR);
  VAR I: CARDINAL;
  BEGIN
    FOR I := 0 TO HIGH(S) DO Write(S[I]) END
  END WriteString;
```

However, the actual parameter passed to S may be a string *variable* which has previously been assigned a shorter string value, in which case the assigned value will have been terminated with a *NUL* control character. To output only the significant characters of such strings, the action of the WriteString procedure may be rewritten as:

```
PROCEDURE WriteString(S: ARRAY OF CHAR);
  CONST NUL = 0C;
  VAR I: CARDINAL;
  BEGIN
    I := 0;
    WHILE (I <= HIGH(S)) AND (S[I] <> NUL) DO
      Write(S[I]); I := I+1
    END
  END WriteString;
```

The implementation of the ReadString procedure in terms of the procedure Read is left as an exercise for the reader.

The following restrictions apply to the use of open array parameters:

(a) Multi-dimensional open array parameters are not permitted.

(b) Open array parameters may only be accessed element-wise and so it is not permitted to assign the value of an array to another array which is an open array parameter. Hence, within the procedure Encode, it is illegal to assign a string constant or variable to the parameter S.

Suppose we wish to write a procedure which maximizes the contents of two
open array parameters by assigning to both whichever of the initial array values
has the greater element sum. This procedure might take the following fc :m:

```
PROCEDURE Maximize(VAR X, Y: ARRAY OF INTEGER);
  BEGIN
    IF Sum(X) > Sum(Y) THEN assign Y to X
    ELSE assign X to Y
    END
  END Maximize;
```

Because X and Y are open array parameters they may not be assigned by
assignment-statements such as

```
Y := X  or  X := Y
```

Instead the assignment must be programmed element-by-element, thus:

```
PROCEDURE Maximize(VAR X, Y: ARRAY OF INTEGER);
  VAR I, XUpper, YUpper: CARDINAL;
  BEGIN
    XUpper := HIGH(X); YUpper := HIGH(Y);
    IF XUpper = YUpper THEN
      IF Sum(X) > Sum(Y) THEN
        FOR I := 0 TO XUpper DO X[I] := Y[I] END
      ELSE
        FOR I := 0 TO XUpper DO Y[I] := X[I] END
      END
    ELSE
      WriteString("ERROR in Maximize: arrays of different sizes");
      WriteLn; HALT
    END
  END Maximize;
```

Between them, the examples presented so far illustrate the range of operations
that can be applied to open array parameters; these are as follows:

(a) The individual elements of an open array parameter may be accessed using
    the formal notation for indexed-variables, as in Sum, Encode and Maxim-
    ize.

(b) An open array parameter may be passed as a parameter to another pro-
    cedure or function that expects a similar open array parameter, as X and Y
    are passed to Sum within Maximize.

An *open-array-schema* may be used to declare either *variable* or *value* parameters, with the usual consequent differences in how such parameters are used. For
a variable open array parameter the corresponding actual parameter must be an

array variable (or another open array parameter), and operations on the formal parameter within the procedure or function are applied directly to this actual parameter. Thus in the procedure Maximize, which is intended to alter one or other of its actual parameters, the formals X and Y are declared as *variable* open array parameters.

For a formal value open array parameter the corresponding actual parameter may be any expression that produces an array value. (In practice, the only expressions in Modula-2 that produce array values are array variables themselves, or strings). This value is assumed by the formal parameter when the procedure or function is called, and subsequent operations on the formal parameter do not alter the actual parameter itself. The procedure Encode is not intended to alter its actual array parameter, and therefore the formal parameter S is declared as a *value* open array parameter. This means that Encode may be called with any character array or string variable V as parameter, thus,

Encode(V, ...)

or with a string constant as parameter, thus

Encode("Mata Hari", ...)

All the examples show that the open array mechanism enables flexible procedures and functions to be defined, but it is also the case that greater programming care may be required in writing and using these procedures than is the case with "fixed" array parameters. In discussing fixed array parameters in an earlier section, we noted that the programmer must consider the overhead of copying large arrays that are passed by value. The same considerations apply in the case of open array parameters, but in this case, overheads may also arise from the use of the open array mechanism itself. For many implementations, the time taken to access an element of an open array parameter may be greater than that taken to access the element of a corresponding array parameter of fixed type, and the time taken to check that the subscript involved lies in the correct range may be much greater. For all of these reasons, the open array parameter mechanism is one to be used with some caution. In general, it should be used only in those situations where a procedure or function must handle arrays of varying sizes during a single execution of the program involved. In all other cases, the use of the normal parameter mechanism for arrays is simpler to understand, less prone to error, and in many cases, more efficient.

DATA VALIDATION

The open array parameter mechanism provides us with an opportunity to overcome one of the shortcomings of the example programs presented so far, namely, that they will only function correctly if the user supplies valid input data. What the programs ought to do is check the data supplied by the user and, if it does not appear to be valid, ask the user to re-input it. An input value may be invalid because, e.g., a number is required and the characters supplied may not form a number, or the value of the number may not be within the required range. This process of checking the validity of input data is known as *data validation*.

The procedure GetCardinal outputs a given prompt message to the user, reads in a response which is intended to be a CARDINAL value, and checks whether the input value lies within the specified limits Lower and Upper. Should the response be unacceptable then the process will be repeated until an acceptable value is finally input.

```
PROCEDURE GetCardinal(Prompt: ARRAY OF CHAR;
                      VAR Value: CARDINAL;
                      Lower, Upper: CARDINAL);
  (* This procedure gets a cardinal value in the range Lower .. Upper from
     the terminal user, using the prompt given, which should be of the form
            "Input <description of value required>"                        *)
  CONST BELL = 07C;
  VAR Ch: CHAR; Status: (Valid, Invalid, OutOfRange, UnexpectedChars);
  BEGIN
    REPEAT
      (* use prompt to obtain value *)
      WriteString(Prompt); WriteString(" in range "); WriteCard(Lower, 1);
      WriteString(".."); WriteCard(Upper, 1); WriteString(": ");
      ReadCard(Value);

      (* check validity of response *)
      IF NOT Done THEN Status := Invalid
      ELSIF (Value < Lower) OR (Value > Upper) THEN Status := OutOfRange
      ELSE Status := Valid
      END;

      (* skip to end of line, checking blankness *)
      Ch := termCH;
      WHILE Ch <> EOL DO
        IF (Ch <> " ") AND (Status = Valid) THEN
          Status := UnexpectedChars
        END;
        Read(Ch)
      END;
```

```
        IF Status <> Valid THEN
          Write(BELL);
          WriteString("ERROR -- ");
          CASE Status OF
            Invalid: WriteString("invalid number") |
            OutOfRange: WriteString("value out of range") |
            UnexpectedChars: WriteString("unexpected characters after value")
          END;
          WriteString(" -- TRY AGAIN"); WriteLn;
        END;
      UNTIL Status = Valid
    END GetCardinal;
```

This procedure could be used in any of the earlier programs that required input from the keyboard of a CARDINAL number in any range, and its use will guarantee that the program receives a valid number from the user. For instance, in the Towers of Hanoi program the user must supply the number of disks for which a particular solution is required—this number must be in the range 1..Maximum-Disks. Hence the statements which obtain the input, viz.,

WriteString("Input number of disks: "); ReadCard(N);

could be replaced with

GetCardinal("Input number of disks: ", N, 1, MaximumDisks);

and the program will only proceed once the user has supplied a value in the range 1..MaximumDisks.

Similarly, some of the programs ask the user if he wishes to continue supplying data, by outputting a string in the form of a question to which the user must supply an answer ("Y" or "N", or their lower-case equivalents). The procedure GetBoolean will display a specified question, and check that the reply is an acceptable character. If it is not, then it will require the user to answer the question until an acceptable answer is input. The value assigned to the variable parameter ReplyIsYes indicates the nature of the reply. This procedure could have been used in the program FindNearestPrime where the user's wish to continue was determined by the statement-sequence

WriteString("Are you finished ? ");
Read(Reply); WriteLn;
UserIsFinished := (Reply = "Y") OR (Reply = "y")

which accepted any reply other than "Y" or "y" as a negative reply. This could be replaced by the call

GetBoolean("Are you finished ? ", UserIsFinished)

```
PROCEDURE GetBoolean(Question: ARRAY OF CHAR;
                     VAR ReplyIsYes: BOOLEAN);
  (* This procedure gets a yes/no answer to
     the given question from the terminal user. *)
  CONST BELL = 07C;
  VAR ReplyCh: CHAR;
  PROCEDURE GetReplyCh;
    VAR Ch: CHAR;
    BEGIN
      (* ask question and obtain reply, ignoring blanks *)
      WriteString(Question); WriteString(" : ");
      REPEAT Read(ReplyCh) UNTIL ReplyCh <> " ";
      (* skip to end of line *)
      Ch := ReplyCh;
      WHILE Ch <> EOL DO Read(Ch) END;
    END GetReplyCh;
  BEGIN
    GetReplyCh;
    WHILE (ReplyCh <> "Y") AND (ReplyCh <> "y") AND
          (ReplyCh <> "N") AND (ReplyCh <> "n") DO
      Write(BELL);
      WriteString("ERROR - press only Y or N keys - TRY AGAIN");
      WriteLn;
      GetReply(Ch)
    END;
    ReplyIsYes := (Ch = "Y") OR (Ch = "y")
  END GetBoolean;
```

The same program required input of an integer value greater than 1, and could be simplified by replacing the statements which obtained the input value with a call

```
GetCardinal("Input a number: ", J, 2, MAX(CARDINAL))
```

With this change, the program would no longer have to test that the input value is greater than 1.

Note that the procedures GetCardinal and GetBoolean each ensure that the input is aligned at the first character of the next line after each interaction. In some of our previous programs this was not done—the programs relied on a subsequent ReadCard, ReadInt, or ReadReal statement to skip over the EOL and any blank characters remaining from the user's response. However, if a user of the original program FindNearestPrime types "*no*" rather than just "*n*" in response to the question *Are you finished?* the subsequent ReadCard statement fails to read the next number because of the residual "*o*" in the input, and the program therefore malfunctions. By use of carefully programmed procedures such as GetCardinal and GetBoolean, programs for interactive use become

(a) more *robust,* in that the programs do not malfunction in the event of user errors, and

(b) more *user-friendly,* in that the user is given some flexibility in the way responses are typed, and help when unacceptable inputs are made.

Similar procedures for acquisition of real or integer values from the user can also be programmed. As these procedures are of use in a wide range of programs we shall henceforth assume that they are available in a library module named ValidInput. In Chapter 12 we describe how such a module may be constructed.

OTHER STRUCTURED TYPES

Array types are just one of a number of ways in which composite, or *structured,* data items may be defined in Modula-2. In Chapter 3 we defined *type* as follows

$$type = simple\text{-}type \mid structured\text{-}type \mid pointer\text{-}type \mid procedure\text{-}type.$$

Simple-types were discussed in Chapter 3, *procedure-types* in Chapter 7, and *pointer-types* are introduced in Chapter 11. For *structured-types* there are in fact three possible forms, as the following definition shows

$$structured\text{-}type = array\text{-}type \mid record\text{-}type \mid set\text{-}type.$$

Array-types have been the subject of this chapter; *record-* and *set-types* are discussed in Chapters 9 and 10 respectively.

Variables of a *structured-type* may be manipulated as a whole, or their individual components may be manipulated by appropriate selection constructs.

For arrays the indexed-variable notation enabled individual elements to be referenced and manipulated as individual variables. In Chapter 4 we defined *variable* as follows

$$variable = entire\text{-}variable \mid component\text{-}variable \mid referenced\text{-}variable.$$
$$entire\text{-}variable = variable\text{-}identifier \mid field\text{-}identifier.$$

An *entire-variable* is simply an identifier introduced in a variable-declaration to denote a variable—it may thus denote a variable of a simple (or a pointer or procedure) type, or a variable of a structured type as a whole. A *component-variable* is used to denote a particular component of a variable of a structured-type and takes one of two forms

$$component\text{-}variable = indexed\text{-}variable \mid field\text{-}designator.$$

As we have already seen, *indexed-variables* are used to denote the components of variables of array-types.

Field-designators are used to denote the accessible components of variables of *record-types*. The components of a variable of set-type are not individually accessible as variables, although they can be manipulated in other ways, as Chapter 10 describes.

EXERCISES

8.1 Extend the text analysis program specified by Exercise 6.6, to determine the number of occurrences of each of the letters **A** to **Z** (in either lower case or upper case form) in the input text.

8.2 Write a program which reads a sequence of ten positive integers and then finds the maximum of the sequence, outputs its value, the number of times that it occurs, and the positions in which it appears. The process is then repeated to find the next largest value, and so on.

```
Sample input:     7 10 143 10 52 143 72 10 143 7
Sample output:    143 occurs 3 times, at positions  3  6  9
                  ...
                  7 occurs 2 times, at positions  1 10
```

8.3 Write a program which reads an input text and prints out the number of occurrences of each adjacent letter pair which appears within the text.

8.4 Write a program which reads a sequence of word pairs from an input file and prints each pair in dictionary order. You may assume that each word pair is on a separate input line, the words of each pair are separated by at least one blank, and each word is not more than 16 letters long. Use a similar format for the output.

8.5 Given the procedure-type

TYPE RealFuncType = PROCEDURE(REAL): REAL;

write a procedure

PROCEDURE Plot(F: RealFuncType; XLower, XUpper: REAL)

which "plots" a graph of the function $F(x)$ over the range XLower to XUpper, with the x axis horizontal. The plot should be scaled to use 50 horizontal and 20 vertical output positions, and both axes should be displayed. Use this procedure in a program which plots a graph of $sin(x)$ over the range 0 to 2π. (The library module MathLib0 should provide a function for computing $sin(x)$.)

9

Records

THE RECORD CONCEPT

An array consists of a number of components which are *identical* in nature, and hence in type. It is often the case that an item of data is made up of a number of components which are *distinct* in nature and, perhaps, also of different types. In Case Study 3 we introduced three variables to denote a calendar date, as follows:

Month: [1..12]; Day: [1..31]; Year: [1900..2000];

with an implicit assumption that the three variables represented the different components of the same date.

A date may therefore be considered as the composition of exactly three values, one from each of the three types above. Modula-2 provides a means of defining a data type whose values are the composition of values of other, differing, data types—as a *record-type*. For dates we may define a record-type:

Date = RECORD Month: [1..12]; Day: [1..31]; Year: [1900..2000] END

This definition specifies that a value of type Date consists of exactly three component values, of type [1..12], [1..31], and [1900..2000], respectively. The identifiers Month, Day and Year introduced in the record-type definition are names given to the individual components, or *fields*, and they enable reference to be made to the component values of a variable of type Date.

The general form of a Modula-2 *record-type* is defined syntactically as

> *record-type* = "RECORD" *field-list-sequence* "END".
> *field-list-sequence* = *field-list* {";" *field-list*}.
> *field-list* = [*fixed-part* | *variant-part*].

For the time being we ignore record-types containing *variant-parts*, which are discussed later in this chapter.

$$fixed\text{-}part = identifier\text{-}list ":" type.$$

Thus, for the present, a *record-type* consists of the symbols RECORD and END enclosing a sequence of zero or more *fixed-parts*. Each *fixed-part* introduces a list of one or more identifiers (separated by commas) and a specification of their type. These identifiers are known as *field-identifiers* and hereafter the syntax category

$$field\text{-}identifier = identifier.$$

is used to denote the class of identifiers introduced in this way. The examples below further illustrate record-type declarations.

```
TYPE Cartesian = RECORD X, Y: REAL END;

     Suit = (Clubs, Diamonds, Hearts, Spades);
     Rank = (Two, Three, Four, Five, Six, Seven, Eight,
             Nine, Ten, Jack, Queen, King, Ace);
     Card = RECORD S: Suit; R: Rank END;

     Time = RECORD Hours: [0..24]; Minutes, Seconds: [0..59] END;
```

The scope of the field-identifiers introduced in a record-type declaration is the record-type itself, and so the field-identifiers must be distinct from any other field-identifier of the same record-type, but not necessarily distinct from any other identifiers declared outside the record-type.

Having defined and named a record-type in a type declaration such as those above, variables of the named type may be declared in a variable-declaration-part in the usual way, for example:

```
VAR Focus1, Focus2: Cartesian;
    CardLed: Card;
    TakeOff, Landing: Time;
```

A record-type might of course be defined in a variable-declaration itself, as in

```
VAR Date1, Date2:
    RECORD Month: [1..12]; Day: [1..31]; Year: [1900..2000] END;
```

but in this case variables of the same type cannot be declared elsewhere in the program. The introduction of type-identifiers to denote shared types is often necessary, and is always good programming practice.

Data held as record variables within a program must be manipulated in some way. The simplest operation which may be applied to a record variable is to assign it the value of another variable of the same record-type, e.g.,

```
TakeOff := Landing
```

which has the effect of assigning the value of each field of the variable Landing
to the corresponding field of the variable TakeOff.

To refer to one of the component fields of a record, a *field-designator* is
used, in which the record variable is qualified by the required field-identifier.

> *field-designator = record-variable "." field-identifier.*
> *record-variable = variable.*

Thus, given a variable Date1 of type Date as above

    Date1.Month   denotes the month component, of type [1..12];
    Date1.Day   denotes the day component, of type [1..31];
    Date1.Year   denotes the year component, of type [1900..2000].

The following are examples of field-designators assuming the variable declarations given earlier:

    Focus1.X
    CardLed.S
    TakeOff.Hours

A component of a record variable may be used anywhere that a variable of that
component's type may be used, e.g.,

    XX := (Focus1.X + Focus2.X)/2.0;
    IF CardLed.S = Hearts THEN ... END;
    WriteCard(TakeOff.Hours, 4)

An individual component of a record may thus have its value changed, leaving
the values of all other components unchanged, by naming the required component in an assignment-statement, e.g.,

    Focus1.X := 0.0;
    Date1.Year := 1949;
    TakeOff.Hours := TakeOff.Hours + 2

This is known as *selective updating*. The record-variable assignment

    Date1 := Date2

where Date1 and Date2 are variables of type Date, is thus equivalent to the following sequence of selective updating assignments:

    Date1.Month := Date2.Month;
    Date1.Day := Date2.Day;
    Date1.Year := Date2.Year

In such a case the record-variable assignment is to be preferred, since it is
clearer, more succinct, and more efficient in many implementations.

The use of field-designators is illustrated by the following procedure Bisect, which determines the mid-point M of the line joining two points P1, P2, where all the points are represented as records of type Cartesian:

```
PROCEDURE Bisect(P1, P2: Cartesian; VAR M: Cartesian);
BEGIN
    M.X := (P1.X + P2.X)/2.0;
    M.Y := (P1.Y + P2.Y)/2.0
END Bisect
```

The With-statement

When processing a record variable it is quite usual to make several references to its components within a small region of the program. For instance, to initialize the variable Date1 one might write

```
Date1.Month := 1; Date1.Day := 1; Date1.Year := 1986;
```

In these circumstances repeated reference to fields of a record by writing the record variable name qualified by the required field-identifier soon becomes tedious, particularly if long identifiers are used. Modula-2 provides a statement for use with record variables that enables reference to record components without having to repeat the record variable-identifier at each reference. This is the *with-statement*, which is defined as follows:

with-statement = *"WITH" record-variable "DO" statement-sequence "END"*.

Within the *statement-sequence* controlled by a *with-statement* a field of the indicated record-variable may be denoted by use of the *field-identifier* alone. The effect of a *with-statement* is to open a new scope which contains the corresponding field-identifiers of the named record variable, thereby permitting the use of the field-identifiers as variables. The initialization of the variable Date1 may thus be written as

```
WITH Date1 DO Month := 1; Day := 1; Year := 1986 END
```

If with-statements are nested, e.g.,

```
WITH V1 DO
    ...
    WITH V2 DO
        SS
    END;
    ...
END
```

the scopes are opened, and therefore nested, in the order in which the with-statements appear. Thus, if the record variables V1 and V2 each have a field identified by F, then a simple occurrence of F within the statement-sequence *SS* denotes the corresponding field of V2, not that of V1, by the rules of nested scopes. The field F of V1 can be denoted within *SS* only by writing V1.F explicitly.

The use of a with-statement not only reduces the length of the text of a program, but increases its readability, and in some cases may produce a more efficient program.

The use of records and with-statements is illustrated in the re-formulation of the program NextDay shown below. Dates are now held as variables of the record-type Date. Procedures ReadDate and WriteDate handle the input and output of date values to and from variables of type Date and procedure Update updates its variable parameter of type Date to the day following its original date value. The main program now reads in a sequence of dates, and outputs, for each, the date of the next day.

```
MODULE NextDay2;

  FROM InOut IMPORT WriteString, WriteCard, Write, WriteLn;
  FROM ValidInput IMPORT GetCardinal, GetBoolean;

  (* This program inputs a sequence of dates from the user,
     and outputs the date of the day following for each.    *)

  TYPE Date = RECORD
                  Month: [1..12];
                  Day: [1..31];
                  Year: [1900..2000]
              END;

  VAR  Day: Date; Finished: BOOLEAN;

  PROCEDURE ReadDate(VAR D: Date);
    (* get date D by interactive dialogue *)
    VAR C: CARDINAL;
    BEGIN
      WITH D DO
        GetCardinal("Input month", C, 1, 12); Month := C;
        GetCardinal("Input day", C, 1, 31); Day := C;
        GetCardinal("Input year", C, 1900, 1999); Year := C
      END
    END ReadDate;
```

```
PROCEDURE WriteDate(D: Date);
  (* output date D in format mm/dd/yyyy *)
  BEGIN
    WITH D DO
      WriteCard(Month, 2); Write("/"); WriteCard(Day, 2);
      Write("/"); WriteCard(Year, 4)
    END
  END WriteDate;

PROCEDURE Update(VAR D: Date);
  (* advance date D to day following *)
  VAR DaysInMonth: [28 .. 31];
  BEGIN
    WITH D DO
      CASE Month OF
        1, 3, 5, 7, 8, 10, 12: DaysInMonth := 31 |
        4, 6, 9, 11 : DaysInMonth := 30 |
        2: IF (Year MOD 4 = 0) AND (Year <> 1900) THEN DaysInMonth := 29
           ELSE DaysInMonth := 28
           END
      END;
      IF Day = DaysInMonth THEN
        Day := 1;
        IF Month = 12 THEN Month := 1; Year := Year + 1
        ELSE Month := Month + 1
        END
      ELSE Day := Day + 1
      END
    END
  END Update;

BEGIN
  REPEAT
    ReadDate(Day);
    WriteString("The day following ");
    WriteDate(Day); WriteString(" is ");
    Update(Day);
    WriteDate(Day); WriteLn; WriteLn;
    GetBoolean("Are you finished ?", Finished)
  UNTIL Finished
END NextDay2.
```

MIXED STRUCTURES

The definition of a *fixed-part* indicates that a field of a record may be of any type—not only a simple type, as in the examples so far, but also a structured type such as an array-type or another record-type. For example, we might define a record-type to describe the details of a person as follows:

```
TYPE Person = RECORD
                Name: ARRAY [1..20] OF CHAR;
                DateOfBirth: Date
              END;
```

A value of type Person consists of two component values—a field Name which is itself an array of 20 characters, and a field DateOfBirth which is itself a record made up of three component values, Month, Day and Year.

Likewise a record may occur as a component of other structured types. Thus an array-type may be defined whose elements are records. For example, we may define a type

```
TYPE BridgeHand = ARRAY [1 .. 13] OF Card;
```

where the record-type Card has already been defined as before.

In this way we can describe data structures of arbitrary complexity in terms of previously defined simple and structured data types. These structures and their components can be manipulated at several levels using the notation for variables and variable components already introduced.

For example, if we have a declaration

```
VAR P: Person;
```

then

P itself	denotes a variable of type Person which might be assigned to other variables of the same type;
P.Name	denotes an array of 20 characters which might be input, assigned, or output, as any such character array might be;
P.Name[I]	denotes the *I*th character of P.Name, which might be used in any way appropriate to a character variable;
P.DateOfBirth	denotes a record variable of type Date which might be assigned to or from other variables of type Date;
P.DateOfBirth.Day	denotes a variable of type [1..31];

and so on. Thus the statement-sequence

```
WriteString(P.Name); WriteCard(P.DateOfBirth.Year, 5);
```

prints out the name and year of birth of the person described by the variable P.

The statement

WITH P DO WriteString(Name); WriteCard(DateOfBirth.Year, 5) END

has exactly the same effect.

If the record-variable appearing in a with-statement involves the use of any array indices to identify it, then the indices are evaluated once only (before the execution of the statement-sequence controlled by the with-statement). Thus the statement-sequence:

```
I := 1;
WITH BridgeHand[I] DO
  WHILE I <= 13 DO
    process S and R;
    I := I+1
  END
END
```

does not process the S and R fields of the thirteen records BridgeHand[1] to BridgeHand[13] as we might expect, but processes the same record Bridge-Hand[1] thirteen times. To process the thirteen records, the sequence should be written as:

```
I := 1;
WHILE I <= 13 DO
  WITH BridgeHand[I] DO
    process S and R
  END;
  I := I+1
END
```

In general it is confusing, and hence bad programming practice, if the statement-sequence controlled by a with-statement reassigns any variable used in determining the record-variable involved.

CASE STUDY 10

In a soccer league, each team plays each other team twice. A program is required whose input is two text files. The first is a file named *LEAGUE* containing a league table consisting of one line for each team, where each line contains the following information:

(a) the team name, as 12 characters;
(b) the number of games played, won, lost and drawn so far, as four integer numbers each followed by at least one blank;

(c)   the number of points gained, where each win gains two points, each draw
      one point and each defeat none.

The second is a file named *RESULTS* which contains the results of the latest
round of matches, where each result is on a separate line consisting of

(a)   the home team's name;
(b)   the home team's score;
(c)   the away team's name;
(d)   the away team's score;

each separated by at least one blank. The program is required to read in the
league table and results, and output an updated league table in which the teams
and their playing records are listed in the order of their new league position, i.e.
in descending points order.

The basic structure of the program may be expressed as:

read in table;
update table from results;
sort table;
print table

All of these processes manipulate the league table and so we must first define a
suitable structure for the representation of this table within the program. Since
there will be one set of details in the table for each of the teams in the league, a
suitable structure might be an array

    VAR LeagueTable: ARRAY TablePosition OF TeamDetails;

where the type TablePosition is defined as

    TYPE TablePosition = [1..MaxNumberOfTeams];

The details associated with the team at each position are its name, the number of
games played, won, lost and drawn and the points gained so far. Thus, defining
the following constants

    CONST NameLength = 12;
          MaxNumberOfTeams = 20;
          MaximumGames = 2 * (NumberOfTeams – 1);
          MaximumPoints = 2 * MaximumGames;

and the following types

    TYPE NameRange = [1 .. NameLength];
         TeamName = ARRAY NameRange OF CHAR;
         GamesRange = [0 .. MaximumGames];
         PointsRange = [0 .. MaximumPoints];

the type TeamDetails may be defined as a record-type with six fields:

```
TYPE TeamDetails = RECORD
              Name: TeamName;
              Played, Won, Drawn, Lost: GamesRange;
              Points: PointsRange
           END;
```

With this data structure we can now proceed to design each of the four main processes of the program.

The process *read in table* simply involves reading the lines of the input file containing the current table and storing the details for each team in a corresponding element of the array LeagueTable:

```
PROCEDURE ReadInTable;
BEGIN
   FOR each team DO
      read name and playing details
      into the next element of LeagueTable
   END;
   record number of teams entered
END ReadInTable
```

The details of this process are easily programmed, but since team names also have to be read in from the results file it is useful to introduce a shared procedure for this task, of the form

```
PROCEDURE ReadName(VAR Name: TeamName)
```

The process *update table from results* consists of reading in the latest results from the results file and, for each match, updating the league records of the teams involved according to the result of the match. Remembering that a win is worth 2 points, a draw 1 point, and a defeat 0 points, the procedure UpdateTable may be expressed informally as:

```
PROCEDURE UpdateTable;
BEGIN
   FOR each match DO
      read the team names and scores;
      add 1 to games played by both teams;
      CASE result OF
      home win:
         for home team add 1 to wins and 2 to points;
         for away team add 1 to losses |
      away win:
         for home team add 1 to losses;
         for away team add 1 to wins and 2 to points |
```

> *draw:*
>> *for both teams add 1 to draws;*
>> *for both teams add 1 to points*
> END
> END
> END UpdateTable

For each team in the results lines it is necessary to locate the corresponding details record in the existing league table. This is a simple search process which may be abstracted as a function of the form

```
PROCEDURE Position(Name: TeamName): TablePosition
```

Using this function the remaining details of the update process may easily be programmed.

Sorting the league table into descending points order can be accomplished, using the *selection sorting* strategy, by a procedure with the following outline:

```
PROCEDURE SortTable;
VAR I: TablePosition;
BEGIN
  FOR I := 1 TO NumberOfTeams − 1 DO
    find team with maximum points from position I onwards;
    swap details with position I if necessary
  END
END SortTable;
```

To find the team with maximum points we introduce working variables Max-Points and MaxPosition to record the maximum points and position seen so far.

```
MaxPosition := I;
MaxPoints := LeagueTable[I].Points;
FOR J := I + 1 TO NumberOfTeams DO
  IF LeagueTable[J].Points > MaxPoints THEN
    MaxPoints := LeagueTable[J].Points;
    MaxPosition := J
  END
END
```

Swapping the team details if necessary then involves the sequence

```
IF MaxPosition <> I THEN
  DetailsSaved := LeagueTable[I];
  LeagueTable[I] := LeagueTable[MaxPosition];
  LeagueTable[MaxPosition] := DetailsSaved
END
```

The process *print table* simply involves printing out the details from each record in the sorted LeagueTable array in turn.

The final program UpdateLeagueTable is shown together with the output produced by its execution using input files whose contents correspond to the initial league table and results shown in Figure 9.1.

	P	W	D	L	PTS
Red Rovers	3	2	1	0	5
Silver City	3	1	2	0	4
Blue United	3	1	1	1	3
Black Forest	3	1	1	1	3
Green Villa	3	1	0	2	2
Brown Town	3	0	1	2	1

Black Forest	3	Brown Town	4
Green Villa	2	Red Rovers	2
Blue United	1	Silver City	0

Figure 9.1   League table and results

```
MODULE UpdateLeagueTable;
  FROM InOut IMPORT
    EOL, Done, termCH, OpenInput, CloseInput, Read, ReadCard,
    WriteString, WriteLn, WriteCard;
(* This program
    (a) reads a text file containing the playing records of the teams
        in a soccer league, as a sequence of lines of the form:
        team-name games-played games-won games-lost games-drawn
    (b) reads a text file containing the results of matches played on
        a given day, as a sequence of lines of the form:
        home-team-name goals-scored away-team-name goals-scored
    (c) outputs a league table showing the amended playing records of
        each team in descending points order, where 2 points are
        awarded for a win and 1 point for a draw.
    In the input data team-names are represented as 12 characters,
    starting from an initial non-blank character. All other data values
    are cardinal numbers.                                            *)
  CONST NameLength = 12; MaxNumberOfTeams = 20;
        MaximumGames  = 2 * (MaxNumberOfTeams – 1);
        MaximumPoints = 2 * MaximumGames;
```

```
TYPE NameRange = [1 .. NameLength];
     TeamName = ARRAY NameRange OF CHAR;
     TablePosition = [1 .. MaxNumberOfTeams];
     GamesRange = [0 .. MaximumGames];
     PointsRange = [0 .. MaximumPoints];
     TeamDetails = RECORD
                        Name: TeamName;
                        Played, Won, Drawn, Lost: GamesRange;
                        Points: PointsRange
                   END;

VAR LeagueTable: ARRAY TablePosition OF TeamDetails;
    NumberOfTeams: TablePosition;

PROCEDURE ReadName(VAR Name: TeamName);
  (* read team name if available, skipping preceding blanks;
     otherwise leave Done false                           *)
  VAR Ch: CHAR; I: NameRange;
  BEGIN
    REPEAT Read(Ch) UNTIL NOT Done OR (Ch <> " ");
    IF Done THEN
      Name[1] := Ch;
      FOR I := 2 TO NameLength DO Read(Name[I]) END
    END
  END ReadName;

PROCEDURE SkipRestOfLine;
  (* skip input from last cardinal read to end of line *)
  VAR Ch: CHAR;
  BEGIN
    Ch := termCH;
    WHILE Ch <> EOL DO Read(Ch) END
  END SkipRestOfLine;

PROCEDURE ReadInTable;
  (* read playing records into LeagueTable *)
  VAR I: [0..MaxNumberOfTeams]; NextName: TeamName; C: CARDINAL;
  BEGIN
    I := 0;
    LOOP
      ReadName(NextName);
      IF NOT Done THEN (* no more playing records *) EXIT END;
```

```
      I := I+1;
      WITH LeagueTable[I] DO
        Name := NextName;
        ReadCard(C); Played := C; ReadCard(C); Won := C;
        ReadCard(C); Drawn := C; ReadCard(C); Lost := C;
        Points := 2*Won + Drawn
      END;
      SkipRestOfLine
    END;
    NumberOfTeams := I
  END ReadInTable;

PROCEDURE UpdateTable;

  (* read results and update playing records accordingly *)

  VAR Name: TeamName; Team1, Team2: TablePosition;
      Goals1, Goals2: CARDINAL;

  PROCEDURE Position(Name: TeamName): TablePosition;

    (* returns position of named team in LeagueTable *)

    VAR I: TablePosition;

    PROCEDURE EqualNames(Name1, Name2: TeamName): BOOLEAN;
      (* returns true if Name1 = Name2, false otherwise *)
      VAR I: NameRange;
      BEGIN
        FOR I := 1 TO NameLength DO
          IF Name1[I] <> Name2[I] THEN RETURN FALSE END
        END;
        RETURN TRUE
      END EqualNames;

    BEGIN
      FOR I := 1 TO NumberOfTeams DO
        IF EqualNames(LeagueTable[I].Name, Name) THEN
          RETURN I
        END
      END;
      (* Name sought is not in LeagueTable - report and abort *)
      WriteString("Invalid team name: "); WriteString(Name); WriteLn;
      CloseInput;
      HALT
    END Position;
```

```
    BEGIN
     LOOP
       ReadName(Name);
       IF NOT Done THEN (* no more results *) EXIT END;
       Team1 := Position(Name); ReadCard(Goals1); ReadName(Name);
       Team2 := Position(Name); ReadCard(Goals2); SkipRestOfLine;
       WITH LeagueTable[Team1] DO Played := Played + 1 END;
       WITH LeagueTable[Team2] DO Played := Played + 1 END;
       IF Goals1 > Goals2 THEN (* home win *)
         WITH LeagueTable[Team1] DO
           Won := Won + 1; Points := Points + 2
         END;
         WITH LeagueTable[Team2] DO Lost := Lost + 1 END
       ELSIF Goals2 > Goals1 THEN (* away win *)
         WITH LeagueTable[Team1] DO Lost := Lost + 1 END;
         WITH LeagueTable[Team2] DO
           Won := Won + 1; Points := Points + 2
         END
       ELSE (* drawn *)
         WITH LeagueTable[Team1] DO
           Drawn := Drawn + 1; Points := Points + 1
         END;
         WITH LeagueTable[Team2] DO
           Drawn := Drawn + 1; Points := Points + 1
         END
       END
     END
   END UpdateTable;
 PROCEDURE SortTable;
   (* sort league table into descending points order *)
   VAR I, J, MaxPosition: TablePosition; MaxPoints: PointsRange;
       DetailsSaved: TeamDetails;
   BEGIN
     FOR I := 1 TO NumberOfTeams – 1 DO
       (* find team with maximum points from position I onwards *)
       MaxPosition := I; MaxPoints := LeagueTable[I].Points;
       FOR J := I + 1 TO NumberOfTeams DO
         IF LeagueTable[J].Points > MaxPoints THEN
           MaxPoints := LeagueTable[J].Points; MaxPosition := J
         END
       END;
```

```
      (* if necessary, swap with entry I *)
      IF MaxPosition <> I THEN
        DetailsSaved := LeagueTable[I];
        LeagueTable[I] := LeagueTable[MaxPosition];
        LeagueTable[MaxPosition] := DetailsSaved
      END
    END
  END SortTable;

PROCEDURE PrintTable;
  VAR I: TablePosition;
  BEGIN
    WriteLn; WriteString("         P   W   D   L   PTS"); WriteLn;
    FOR I := 1 TO NumberOfTeams DO
      WITH LeagueTable[I] DO
        WriteString(Name); WriteCard(Played, 4); WriteCard(Won, 4);
        WriteCard(Drawn, 4);  WriteCard(Lost, 4); WriteCard(Points, 6);
        WriteLn
      END
    END
  END PrintTable;

BEGIN
  WriteString("Playing records to date ..."); WriteLn; OpenInput("");
  IF Done THEN
    ReadInTable; CloseInput;
    WriteString("Results of latest matches ..."); WriteLn; OpenInput("");
    IF Done THEN
      UpdateTable; CloseInput; SortTable; PrintTable
    END
  END
END UpdateLeagueTable.
```

```
Playing records to date ...
Enter Input File Name: LEAGUE
Results of latest matches ...
Enter Input File Name: RESULTS

                 P    W    D    L    PTS
Red Rovers       4    2    2    0     6
Blue United      4    2    1    1     5
Silver City      4    1    2    1     4
Black Forest     4    1    1    2     3
Green Villa      4    1    1    2     3
Brown Town       4    1    1    2     3
```

VARIANT RECORDS

The nature and types of some components of a data item sometimes depend on the values of other components. For instance, consider the following record-type declaration describing information associated with a register of all persons in a country at a given time.

```
TYPE Person = RECORD
              Name: PersonName;
              DateOfBirth: Date;
              Origin: (National, Alien)
          END;
```

The types PersonName and Date are assumed to be defined elsewhere. The field Origin distinguishes between nationals of the country, and aliens temporarily visiting the country.

Suppose that we wish to extend this type-declaration to provide extra information about each person. In the case of nationals we wish to record their place of birth while, for aliens, the country of origin and date and port of entry to the country are required.

The record-type Person now has two alternative structures, or *variants*, according as to whether the person's origin is National or Alien. In both cases the name and date of birth are still required but we have a different number, and different types, of further components in the record depending on the value of the Origin field.

Records with alternative structures are catered for in a Modula-2 record-type definition by introduction of so-called *variant-parts*. A *variant-part* consists of a *tag-field*, of a previously-defined type whose values distinguish the possible alternative structures or variants, followed by further *field-lists* corresponding to each of these alternative structures. Each *field-list* is labeled with the tag-field values to which it corresponds.

> *variant-part =*
> *"CASE" [tag-field] ":" type-identifier "OF"*
> *variant {"/" variant}*
> *["ELSE" field-list-sequence]*
> *"END".*
> *tag-field = identifier.*
> *variant = [case-label-list ":" field-list-sequence].*

The *tag-field* type must be an ordinal type. Thus our augmented type Person might be defined as

```
TYPE PersonKind = (National, Alien);
     Person = RECORD
```

```
        Name: PersonName; DateOfBirth: Date;
        CASE Origin: PersonKind OF
          National:
            BirthPlace: PlaceName |
          Alien:
            CountryOfOrigin: PlaceName;
            DateOfEntry: Date; PortOfEntry: PlaceName
        END
      END;
```

In a variant record definition such as the above, the tag-field is an explicit field of the record which may be selected and updated in the same way as other fields. If ThisPerson is a variable of type Person, one may write statements such as

```
    ThisPerson.Origin := National
```

or

```
    IF ThisPerson.Origin <> Alien THEN WriteString(ThisPerson.Name) END
```

Field names appearing within each variant must be unique throughout the entire record. Use of such a field name then implies the variant (and hence the tag-field value) assumed, and no explicit indication of this is necessary. Thus fields within variants may be selected in the same way as fields within a fixed-part. For example, we might write

```
    ThisPerson.CountryOfOrigin := Italy
```

or

```
    IF ThisPerson.BirthPlace = USA THEN ... END
```

However, these field selections are valid only when the tag-field Origin does indeed have the assumed value (Alien in the first case, National in the second). For reasons of efficiency, few implementations of Modula-2 actually check the tag-field value when a field of a variant is selected. It is the responsibility of the programmer to ensure that the variant fields are accessed correctly, and failure to do so will generally produce incorrect programs.

Unfortunately no explicit language facility is provided in Modula-2 to aid the programmer in this respect. However, systematic use of the *case-statement* in conjunction with a *with-statement* can reduce the likelihood of error. For instance, if we write the sequence

```
    WITH ThisPerson DO
      ...
      CASE Origin OF
        National:
          BirthPlace := ... |
```

```
    Alien:
        CountryOfOrigin := ...;
        DateOfEntry := ...;
        PortOfEntry := ...
    END;
    ...
    END
```

then it is apparent that the field BirthPlace should be accessed only within the case-statement limb labeled National, while the fields CountryOfOrigin, DateOfEntry and PortOfEntry should be accessed only in the limb labeled Alien.

In some cases no further variant fields may be required for a particular variant of a record-type, in which case the variant is defined with an *empty* field-list. For example, if we wished to record no further information on aliens, the record-type Person might be defined as

```
TYPE PersonKind = (National, Alien);
     Person = RECORD
                 Name: PersonName; DateOfBirth: Date;
                 CASE Origin: PersonKind OF
                 National: BirthPlace: PlaceName |
                 Alien:
                 END
              END;
```

A record structure may have no fields common to all of its alternative structures and consist solely of one or more variant-parts. For example, when playing poker with the jokers wild, any card dealt may be either one of the 52 suit cards, or a joker. To describe a poker card we might define the types specified below:

```
TYPE Suit = (Clubs, Diamonds, Hearts, Spades);
     Rank = (Two, Three, Four, Five, Six, Seven, Eight,
             Nine, Ten, Jack, Queen, King, Ace);
     Joker = (RedJoker, BlackJoker);
     CardType = (Normal, Wild);
     PokerCard = RECORD
                    CASE Which: CardType OF
                    Normal: S: Suit; R: Rank |
                    Wild: J: Joker
                    END
                 END;
```

In our examples so far the tag-field is an assignable component of the variant record-type, and record processing involves inspecting this tag-field to determine the variant involved. However, the syntax of *tag-field* allows omission of the tag-field identifier, in which case the programmer has no means of assigning or inspecting the tag-field—the variant in force for any record is implied by the fields accessed. Such a record-type might be useful in programs where the variant which any record takes is always implied by context. For example, we might consider the pages of a book as records defined as:

```
TYPE PageKind = (First, Following);
     Page = RECORD
                CASE : PageKind OF
                First:
                    Title: BookName; Author: PersonName;
                    ISBN: ARRAY [1..10] OF CHAR |
                Following:
                    Text: ARRAY [1..PageSize] OF Line
                END
            END;
```

By implication only those records representing the first pages of books will take the first variant; all others will take the second. If the program is always aware of which records represent first pages (by the order in which they are processed, say) then inclusion of an assignable tag-field is unnecessary.

(On implementations which conform to the second or earlier editions of *Programming on Modula-2* the colon preceding the tag-field type-identifier is also omitted when the tag-field identifier is omitted.)

A variant record may contain more than one variant part. Returning to our person register example, we might wish to record an appropriate relationship for each person who is either married or a minor, as well as their origin as before. This might be done as follows:

```
TYPE PersonKind = (National, Alien);
     RelationKind = (Single, Married, Minor);
     Person = RECORD
                Name: PersonName; DateOfBirth: Date;
                CASE Origin: PersonKind OF
                National:
                   BirthPlace: PlaceName;
                Alien:
                   CountryOfOrigin: PlaceName;
                   DateOfEntry: Date; PortOfEntry: PlaceName
                END;
                CASE Relation: RelationKind OF
                Single: |
                Married: Spouse: PersonName |
                Minor: Guardian: PersonName
                END
            END;
```

A *field-list* is either empty, a *fixed-part*, or a *variant-part*. Since each *variant* in a *variant-part* in turn contains a *field-list* it is thus possible for the variant-parts of a record to contain nested variant-parts. This is illustrated by expanding the definition of the record-type Person to distinguish between nationals who were actually born in the country and those whose nationality was obtained by naturalization.

```
TYPE PersonKind = (National, Alien);
     Status = (ByBirth, Naturalization);
     Person = RECORD
                   Name: PersonName; DateOfBirth: Date;
                   CASE Origin: PersonKind OF
                   National:
                     BirthPlace: PlaceName;
                     CASE Qualification: Status OF
                     ByBirth: |
                     Naturalization:
                         Number: CARDINAL;
                         DateOfNaturalization: Date
                     END |
                   Alien:
                     CountryOfOrigin: PlaceName;
                     DateOfEntry: Date; PortOfEntry: PlaceName
                   END
              END;
```

The fields within the nested variant-part are selected in the same way as any other fields of the record, e.g., one may write

```
IF ThisPerson.Qualification = Naturalization THEN
   WriteCard(ThisPerson.Number, 10)
END
```

or

```
ThisPerson.DateOfNaturalization.Y := 1985
```

In both cases the tag-field Origin is assumed to have the value National, while in the latter case the tag-field Qualification is assumed to have the value Naturalization.

Variant records are a convenient means of describing the data that arise in many practical programming applications. However, as already indicated, considerable care is required in programming their manipulation, particularly where changes of variant of a given record occur. For a variant record that has a tag-field identifier, a change of variant occurs when a new value is assigned to the tag-field. For a variant record without a tag-field identifier, a change of variant is implied when a field of a different variant is referenced. In either case, the variant fields of the old variant cease to exist at this point, and the variant fields of the new variant come into existence with undefined values. The manipulation of fields must be consistent with the destruction and creation that occurs at each change of variant. Unfortunately, implementations rarely detect inconsistent manipulation of variant fields when it occurs. More often the result is an undetected error whose effect is baffling and whose origin is difficult to diagnose. To minimize the likelihood of such errors, great care is recommended in programming the manipulation of variant records.

CASE STUDY 11

In printing text the textual information must be formatted to suit the available line length of the printing device involved. A program is required to read a series of lines of text containing any number of characters, and output this text as a series of lines containing not more than N characters, where the value of N is provided by the user of the program. The input text consists of words (of not more than 16 characters), commas, semicolons, full stops (periods) and "layout devices" such as blank lines and new paragraphs. Any non-blank line having three or more leading blanks is considered to be the start of a new paragraph.

The output is to retain the blank lines and paragraph layout of the input text. Normal conventions are to be observed in positioning punctuation symbols—a punctuation symbol must immediately follow the preceding word and both must appear on the same line, with the punctuation symbol being followed by a blank, unless it is the last character of a line.

We might initially conceive the program as a loop which identifies the next item in the input text and transfers it to the output text:

> *obtain required output line width*;
> *read item*;
> REPEAT
> *write item*;
> *read item*
> UNTIL *end of text*

It is convenient to think of the end of the text as a special "item" which is read but not written in this process. However, this scheme is inadequate when we realize that how a word item is written depends on whether the next item is a punctuation symbol. The program input must thus be one item ahead of its output and so we rewrite it as:

> *obtain required output line width*;
> *read NextItem*;

```
REPEAT
    ThisItem := NextItem;
    read NextItem;
    write ThisItem
UNTIL NextItem is EndOfText
```

This process is expressible using calls of two procedures ReadNextItem and WriteThisItem, where the latter now has access to the details of the next item to carry out its task.

How should we represent the items which appear in the text? They may be words of up to 16 letters, punctuation symbols (comma, semicolon, or full stop), "layout devices" (a blank line or new paragraph), or the end of text item. We may thus define a variant record-type to describe these possibilities.

```
TYPE ItemKind = (Word, Punctuation, Layout, EndOfText);
    TextItem = RECORD
                CASE Kind: ItemKind OF
                    Word: Length: WordRange; Spelling: WordSpelling |
                    Punctuation: Symbol: CHAR |
                    Layout: Device: (BlankLine, Paragraph) |
                    EndOfText:
                END
            END;
```

where

```
CONST MaxWordLength = 16;

TYPE WordRange = [1 .. MaxWordLength];
    WordSpelling = ARRAY WordRange OF CHAR;
```

Two variables of type TextItem can now be used to hold the details of the items processed by ReadNextItem and WriteThisItem:

```
VAR   ThisItem, NextItem: TextItem;
```

The procedure ReadNextItem must read the characters which make up the next item from the input, and leave its description in the variable NextItem. For some items such as words and new paragraphs it is not apparent that the item is complete until the following character has been read—hence we program ReadNextItem so that it is always one character ahead.

```
PROCEDURE ReadNextItem;
BEGIN
    skip blanks if necessary;
    IF next character is EOL THEN
        IF input is exhausted THEN item is EndOfText
        ELSE
```

```
        skip and count leading blanks on next line;
        IF next character is EOL THEN item is a blank line
        ELSIF more than 2 leading blanks THEN item is a paragraph
        ELSE scan first non-blank item in line
        END
    END
    ELSE scan next non-blank item in line
    END
END ReadNextItem
```

Now, *scan next non-blank item in line* can be expressed as a call of a procedure whose action depends on the character currently under consideration. Denoting this character by the variable

```
    VAR NextCh: CHAR;
```

we have:

```
    PROCEDURE ScanNonBlankItem;
    BEGIN
        WITH NextItem DO
        CASE NextCh OF
        "A".."Z", "a".."z" ...:
            item is a word;
            scan word and record its length and spelling |
        " ", ",", ".":
            item is a punctuation symbol;
            scan and record symbol
        ELSE  illegal character!
        END
    END
    END ScanNonBlankItem
```

In practice we will allow any sequence of letters or digits as a "word". For simplicity the program will report and abort on encountering any other illegal character.

Note that NextCh must be a global variable since its value must be retained between calls of ReadNextItem and ScanNonBlankItem. Initializing NextCh as follows ensures that the first input item is processed correctly by the first call of ReadNextItem:

```
    NextCh := EOL
```

The structure required for the procedure WriteThisItem is a case-statement which discriminates among the various kinds of text item, thus:

```
WITH ThisItem DO
  CASE Kind OF
  Word:
    IF no room on line THEN take a new line
    ELSIF NOT start of line THEN precede word by a blank
    END;
    write out the word |
  Punctuation:
    write out the symbol |
  Layout:
    IF line partially full THEN take a new line END;
    IF device = BlankLine THEN take a new line
    ELSE take a new paragraph
    END
  END
END
```

Introducing a global variable SpaceLeftOnLine to record the number of available character positions remaining on the current output line, this procedure is easily expressed in Modula-2. Splitting a word and a punctuation symbol over two lines is avoided by inspecting NextItem when ThisItem is a word.

TextFormatter is the final program that results. The sample output file shown corresponds to its execution for output line width 50, using the same input file as was used in Case Study 9.

```
MODULE TextFormatter;

FROM InOut IMPORT
  Done, EOL, OpenInput, CloseInput, Read,
  OpenOutput, CloseOutput, Write, WriteString, WriteLn;
FROM ValidInput IMPORT GetCardinal;

(* This program reads an input text file, reformats its contents
   to a user-specified line-length, and outputs it to another file.
   All blank lines and paragraph structure in the input text are
   preserved. A line starting with two or more blanks is taken to
   be the start of a new paragraph. Punctuation symbols ".", "," and
   ";" are recognized, and words consist of up to 16 letters or digits *)

CONST MaxWordLength = 16;

TYPE WordRange = [1 .. MaxWordLength];
     ItemKind = (Word, Punctuation, Layout, EndOfText);
     WordSpelling = ARRAY WordRange OF CHAR;
```

```
              TextItem = RECORD
                      CASE Kind: ItemKind OF
                        Word: Length: WordRange; Spelling: WordSpelling |
                        Punctuation: Symbol: CHAR |
                        Layout: Device: (BlankLine, Paragraph) |
                        EndOfText:
                      END
                      END;

VAR ThisItem, NextItem: TextItem; NextCh: CHAR;

PROCEDURE ReadNextItem;

  (* read the next item from the input file, and leave
    its description in the global variable NextItem.   *)

  PROCEDURE ScanNonBlankItem;

    (* scan and record word or punctuation symbol *)

    PROCEDURE WordChar(Ch: CHAR): BOOLEAN;
      BEGIN
        RETURN (Ch >= "A") AND (Ch <= "Z") OR
               (Ch >= "a") AND (Ch <= "z") OR
               (Ch >= "0") AND (Ch <= "9")
      END WordChar;

    VAR L: [0 .. MaxWordLength];
    BEGIN
      WITH NextItem DO
        CASE NextCh OF
          "A".."Z", "a".."z", "0".."9":
            Kind := Word; L := 0;
            REPEAT
              L := L + 1; Spelling[L] := NextCh; Read(NextCh)
            UNTIL NOT WordChar(NextCh);
            Length := L |
          ",", ".", ";":
            Kind := Punctuation; Symbol := NextCh; Read(NextCh)
        ELSE
          (* illegal character: report and abort *)
          CloseOutput; WriteString("Illegal character: '");
          Write(NextCh); Write("'"); WriteLn; HALT
        END
      END
    END ScanNonBlankItem;
```

```
    VAR LeadingBlanks: CARDINAL;
    BEGIN (* ReadNextItem *)
      WHILE NextCh = " " DO Read(NextCh) END;
      IF NextCh = EOL THEN
        Read(NextCh);
        IF NOT Done THEN NextItem.Kind := EndOfText
        ELSE
          LeadingBlanks := 0;
          WHILE NextCh = " " DO
            LeadingBlanks := LeadingBlanks + 1; Read(NextCh)
          END;
          WITH NextItem DO
            IF NextCh = EOL THEN Kind := Layout; Device := BlankLine
            ELSIF LeadingBlanks > 2 THEN
              Kind := Layout; Device := Paragraph
            ELSE ScanNonBlankItem
            END
          END
        END
      ELSE ScanNonBlankItem
      END
    END ReadNextItem;

  VAR SpaceLeftOnLine, OutputMax: CARDINAL;
  PROCEDURE WriteThisItem;
    (* write item described by global variable ThisItem,
       assuming it is to be followed by item NextItem    *)
    PROCEDURE TakeNewLine;
    BEGIN
      WriteLn; SpaceLeftOnLine := OutputMax
    END TakeNewLine;
    VAR SpaceNeeded: [1 .. MaxWordLength+2]; I: WordRange;
    BEGIN
      WITH ThisItem DO
        CASE Kind OF
          Word:
          IF NextItem.Kind = Punctuation THEN SpaceNeeded := Length + 2
          ELSE SpaceNeeded := Length + 1
          END;
```

```
              IF SpaceNeeded > SpaceLeftOnLine THEN TakeNewLine
              ELSIF SpaceLeftOnLine <> OutputMax THEN
                Write(" "); SpaceLeftOnLine := SpaceLeftOnLine – 1
              END;
              FOR I := 1 TO Length DO Write(Spelling[I]) END;
              SpaceLeftOnLine := SpaceLeftOnLine – Length |
            Punctuation:
              Write(Symbol); SpaceLeftOnLine := SpaceLeftOnLine – 1 |
            Layout:
              IF SpaceLeftOnLine < OutputMax THEN TakeNewLine END;
              IF Device = BlankLine THEN TakeNewLine
              ELSE WriteString(" "); SpaceLeftOnLine := SpaceLeftOnLine – 2
              END
          END
        END
      END WriteThisItem;

BEGIN
  GetCardinal("Give required line width for output: ", OutputMax, 40, 120);
  OpenInput(""); WriteLn;
  IF Done THEN
    OpenOutput(""); WriteLn;
    IF Done THEN
      NextCh := EOL; SpaceLeftOnLine := OutputMax; ReadNextItem;
      REPEAT
        ThisItem := NextItem; ReadNextItem; WriteThisItem
      UNTIL NextItem.Kind = EndOfText;
      IF SpaceLeftOnLine <> OutputMax THEN WriteLn END;
      CloseOutput
    END;
    CloseInput
  END
END TextFormatter.
```

THE PROFILE

  The profile is an edited, automatically
formatted, listing of the source program which
displays the frequency of execution of each
statement of the program.

EXERCISES

9.1 Extend the program from Case Study 10 to record the goals for and against each team, and to use goal difference (goals for – goals against) to determine the league positions of teams with the same number of points.

9.2 Define a record-type, each value of which denotes a point on an x-y grid where x and y take integer values in the range 1 to 100. Write a program which reads four pairs of values representing the vertices A, B, C, D of a quadrilateral in cyclic order, and determines whether $ABCD$ is a square, a rectangle, or otherwise.

9.3 Define a record-type enabling the name, grades, and grade total for each student processed by the program Grades2 to be held as a record variable. Write a procedure which reads a student's performance from one line of input and stores it as a record of this type. Use this procedure in a revised version of Grades2 which tabulates the class performance as before, but in descending order of grade total.

9.4 Define a variant record-type whose values describe the shape and dimensions of geometric figures which may be circles, squares, rectangles or triangles. Write a procedure which reads a description of a geometric figure and stores it as a record of this type. Each input description starts with a letter C, S, R, or T denoting the shape. This is followed by one, two or three real numbers which specify the length of the radius, side or sides as appropriate, e.g.,

```
C 12.1
R 30.4   17.5
S 16.7
T 40.6   27.9   21.8
```

Write a function which determines the area of the figure described by such a record. Use the procedure and function in a program which reads a sequence of descriptions of figures, and prints out the description of the figure of largest area.

10

Sets

THE SET CONCEPT

In Chapter 3 we defined the concept of type as the set of values which a data item of that type may take. Each item has at any moment a value which is exactly one of the members of this set. In many practical situations data items arise whose values are themselves sets of the values of some other type.

Consider the familiar phenomenon of mixing colors from monochromatic sources, such as occurs on the screen of a color television set. We might have primary sources for three colors—red, yellow and blue, say—which we consider as the possible values of a type:

    TYPE PrimaryColor = (Red, Yellow, Blue);

These primary colors can be mixed in any combination. For example, at some point we might use a mix of all three colors, and denote this as follows

    {Red, Yellow, Blue}

(Since the order of mixing is not important, the order in which we write the primary colors is not important. We might have written {Yellow, Red, Blue}, or {Blue, Yellow, Red} or any of the other possible orderings—there are six possible ways of denoting this mix of three sources, all of which are equivalent.)

Alternatively, we might use a mix of only two of the three primary colors, i.e., one of the following:

    {Red, Yellow}
    {Red, Blue}
    {Yellow, Blue}

(In this case there are two equivalent ways of denoting each distinct mix of two colors.)

Again we might use a "mix" of only one of the three possible sources (i.e., use that primary color on its own), i.e., one of the following:

{Red}
{Yellow}
{Blue}

Finally, at some point we may require no coloring at all, i.e., a "mix" involving none of the three primary colors, which we denote as

{ }

The eight possible mixes which we have listed are the only possible *sets* or unordered combinations of the three primary colors Red, Yellow, Blue and are in fact the possible values of a type which we might define as

TYPE Mix = SET OF PrimaryColor;

where PrimaryColor is said to be the *base-type* of the *set-type* Mix.

Modula-2 allows the description of such set-types, for a restricted range of base-types, as follows

$$set\text{-}type = "SET" "OF" base\text{-}type.$$
$$base\text{-}type = simple\text{-}type.$$

Each implementation of Modula-2 places an upper limit N on the *cardinality* (i.e., number of values) of any acceptable base-type. This constant N is usually equal to the word length of the computer concerned (i.e., number of binary digits in a storage location), or is a small multiple of the word length. Typically N is 16 or 32. The *base-type* must be either

(a) a subrange of the non-negative integers within the range $0..N-1$, or
(b) (a subrange of) an enumerated-type with a cardinality of not more than N.

As a further example of a set-type consider the data required by the control mechanism of a lift in a multistorey building. At any moment the mechanism must be aware of the outstanding calls for the lift from all floors, which may vary from no calls at all (when no-one wants the lift) to calls from all floors (at a rush period). The outstanding calls can be thought of as a value of the set-type LiftCalls defined as follows

TYPE Floor = [1 .. Top];
     LiftCalls = SET OF Floor;

Variables of type Mix and LiftCalls may then be declared, e.g.,

VAR Mix1: Mix;
    ThisJourney, CallsNow: LiftCalls;

MANIPULATING SETS

Once a set-type has been defined, variables of that type may be declared and manipulated in a Modula-2 program. Besides copying or assignment, Modula-2 provides a number of special operations which may be applied to values of set-types.

Construction

A value of a set-type may be constructed by specifying its elements, or members. This is done by using the syntactic form *set*, which was noted in Chapter 4 as one alternative for a *factor* within an *expression*. This is defined as follows:

> *set = [type-identifier] "{" element-list "}".*
> *element-list = [element{"," element}].*
> *element = expression [".." expression].*

The form

   S{ }

where S is the identifier of a set-type, denotes a set of no elements, and is known as the *empty* set.

A non-empty set consists of one or more *element* specifications, separated by commas, enclosed by curly brackets, and prefixed by the name of the set-type. All expressions appearing in the *element* specifications must be of the same type, which is the base-type of the set.

An *element* specification consists either of a single *expression* whose value determines the corresponding element of the set, or of two *expressions* which determine a consecutive range of elements for the set. For example,

Mix{Red}   denotes the set of type Mix containing one element Red;
Mix{Red..Blue}   denotes the set of type Mix containing all three elements Red, Yellow, Blue;
LiftCalls{1..3, T} denotes the set of type LiftCalls containing floors 1, 2, 3 and T, where T is a variable of type Floor.

Note that two distinct element specifications may indicate the same element value. By definition an element may occur at most once in a set. Thus a constructed set

   S{I, J}

where S is a set-type identifier and the values of the expressions I and J are found to be equal, yields a set of one element.

An element specification I..J, where the values of the expressions I and J are such that I>J, is interpreted as specifying no elements. Thus S{I..J} would yield the empty set in this case.

In some Modula-2 implementations constructed sets may contain *constant* values only, as required by early editions of Professor Wirth's *Programming in Modula-2*. Such *constant-sets* are simply *sets* in which the *element* specifications involve constant-expressions. Constant-sets are often used in constant-declarations, e.g.,

```
CONST Green = Mix{Blue, Yellow};
      AllFloors = LiftCalls{1..Top};
      NoCalls = LiftCalls{ };
```

Constructed sets, constant or otherwise, are used to initialize set-variables, e.g.,

```
CallsNow := LiftCalls{Top}
Mix1 := Mix{Red, Blue}
```

The empty set also plays a frequent role in set comparison, and the singleton sets (sets of one element) may be used in set updating as described below.

Membership Testing

Modula-2 provides five relational operators by which the membership of set values can be investigated. Four of these are the familiar operators =, <>, <=, >=, which are used with two operands of the same set-type. The fifth is the operator IN, which is used with one operand of a base-type and a second operand of the corresponding set-type.

The operators = and <> are used to test set equality. Two sets are equal if they contain exactly the same elements. Thus

Mix{Red, Blue} = Mix{}	gives	FALSE
Mix{Red} <> Mix{Blue}	gives	TRUE
Mix{Red, Yellow, Blue} = Mix{Red..Blue}	gives	TRUE

The operators <= and >= are used to test set *containment* or *inclusion*. Assuming that A and B are sets of a type

```
TYPE S = SET OF T;
```

the set A is *contained*, or *included*, by the set B, written A <= B, if each member of A is also a member of B. Thus

Mix{Red, Blue} <= Mix{Red, Yellow, Blue}	gives	TRUE
Mix{Red, Blue} <= Mix{Red, Blue}	gives	TRUE
Mix{Red, Blue} <= Mix{Red, Yellow}	gives	FALSE
Mix{Red, Blue} <= Mix{Blue}	gives	FALSE

Note that the empty set is included by any other set, so

$$S\{\} <= B \quad gives \quad TRUE$$

whatever the value of the set B.

The relation A >= B is read as A *includes* B, and is TRUE if each member of B is a member of A, and FALSE otherwise. Thus

Mix{Red, Blue} >= Mix{Red, Yellow, Blue}	gives	FALSE
Mix{Red, Blue} >= Mix{Red, Blue}	gives	TRUE
Mix{Red, Blue} >= Mix{Red, Yellow}	gives	FALSE
Mix{Red, Blue} >= Mix{Blue}	gives	TRUE

Note that both operators may give FALSE for the same operand pair. In this respect they differ from their arithmetic counterparts—if A and B are integers, then ((A <= B) OR (A >= B)) must be TRUE but when A and B are sets it may be FALSE.

The operator IN is used to test the presence of an individual member in a set. If X is a value of the base-type and A is a value of the corresponding set-type then

$$X \ IN \ A \quad gives \quad TRUE \ if \ X \ is \ a \ member \ of \ A,$$
$$FALSE \ otherwise$$

For example,

Red IN Mix{Red, Yellow}	gives	TRUE
Red IN Mix{Red}	gives	TRUE
Red IN Mix{Yellow, Blue}	gives	FALSE
Red IN Mix{ }	gives	FALSE

As we shall see, the membership testing operators are commonly used to control the processing of set data, e.g.,

```
IF ThisFloor IN CallsNow THEN ... ELSE ... END
WHILE CallsNow <> NoCalls DO ... END
```

However, the IN operator is often useful in contexts where explicit set manipulation is not involved, as a means of expressing an equality test with several alternatives. Thus, if

```
TYPE DaySet = SET OF DaysOfWeek;
```

and D is a variable of type DaysOfWeek, writing

```
IF D IN DaySet{Monday, Wednesday, Friday} THEN ... END
```

is clearer, and for most implementations more efficient, than the clumsy

```
IF (D = Monday) OR (D = Wednesday) OR (D = Friday) THEN ... END
```

Set Arithmetic

Mathematical manipulation of sets is commonly expressed in terms of four operations, each of which takes two set operands and yields a set result, namely *union, intersection, set difference* (or *relative complement*) and *symmetric difference*. Modula-2 also provides these operations, denoting them by the operators +, *, – and / respectively. When used with two operands of a common set-type these produce a result of the same set-type, as follows:

A + B gives the *union* of A and B, i.e., the set of all values which are either in A, or in B, or in both

A * B gives the *intersection* of A and B, i.e., the set of all values which are in A, and also in B

A – B gives the *relative complement* of A and B, i.e., the set of values which are in A but not in B

A / B gives the *symmetric difference* of A and B, i.e., the set of values which are in A, or in B, but not in both.

For example,

Mix{Red, Blue} + Mix{Red, Yellow}	gives	Mix{Red, Yellow, Blue}
Mix{Red, Blue} * Mix{Red, Yellow}	gives	Mix{Red}
Mix{Red, Blue} – Mix{Red, Yellow}	gives	Mix{Blue}
Mix{Red, Blue} / Mix{Red, Yellow}	gives	Mix{Yellow, Blue}

The operators + and – may be used with singleton sets as a means of adding or removing a given value to or from an existing set. Thus

A := A+S{X}   *adds* a value X to set A – if A already contains X the operation has no effect

A := A–S{X}   *removes* a value X from set A – if A does not contain X the operation has no effect.

As noted earlier, in some Modula-2 implementations constructed sets may contain *constant* values only. For such implementations, if we wish to add the value of a *variable* V to a set A, it is illegal to write

A := A + S{V}

Instead, the standard procedures INCL and EXCL must be used, where

INCL(S, e)   *adds the value of the expression e to the set S if not already present*
EXCL(S, e)   *removes the value of the expression e from the set S if present*

e may be any expression giving a value of the base-type of S.

The function DistinctDigits accepts a non-negative integer N as parameter and
counts the number of distinct digits in its decimal representation.

```
PROCEDURE DistinctDigits(N: CARDINAL): CARDINAL;
  TYPE Digit = [0 .. 9]; DigitSet = SET OF Digit;
  VAR ThisDigit: Digit; PreviousDigits: DigitSet; Count: CARDINAL;
  BEGIN
    PreviousDigits := DigitSet{};
    Count := 0;
    REPEAT
      ThisDigit := N MOD 10;
      IF NOT (ThisDigit IN PreviousDigits) THEN
        Count := Count + 1;
        INCL(PreviousDigits, ThisDigit)
      END;
      N := N DIV 10
    UNTIL N = 0;
    RETURN Count
  END DistinctDigits
```

CASE STUDY 12

A computer-dating service maintains files which record data on each of its
clients in a given area as a line of text with the following format:

characters	1 – 40	name and telephone number
character	41	sex (denoted by M or F)
characters	42 – 43	age (recorded as two decimal digits)
characters	44 – 49	interests (a 1 in the corresponding position denotes an interest in art, books, music, theatre, politics, sport)

For example, the first few lines of a typical file might be as shown:

```
Alex Anderson          062-376-4692 M24 1   1
Anne English           062-374-6699 F19  11
Julia Monteith         065-280-3321 F33  1 1
Maurice Short          062-467-5490 M181    11
Kathleen Bryans        061-271-5550 F21 11
```

A program is required which will ascertain the sex, age and interests of a new
client, then scan a selected file of existing clients, and print out a list of all existing clients who are "compatible" with the new client, i.e., of opposite sex, with
an age difference less than ten years, and with at least one common interest.

The overall form of the program required is thus

input new client details;
read first client details from file;
WHILE *all clients not processed* DO
  IF *this client compatible with new client* THEN
    print name and telephone number
  END;
  read next client details
END

To refine this further we must decide how the data on each client is to be represented. Clearly the overall form is a record, with fields representing the name and telephone number, sex, age and interests of the client concerned. The name and telephone number can be held as a character array of length 40, the sex as a value of some suitable two-valued type, and the age as a suitable integer subrange. Since the interests are any combination of a predefined list of topics, a convenient representation is a set over a corresponding base-type Topics. The complete representation is given by the following type declarations:

```
TYPE  IdentityRange = [1 .. IdentityLength];
      AgeRange = [LowerAge .. UpperAge];
      Sexes = (Male, Female);
      Topics= (Art, Books, Music, Theatre, Politics, Sport);
      SetOfTopics = SET OF Topics;

      Client = RECORD
              Identity: ARRAY IdentityRange OF CHAR;
              Sex: Sexes;
              Age: AgeRange;
              Interests: SetOfTopics
          END;
```

With this representation the process of reading the data on an existing client from a relevant file can be expressed as the procedure ReadDetails:

```
PROCEDURE ReadDetails(VAR C: Client);
  VAR I: IdentityRange; Ch: CHAR;  T: Topics;
  BEGIN
    WITH C DO
      Read(Identity[1]);
      IF NOT Done THEN RETURN END;
      FOR I := 2 TO IdentityLength DO Read(Identity[I]) END;
      Read(Ch);
      IF Ch = "M" THEN Sex := Male ELSE Sex := Female END;
      read age;
```

```
Interests := SetOfTopics{ };
FOR T := Art TO Sport DO
  Read(Ch);
  IF Ch = "1" THEN INCL(Interests, T) END
END
END;
REPEAT Read(Ch) UNTIL Ch = EOL
END ReadDetails
```

ReadDetails begins by first ensuring that there is indeed another line of input data to be read—it does so by attempting to read the first character of the next line. If no such character exists then the Boolean variable Done provided by the InOut module will be assigned FALSE, in which case ReadDetails immediately executes a return-statement and control returns to the main program. Hence the terminating condition of the while-statement

WHILE *all clients not processed* DO ... END

in the main program is expressed as

WHILE Done DO ... END

Input of the client's age cannot be programmed using the procedure ReadCard provided by InOut because the immediately following character may also be the digit 1. Instead we must read the age as two character values and do the conversion to an equivalent cardinal value explicitly.

The set of interests is accumulated by adding a new member to an initially empty set for each "1" found in a corresponding input position. The final repeat-statement in ReadDetails ensures that the input is correctly aligned at the start of the next line for the next call to ReadDetails.

Although this program does not need the identity information on the new client, for convenience we store the sex, age, and interests data in another record of type Client. Using the data validation facilities of our module ValidInput, the process of obtaining these details is expressed as the following procedure:

```
PROCEDURE GetNewDetails(VAR C: Client);
VAR ReplyIsYes: Boolean; A: CARDINAL;
BEGIN
  WITH C DO
    Identity := "";
    GetBoolean("Is client male?", ReplyIsYes);
    IF ReplyIsYes THEN Sex := Male ELSE Sex := Female END;
    GetCardinal("Input client's age", A, LowerAge, UpperAge); Age := A;
    Interests := SetOfTopics{ };
    WriteString("Input Y or N for each interest:"); WriteLn;
    GetBoolean("Art?", ReplyIsYes);
```

```
        IF ReplyIsYes THEN INCL(Interests, Art) END;
        GetBoolean("Books?", ReplyIsYes);
        IF ReplyIsYes THEN INCL(Interests, Books) END;
        ...
        GetBoolean("Sport?", ReplyIsYes);
        IF ReplyIsYes THEN INCL(Interests, Sport) END
    END
END GetNewDetails
```

Input of the client's interests could be expressed as a loop by introducing an array of strings to hold the name of each interest. This is left as an exercise for the reader.

How is the compatibility of two clients tested? The sex and age tests are easily programmed. To determine that the two clients concerned have at least one common interest we form the intersection of their sets of interests, and test that this is not empty. Compatibility can thus be expressed as the function:

```
PROCEDURE Compatible (C1,C2: Client): BOOLEAN;
BEGIN
    RETURN (C1.Sex <> C2.Sex) AND
           (ABS(INTEGER(C1.Age)-INTEGER(C2.Age)) < 10) AND
           (C1.Interests * C2.Interests <> SetOfTopics{ })
END Compatible
```

The complete program DatingService is shown, together with the output produced by a sample run.

```
MODULE DatingService;

FROM InOut IMPORT
  EOL, Done, OpenInput, CloseInput, Read, WriteString, WriteLn;
FROM ValidInput IMPORT GetBoolean, GetCardinal;

(* This program obtains relevant details of a new dating-service client
   by interactive dialogue, scans a selected file of existing clients,
   and prints out a list of all those "compatible" with the new client.

   The client file records data on each client as a line of text thus:

   characters  1-40    name and telephone number
   character   41      sex (denoted by M or F)
   characters  42-43   age (recorded as two decimal digits)
   characters  44-49   interests (a 1 in the corresponding position
                       denotes an interest in art, books, music,
                       theatre, politics, sport)
```

```
    Compatible clients are of opposite sex, with an age difference
    less than ten years, and with at least one common interest.        *)

CONST IdentityLength = 40;
        LowerAge = 16; UpperAge = 99; MaximumAgeDifference = 10;

TYPE   IdentityRange = [1 .. IdentityLength];
       AgeRange = [LowerAge .. UpperAge];
       Sexes = (Male, Female);
       Topics= (Art, Books, Music, Theatre, Politics, Sport);
       SetOfTopics = SET OF Topics;
       Client = RECORD
                 Identity: ARRAY IdentityRange OF CHAR;
                 Sex: Sexes;
                 Age: AgeRange;
                 Interests: SetOfTopics
               END;

CONST EmptySet = SetOfTopics{ };

VAR   NewClient, NextClient: Client;

PROCEDURE ReadDetails(VAR C: Client);
  VAR I: IdentityRange; Ch: CHAR;  T: Topics;

  PROCEDURE ReadAge;
    VAR d1, d2: CHAR;
    BEGIN
      Read(d1); Read(d2);
      C.Age := 10*(ORD(d1)–ORD("0")) + ORD(d2)–ORD("0")
    END ReadAge;

  BEGIN
    WITH C DO
      Read(Identity[1]);
      IF NOT Done THEN (* no more clients *) RETURN END;
      FOR I := 2 TO IdentityLength DO Read(Identity[I]) END;
      Read(Ch);
      IF Ch = "M" THEN Sex := Male ELSE Sex := Female END;
      ReadAge;
```

```
    Interests := EmptySet;
    FOR T := Art TO Sport DO
      Read(Ch);
      IF Ch = "1" THEN INCL(Interests, T) END
    END
  END;
  REPEAT Read(Ch) UNTIL Ch = EOL
END ReadDetails;

PROCEDURE GetNewDetails(VAR C: Client);
  VAR ReplyIsYes: Boolean; A: CARDINAL;
  BEGIN
    WITH C DO
      Identity := "";
      GetBoolean("Is client male?", ReplyIsYes);
      IF ReplyIsYes THEN Sex := Male ELSE Sex := Female END;
      GetCardinal("Input client's age", A, LowerAge, UpperAge); Age := A;
      Interests := SetOfTopics{ };
      WriteString("Input Y or N for each interest:"); WriteLn;
      GetBoolean("Art?", ReplyIsYes);
      IF ReplyIsYes THEN INCL(Interests, Art) END;
      GetBoolean("Books?", ReplyIsYes);
      IF ReplyIsYes THEN INCL(Interests, Books) END;
      GetBoolean("Music?", ReplyIsYes);
      IF ReplyIsYes THEN INCL(Interests, Music) END;
      GetBoolean("Theatre?", ReplyIsYes);
      IF ReplyIsYes THEN INCL(Interests, Theatre) END;
      GetBoolean("Politics?", ReplyIsYes);
      IF ReplyIsYes THEN INCL(Interests, Politics) END;
      GetBoolean("Sport?", ReplyIsYes);
      IF ReplyIsYes THEN INCL(Interests, Sport) END
    END
  END GetNewDetails;

PROCEDURE Compatible(C1,C2: Client): BOOLEAN;
  BEGIN
    RETURN (C1.Sex <> C2.Sex) AND
           (ABS (INTEGER(C1.Age)-INTEGER(C2.Age))
                   < MaximumAgeDifference) AND
           (C1.Interests * C2.Interests <> EmptySet)
  END Compatible;
```

```
BEGIN
  WriteString("Enter details of new client:"); WriteLn;
  GetNewDetails(NewClient); WriteLn;
  WriteString("Choose file of existing clients:"); WriteLn;
  OpenInput (""); WriteLn;
  IF Done THEN
    WriteString("Compatible existing clients:"); WriteLn; WriteLn;
    ReadDetails(NextClient);
    WHILE Done DO
      IF Compatible(NewClient, NextClient) THEN
        WriteString (NextClient.Identity); WriteLn
      END;
      ReadDetails(NextClient)
    END;
    CloseInput
  END
END DatingService.
```

```
Enter details of new client:
Is client male? : y
Input client's age in range 16..99: 24
Input Y or N for each interest:
Art? : n
Books? : y
Music? : n
Theatre? : n
Politics? : n
Sport? : y

Choose file of existing clients:

Enter Input File Name: Newtown-north

Compatible existing clients:

Julia Monteith            065-280-3321
Kathleen Bryans           061-271-5550
Mary Stewart              061-313-2827
```

CASE STUDY 13

A continent comprises countries each of which borders one or more of the others. A map of the continent showing these countries must be colored such that no two countries with a common border are the same color. A computer program is required which will find a suitable coloring. (It has been shown that four colors are always sufficient to color any possible arrangement of countries.)

The problem is typical of a wide class of problems which are solved by *trial and error*. The method involves successively improving a partial solution by considering one country at a time, picking a suitable color for that country, and then proceeding to consider the next country. If it proves impossible to find a suitable color for the current country the method must *backtrack* to the last country for which a further alternative exists and restart from that point. This backtracking process is conveniently expressed as a recursive procedure which for the map coloring problem has the general form:

```
PROCEDURE ColorCountry(I: Country);
  BEGIN
    FOR each available color DO
      IF this color has not been chosen for
        a country bordering country I THEN
        choose this color for country I;
        IF I = NumberOfCountries THEN PrintSolution
        ELSE ColorCountry(I+1)
        END;
        reject this color for country I
      END
    END
  END ColorCountry
```

The procedure must be used by a program sequence which initializes the data to indicate that no colors have been chosen so far and then calls the procedure to color country number 1.

As it stands this procedure is capable of finding all possible solutions, since it continues to consider alternative colorings even after a complete solution has been output. If only one solution is required, resumption of the recursive process can be avoided by executing the standard procedure HALT in the PrintSolution procedure.

To refine the procedure further we must decide how the data on which it operates are to be represented.

The countries which border each country of the continent are conveniently represented as a table

```
VAR CountriesBordering: ARRAY Country OF CountrySet;
```

where the types Country and CountrySet are defined as

```
TYPE Country = [1 .. MaxNumberOfCountries];
     CountrySet = SET OF Country;
```

and it is assumed that the value of the constant MaxNumberOfCountries is not greater than the maximum set size permitted by the Modula-2 implementation used to run this program.

A possible coloring scheme for the continent can then be represented as a table

```
VAR Colored: ARRAY Color OF CountrySet;
```

where the type Color is defined, say, as

```
TYPE Color = (Red, Blue, Green, Yellow);
```

The unrefined steps in our recursive procedure are easily expressed in terms of this representation. To test whether a color C has already been chosen for a country bordering country I we form the intersection of the countries which border country I and the countries colored C, and test the non-emptiness of the result. The other steps are trivially programmed to give a final version of the procedure as shown.

```
PROCEDURE ColorCountry(I: Country);
VAR C: Color;
BEGIN
  FOR C := Red TO Yellow DO
    IF CountriesBordering[I] * Colored[C] = EmptySet THEN
      INCL(Colored[C], I);
      IF I = NumberOfCountries THEN PrintSolution
      ELSE ColorCountry(I + 1)
      END;
      EXCL(Colored[C], I)
    END
  END
END ColorCountry
```

Program MapColoring uses this procedure together with a suitable means of input of the border table from a file, and output for the solution found. Output is shown for input data corresponding to Table 10.1, which represents the border relationships for the continent of Europe. If a country A has a border with some other country B, then a "1" appears in column number B of the border relationships for country A, otherwise that column contains a "0". Thus, Albania (country 1) borders only Greece (country 12) and Yugoslavia (country 30). The border relationships are duplicated, i.e., the rows for Greece and Yugoslavia also indicate that these countries have a border with Albania.

		1111111111122222222223
		123456789012345678901234567890
1	ALBANIA	000000000001000000000000000001
2	ANDORRA	000000000010000000000001000000
3	AUSTRIA	000001000000101100000000010011
4	BELGIUM	000000000010000011000000000010
5	BULGARIA	000000000010000000000100001001
6	CZECHOSLOVAKIA	001000010000100000010010000010
7	DENMARK	000000000000000000000000000010
8	EAST GERMANY	000001000000000000010000000010
9	EIRE	000000000000000000000000000100
10	FINLAND	000000000000000000100010100000
11	FRANCE	010100000000001010000001010010
12	GREECE	100010000000000000000000001001
13	HUNGARY	001001000000000000000110000001
14	ICELAND	000000000000000000000000000000
15	ITALY	001000000010000000000000010001
16	LIECHTENSTEIN	001000000000000000000000010000
17	LUXEMBOURG	000100000010000000000000000010
18	NETHERLANDS	000100000000000000000000000010
19	NORWAY	000000000100000000000010100000
20	POLAND	000001010000000000000010000000
21	PORTUGAL	000000000000000000000001000000
22	ROMANIA	000010000000100000000010000001
23	U.S.S.R.	000001000100100000110100001000
24	SPAIN	010000000010000000001000000000
25	SWEDEN	000000000100000000100000000000
26	SWITZERLAND	001000000010001100000000000010
27	TURKEY	000010000010000000000010000000
28	U.K.	000000001000000000000000000000
29	WEST GERMANY	001101110010000011000000010000
30	YUGOSLAVIA	101010000011010000001000000000

Table 10.1   Border relationships for Europe

The actual file (*EUROMAP*) input to the program consists of a sequence of lines, one for each country in the above table. Each line consists of the name of the country (18 characters), and then as many characters as there are countries (each character either a "1" or a "0") representing the border relationships between that country and the other countries.

```
MODULE MapColoring;

  FROM InOut IMPORT
    EOL, OpenInput, CloseInput, Done, Read, WriteString, WriteLn;

  (* This program finds a suitable coloring for the countries on a map of
     a continent, using four colors. The names and border relationships of
     the countries are input from a file of N lines, one for each country.
     Each line consists of the name of a country (18 characters), and then
     N characters (each either a "1" or a "0"). A "1" in the Ith position
     indicates that the country named has a common border with the
     country represented by the Ith line of input.                      *)

  CONST MaxNumberOfCountries = 31; NameLength = 18;

  TYPE NameRange = [1 .. NameLength];
       Country = [1 .. MaxNumberOfCountries];
       CountrySet = SET OF Country;
       Color = (Red, Blue, Green, Yellow);

  CONST EmptySet = CountrySet{ };

  VAR CountriesBordering: ARRAY Country OF CountrySet;
      Colored: ARRAY Color OF CountrySet;
      Name: ARRAY Country OF ARRAY NameRange OF CHAR;
      NumberOfCountries: Country; C: Color;

  PROCEDURE ReadBorderTable;
    (* read country names and border data, setting NumberOfCountries *)
    VAR J, M: CARDINAL; K: NameRange; Ch: CHAR;
    BEGIN
      J := 0;
      LOOP
        Read(Ch);
        IF NOT Done THEN (* no more countries *) EXIT END;
        J := J+1; Name[J][1] := Ch;
        FOR K := 2 TO NameLength DO Read(Name[J][K]) END;
        CountriesBordering[J] := EmptySet; M := 0;
        REPEAT
          Read(Ch); M := M+1;
          IF Ch = "1" THEN INCL(CountriesBordering[J], M) END
        UNTIL Ch = EOL
      END;
      NumberOfCountries := J
    END ReadBorderTable;
```

```
PROCEDURE PrintSolution;
  (* print solution found (and terminate execution) *)
  VAR I: Country; C: Color;
  BEGIN
    WriteString ("COLORING OF MAP:"); WriteLn; WriteLn;
    FOR I := 1 TO NumberOfCountries DO
      WriteString(Name[I]); WriteString("   ");
      (* find color chosen for country I *)
      C := Red; WHILE NOT (I IN Colored[C]) DO INC(C) END;
      CASE C OF
        Red: WriteString("red") |
        Blue: WriteString("blue") |
        Green: WriteString("green") |
        Yellow: WriteString("yellow")
      END;
      WriteLn
    END;
    HALT
  END PrintSolution;
PROCEDURE ColorCountry(I: Country);
  (* extend solution for countries I to NumberofCountries *)
  VAR C: Color;
  BEGIN
    FOR C := Red TO Yellow DO
      IF CountriesBordering[I] * Colored[C] = EmptySet THEN
        INCL(Colored[C], I);
        IF I = NumberOfCountries THEN PrintSolution
        ELSE ColorCountry(I+1)
        END;
        EXCL(Colored[C], I)
      END
    END
  END ColorCountry;
BEGIN
  OpenInput(""); WriteLn;
  IF Done THEN
    ReadBorderTable;
    FOR C := Red TO Yellow DO Colored[C] := EmptySet END;
    ColorCountry(1); CloseInput
  END
END MapColoring.
```

```
Enter Input File Name: EUROMAP

COLORING OF MAP:

ALBANIA              red
ANDORRA              red
AUSTRIA              red
BELGIUM              red
BULGARIA             red
CZECHOSLOVAKIA       blue
DENMARK              red
EAST GERMANY         red
EIRE                 red
FINLAND              red
FRANCE               blue
GREECE               blue
HUNGARY              green
ICELAND              red
ITALY                green
LIECHTENSTEIN        blue
LUXEMBOURG           yellow
NETHERLANDS          blue
NORWAY               blue
POLAND               green
PORTUGAL             red
ROMANIA              blue
U.S.S.R              yellow
SPAIN                green
SWEDEN               green
SWITZERLAND          yellow
TURKEY               green
U.K.                 blue
WEST GERMANY         green
YUGOSLAVIA           yellow
```

THE TYPE BITSET

Modula-2 provides a predefined set-type BITSET whose values are sets of integers between 0 and W–1, where W is a constant defined by the implementation—usually the value of W is equal to the *word length* of the computer used, i.e.,

　　TYPE BITSET = SET OF [0..W-1];

Sets of type BITSET are constructed in the usual manner, except that the prefixing type-identifier BITSET may be omitted. Assuming W equals 16 say, then the following are values of type BITSET:

```
BITSET{2, 4, 9}
{0..3, 15}
{ }
```

All the operations of set arithmetic and membership testing described previously are applicable to sets of type BITSET.

The provision of BITSET as a predefined set-type is mainly of importance for *low-level programming*, a topic which is considered in Chapter 13, but its availability is also a convenience in many situations involving the manipulation of sets of small cardinal numbers. Thus the function DistinctDigits given earlier in this chapter may be re-expressed using a variable of type BITSET as:

```
PROCEDURE DistinctDigits(N: CARDINAL): CARDINAL;
   VAR ThisDigit: [0..9]; Count: CARDINAL; PreviousDigits: BITSET;
   BEGIN
     PreviousDigits := {};
     ...
   as before
     ...
   END DistinctDigits;
```

EXERCISES

10.1 Given type-declarations

```
TYPE Country = (Austria, Belgium, Denmark, Eire, France, Germany,
                Greece, Italy, Luxembourg, Netherlands, Norway,
                Portugal, Spain, Sweden, Switzerland, UK);
     SetOfCountries = SET OF Country;
```

and a variable-declaration

```
VAR Alpine, Mediterranean, Atlantic, NorthSea, EEC: SetOfCountries;
```

write assignment-statements to assign appropriate values to the variables. Use the variables to construct expressions which denote the following sets:

(a) the countries with both Atlantic and Mediterranean coastlines;
(b) EEC countries with Atlantic or North Sea coastlines;
(c) Alpine countries which are not in the EEC.

Write down Boolean expressions which determine whether

(d)   a country C is in the EEC;
(e)   a country C has a Mediterranean, but not an Atlantic, coastline;
(f)   all Alpine countries with a Mediterranean coastline are in the EEC.

10.2   Modify the computer-dating program developed in Case Study 12 to require at least two common interests for compatibility.

10.3   A college offers ten final-year courses in Art, English, French, German, History, Geography, Mathematics, Physics, Chemistry and Biology. Each student's enrolment is recorded as a line of text with the student's name in the first 20 positions. Each course to be taken by the student is shown by an X in the corresponding column of character positions 21-30. Write a program which reads the enrolment data and prints a student list for each course. You may assume that there are not more than 100 final-year students.

10.4   A factory produces steel bars whose exact length is unknown until after production. Its cutting shop receives orders for cut lengths of bar which must be met by cutting up the manufactured bars. For a given manufactured bar of length L a set C of orders is chosen from the order list, which can be met by cutting up this bar, and with minimum wastage. Design a recursive backtracking procedure which will construct C for given L and order list.

Incorporate the procedure in a program which constructs C from the following order list:

order 1	773 mm
order 2	548 mm
order 3	65 mm
order 4	929 mm
order 5	548 mm
order 6	163 mm
order 7	421 mm
order 8	37 mm

and a manufactured bar length $L = 1848$ mm.

11

Pointers

THE POINTER CONCEPT

The array-, record-, and set-types introduced in Chapters 8–10 permit the description of data structures whose form and size are predetermined and whose components are accessed in a standard way. However, many programming situations give rise to data structures which vary in size and form during their lifetime and whose means of access is particular to the programming problem involved.

Such structures are often realized as *linked data structures* in which the individual components of the structure are linked to, or point to, other related components of the structure. Some typical linked structures are illustrated in Figure 11.1.

Such structures usually grow and contract dynamically during the execution of a program. Because the number of components in the structure is not fixed and the connections between the components are also not fixed, the component data items of the structure must be created and linked dynamically during the execution of the program.

It is impractical for a general-purpose language such as Modula-2 to provide a range of data types which cover each of the possible classes of linked structures. Instead, Modula-2 provides a single mechanism, called the *pointer*, which allows the programmer to realize such structures himself, and to program the operations applicable to them.

Whereas variables of all the Modula-2 data types we have considered so far are *static* variables in the sense that they are declared in the program, denoted by means of their declared identifier, and their associated storage remains in existence throughout the lifetime of the block in which they are declared, this is not the case for the component variables of linked structures. These component variables are generated and destroyed *dynamically* during the execution of the program, and are not referred to by a user-declared identifier. Instead, they are referenced by means of auxiliary *pointer-variables* which point to the

Linked list

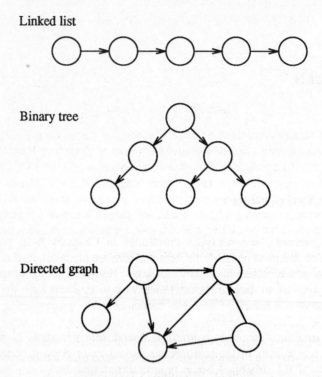

Binary tree

Directed graph

Figure 11.1   Linked data structures

dynamically created variables. For example, the pointer variable *p* in Figure 11.2 is said to *point to*, or *reference*, the variable whose value is *x*. The means of dynamically creating the variable with value *x* is described later.

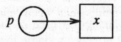

Figure 11.2   A pointer variable

A *pointer-type* is defined in Modula-2 as follows

$$pointer\text{-}type = \text{"POINTER" "TO" } type.$$

Thus, a Modula-2 program may include a type-declaration of the form

    TYPE P = POINTER TO T;

Values of the type P so defined are said to reference, or point to, variables of the type denoted by T. The type P is said to be *bound* to the type T.

Consider the example of a list of integers in which each component of the list points to its successor in the list, as in Figure 11.3.

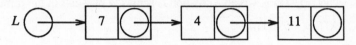

Figure 11.3   A list of integers

This structure consists of a pointer L to the first component of the list and a number of components linked together by means of pointers. Thus each component of the list consists of two data items, a value of type INTEGER and a pointer value which refers to another component of the list. Hence the components of the list belong to a record-type, which we shall choose to name ListComponent, consisting of two fields, an integer Value and a pointer Next. Choosing to name the pointer-type ListPointer, we may thus define it as:

```
TYPE ListPointer = POINTER TO ListComponent;
     ListComponent = RECORD
                        Value: INTEGER;
                        Next: ListPointer
                     END;
```

Note that the definition of the type ListComponent follows that of the type List-Pointer even though the definition of ListPointer refers to ListComponent. This situation generally arises in the definition of pointer-types and pointed-to types and for this reason Modula-2 allows the use of a type-identifier before its declaration in these circumstances. The declaration must appear later in the same block. This is the only case in Modula-2 where an identifier may be used in a declaration before it is declared.

Thus, in our example above, the inclusion of a pointer field of type List-Pointer in each record of type ListComponent enables a linear chain of records to be established, with an item component Value held in each. As we shall see, inclusion of two or more pointers in a component enables a variety of non-linear structures to be realized in the same way.

The variable L which points to the first component of the list is declared as a static variable—like any other type a pointer-type may be used to declare a static pointer-variable, thus:

```
VAR p: P;
```

However, the declaration of a pointer-variable p does not create any variable to which p points, only the capability to do so. Creation of such a variable is achieved by use of an implementation-defined procedure, but unfortunately some variation currently exists on how this is done.

In the third edition of *Programming in Modula-2* Professor Wirth indicates that implementations should provide a library module Storage, which provides two procedures ALLOCATE and DEALLOCATE. Given a pointer variable p of type P = POINTER TO T, variable creation is achieved by a call of the form

ALLOCATE(p, SIZE(T))

where SIZE is a standard function defined as follows:

SIZE(T) *gives the number of (implementation-defined) storage units occupied by a value of type* T, *or by a variable* T.

Further discussion on the units of storage measurement used by each implementation is given in Chapter 13.

On implementations which conform to earlier editions of *Programming in Modula-2*, however, the above call to ALLOCATE may be abbreviated to a call to a standard procedure NEW, thus:

NEW(p)

Note also that for such implementations SIZE is not a standard function, though a similar function, applicable only to variables, is available for import from the module SYSTEM which is discussed in Chapter 13.

It follows that Modula-2 programmers must be careful to ascertain which convention is observed by a particular implementation of Modula-2. In this book we follow the third edition convention based on ALLOCATE in the programs and program fragments illustrated. Such programs may need appropriate adaptation for those implementations on which NEW is supported.

The effect of a call ALLOCATE(p, SIZE(T)) or NEW(p), where p is of type P = POINTER TO T, is to create a new variable of type T, and to set the pointer variable p to point to it.

Variables created in this way are subsequently denoted as *referenced-variables*, which are defined as follows:

referenced-variable = pointer-variable "^".
pointer-variable = variable.

A *referenced-variable*, i.e., a *pointer-variable* followed by an upward arrow ^, denotes the variable to which the pointer variable points.

Suppose L is a variable of type ListPointer as above. After a call ALLOCATE(L, SIZE(ListComponent)) or its second edition equivalent NEW(L)

L^   denotes the variable of type ListComponent created,
L^.Value   denotes the integer component of that variable, and
L^.Next   denotes the pointer component, as shown in Figure 11.4.

Pointer values, and the variables which they reference, are thus created by means of the procedure ALLOCATE or its equivalent in other implementations.

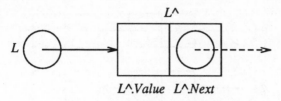

$$L\text{^}$$

$$L\text{^}.Value \quad L\text{^}.Next$$

Figure 11.4   Pointer referencing

They are used thereafter to reference these variables. Pointer values may also be copied, by assignment to another pointer variable.

Suppose p and q are pointer variables pointing to different list components, as shown in Figure 11.5(a). Execution of the assignment

 q := p

would produce the situation in Figure 11.5(b). Note the difference between this and assignment of the referenced variables. With the same initial situation, execution of

 q^ := p^

would result in the situation shown in Figure 11.5(c).

Several pointer-variables may thus have the same value, i.e., point to the same referenced-variable. To test whether two pointers reference the same variable they may be compared using the equality and inequality operators =, <>, e.g.,

 IF p = q THEN p^.Value := 0 END

In Figure 11.5(b) p = q is TRUE, but in Figure 11.5(c) p = q is FALSE.

In some cases it is necessary to indicate explicitly that a pointer does not point to anything. For this purpose Modula-2 provides a special value, denoted by the standard identifier NIL, which may be assigned to any pointer variable, thus

 p := NIL

For example, the value NIL might be used in the final list component of a list of integers, to indicate that no further integers follow, as in Figure 11.6(a), or it might be assigned to the variable L itself, to indicate that the list is empty, as in Figure 11.6(b). In processing a list, the occurrence of a NIL value must be tested for, e.g.,

 IF p <> NIL THEN ... END

The effect of attempting to access the variable referenced by a pointer variable whose value is NIL is undefined in Modula-2 but is clearly a programming error.

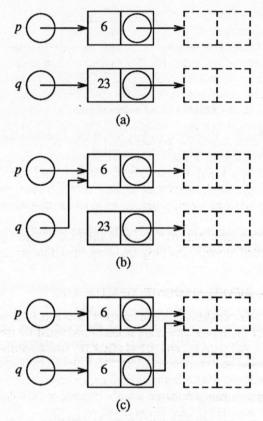

Figure 11.5 Pointer manipulation

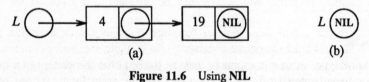

Figure 11.6 Using **NIL**

Implementations may provide a means of detecting any such attempt during the execution of a program.

Once created, a referenced-variable remains in existence until it is destroyed explicitly by a call of the form

DEALLOCATE(p, SIZE(T))

or its second edition equivalent

    DISPOSE(p)

where p is a pointer (of type P = POINTER TO T) to the variable to be destroyed.

    Note that the lifetime of a variable created by ALLOCATE or NEW is not related either to the block in which it is created, or to the block in which pointer variables referencing it are declared. To maintain storage economy it is the programmer's responsibility to ensure that all such unwanted variables are disposed of, or deallocated, before the pointers to them are lost.

    After a referenced-variable has been deallocated, the values of any pointer variables which pointed to it are conceptually undefined. It is a serious programming error to use such a *dangling* pointer value in any way. For the same reason it is an error to dispose of a referenced-variable while it, or any of its components, is in use as a variable parameter, or as the record variable of a with-statement. However, implementations usually do not detect such errors, so extreme care must be taken by the programmer to ensure that these errors are not made.

    Since the procedures ALLOCATE and DEALLOCATE are provided by a library module called Storage, any program using them must include in its heading an import-list:

    FROM Storage IMPORT ALLOCATE, DEALLOCATE;

    On most implementations which support the abbreviations NEW and DISPOSE, calls of these procedures are actually translated by the implementation into calls of ALLOCATE and DEALLOCATE which perform the actual storage allocation and deallocation required. Thus, although NEW and DISPOSE are *standard* identifiers in such implementations, and do not themselves have to be imported, programs using them are usually required to include an import-list citing ALLOCATE and DEALLOCATE, as above.

PROGRAMMING A STACK

To illustrate the use of these pointer facilities, consider the organization of a *stack*. A stack is a data structure consisting of a variable number of components of the same type. A new component may be *pushed* onto the stack, or an existing component *popped* off the stack, such that the component popped off is always that most recently pushed onto the stack.

    To represent a stack, of characters say, we use a chain of record variables, each of which holds one character and a pointer to the next record in the chain. The necessary type definitions are

```
TYPE StackPointer = POINTER TO StackComponent;
     StackComponent = RECORD
                        Ch: CHAR;
```

            Next: StackPointer
            END;

The records will be chained in the order in which the characters are to be popped off the stack, with a pointer variable Stack pointing to the next record for popping at all times

    VAR Stack: StackPointer;

Thus, if characters *A*, *B*, and *C* have been pushed onto the stack in that order the representation will be as shown in Figure 11.7. Note that the value NIL is held in the pointer field of the last record to indicate that no further records exist in the chain. An empty stack, i.e., one containing no components, is represented by assigning the value NIL to the variable Stack itself.

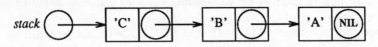

Figure 11.7   A stack of characters

The operation of pushing a new character X onto the stack can be expressed as a call of a procedure Push, defined as follows:

    PROCEDURE Push(X: CHAR);
    VAR NewComponent: StackPointer;
    BEGIN
      ALLOCATE(NewComponent, SIZE(StackComponent));
      WITH NewComponent^ DO Ch := X; Next := Stack END;
      Stack := NewComponent
    END Push;

Assuming a stack representation as shown in Figure 11.7, execution of the call Push('D') would produce the representation shown in Figure 11.8.

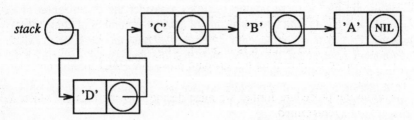

Figure 11.8   After *Push('D')*

The operation of popping a character value off the stack and assigning it to a character variable X can be expressed as a procedure Pop, defined as follows:

```
PROCEDURE Pop(VAR X: CHAR);
  VAR OldComponent: StackPointer;
  BEGIN
    OldComponent := Stack;
    WITH OldComponent^ DO X := Ch; Stack := Next END;
    DEALLOCATE(OldComponent, SIZE(StackComponent))
  END Pop;
```

Executing this procedure on the stack representation shown in Figure 11.8 would restore that shown in Figure 11.7. The procedure Pop should only be executed when Stack <> NIL, i.e., when the stack is not empty. Execution of any equal number of pushes and pops on an initially empty stack will restore the empty condition Stack = NIL.

Use of this stack is illustrated by the following statement-sequence which reads a sequence of characters up to a period and prints out the sequence in reverse order.

```
Stack := NIL;
REPEAT Read(Ch); Push(Ch) UNTIL Ch = ".";
REPEAT Pop(Ch); Write(Ch) UNTIL Stack = NIL
```

This sequence thus achieves the same effect as the recursive procedure ReverseInput which was given in Chapter 7. Furthermore it achieves a similar economy of storage, in that the stack grows to the exact size required for reversal of the input sequence involved. In general, using records linked by pointers to realize a stack ensures that only as much storage is used by the stack at any moment as its current number of components requires. Using an array for the same purpose would involve setting aside a fixed amount of storage throughout the stack's lifetime, which is sufficient for the maximum height of stack expected. This flexible use of storage is a significant advantage of the pointer mechanism. Case Study 14, which follows, illustrates two further situations in which this flexibility is exploited.

CASE STUDY 14

The program developed in Case Study 9 produced a sorted concordance of the words found in an input text. Let us now extend the specification of the program as follows. The output is to list all the words used, sorted in dictionary order, and give, for each word, a list of the numbers of all lines on which it occurs, where the lines in the input text are assumed to be numbered from 1. Upper-case and lower-case spellings will again be considered identical, and the concordance will record the spelling of each word in upper-case form.

Using the basic notions conceived in Case Study 9, the overall program structure required is clearly:

```
GetNextWord;
WHILE NOT EndOfWords DO
  record word occurrence;
  GetNextWord
END;
print sorted list of words and occurrences
```

The development of the procedure GetNextWord remains as before, except that it must now keep track of the number of the line on which each word occurs. This is easily accomplished by introducing a global variable

```
VAR Line: CARDINAL;
```

to represent the number of the line being read at any moment, and extending the procedure GetNextWord as shown below:

```
PROCEDURE GetNextWord;
  VAR I, Length: [0..MaxWordLength];
  BEGIN
    IF Done THEN
      REPEAT
        IF NextCh = EOL THEN INC(Line) END;
        Read(NextCh)
      UNTIL NOT Done OR Letter(NextCh);
    END;
    IF Done THEN
      Length := 0;
      REPEAT
        Word[Length] := CAP(NextCh); Length := Length + 1;
        Read(NextCh)
      UNTIL NOT Done OR NOT Letter(NextCh);
      FOR I := Length TO MaxWordLength - 1 DO Word[I] := " " END
    ELSE EndOfWords := TRUE
    END
  END GetNextWord;
```

To remember if the preceding word was immediately followed by an EOL, the variable NextCh must also be global, and to number the first line correctly these global variables are initialized thus:

```
Line := 1; NextCh := " ";
```

Now consider the additional processes of recording and printing the cross-reference of words occurring in the text. Clearly a data structure is required in which word occurrences are recorded during text printing for subsequent printing.

A logical structure for this list is to create one record for each distinct word encountered, each record holding a list of occurrences for that word. The process of recording each occurrence of a word in the list then breaks down into two steps

locate word in list;
add this line to its list of occurrences

where *locate word in list* is assumed to create a new record for a word not previously recorded, and initialize its list of occurrences as empty.

In Case Study 9 we used a simple one-dimensional array to record the distinct words found in the input text. This had the disadvantage that some limit had to be placed on the number of distinct words which might occur, and an array of this limiting size had to be used, whatever the number of distinct words in the actual input might be. With pointers we can now construct an alternative form of list in which the number of entries provided is exactly that required by the input at any moment. We might use a linear chained list of word records by defining the types

```
TYPE WordPointer = POINTER TO WordRecord;
     WordRecord  = RECORD
                       Spelling: WordSpelling;
                       Occurrences: ListOfOccurrences;
                       Next: WordPointer
                   END;
```

The complete list of words is then represented by a single pointer variable pointing to the first word in the list:

```
VAR WordList: WordPointer;
```

and the recording of a word occurrence can now be expressed as a call to the procedure:

```
PROCEDURE RecordWord(Word: WordSpelling; Line: CARDINAL);
VAR ThisWord: WordPointer;
BEGIN
  LocateWordInList(Word, ThisWord);
  AddOccurrence(Line, ThisWord^.Occurrences)
END RecordWord;
```

Since the words have to be printed out in dictionary order it is logical to build the list in this order. The procedure LocateWordInList therefore takes the form:

```
PROCEDURE LocateWordInList(WordSought: WordSpelling;
                            VAR WordFound: WordPointer);
BEGIN
  search word list until either a word >= WordSought
  is encountered or the end of the list is reached;
  create a new word record if necessary
END LocateWord;
```

Searching the list involves a repetition which terminates when either a word spelling alphabetically greater than or equal to WordSought is encountered, or the list has been completely searched. In either case a pointer to the previous word may be needed for the subsequent insertion, so a suitable coding is as shown below, where we assume the function Compare used in Case Study 9.

```
ThisWord := WordList; PreviousWord := NIL;
WHILE (ThisWord <> NIL) AND
      Compare(ThisWord^.Spelling, WordSought) = LessThan DO
  PreviousWord := ThisWord; ThisWord := ThisWord^.Next
END
```

Note that since the second operand of the AND operator in the while-statement is not evaluated when ThisWord = NIL, no attempt to access the Spelling field of the variable referenced by ThisWord will occur in this case.

The step *create a new word record if necessary* is then expressible as:

```
IF ThisWord <> NIL THEN
  IF Compare(ThisWord^.Spelling, WordSought) = Equals THEN
    WordFound := ThisWord
  ELSE insert a new record (before ThisWord^)
  END
ELSE insert a new record at end of list
END
```

In either case the entries to precede and follow the new record are indicated by PreviousWord and ThisWord, so each insertion process is expressible as a call to a local procedure InsertWord:

```
PROCEDURE InsertWord;
  VAR NewWord: WordPointer;
  BEGIN
    ALLOCATE(NewWord, SIZE(WordRecord));
    WITH NewWord^ DO
      Spelling := WordSought;
      Occurrences := none;
      Next := ThisWord
    END;
```

```
      IF PreviousWord = NIL THEN WordList := NewWord
      ELSE PreviousWord^.Next := NewWord
      END;
      WordFound := NewWord
   END InsertWord;
```

Note that the insertion of a new record in the ordered list is achieved without any movement or copying of existing records—a significant advantage of the linked-list representation.

The informal statement

Occurrences := none

cannot be programmed until we determine a representation for the list of occurrences. How should we represent the list of occurrences for each word? The length of these lists may vary considerably—for some words only one or two occurrences may be recorded, while for other commonly used words long lists may be built up. This variation in length can again be accommodated in a representation based on pointers. The components of each list of occurrences (which are simply line numbers) are added to the list in the same order as they are to be printed, i.e., in ascending order of line number. Such a linear list is known as a *queue*, and can be represented as a chain of records with pointers leading from the first to the last, and two auxiliary pointers which indicate these first and last records at all times. Such a list of occurrences can be realized in Modula-2 by the following type definitions:

```
TYPE LinePointer = POINTER TO LineRecord;
     LineRecord = RECORD
                     Line: CARDINAL;
                     NextLine: LinePointer
                  END;
     ListOfOccurrences = RECORD First, Last: LinePointer END;
```

The list of occurrences for a word occurring on lines 3, 21 and 247 would be represented as in Figure 11.9.

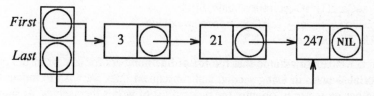

Figure 11.9   A list of occurrences

The process of adding the current line number to a given list of occurrences is then expressible as a call of a procedure AddOccurrence:

```
PROCEDURE AddOccurrence( NewLine: CARDINAL;
                            VAR List: ListOfOccurrences);
  VAR Occurrence: LinePointer;
  BEGIN
    ALLOCATE(Occurrence, SIZE(LineRecord));
    WITH Occurrence^ DO Line := NewLine; NextLine := NIL END;
    WITH List DO
      IF First = NIL THEN First := Occurrence
      ELSE Last^.NextLine := Occurrence
      END;
      Last := Occurrence
    END
  END AddOccurrence;
```

The process of printing out a sorted list held in linked list format is also a simple list traversal loop:

```
PROCEDURE PrintWords;
  VAR ThisWord: WordPointer;
  BEGIN
    WriteString("Crossreference of words and occurrences");
    WriteLn; WriteLn;
    ThisWord := WordList;
    WHILE ThisWord <> NIL DO
      print spelling and occurrences of ThisWord^;
      ThisWord := ThisWord^.Next
    END
  END PrintWords;
```

Printing the list of occurrences is in principle a simple loop process of the form:

```
ThisOccurrence := List.First;
REPEAT
  WriteCard(ThisOccurrence^.Line, 6);
  ThisOccurrence := ThisOccurrence^.NextLine
UNTIL ThisOccurrence = NIL
```

However, we cannot assume that the list of line numbers for any word fits on a single printed line. In using second and subsequent lines we wish to indent the first number so as not to obscure the ordered list of words themselves, as shown in Figure 11.10.

If we assume the output concordance may use a maximum of Max-LineLength characters per line, we have MaxWordLength characters for the

```
        .
        .
        .
TAMELY       9    113
THE          1      5    11   . . .
            93     99   106   . . .
           111
TOWN        46
        .
        .
        .
```

Figure 11.10

words themselves, and MaxListLength (= MaxLineLength–MaxWordLength) characters for the occurrence lists. Using a variable SpaceLeftOnLine, as in Case Study 11, to indicate the number of remaining print positions on the current line of the printout, the complete task of printing one word and its list of occurrences is thus

```
PROCEDURE PrintOccurrences(Word: WordSpelling;
                           List: ListOfOccurrences);
  VAR SpaceLeftOnLine: CARDINAL; I: [0..MaxWordLength–1];
      ThisOccurrence: LinePointer;
  BEGIN
    WriteString(Word); SpaceLeftOnLine := MaxListLength;
    ThisOccurrence := List.First;
    REPEAT
      IF SpaceLeftOnLine < 6 THEN
        WriteLn;
        FOR I := 0 TO MaxWordLength – 1 DO Write (" ") END;
        SpaceLeftOnLine := MaxListLength
      END;
      WriteCard(ThisOccurrence^.Line, 6);
      SpaceLeftOnLine := SpaceLeftOnLine – 6;
      ThisOccurrence := ThisOccurrence^.NextLine
    UNTIL ThisOccurrence = NIL;
    WriteLn
  END PrintOccurrences;
```

Any program which creates a data structure using dynamically created variables should deallocate those variables as soon as they are no longer needed. In this case the word list and each list of occurrences could be disposed of as they are printed, but in general a program is more flexible and less complex if such disposal is programmed as a separate process. Thus disposal may be expressed as a procedure DisposeWords to be called immediately after the call to Print-Words:

```
PROCEDURE DisposeWords;
 VAR ThisWord, NextWord: WordPointer;
 BEGIN
   NextWord := WordList;
   WHILE NextWord <> NIL DO
     ThisWord := NextWord;
     dispose of occurrences of ThisWord^;
     NextWord := ThisWord^.Next;
     DEALLOCATE(ThisWord, SIZE(WordRecord))
   END
 END DisposeWords;
```

Note that the list disposal loop requires *two* pointer variables—one of which holds the pointer to the next record on the list while the current record is deallocated using the other. Deallocation of each list of occurrences can be expressed as a call to a similar procedure DisposeOccurrences.

The complete program CrossReference is shown, together with the output produced by it for the same input file as was used for Case Studies 9 and 11.

```
MODULE CrossReference;

FROM InOut IMPORT
  EOL, Done, OpenInput, CloseInput, Read, ReadCard,
  OpenOutput, CloseOutput, Write, WriteString, WriteCard, WriteLn;
FROM Storage IMPORT ALLOCATE, DEALLOCATE;

(* This program reads an input text file, whose lines are assumed
   to be numbered from 1, and outputs a sorted concordance
   showing all words occurring in the text, with a list of the
   line numbers at which each word occurs.                          *)

CONST LineNumberWidth = 6; MaxLineLength = 50;
      MaxListLength = MaxLineLength–MaxWordLength;


(* —— Input of words from the input text file —— *)

CONST MaxWordLength = 16;

TYPE WordSpelling = ARRAY [0..MaxWordLength–1] OF CHAR;

VAR Word: WordSpelling; Line: CARDINAL;
    EndOfWords: BOOLEAN; NextCh: CHAR;
```

```
PROCEDURE Letter(Ch: CHAR): BOOLEAN;
BEGIN
  RETURN ((Ch >= 'A') AND (Ch <= 'Z')) OR ((Ch >= 'a') AND (Ch <= 'z'))
END Letter;

PROCEDURE GetNextWord;
(* This procedure puts the next word from the input in the global variable
  Word, if one exists; otherwise it sets the global EndOfWords true.
  The line number at which the next word occurs is maintained in the
  global Line. The global NextCh is used to remember the character
  following each word. These two variables should be initialized thus:
  Line := 1; NextCh := " "; before the first call to GetNextWord.        *)
VAR I, Length: [0..MaxWordLength];
BEGIN
  IF Done THEN
    REPEAT
      IF NextCh = EOL THEN INC(Line) END;
      Read(NextCh)
    UNTIL NOT Done OR Letter(NextCh);
  END;
  IF Done THEN
    Length := 0;
    REPEAT
      Word[Length] := CAP(NextCh); Length := Length + 1;
      Read(NextCh)
    UNTIL NOT Done OR NOT Letter(NextCh);
    FOR I := Length TO MaxWordLength – 1 DO Word[I] := " " END
  ELSE EndOfWords := TRUE
  END
END GetNextWord;

(* —— Representation and manipulation of lists of occurrences —— *)

TYPE LinePointer = POINTER TO LineRecord;
     LineRecord  = RECORD Line: CARDINAL; NextLine: LinePointer END;
     ListOfOccurrences = RECORD First, Last: LinePointer END;

PROCEDURE InitOccurrences(VAR List: ListOfOccurrences);
  (* initialize list of occurrences List as empty *)
BEGIN
  WITH List DO First := NIL; Last := NIL END
END InitOccurrences;
```

```
PROCEDURE AddOccurrence(NewLine: CARDINAL;
                              VAR List: ListOfOccurrences);
  (* append line number NewLine to list of occurrences List *)
  VAR Occurrence: LinePointer;
  BEGIN
    ALLOCATE(Occurrence, SIZE(LineRecord));
    WITH Occurrence^ DO Line := NewLine; NextLine := NIL END;
    WITH List DO
      IF First = NIL THEN First := Occurrence
      ELSE Last^.NextLine := Occurrence
      END;
      Last := Occurrence
    END
  END AddOccurrence;

PROCEDURE PrintOccurrences(Word: WordSpelling;
                              List: ListOfOccurrences);

  (* prints the word Word and the given occurrence list in format

      wwwwwwwwww  ooo ooo ooo ...
                      ooo ooo ...

    where LineNumberWidth defines the fieldwidth for each occurrence,
    and MaxListLength the maximum length of each occurrences line.   *)

  VAR SpaceLeftOnLine: CARDINAL; I: [0..MaxWordLength−1];
      ThisOccurrence: LinePointer;

  BEGIN
    WriteString(Word); SpaceLeftOnLine := MaxListLength;
    ThisOccurrence := List.First;
    REPEAT
      IF SpaceLeftOnLine < LineNumberWidth THEN
        WriteLn;
        FOR I := 0 TO MaxWordLength − 1 DO Write(" ") END;
        SpaceLeftOnLine := MaxListLength
      END;
      WriteCard(ThisOccurrence^.Line, LineNumberWidth);
      SpaceLeftOnLine := SpaceLeftOnLine−LineNumberWidth;
      ThisOccurrence := ThisOccurrence^.NextLine
    UNTIL ThisOccurrence = NIL;
    WriteLn
  END PrintOccurrences;
```

```
PROCEDURE DisposeOccurrences(List: ListOfOccurrences);
  (* dispose of given occurrence list *)
  VAR ThisOccurrence, NextOccurrence: LinePointer;
  BEGIN
    NextOccurrence := List.First;
    WHILE NextOccurrence <> NIL DO
      ThisOccurrence := NextOccurrence;
      NextOccurrence := ThisOccurrence^.NextLine;
      DEALLOCATE(ThisOccurrence, SIZE(LineRecord))
    END
  END DisposeOccurrences;


(* —— Representation and manipulation of the list of words —— *)

TYPE WordPointer = POINTER TO WordRecord;
     WordRecord  = RECORD
                        Spelling: WordSpelling;
                        Occurrences: ListOfOccurrences;
                        Next: WordPointer
                   END;

VAR WordList: WordPointer;

PROCEDURE LocateWordInList(WordSought: WordSpelling;
                           VAR WordFound: WordPointer);
  (* Locate entry for word sought in the ordered list pointed
     to by WordList, creating a new entry if necessary, and
     returning a pointer to the entry located in WordFound.   *)
  VAR  ThisWord, PreviousWord: WordPointer;
  TYPE Relation = (LessThan, Equals, GreaterThan);
  PROCEDURE Compare(W1, W2: WordSpelling): Relation;
    VAR I: [0..MaxWordLength–1];
    BEGIN
      I := 0;
      LOOP
        IF W1[I] < W2[I] THEN RETURN LessThan
        ELSIF W1[I] > W2[I] THEN RETURN GreaterThan
        ELSIF I = MaxWordLength–1 THEN RETURN Equals
        ELSE I := I + 1
        END
      END
    END Compare;
```

```
    PROCEDURE InsertWord;
    (* create new entry for WordSought at list position
       delimited by PreviousWord and ThisWord pointers. *)
    VAR NewWord: WordPointer;
    BEGIN
      ALLOCATE(NewWord, SIZE(WordRecord));
      WITH NewWord^ DO
        Spelling := WordSought;
        InitOccurrences(Occurrences);
        Next := ThisWord
      END;
      IF PreviousWord = NIL THEN WordList := NewWord
      ELSE PreviousWord^.Next := NewWord
      END;
      WordFound := NewWord
    END InsertWord;

  BEGIN (* LocateWordInList *)
    ThisWord := WordList;  PreviousWord := NIL;
    WHILE (ThisWord <> NIL) AND
            (Compare(ThisWord^.Spelling, WordSought) = LessThan) DO
      PreviousWord := ThisWord; ThisWord := ThisWord^.Next
    END;
    IF ThisWord <> NIL THEN
      IF Compare(ThisWord^.Spelling, WordSought) = Equals THEN
        WordFound := ThisWord
      ELSE InsertWord
      END
    ELSE InsertWord
    END
  END LocateWordInList;

PROCEDURE RecordWord(Word: WordSpelling; Line: CARDINAL);
(* record occurrence of word Word on line Line *)
VAR ThisWord: WordPointer;
BEGIN
  LocateWordInList(Word, ThisWord);
  AddOccurrence(Line, ThisWord^.Occurrences)
END RecordWord;
```

```
PROCEDURE PrintWords;
  (* print words and occurrence lists from list WordList *)
  VAR ThisWord: WordPointer;
  BEGIN
    WriteString("Crossreference of words and occurrences:");
    WriteLn; WriteLn;
    ThisWord := WordList;
    WHILE ThisWord <> NIL DO
      WITH ThisWord^ DO PrintOccurrences(Spelling, Occurrences) END;
      ThisWord := ThisWord^.Next
    END
  END PrintWords;

PROCEDURE DisposeWords;
  (* dispose of words and occurrence lists in list WordList *)
  VAR ThisWord, NextWord: WordPointer;
  BEGIN
    NextWord := WordList;
    WHILE NextWord <> NIL DO
      ThisWord := NextWord;
      DisposeOccurrences(ThisWord^.Occurrences);
      NextWord := ThisWord^.Next;
      DEALLOCATE(ThisWord, SIZE(WordRecord))
    END
  END DisposeWords;

(* —— The controlling program —— *)
BEGIN
  OpenInput(""); WriteLn;
  IF Done THEN
    WordList := NIL;
    Line := 1; NextCh := " "; EndOfWords := FALSE; GetNextWord;
    WHILE NOT EndOfWords DO
      RecordWord(Word, Line); GetNextWord
    END;
    PrintWords; DisposeWords; CloseInput
  END
END CrossReference.
```

```
Enter Input File Name: PROFILE

Crossreference of words and occurrences:

AN                 3
AUTOMATICALLY      3
DISPLAYS           5
EACH               6
EDITED             3
EXECUTION          5
FORMATTED          4
FREQUENCY          5
IS                 3
LISTING            4
OF                 4      6
PROFILE            1      3
PROGRAM            4      6
SOURCE             4
STATEMENT          6
THE                1      3      4      5      6
WHICH              5
```

NON-LINEAR STRUCTURES

In our use of pointers so far we have illustrated three forms of *linear* structure:

(a) a *stack*, which is extended and reduced at one end only;
(b) a *queue*, which is extended at one end but accessed from the other;
(c) an *ordered list*, whose extension may involve an insertion at any point in the existing list.

All of these structures can be realized as a sequence of records, each of which contains a single pointer to the next record in the list.

However, each record of the ordered list of words built by the program CrossReference in Case Study 14 also contained a pointer (or rather two pointers) to the corresponding queue of occurrences. The overall structure was thus as illustrated in Figure 11.11. Viewed as a whole this is not a linear structure, and it shows clearly that any node or record within a linked structure which contains two or more pointers to other nodes creates a potential non-linearity. Modula-2's pointers can thus be used without further extension to realize non-linear structures of arbitrary complexity.

The program CrossReference provides a further opportunity to illustrate the (judicious) use of pointers in creating non-linear structures. Representation of the ordered list of words as a linked linear list enabled the amount of storage

Words

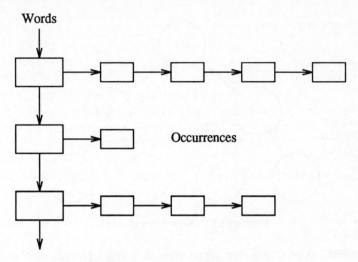

Figure 11.11   Words and occurrences: overall structure

used to be limited to that required by the list at any moment, and allowed insertion of new words in the ordered list without any movement or copying of existing words. However, the simple linear linkage meant that the list could only be
searched for an existing word, or to determine the correct position for a new one,
by a linear traversal of the list. For long lists such a linear search is a time-
consuming process.

A faster search can be achieved, and the storage and insertion flexibility of
the linked list retained, by holding the list as a *binary tree*. Figure 11.12 shows
how the words of the sentence

the white dog chased the little yellow van

might be held as a binary tree. The node for the word *the* is called the *root* of
the tree, while those for *chased, little, van* and *yellow* are called its *leaves*. The
tree is *sorted* in that for each node the words in its left subtree precede, in dictionary order, the word at that node, while the words in the right subtree succeed
that word.

Such a tree can be represented in Modula-2 using records connected by
pointers defined as

```
TYPE WordPointer = POINTER TO WordRecord;
     WordRecord  = RECORD
                        Spelling: WordSpelling;
                        Occurrences: ListOfOccurrences;
                        Predecessors, Successors: WordPointer
                   END;
```

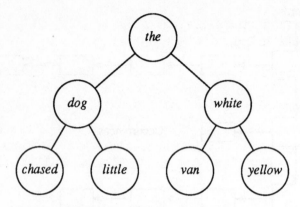

Figure 11.12   Binary tree of words

The complete word tree is then represented as a single pointer variable which points to its root:

    VAR WordTree: WordPointer;

An empty tree, and hence the subtrees of each leaf node, are represented by the value NIL.

A binary tree is inherently recursive in structure, since each node is defined in terms of two further trees of the same form. The process of locating an existing entry, or creating a new entry, in such a tree is simply expressed as a recursive procedure with the following outline:

```
PROCEDURE LocateWordIn(VAR ThisTree: WordPointer);
  BEGIN
    IF ThisTree is empty THEN
      create a leaf node as ThisTree
    ELSIF root word > word sought THEN
      LocateWordIn(Predecessors)
    ELSIF root word < word sought THEN
      LocateWordIn(Successors)
    ELSE root is word sought
    END
  END LocateWordIn;
```

Each step in the searching process which this procedure implements halves the area of subsequent search, since it chooses either the predecessors or successors subtree of the current node. This halving process leads to an average search time proportional to $log_2 N$, where there are N words in the tree. In practice this logarithmic performance is guaranteed only if the tree is *balanced*, i.e., there is an equal number of words in the predecessors and successors subtrees at each node. With the simple insertion process outlined above, the balance of the tree depends upon the order of insertion of the words involved. The example sentence used in Figure 11.12 leads to an exactly balanced tree, but not all data are so well chosen. However, the words encountered in any sizeable natural text are sufficiently random in order to produce a reasonably balanced tree, and hence an average search time which is close to the ideal log_2N.

The procedure LocateWord of the program CrossReference may now therefore be written using a local recursive procedure of this form, as shown below.

```
PROCEDURE LocateWord(WordSought: WordSpelling;
                     VAR WordFound: WordPointer);

  PROCEDURE LocateWordIn (VAR ThisTree: WordPointer);
  ... as outlined above ...

BEGIN
  LocateWordIn (WordTree)
END LocateWord;
```

In this context the details of the recursive procedure are easily settled, thus

```
PROCEDURE LocateWordIn(VAR ThisTree: WordPointer);
BEGIN
  IF ThisTree = NIL THEN
    ALLOCATE(ThisTree, SIZE(WordRecord));
    WITH ThisTree^ DO
      Spelling := WordSought; InitOccurrences(Occurrences);
      Predecessors := NIL; Successors := NIL
    END;
    WordFound := ThisTree
  ELSE
    WITH ThisTree^ DO
      IF Compare(Spelling, WordSought) = GreaterThan THEN
        LocateWordIn(Predecessors)
      ELSIF Compare(Spelling, WordSought) = LessThan THEN
        LocateWordIn(Successors)
      ELSE WordFound := ThisTree
      END
    END
  END
END LocateWordIn;
```

The process of printing out a sorted list held as a binary tree is also expressible as a recursive procedure. For any non-empty tree the predecessors in the left subtree must be printed before the word at the root node itself, and the successors in the right subtree after it:

```
PROCEDURE PrintWordsIn(ThisTree: WordPointer);
  BEGIN
    IF ThisTree <> NIL THEN
      WITH ThisTree^ DO
        PrintWordsIn(Predecessors);
        PrintOccurrences(Spelling, Occurrences);
        PrintWordsIn(Successors)
      END
    END
  END PrintWordsIn;
```

The body of the procedure PrintWords used in Case Study 14 then becomes

```
BEGIN
  WriteString("Crossreference of words and occurrences"); WriteLn; WriteLn;
  PrintWordsIn(WordTree)
END
```

Disposal of the word list is accomplished by a similarly recursive procedure:

```
PROCEDURE DisposeWords(ThisTree: WordPointer);
  BEGIN
    IF ThisTree <> NIL THEN
      WITH ThisTree^ DO
        DisposeWords(Predecessors);
        DisposeOccurrences(Occurrences);
        DisposeWords(Successors)
      END;
      DEALLOCATE(ThisTree, SIZE(WordRecord))
    END
  END DisposeWords;
```

The linear word list used in Case Study 14 may thus be replaced by a binary tree, simply by redefining the record-type WordRecord, and rewriting the procedures LocateWord, PrintWords and DisposeWords which manipulate these records. The resultant program should run faster on texts of significant length.

The binary tree structure was achieved simply by introducing two components of type WordPointer into each WordRecord rather than one. In a similar way a variety of non-linear structures can be realized, by including an appropriate set of linking pointers in each component node. This power which the pointer mechanism provides should be used with caution, however, as the complexity of the data structures realized can quickly go beyond our intellectual grasp, and errors in the programs which manipulate them are difficult to diagnose.

EXERCISES

11.1 The program developed in Case Study 14 uses a single pointer variable
WordList. Modify the program to use an array

VAR WordList: ARRAY ["A".."Z"] OF WordPointer;

each element of which is a pointer to the head of a linked list of words
beginning with the corresponding letter.

11.2 An office block accommodates employees in rooms occupied by one or
more people, each room having one telephone. An internal telephone
directory for the block is available as an input file, each line of which contains an employee's name (a 16 character string) and telephone number.
The lines are in alphabetic order of employee's names. Write a program
which will read the directory and output a series of lists of the employees
in each room (together with the number of the telephone in that room).
The lists are to be output in ascending order of telephone number, and the
names of the employees in each room are to be output in alphabetic order.

11.3 Rewrite the program developed in Case Study 10 to hold the league table
as an array of pointers, each element of which points to the corresponding
TeamDetails record. What effect does this change have on the efficiency
of the program?

11.4 A polynomial of arbitrary degree is representable as a sequence of
coefficient-degree pairs, preferably held in descending order of degree.
For example, the polynomial

$$x^8 + 5x^6 - 7x^5 + 6x + 1$$

may be represented as

$$(1,8), (5,6), (-7,5), (6,1), (1,0)$$

Define a pointer-type which enables such a sequence to be held in a linked
list.
Write a procedure ReadPolynomial which reads a positive integer indicating the number of terms in a polynomial, followed by the ordered
coefficient-degree pairs. For example, the above polynomial would be
input as

$$5\ 1\ 8\ 5\ 6\ -7\ 5\ 6\ 1\ 1\ 0$$

The procedure should build the linked-list representation of the polynomial.
Write two functions Sum and Product, each of which takes two pointers
representing polynomials as parameters, and returns as result a polynomial

which is the sum and product, respectively, of the parameters. Use these in a program which reads the input representations of the following polynomials

$$3x^2 + 9x + 1$$
$$x^3 - 3x^2 - 5x$$

calculates their sum and product, and outputs the results in the form

```
SUM = x^3 + 4x + 1
PRODUCT = 3x^5 - 41x^3 - 48x^2 - 5x
```

12

Modules

THE MODULE CONCEPT

The program developed in Case Study 14 is significantly more complex than those before it in this book, mainly because it involves several subproblems whose solutions must be combined to achieve the required effect. The overall form of the program can be expressed as follows:

initialize input of text;
initialize list of words;
REPEAT
  get word and its line number from input text;
  record word and line number in list
UNTIL *end of words;*
print words in list

At this level we may identify two abstractions involved:

(a) a stream of word and line number pairs which are extracted from the input text one by one, and
(b) a list of the words extracted so far which will record all occurrences of each.

Solution of the overall problem involves some realization, in terms of the concepts provided by Modula-2, of each of these abstractions.

In practice, the stream of word and line number pairs was expressed as a procedure GetNextWord which updated the variables Word, Line and EndOf-Words to represent the next word, if any, in the input stream when required. To enable proper detection of an end of line immediately following any word, a further global variable NextCh was also required by GetNextWord, so that the total contribution of the word stream abstraction to the program may be summarized as the declarations:

```
CONST MaxWordLength = ...;

TYPE WordSpelling = ...;

VAR Word: WordSpelling; Line: CARDINAL;
    EndOfWords: BOOLEAN; NextCh: CHAR;

PROCEDURE GetNextWord; ...;
```

together with an initialization sequence

```
NextCh := " "; Line := 1; EndOfWords := FALSE;
```

Now consider how we implemented the list of words. To achieve the required program effect the word list abstraction must allow operations to record a word and line number pair and to print the entire list contents in dictionary order, together with whatever initial action is required to start an empty list.

Since the number of words in the list is unpredictable and may vary widely from one use of the program to the next, the list was represented as a chain of records connected by pointers defined as follows:

```
WordPointer = POINTER TO WordRecord;
WordRecord  = RECORD
                  Spelling: WordSpelling;
                  Occurrences: ListOfOccurrences;
                  Next: WordPointer
              END;
```

The complete word list is then represented as a single pointer variable which points to the first record in the list:

```
VAR WordList: WordPointer;
```

The processes of recording a word in the word list, and of printing the ordered list of words and their occurrences, were then expressed as calls to the following procedures:

```
PROCEDURE RecordWord(Word: WordSpelling; Line: CARDINAL); ...;

PROCEDURE PrintWords; ...;
```

With the chained representation the list is trivially initialized as empty:

```
WordList := NiL
```

but the chained representation also required the introduction of a procedure

```
PROCEDURE DisposeWords; ...;
```

to dispose of the dynamically created variables involved.

Together, these declarations form the contribution of the word list abstraction to our cross-reference program. In implementing them, however, we isolated a further abstraction, which is the list of occurrences associated with each word. The operations required on each list of occurrences are as follows:

(a)   initializing it to represent no occurrences;
(b)   adding a line number as a new occurrence; and
(c)   printing a word and its list of occurrences in some suitable form.

Such a list of occurrences was realized by the following declarations:

```
ListPointer = POINTER TO LineRecord;
LineRecord  = RECORD Line: CARDINAL; NextLine: ListPointer END;
ListOfOccurrences = RECORD First, Last: ListPointer END;

PROCEDURE InitOccurrences(VAR List: ListOfOccurrences); ...;
PROCEDURE AddOccurrence(Line: CARDINAL;
                        VAR List: ListOfOccurrences); ...;
PROCEDURE PrintOccurrences(Word: WordSpelling;
                        Occurrences: ListOfOccurrences); ...;
PROCEDURE DisposeOccurrences(List: ListOfOccurrences); ...;
```

where the final procedure is again required to enable disposal of the dynamically created variables involved in each list.

Consider now what happens when we bring these implementations together to form the cross-reference program. The overall form of the program is as follows:

```
MODULE CrossReference;

CONST MaxWordLength = ...;
TYPE WordSpelling = ...;
VAR Word: WordSpelling; Line: CARDINAL;
    EndOfWords: BOOLEAN; NextCh: CHAR;
PROCEDURE GetNextWord; ...;

TYPE  LinePointer = ...;
      LineRecord = ...;
      ListOfOccurrences = ...;
PROCEDURE InitOccurrences(...); ...;
PROCEDURE AddOccurrence(...); ...;
PROCEDURE PrintOccurrences(...); ...;
PROCEDURE DisposeOccurrences(...); ...;

TYPE WordPointer = ...;
     WordRecord = ...;
VAR WordList: WordPointer;
PROCEDURE RecordWord(...); ...;
PROCEDURE PrintWords; ...;
PROCEDURE DisposeWords; ...;
```

```
BEGIN
...;
initialize word input;
initialize word list;
GetNextWord;
WHILE NOT EndOfWords DO
  RecordWord(Word, Line);
  GetNextWord
END;
PrintWords; DisposeWords;
...
END CrossReference.
```

The bulk of the final program is taken up with the implementation of the abstractions of an input word stream, a word list and of a list of occurrences. While introduction of these abstractions makes the main program loop very simple, and clearly benefited our derivation of the program, in its final form it has a number of significant disadvantages:

(a) Although the main program does not and should not make any use of it, the declaration of the variable NextCh appears in the main program block. This is necessary to ensure that the variable holds its value from one call of GetNextWord to the next.

(b) Although the main program does not and should not make any use of the way in which the abstraction of a word list is implemented, i.e., by using pointers, the corresponding pointer type declarations must appear in the main program block. This is the only way in Modula-2 that these definitions may be shared by the corresponding abstract operations Record-Word, PrintWords and DisposeWords.

(c) Similarly, although the abstraction of a list of occurrences is a secondary component of the word list abstraction itself, the type declarations supporting its implementation also have to appear in the main program block. The abstract operations AddOccurrence, PrintOccurrences and DisposeOccurrences could each be hidden within the respective procedures Record-Word, PrintWords and DisposeWords, but the type declarations that they share would still have to appear in the outermost block.

The presence of these declarations in the outermost block means that the main program body may inadvertently inspect and even alter the pointers involved in realizing the abstractions without violating any of the rules of Modula-2. Thus, in contrast to the built-in abstractions of the language, these program-defined abstractions are not protected from accidental misuse, since the program using them is not strictly confined to making calls on the procedures realizing the abstract operations.

For large programs that involve many more than two independent abstractions the danger of such unwanted interactions is greatly increased, and diagnosing the nature of such errors when they occur is extremely difficult because the assumed independence of the abstractions involved is no longer guaranteed. If the systematic use of program-defined abstractions is to be an effective tool in the construction of large programs it is desirable, therefore, that the programming language supports the mutual security of such abstractions. In the following sections we explore the *module* construct, which has precisely this property.

LOCAL MODULES

From the syntax definition of a *block* (given in Chapters 2 and 7), we see that a *module* may be declared anywhere in a program that a *procedure-declaration* may appear, and its syntax is similar to that of a *program-module*, viz.,

> *module-declaration* =
> *"MODULE" identifier [priority] ";"*
> *{import-list ";"} [export-list ";"]*
> *block identifier.*
> *import-list = ["FROM" identifier] "IMPORT" identifier-list.*
> *export-list = "EXPORT" ["QUALIFIED"] identifier-list.*

A module whose declaration is imbedded in an enclosing program, procedure, or module block is called a *local* module. For the moment we concentrate on such modules. We will see in later sections how *separately compiled* modules, such as InOut, ValidInput, etc. can be constructed.

The essential feature of modules is that they provide a tighter control over the scope and visibility of identifiers. The following subsections show how this facility can be used to overcome the program deficiencies noted above.

A Module for Word Input

In its simplest form the module construct acts as a bracket which controls the visibility of identifiers declared inside and outside the module. In the case of the word input abstraction this property can be exploited by enclosing the relevant declarations in a module of the following form:

```
MODULE WordInput;

    IMPORT EOL, Done, Read;

    EXPORT MaxWordLength, WordSpelling,
            Word, Line, EndOfWords, GetNextWord;

    CONST MaxWordLength = ...;
```

```
TYPE WordSpelling = ...;
VAR Word: WordSpelling; Line: CARDINAL;
    EndOfWords: BOOLEAN; NextCh: CHAR;
PROCEDURE GetNextWord; ...;
BEGIN
   NextCh := " "; Line := 1; EndOfWords := FALSE
END WordInput
```

The significant properties of this module are as follows:

(a) Identifiers declared outside the module are not visible inside it except those appearing in the import-list. In this case the module uses only the identifiers EOL, Done and Read as provided by the library module InOut. These must therefore be available in the enclosing block, i.e. they must already have been imported by the program module from InOut.

(b) Standard identifiers, such as CARDINAL, BOOLEAN, CHAR and FALSE, are an exception to (a). Their definitions are said to be *pervasive,* and are available in any module without explicit mention in an import-list.

(c) Identifiers declared within a module are not visible in the enclosing block, except those which appear in the export-list. In this case the enclosing program needs access to all identifiers declared within the module except NextCh, so all other identifiers are listed in the export-list. By omitting NextCh from this list access to it by the program block is precluded.

(d) The lifetime of variables declared within the module is the lifetime of the module itself, which is in turn the lifetime of all objects declared in the enclosing block. Thus in this case the variables Word, Line, EndOfWords, and NextCh all persist, and hold their values, between calls to GetNext-Word, even though NextCh is inaccessible to the program which makes these calls.

(e) The statement-part of the module itself acts as an initialization sequence for the variables declared within it. By definition this is executed before the enclosing program can make any use of the variables or procedures exported by the module. Thus, in this case the initialization of Line, EndOf-Words and NextCh is guaranteed and is no longer the main program's responsibility.

The WordInput module is said to *encapsulate* the declarations used to realize our original word input abstraction. This encapsulation has the two-fold advantage of protecting the variable NextCh from misuse by the main program, and of relieving the main program of the responsibility for initialization of the variables involved. Both properties reduce the likelihood of misuse of the abstraction by the program which uses it.

In addition, of course, the bringing together in an explicit module construct of all declarations and statements involved in realizing the word input abstraction emphasizes the relationship between them, and delimits them clearly from other parts of the program. This *separation of concerns* is a considerable clarification for anyone who has to read and understand the program, including its author!

A Word List Module

Now we consider the word list abstraction required in the cross-reference program. In principle, we can tackle the abstraction problem in exactly the same way, that is, we might produce a module with the following overall form:

```
MODULE WordList;

    IMPORT MaxWordLength, WordSpelling, Write, WriteString,
            WriteCard, WriteLn, ALLOCATE, DEALLOCATE;
    EXPORT RecordWord, PrintWords, DisposeWords;

    TYPE LinePointer = ...;
            LineRecord = ...;
            ListOfOccurrences = ...;
    PROCEDURE InitOccurrences(...); ...;
    PROCEDURE AddOccurrence(...); ...;
    PROCEDURE PrintOccurrences(...); ...;
    PROCEDURE DisposeOccurrences(...); ...;

    TYPE WordPointer = ...;
            WordRecord = ...;
    VAR FirstWord: WordPointer;
    PROCEDURE RecordWord(...); ...;
    PROCEDURE PrintWords; ...;
    PROCEDURE DisposeWords; ...;

    BEGIN
      FirstWord := NIL
    END WordList
```

The significant aspects of this module are as follows:

(a) The module depends explicitly on the constant identifier MaxWordLength, on the type identifier WordSpelling, and on the procedure identifiers Write, WriteString, WriteCard, WriteLn, ALLOCATE and DEALLOCATE. It must therefore import these from the enclosing program block. All such identifiers must be available for import in the enclosing program block, whether or not they are used in that block.

(b) The type definitions which realize the word list representation, and the pointer variable that indicates the first word of that list, are now declared within the module, and not exported, so that the representation of the word list is totally invisible to the using program. Only the necessary operations RecordWord, PrintWords and DisposeWords are exported.

(c) As in the case of NextCh, the lifetime of the variable FirstWord is the lifetime of the module itself which, as we have seen, is the lifetime of its enclosing block.

(d) The initialization of the word list has been expressed as the statement-part of the module itself. By definition this will be executed before the user program can make any call on RecordWord, PrintWords or DisposeWords. Thus, the initialization is again guaranteed and is no longer the main program's responsibility.

Thus the encapsulation of our word list abstraction as the module WordList has similar advantages to those of the WordInput module. In this case, however, all data and data types involved in representing the list are hidden from the main program. To the program using it, the module itself *is* the word list, and the only possible operations on it are those defined by the exported procedures RecordWord, PrintWords and DisposeWords. In this sense the WordList module is more secure against misuse than the WordInput module.

As outlined above, this encapsulation of the word list achieves the necessary separation of its implementation details from the program that uses it, but it is still unsatisfactory in that the details of representing lists of occurrences are mixed up with the details of the word list itself. Ideally, therefore, we want to further isolate these details in a module concerned only with lists of occurrences. Since these lists are used only as components of the word list itself, the natural place to locate such a module is within the WordList module, thus:

```
MODULE WordList;

    IMPORT MaxWordLength, WordSpelling, Write, WriteString,
            WriteCard, WriteLn, ALLOCATE, DEALLOCATE;
    EXPORT RecordWord, PrintWords, DisposeWords;

    MODULE Occurrences; ...;

    TYPE WordPointer = ...;
         WordRecord = ...;

    VAR FirstWord: WordPointer;

    PROCEDURE RecordWord(...); ...;
    PROCEDURE PrintWords; ...;
    PROCEDURE DisposeWords; ...;

    BEGIN
      FirstWord := NIL
    END WordList
```

Since the syntax of Modula-2 permits the nesting of module declarations, this is exactly what we do.

A List of Occurrences Module

Both the WordInput module and the WordList module declare variables on which their exported procedures operate. For the lists of occurrences, however, the requirements are somewhat different. Each occurrence list must be imbedded in a corresponding word record created by the WordList module. To enable this our Occurrences module therefore exports the *type* ListOfOccurrences together with a set of procedures which take variables of this type as parameter:

```
MODULE Occurrences;

    IMPORT MaxWordLength, WordSpelling, Write, WriteString,
        WriteCard, WriteLn, ALLOCATE, DEALLOCATE;
    EXPORT ListOfOccurrences, InitOccurrences, AddOccurrence,
        PrintOccurrences, DisposeOccurrences;

    CONST ...;

    TYPE LinePointer = ...;
        LineRecord = ...;
        ListOfOccurrences = ...;

    PROCEDURE InitOccurrences(...); ...;
    PROCEDURE AddOccurrence(...); ...;
    PROCEDURE PrintOccurrences(...); ...;
    PROCEDURE DisposeOccurrences(...); ...;

    END Occurrences
```

A module of this form, which exports a data type together with a set of procedures which operate on variables of that type is often known as a *package*. Since no data is declared within the module itself, no initialization is required, and the module has an empty statement-part. However, for each variable of the exported type created by the program using the module, the procedure InitOccurrences must be called before any other operation can be applied to it. These characteristics are typical of package modules in general.

The module imports a range of identifiers from the enclosing WordList module, which must again insure that they are available. Note, however, that the constant identifiers which control the format in which lists of occurrences are printed, namely MaxLineLength, MaxListLength and LineNumberWidth, have been localized within this module, since they are not relevant to any other part of the program.

The Overall Modular Program

With these three modules to realize the major abstractions involved in its creation, the overall form of the cross-reference program is now:

```
MODULE CrossReference;

FROM InOut IMPORT
  EOL, Done, OpenInput, CloseInput, Read,
  Write, WriteString, WriteCard, WriteLn;
FROM Storage IMPORT ALLOCATE, DEALLOCATE;

MODULE WordInput; ...;

MODULE WordList; ...;

BEGIN
  OpenInput(""); WriteLn;
  IF Done THEN
    GetNextWord;
    WHILE NOT EndOfWords DO
      RecordWord(Word, Line); GetNextWord
    END;
    PrintWords; DisposeWords; CloseInput
  END
END CrossReference.
```

The program module now consists entirely of

(a) the module declarations for the modules WordInput and WordList (the latter containing the nested declaration of the Occurrences module);
(b) a statement part which expresses the overall program action in terms of the facilities exported by these modules; and
(c) the import lists necessary to provide all library module facilities required by the program.

The program module is thus a direct reflection of the abstract model originally conceived for it, i.e., of a simple main program loop expressed in terms of two major abstractions, the detailed implementation of which are 'hidden' by the modules introduced. As such, the program structure both reinforces and protects this abstract model, contributing both to its clarity and to its security against programming error. These two properties, clarity and error security, are the essential benefits of the modularity introduced.

The cost of these benefits may be seen as the explicit definitions of the relationship between each module and the block containing it, as expressed in its import and export lists. If we include the nested Occurrences module, this cost may be summarized as follows:

```
MODULE CrossReference;
...
  MODULE WordInput;
    IMPORT EOL, Done, Read;
    EXPORT MaxWordLength, WordSpelling,
            Word, Line, EndOfWords, GetNextWord;
    ...
  END WordInput;

  MODULE WordList;
    IMPORT MaxWordLength, WordSpelling, Write, WriteString,
            WriteCard, WriteLn, ALLOCATE, DEALLOCATE;
    EXPORT RecordWord, PrintWords;

    ...
    MODULE Occurrences;
      IMPORT MaxWordLength, WordSpelling, Write, WriteString,
              WriteCard, WriteLn, ALLOCATE, DEALLOCATE;
      EXPORT ListOfOccurrences, InitOccurrences, AddOccurrence,
              PrintOccurrences, DisposeOccurrences;
      ...
    END Occurrences;

    ...
  END WordList;

  BEGIN
  ...
END CrossReference.
```

The import and export lists within each module delimit the interdependence
between the module and the surrounding block. Together with the declarations
of the identifiers concerned they define the *interface* between the module and
the surrounding block.

When compared with an unmodularized program, these import and export
lists represent the programming overhead involved in achieving modularity in
Modula-2. However, this overhead is more than outweighed by the clarification
of intermodular relationships which the lists provide. In large programs with
many modules, these lists play a significant role in guiding a programmer who
has to make changes or extensions to the existing program. By providing a precise identification of the interface involved, the lists reduce the likelihood of
changes being made which violate the intended interdependence of the module
and the block in which it is used. From the programmer's viewpoint the

modular structure delimits those parts of the program which are relatively independent of one another, while the import and export lists identify the necessary interdependencies that remain. Provided the programmer takes due account of this interdependence, changes within any module can be made without risk of causing unintended side-effects elsewhere in the program.

Qualified Export

Our modular cross-reference program illustrates the basic principles of identifier import and export as a means of delimiting the interface between a module and the block that uses it. In this subsection we look at additional aspects of import and export as defined in Modula-2, which have not been illustrated so far.

Since the modular cross-reference program was constructed from a valid unmodularized program, the identifiers exported from the modules introduced are necessarily distinct, and produce no conflicts with each other or with identifiers declared in the enclosing block.

Thus, the identifiers which are exported by the Occurrences module, namely ListOfOccurrences, InitOccurrences, AddOccurrence and PrintOccurrences, are distinct from any declared by the enclosing WordList module, and may be referred to in that module as though they had been declared there, i.e. simply as

```
ListOfOccurrences
AddOccurrence
etc.
```

These identifiers are said to be exported from Occurrences in *unqualified* form.

In general, however, it is possible that the identifiers chosen to denote the exported entities of a module clash with those exported by another module enclosed by the same block, or with those declared in the enclosing block itself—in some cases good reasons may exist for using the same identifiers in this way. Consider, for example, a program which contains two modules, one which maintains a stack of real numbers, and another which maintains a stack of integers:

```
MODULE Example1;
    ...
    MODULE RealStack;
        ...
        PROCEDURE Push(X: REAL); ...;
        PROCEDURE Pop(VAR X: REAL); ...;
        ...
    END RealStack;
```

```
MODULE IntegerStack;
...
PROCEDURE Push(X: INTEGER); ...;
PROCEDURE Pop(VAR X: INTEGER); ...;
...
END IntegerStack;
...
END Example1
```

It is natural to use the identifiers Push and Pop for the procedures defined by each module, but clearly both modules cannot export these procedures in unqualified form, since the meaning of either identifier would be ambiguous in the enclosing program block.

In such cases, identifiers may be exported in *qualified* form, by writing the export-list in the form:

```
EXPORT QUALIFIED Push, Pop;
```

in which case, in the surrounding block, these exported identifiers must be referred to as *qualified-identifiers*, in which the exported identifiers are prefixed with the exporting module's identifier, thus:

```
RealStack.Push(1.0)
IntegerStack.Push(0)
```

and the ambiguity is resolved.

Such qualified export may also be used to resolve a clash between an exported identifier and one which is declared in the enclosing block, thus:

```
MODULE Example2;

VAR X: INTEGER;

MODULE M1;
    EXPORT QUALIFIED X, Y, Z;
    VAR X, Y, Z: REAL;
    ...
    END M1;
...
END Example2
```

Throughout the module Example2 the identifier X denotes the integer variable declared by the module itself, while the qualified identifier M1.X denotes the real variable declared within the nested module M1.

Suppose now Example2 contains a second module M2 which needs to use the real variable X exported by M1. The module M2 cannot use an import-list of the form

IMPORT M1.X;

since a qualified identifier cannot appear in an import-list. One solution is for M2 to import the module name M1, thus

IMPORT M1;

and denote the real variable required as M1.X, but this has the effect of making M1.Y and M1.Z available as well, which may not be necessary. An alternative is to use *unqualifying import* thus:

FROM M1 IMPORT X;

in which case the real variable required may be denoted simply by X within M2. This unqualifying import thus has the twin advantages of being selective about which of the identifiers exported by M1 are imported by M2, and of eliminating the need for use of the qualified-identifier M1.X within M2.

These twin features, of qualified export and unqualifying import, enable the consequences of identifier conflicts to be minimized in modular programming. For programs which are built entirely with local modules nested within the program module itself, these problems are normally avoided by judicious choice of identifiers. In such programs qualified export and unqualifying import are only needed in unusual circumstances. As we shall see in later sections, however, the concepts of qualified export and unqualifying import have a more important role to play in programs built from *separately compiled* modules.

Implicit Import and Export

In principle, import and export lists give complete control over the visibility of identifiers across module boundaries. In practice, however, there are a number of situations in which identifiers declared on one side of a module boundary are usable on the other side without explicit mention in an import or export list. Three such situations can be identified in Modula-2:

(a) If a module exports an identifier which denotes a record-type, then the field-identifiers which denote fields of the type can be used outside the module, to access fields of variables of the type. These identifiers need not and cannot be mentioned in the export-list. The same rule applies if variables of a record-type, or types or variables with components of a record-type, are exported.

(b) If a module exports an identifier which denotes an enumerated type, then the constant-identifiers which denote the values of the type can be used outside the module, without explicit mention in the export-list.

(c) If a module A exports an identifier which denotes another module B declared somewhere within A, then the identifiers exported by B can be used outside A without explicit mention in the export-list of A.

Similar rules apply for implicit import of identifiers associated with record-types, enumerated-types, or modules referenced by import-lists.

The availability of field-identifiers, as described in (a), is a special case of the more general property that export of a type T, or of a variable of type T, by a module M automatically makes available all operations applicable to the type T. For a record-type these operations include access of individual fields via the field-identifiers concerned; for an array-type the operations include access of elements by subscripting, for a pointer-type they include dereferencing, and so on. Since all these operations are available for use, or visible, outside M, such an exported type is said to be *transparent*.

In some cases this transparency of an exported type may be contrary to the purpose of modularization, a problem to which we return after discussing separately compiled modules.

SEPARATELY COMPILED MODULES

Most modular programs may be viewed as a *program* module which is responsible for the overall effect required of the program, and one or more *server* modules, which provide facilities for use by the program module in achieving this effect. These server modules may in turn rely on other server modules in providing these facilities.

The cross-reference program fits this pattern in that the word-input and word-list modules are servers whose facilities are used by the program module, while the list-of-occurrences module is a server used by the word list module.

In the version developed so far, each server module has been imbedded in the module that uses it. An alternative modular arrangement is for each module to be developed (and compiled) as a separate text, with the modules being brought together only when an overall executable program is required. The advantages of this approach are

(a) the separation of concerns achieved by each module is emphasized by the textual separation involved;
(b) the cost of editing and recompiling each module is much less than the cost of recompiling the overall program;
(c) the parallel development of separate modules by programmers or teams of programmers becomes much easier;
(d) the construction of new programs from existing separately developed modules becomes a real possibility.

Modula-2 enables this approach to modular programming by allowing programs to be composed from a number of separate *compilation-units* which reflect the modular structure chosen. Such compilation-units are of three kinds:

(a) *program-modules*, which provide the controlling module of each program;
(b) *definition-modules*, which define the facilities and interface provided by each server module in the conceptual modular design; and
(c) *implementation-modules*, which determine how each server module realizes the facilities it provides.

The syntactic form of each class of compilation-unit is defined as follows:

compilation-unit =
program-module | definition-module | implementation-module.

program-module =
"MODULE" identifier [priority] ";" {import-list} block identifier ".".

definition-module =
"DEFINITION" "MODULE" identifier ";"
{import-list} {definition} "END" identifier ".".
definition =
"CONST" {constant-declaration ";"} |
"TYPE" {type-definition ";"} |
"VAR" {variable-declaration ";"} |
procedure-heading ";" |
function-heading ";".
type-definition = type-declaration | opaque-type-declaration.
opaque-type-declaration = identifier.

implementation-module = "IMPLEMENTATION" program-module.

Each of our example programs in earlier chapters consists of a single *program-module*.

As the name implies, each compilation-unit is a separate textual unit which can be submitted for compilation without the other units that make up the overall program. Most implementations impose naming conventions on the files in which these units are stored—in many cases a definition-module X must be stored in a file named $X.def$ while an implementation- or program-module X must be stored in a file named $X.mod$. We will assume these conventions in the examples that follow.

The precise procedure for compilation of the different types of module is also implementation-defined, but in general a definition module must exist (and be compiled) before either the corresponding implementation-module, or any program module that uses it, is compiled.

The role played by each aspect of these compilation-units is now illustrated by recasting the cross-reference program as a set of separately compiled modules.

The Program Module

The program-module for our separately compiled cross-reference program is a minor variation on the outer block of the program previously developed, in which explicit import lists now indicate the identifiers imported from the WordInput and WordList modules, as shown in *CrossReference.mod*.

CrossReference.mod

```
MODULE CrossReference;

    FROM InOut IMPORT Done, OpenInput, CloseInput, WriteLn;
    FROM WordInput IMPORT Word, Line, EndOfWords, GetNextWord;
    FROM WordList IMPORT RecordWord, PrintWords, DisposeWords;

    (* This program reads the sequence of words in an input text file,
       via the module WordInput,  and creates and outputs a sorted
       concordance via the module WordList. This concordance shows
       all words occurring in the text, together with a list of the line
       numbers at which each word occurs.                            *)

    BEGIN
      OpenInput(""); WriteLn;
      IF Done THEN
        GetNextWord;
        WHILE NOT EndOfWords DO
          RecordWord(Word, Line); GetNextWord
        END;
        PrintWords; DisposeWords; CloseInput
      END
    END CrossReference.
```

Note that the import-lists of the original nested-module program are simplified since the program-module no longer has to import the facilities from InOut and Storage that are required by nested modules.

In this form, the program-module is pleasing in that it gives a clear statement of the overall function of our cross-reference program, and of the features of other server modules which it uses. Conversely its validity depends entirely on the definitions of the WordInput and WordList modules. Clearly it cannot be executed until these modules have been implemented, but it cannot even be compiled until the definition-modules for WordInput and WordList have been created. These we now consider.

The Definition Modules

The role of a definition-module is to define the interface provided by the conceptual server module involved. In the case of the WordInput module this takes the form shown as *WordInput.def*.

WordInput.def

```
DEFINITION MODULE WordInput;

  (* This module enables the word by word examination of the words
     found in the current input stream offered by InOut.
     The procedure GetNextWord puts the next word from the input
     in the exported variable Word, if one exists; otherwise it sets the
     exported variable EndOfWords true.

     The line number at which the next word occurs is maintained in
     the exported variable Line. The first character read by the first
     call of GetNextWord is assumed to be on line number 1.        *)

  CONST MaxWordLength = 16;

  TYPE WordSpelling = ARRAY [0..MaxWordLength-1] OF CHAR;

  VAR Word: WordSpelling;
      Line: CARDINAL;
      EndOfWords: BOOLEAN;

  PROCEDURE GetNextWord;

  END WordInput.
```

According to the first and second editions of *Programming in Modula-2*, a definition-module must include a qualified export-list which lists all identifiers exported by the module. In the third edition, however, the convention is adopted that all identifiers defined in a definition-module are implicitly exported with qualification, so that no export-list is required, or indeed permitted. The definition-modules shown in this book follow this third edition convention.

The constant-, type- and variable-declarations provide all details of the exported identifiers MaxWordLength, WordSpelling, Word, Line, and EndOf-Words, that are needed to understand its interface (and to compile any module that uses it). The procedure heading for GetNextWord fulfills the same role for the exported procedure—no details of how the procedure is implemented are needed to understand or compile calls on it.

The definition-module provides all information necessary for compilation of modules that use the server WordInput, but also plays a significant role in documenting the module for programmers who have to understand it. The comments included in a definition-module are therefore important, and should be chosen carefully to describe what the module does, without implying how it does it. The latter information properly belongs in the corresponding implementation-module—the comments included in the implementation-module for WordInput will illustrate this in due course.

The WordInput module is definable without reference to facilities provided by any other module, and in consequence is compilable regardless of whether any other module exists or has been compiled. In general, however, a module interface may depend on features defined by other modules, which must therefore be imported by the definition module. In the case of the WordList module the definition of the procedure RecordWord depends on the type WordSpelling exported by the WordInput module. This must therefore be imported as shown in *WordList.def*.

WordList.def

```
DEFINITION MODULE WordList;

  FROM WordInput IMPORT WordSpelling;

  (* This module enables the creation and output of an ordered list
     of words, together with a list of cardinals for each, which are
     assumed to represent the line numbers at which the word occurs.
     Case differences between word spellings are ignored.          *)

  PROCEDURE RecordWord(Word: WordSpelling; Line: CARDINAL);

    (* record occurrence of word Word on line Line *)

  PROCEDURE PrintWords;

    (* print words and occurrence lists in sorted order *)

  PROCEDURE DisposeWords;

    (* dispose of words and occurrence lists *)

  END WordList.
```

When such a definition-module is compiled, the definition-modules of any modules from which it imports identifiers must have already been compiled. Hence, the definition-module for WordInput must be compiled prior to the compilation of the definition-module for WordList.

Note that although the WordList module depends on the Occurrences module for its implementation, this dependence is not reflected in its definition-module. The import of facilities from Occurrences is necessary only within the implementation-module for WordList.

The definition-module for the Occurrences module follows a similar pattern to the previous two, as shown in *Occurrences.def*.

Occurrences.def

DEFINITION MODULE Occurrences;

FROM WordInput IMPORT WordSpelling;

(* This module enables the creation and output of lists of
   occurrences, i.e., lists of cardinal line numbers. Each list
   is represented as a variable of the type ListOfOccurrences *)

TYPE LinePointer = POINTER TO LineRecord;
     LineRecord = RECORD Line: CARDINAL; NextLine: LinePointer END;
     ListOfOccurrences = RECORD First, Last: LinePointer END;

PROCEDURE InitOccurrences(VAR List: ListOfOccurrences);

   (* initializes List as an empty list *)

PROCEDURE AddOccurrence(NewLine: CARDINAL;
                                  VAR List: ListOfOccurrences);

   (* appends line number NewLine to list List *)

PROCEDURE PrintOccurrences(Word: WordSpelling;
                                  List: ListOfOccurrences);

   (* prints the word Word and the occurrence list List in format

   wwwwwwwwww ooo ooo ooo ...
                    ooo ooo ...   *)

PROCEDURE DisposeOccurrences(List: ListOfOccurrences);

   (* disposes of the dynamic variables used by List *)

END Occurrences.

The Implementation Modules

We turn now to the construction of implementation-modules. The essential role
of an implementation-module is to provide the procedure bodies and initialization statements which were not included in the corresponding definition-module,
together with other hidden data or procedure declarations on which these
depend.

As the syntax rules show, such modules have a form very similar to that of
program-modules. However, the content of an implementation is very much
determined by the corresponding definition-module. To illustrate this
correspondence, consider the implementation module for WordInput, which is
shown as *WordInput.mod*.

WordInput.mod

```
IMPLEMENTATION MODULE WordInput;

FROM InOut IMPORT EOL, Done, Read;

(*This module implements the input of a sequence of words, as specified
  in the corresponding definition module.

  The local variable NextCh holds the last character read by each call
  to GetNextWord, to ensure all ends of line are processed correctly.   *)

VAR NextCh: CHAR;

PROCEDURE Letter(Ch: CHAR): BOOLEAN;
  BEGIN
    RETURN ((Ch >= "A") AND (Ch <= "Z")) OR
           ((Ch >= "a") AND (Ch <= "z"))
  END Letter;

PROCEDURE GetNextWord;
  VAR I, Length: [0..MaxWordLength];
  BEGIN
    IF Done THEN
      REPEAT
        IF NextCh = EOL THEN INC(Line) END;
        Read(NextCh)
      UNTIL NOT Done OR Letter(NextCh);
    END;
    IF Done THEN
      Length := 0;
      REPEAT
        Word[Length] := CAP(NextCh); Length := Length + 1;
        Read(NextCh)
      UNTIL NOT Done OR NOT Letter(NextCh);
      FOR I := Length TO MaxWordLength–1 DO Word[I] := " " END
    ELSE EndOfWords := TRUE
    END
  END GetNextWord;

BEGIN
  Line := 1; NextCh := " "; EndOfWords := FALSE
END WordInput.
```

The following points are characteristic of implementation-modules:

(a) The module-identifier is the same as that of the corresponding *definition-module*.

(b) The implementation-module imports those features of InOut which are required to implement the procedure GetNextWord. This dependence need not appear in the definition-module.

(c) The constants, types, and variables declared in the definition-module are visible without redeclaration in the corresponding implementation-module. In addition, however, the implementation-module declares the variable NextCh which is necessary for implementation of GetNextWord. Since it does not appear in the definition-module this variable is 'hidden' from modules using WordInput.

(d) The implementation-module contains a complete declaration for the procedure GetNextWord. In general, the outermost block of an implementation-module must contain a procedure-declaration for each procedure defined by the corresponding definition-module. Corresponding procedure-headings in the definition-module and implementation-module must be identical.

(e) The statement-part of the implementation-module defines the initial actions to be carried out before any module makes use of the variables or procedures exported by WordInput.

Note also that the comments included in the implementation-module are different in style from those in the definition-module in that they concentrate on *how* the implementation-module achieves the effects specified by the definition-module. In general it is unnecessary to duplicate specification comments in the implementation-module, since the latter must be read in conjunction with its definition-module to be fully understood.

The implementation-module for the WordList module is derived in a similar manner, and is shown in outline as *WordList.mod*.

WordList.mod

```
IMPLEMENTATION MODULE WordList;

   FROM InOut IMPORT WriteString, WriteLn;
   FROM WordInput IMPORT MaxWordLength, WordSpelling;
   FROM Occurrences IMPORT
      ListOfOccurrences, InitOccurrences, AddOccurrence,
      PrintOccurrences, DisposeOccurrences;
   FROM Storage IMPORT ALLOCATE, DEALLOCATE;

   (* This module implements the list of words and occurrences specified
      by the corresponding definition module.
```

The list of words is implemented as a linked list of WordRecords, maintained in sorted order. Case differences between words are ignored by recording all words in upper case.
The list of occurrences for each word is realized via the module Occurrences, which also handles details of printing each word and its list of occurrences. *)

```
TYPE WordPointer = POINTER TO WordRecord;
     WordRecord  = RECORD
                        Spelling: WordSpelling;
                        Occurrences: ListOfOccurrences;
                        Next: WordPointer
                   END;

VAR WordList: WordPointer;

PROCEDURE LocateWordInList(WordSought: WordSpelling;
                           VAR WordFound: WordPointer);
  ...
  END LocateWordInList;

PROCEDURE RecordWord(Word: WordSpelling; Line: CARDINAL);
  ...
  END RecordWord;

PROCEDURE PrintWords;
  ...
  END PrintWords;

PROCEDURE DisposeWords;
  ...
  END DisposeWords;

BEGIN
  WordList := NIL
END WordList.
```

In addition to the points illustrated by the implementation-module for WordInput, the following should be noted with respect to that for WordList:

(a) Identifiers imported by a definition-module are *not* automatically available to the corresponding implementation-module. Those required by the implementation-module must be reimported, together with any additional identifiers which the implementation-module needs from other modules.

(b) Since the Occurrences module is no longer nested within it, WordList need not import those identifiers required by Occurrences.

The implementation-module for Occurrences is handled in a similar form, as shown in outline by *Occurrences.mod*.

Occurrences.mod

```
IMPLEMENTATION MODULE Occurrences;

  FROM WordInput IMPORT MaxWordLength, WordSpelling;
  FROM InOut IMPORT Write, WriteString, WriteCard, WriteLn;
  FROM Storage IMPORT ALLOCATE, DEALLOCATE;

  (* This module implements the manipulation of lists of occurrences,
     as specified in the corresponding definition module.
     The format in which lists are output is controlled by two constants:
     LineNumberWidth defines the field width for each occurrence,
     MaxLineLength defines the maximum length of each output line.   *)

  CONST LineNumberWidth = 6; MaxLineLength = 50;
        MaxListLength = MaxLineLength–MaxWordLength;

  PROCEDURE InitOccurrences(VAR List: ListOfOccurrences);
    BEGIN
      WITH List DO First := NIL; Last := NIL END;
    END InitOccurrences;

  PROCEDURE AddOccurrence(NewLine: CARDINAL;
                          VAR List: ListOfOccurrences);
    ...
    END AddOccurrence;

  PROCEDURE PrintOccurrences(Word: WordSpelling;
                             List: ListOfOccurrences);
    ...
    END PrintOccurrences;

  PROCEDURE DisposeOccurrences(List: ListOfOccurrences);
    ...
    END DisposeOccurrences;

END Occurrences.
```

Since the Occurrences module is essentially a package of procedures which operate on an exported data-type, its implementation module consists of just the implementation of those procedures, with no hidden data definitions, and no initialization code. Note that in such cases the syntax of implementation-modules does not require the BEGIN symbol to appear.

Compiling and Recompiling Modules

As we have already noted, a definition-module cannot be compiled until any other definition-modules whose features it imports have been compiled. Likewise a program-module cannot be compiled until the definition-modules it imports have been compiled. Since an implementation-module depends on its own definition-module, and on any features it imports from other definition-modules, an implementation-module cannot be compiled until all such definition-modules have been compiled. However, the order in which implementation-modules themselves are compiled is not important.

The dependence of each module on the other modules which make up an overall program can be represented by a dependency graph. Figure 12.1 shows the dependency graph for our modular cross-reference program. An arrow from module A to module B means that B depends on A, and hence that A must be compiled before B.

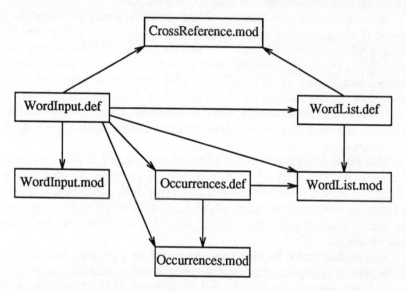

Figure 12.1 Module dependency graph for the cross-reference program

However, the details of how an implementation-module meets the requirements of its definition-module are irrelevant to its users. Hence it is possible to make changes to an implementation-module provided that these changes maintain its consistency with the definition-module. Such changes do not necessitate recompilation of either the definition-module, or of any module that uses it. Thus we could replace the implementation-module for WordList which uses a linear list of word records by one which uses the binary tree outlined in Chapter 11, without any need to recompile its definition module or the CrossReference program-module itself.

It is only when a module interface itself changes, implying a change and recompilation of the corresponding definition-module, that the implementation-module, and all other definition-, implementation- or program-modules that import any feature of the changed definition-module, need to be recompiled. In many Modula-2 implementations, either the compilation system itself, or an auxiliary software tool provided by the implementation, can be used to determine which recompilations are necessary after such a change.

OPAQUE TYPES AND INTERFACE SECURITY

As indicated in an earlier section, export of a type T, or of a variable of type T, by a module M automatically makes available all operations applicable to the type T, and such an exported type is said to be *transparent*.

In some cases this transparency of an exported type may be contrary to the purpose of modularization. For example, in the Occurrences module, this transparency rule means that the fields First and Last of each variable of type ListOfOccurrences are accessible to the WordList module. This in turn means that the contents and linking pointers of the linked list representing each list of occurrences can be altered by the WordList module. Accidental alterations of this kind could lead to malfunction within the module itself, such as infinite looping or access via a dangling pointer. Thus the list of occurrences module as defined so far is not as secure against misuse as we would like.

In the case of separately compiled modules, Modula-2 enables this particular security problem to be solved, by use of an *opaque* type. An opaque type is defined in a definition-module by omitting its type-definition details, i.e., simply by listing its name in the sequence of definitions following TYPE. In the case of the Occurrences module this would be done as shown in the revised Occurrences.def.

In a module which imports such an opaque type, the only operations that can be applied to objects of the type are assignment, passing as parameters and testing for equality. Thus, with the revised definition of ListOfOccurrences, the WordList module can no longer corrupt the representation of the lists of occurrences it creates, so security against such programming errors is achieved.

When an opaque type is defined in a definition-module, the corresponding implementation-module must contain a full definition for the type. Unfortunately, the requirements of separate compilation mean that restrictions must be placed on the forms that an opaque type may take, and the third edition of *Programming in Modula-2* states that opaque types can only be pointer types. This restriction means that an unnecessary level of indirection must be introduced into the representation of the type ListOfOccurrences within the implementation module, with consequent complications of the procedures that manipulate the

Occurrences.def

```
DEFINITION MODULE Occurrences;

FROM WordInput IMPORT WordSpelling;

(* This module enables the creation and output of lists of
   occurrences, i.e., lists of cardinal line numbers. Each list
   is represented as a variable of the type ListOfOccurrences *)

TYPE ListOfOccurrences;

PROCEDURE InitOccurrences(VAR List: ListOfOccurrences);

PROCEDURE AddOccurrence(NewLine: CARDINAL;
                                VAR List: ListOfOccurrences);
...
```
as before
```
...
END Occurrences.
```

type, as shown in the following outline of the revised *Occurrences.mod*.

Occurrences.mod

```
IMPLEMENTATION MODULE Occurrences;

FROM WordInput IMPORT MaxWordLength, WordSpelling;
FROM InOut IMPORT Write, WriteString, WriteCard, WriteLn;
FROM Storage IMPORT ALLOCATE, DEALLOCATE;

(* This module implements the manipulation of lists of occurrences,
   as specified in the corresponding definition module. The opaque
   type ListOfOccurrences is implemented as a linked list, with a
   header record which is pointed to by the opaque type value.

   The format in which lists are output is controlled by two constants:
   LineNumberWidth defines the field width for each occurrence,
   MaxLineLength defines the maximum length of each output line.  *)

CONST LineNumberWidth = 6; MaxLineLength = 50;
      MaxListLength = MaxLineLength–MaxWordLength;

TYPE LinePointer = POINTER TO LineRecord;
     LineRecord  = RECORD Line: CARDINAL; NextLine: LinePointer END;
     ListOfOccurrences = POINTER TO ListHeader;
     ListHeader = RECORD First, Last: LinePointer END;
```

```
PROCEDURE InitOccurrences(VAR List: ListOfOccurrences);
  BEGIN
    ALLOCATE(List, SIZE(ListHeader));
    WITH List^ DO First := NIL; Last := NIL END;
  END InitOccurrences;

PROCEDURE AddOccurrence(NewLine: CARDINAL;
                                VAR List: ListOfOccurrences);
  VAR Occurrence: LinePointer;
  BEGIN
    ALLOCATE(Occurrence, SIZE(LineRecord));
    WITH Occurrence^ DO Line := NewLine; NextLine := NIL END;
    WITH List^ DO
    ...
  END AddOccurrence;

PROCEDURE PrintOccurrences(Word: WordSpelling;
                                List: ListOfOccurrences);
  VAR SpaceLeftOnLine: CARDINAL; I: [1..MaxWordLength];
      ThisOccurrence: LinePointer;
  BEGIN
    WriteString(Word); SpaceLeftOnLine := MaxListLength;
    ThisOccurrence := List^.First;
    ...
  END PrintOccurrences;

PROCEDURE DisposeOccurrences(List: ListOfOccurrences);
  VAR ThisOccurrence, NextOccurrence: LinePointer;
  BEGIN
    NextOccurrence := List^.First;
    WHILE NextOccurrence <> NIL DO
    ...
    END;
    DEALLOCATE(List, SIZE(ListHeader))
  END DisposeOccurrences;

END Occurrences.
```

In this particular case, this complication of the procedures within the
Occurrences module is the cost of achieving error security. In many cases, however, the natural representation for an opaque type is a pointer, so that the necessary restriction causes no complication whatsoever. Note, however, that no
equivalent mechanism for export of opaque types from local modules is provided by Modula-2.

The opaque type facility is a necessary feature for the construction of modules which are secure against one common form of misuse, though, as we shall see clearly later, the fact that Modula-2 permits assignment of variables of opaque types is sometimes undesirable. It is important to realize, however, that there are many other ways in which insecurities may arise, and that, in general, security is a matter of module interface design and module implementation. Other typical sources of insecurity are as follows.

(a) *Export of variables:* In Modula-2, exported variables, such as Word, Line, or EndOfWords, in the WordInput module, can not only be inspected by the user module, but may also be assigned new values. In the case of the WordInput module, this is not only contrary to the module's intention, but could lead to malfunction of the module itself, since subsequent line numbers made available by the module will be affected by any assignment of the Line variable.

(b) *Constraints on the sequence in which operations are used:* The statement-part of a module can be used to guarantee that certain initial actions are carried out before any other facility exported by a module is used, but in general the order in which facilities are used thereafter is determined by the user module. In many cases an incorrect sequence of usage leads to program failure. In the WordList module, for example, any use of RecordWord or PrintWords made after a call to DisposeWords must fail, since the pointer variable FirstWord is now a dangling pointer.

In each of the examples given, the insecurity can be eliminated, either by adjustment of the module interface, or by the inclusion of additional variables and statements within the the the module implementation. In general, however, the security achievable is limited by the security of the language implementation itself—if an implementation does not detect the use of unassigned variables, there is no way that the Occurrences module can detect the user program's failure to call InitOccurrences for a given variable of type ListOfOccurrences.

We conclude, therefore, that the opaque type feature in Modula-2 is important in eliminating one kind of module interface insecurity, but in general the achievement of interface security remains the programmer's problem, and is ultimately limited by the security of the language implementation itself.

SCOPE RULES AND SEMANTICS OF MODULES

The preceding sections have demonstrated the major features of modules as provided in Modula-2. At this point it is appropriate to summarize the scope and semantic rules associated with these features. We begin by clarifying our terminology on declarations, scope and visibility. A *declaration* associates an identifier with a meaning. The *scope* of a declaration is the region of program text in which the identifier may be *used* with the corresponding meaning. The identifier and the declaration are said to be *visible* within the scope.

We now restate the scope rules given for procedures in Chapter 7, in a form that takes account of modules:

(1) *The scope of an identifier declaration within a program- or implementation-module is the block in which the declaration occurs and all procedure blocks enclosed by that block, subject to rules (2), (6) and (7).*

(2) *If an identifier I is visible in a block A, and is redeclared in some block B directly enclosed by A, then block B and all blocks enclosed by B are excluded from the scope of the visible declaration of I in A.*

(3) *The definition of a standard identifier I is said to be pervasive, and its scope includes any block which is not included in the scope of any declaration of identifier I.*

(4) *If an identifier I is used in the declaration of another identifier J and the visible declaration of I is in the same compilation-unit, then the declaration of I must precede the declaration of J in the unit's text.*

It should be noted that import- and export-lists are not declarations in the sense of rule (4), so an import-list in a local module may mention an identifier whose declaration comes later in the enclosing block.

The scope of objects declared in a definition-module is defined by the following rule:

(5) *The scope of a constant-, type- or variable-declaration within a definition-module is the definition-module, the block of the corresponding implementation-module and all procedure blocks enclosed by that block subject to rules (2), (6) and (7).*
     The scope of an opaque-type-declaration is the definition-module in which it occurs, subject to rule (6).
     A procedure- or function-heading in a definition-module acts as a procedure- or function-declaration whose scope is the definition-module itself, subject to rule (6).

If an opaque-type-declaration occurs in a definition-module, a type-declaration for the same identifier must occur in the corresponding implementation-module. If a procedure- or function-heading occurs in a definition-module, a procedure- or function-declaration with an identical heading must occur in the corresponding implementation-module.

The rules to cover import and export by modules are as follows:

(6) *If an identifier I is imported by a module M the scope of the imported declaration of I is extended to include the module M and any procedure-*

blocks enclosed by M, subject to rule (2).

Identifiers imported by M are

(a)   those appearing in an import-list of M;
(b)   the constant-identifiers of an enumerated-type whose type-identifier is imported by M;
(c)   those identifiers exported without qualification by a module N whose module-identifier is itself imported by M.

All identifiers appearing in an import-list of the form

   IMPORT I, ...;

in a module M must be visible in the the environment of M.

   All identifiers following the word IMPORT in an import-list of the form

   FROM N IMPORT I, ...;

in a module M must be exported by a module N which is visible in the environment of M.

   The environment of a local module is the enclosing block. The environment of a compilation-unit is a universe in which the identifiers of all definition-modules are visible.

(7)   *If an identifier I is exported without qualification by a module M, the scope of the visible declaration of I in the block of M is extended to include the block enclosing M and all procedure-blocks enclosed by M, subject to rule (2).*

(8)   *If an identifier I is exported with or without qualification by M, the quantity denoted by I within M may be denoted by M.I throughout the scope of the module identifier M.*

Identifiers exported without qualification by M are

(a)   those appearing in an export-list of the form

   EXPORT I, ...;

   in module M;
(b)   the constant-identifiers of an enumerated-type whose type-identifier is exported without qualification by M;
(c)   those identifiers exported without qualification by a module N whose module-identifier is itself exported without qualification by M.

Identifiers exported with qualification by M are

(a)   all identifiers declared in a definition-module M;
(b)   those appearing in an export-list of the form

EXPORT QUALIFIED I, ...;

in a local module M;
(c) the constant-identifiers of an enumerated-type whose type-identifier is exported with qualification by M;
(d) those identifiers exported without qualification by a module N whose module-identifier is itself exported with qualification by M.

All identifiers appearing in the export-list of a local module M must be visible within the module block, either by being declared there or by being exported from a nested module.

The uniqueness of the meaning of an identifier used in a program is now insured by the following rule:

(9) *If two or more declarations exist for an identifier I, then the scopes of these declarations, as determined by rules (1), (2), (5), (6) and (7), must be disjoint.*

The semantics of programs which include modules are defined by the following additional rules:

(10) *The lifetime of variables declared within a local module is the same as the lifetime of variables declared in the enclosing block. The lifetime of variables declared within a compilation-unit is the duration of execution of the program of which it is a part.*

(11) *The statement-part of a local module is executed before the statement-part of the enclosing block. Where two or more modules are declared within the same enclosing block their statement parts are executed in the order in which the modules appear in the block.*
In general, the statement-part of an implementation-module is executed before the statement-part of any implementation- or program-module that imports the corresponding definition-module. If circular references exist between modules the order of execution of their statement-parts is implementation-dependent, and should not be relied on.

(12) *The operations applicable to objects of an opaque type T are assignment, parameter passing and test of equality, except within the implementation-module corresponding to the definition-module in which T is declared, where the opaque type is considered to be identical to the type declared with identifier T in the implementation-module itself. Given this identity, the effect of a call on a procedure or function declared in a definition-module is identical to that of a call on the corresponding procedure or function declared in the implementation-module.*

When enumerated in this way, the complete set of rules governing the use of modules in Modula-2 may seem complex, but in practice they cause few problems in the construction of modular programs. If the modular structure chosen for the program is logical, and the interfaces between modules and the blocks that use them are defined in a straightforward manner, the precise requirements of the preceding rules are likely to be met without conscious effort on the part of the programmer.

MODULE FLEXIBILITY AND UTILITY PROGRAMMING

The modules making up the CrossReference program were each derived with the specific requirements of that program in mind. However, a separately-compiled module is a potential building block for more than one program, and the economic benefits of assembling new programs from existing modules, or from minor variations of existing modules, is obvious. Given an adequate supply of suitable modules, each new program may be constructed at a fraction of the cost of programming it from scratch. If such *utility programming* is to be fully exploited, however, it is important to avoid all unnecessary dependence of each module on the application for which it is originally constructed.

Consider as an example the Occurrences module in the CrossReference program. The module was conceived as enabling the construction and printout of lists of occurrences or line-numbers, and the names chosen for the types and procedures involved reflect this purpose. In practice, however, each list of occurrences is simply a list of cardinal numbers, and the same types and procedures could be used to construct any list of cardinal numbers, though in this case the names used for them would be better chosen as ListOfCardinals, InitCardinals, AddCardinal, PrintCardinals, and DisposeCardinals.

The effect of the procedure PrintOccurrences is also application-specific in that it provides for prefixing each list with the spelling of the word which occurs on those lines:

```
PROCEDURE PrintOccurrences(Word: WordSpelling;
                           List: ListOfOccurrences);
```

In practice, this dependence can also be eliminated by replacing the formal parameter Word of type WordSpelling by the more general notion of a *list label* which is to prefix the list of cardinals to be printed, declared as an open array of characters, thus:

```
PROCEDURE PrintCardinals(Label: ARRAY OF CHAR;
                         List: ListOfCardinals);
```

Thus, the original Occurrences module can be replaced by a Cardinals module, with the interface shown as *Cardinals.def*.

Using the standard function HIGH defined for use with open array parameters in Chapter 8, the procedure PrintCardinals can be implemented with an

Cardinals.def

```
DEFINITION MODULE Cardinals;

(* This module enables the creation and output of lists of cardinal numbers
   Each list is represented as a variable of the type ListOfCardinals *)

TYPE ListOfCardinals;

PROCEDURE InitCardinals(VAR List: ListOfCardinals);

   (* initializes List as an empty list *)

PROCEDURE AddCardinal(C: CARDINAL;
                              VAR List: ListOfCardinals);

   (* appends number C to list List *)

PROCEDURE PrintCardinals(Label: ARRAY OF CHAR;
                                 List: ListOfCardinals);

   (* prints the label Label and the list List in format

      label  ccc ccc ccc ...
             ccc ccc ...                                    *)

PROCEDURE DisposeCardinals(List: ListOfCardinals);

   (* disposes of the dynamic variables used by List *)

END Cardinals.
```

identical effect to that of the original PrintOccurrences, and with no greater complexity. This is left as a programming exercise for the reader. For all other procedures in the module the same implementation as was used in the Occurrences module is sufficient.

Thus, with no increase in programming effort, a Cardinals module with identical effect to the Occurrences module can be obtained. The only change required in the WordList module that uses it is a systematic change of spelling for the type and procedure identifiers imported. In this new form, however, the module has no particular association with lists of line-numbers, or with words, and may be used in any program which needs to construct and print lists of cardinals. As such it is more flexible, and potentially more labor-saving, than the original Occurrences module.

This example demonstrates that with a little additional thought at module definition stage, and with little or no additional programming effort, a module of greater flexibility may be produced when solving a particular problem such as the list-of-occurrences problem. Conversely, due consideration should be given to the possibility of using an existing module to solve such a problem when it arises. In practice both the word-list and the list-of-occurrences problems might be solved using a general list manipulation module if one were available. It is beyond the scope of this book to develop, or even define, a comprehensive set of such modules, but in the following subsections we look at a number of Modula-2 modules which have a considerable flexibility of purpose, and typify the approach to programming which separately compilable modules encourage.

Utility Modules

As a first example, consider the module ISO, whose sole purpose is to provide a set of constants representing the ISO control characters, for use in Modula-2 programs.

ISO.def

```
DEFINITION MODULE ISO;

   (* This module defines the mnemonics and values of ISO control characters *)

   CONST NUL = 00C;   SOH = 01C;   STX = 02C;   ETX = 03C;
         EOT = 04C;   ENQ = 05C;   ACK = 06C;   BEL = 07C;
         BS = 10C;    HT = 11C;    LF = 12C;    VT = 13C;
         FF = 14C;    CR = 15C;    SO = 16C;    SI = 17C;
         DLE = 20C;   DC1 = 21C;   DC2 = 22C;   DC3 = 23C;
         DC4 = 24C;   NAK = 25C;   SYN = 26C;   ETB = 27C;
         CAN = 30C;   EM = 31C;    SUB = 32C;   ESC = 33C;
         FS = 34C;    GS = 35C;    ES = 36C;    US = 37C;
         SP = 40C;    DEL = 177C;

   END ISO.
```

Such a module is easily provided in any Modula-2 programming environment. Although individual programs or modules may only import a small subset of the constants defined, the provision of a single module of this sort encourages consistency between all programs and modules and the ISO character set itself, both in the character values and in the mnemonics used to denote them.

The module ISO encapsulates a related set of constant definitions. The library module MathLib0 provided by most Modula-2 implementations provides a similar encapsulation of function procedures for evaluating various mathematical functions.

The MathLib0 module provides a convenient package of the most commonly used mathematical functions, from which individual programs may import those that they require. Similar modules could be defined which provide an extended set of mathematical functions (e.g., additional trigonometric and

MathLib0.def

```
DEFINITION MODULE MathLib0;                        .

  (* This module provides basic mathematical functions *)

  PROCEDURE sqrt(x: REAL): REAL;

  PROCEDURE exp(x: REAL): REAL;

  PROCEDURE ln(x: REAL): REAL;

  PROCEDURE sin(x: REAL): REAL;

  PROCEDURE cos(x: REAL): REAL;

  PROCEDURE arctan(x: REAL): REAL;

  PROCEDURE real(x: INTEGER): REAL;

  PROCEDURE entier(x: REAL): INTEGER;

END MathLib0.
```

hyperbolic functions) and could be implemented using the functions provided by
MathLib0.

As a final example of a general-purpose utility module consider the ValidInput module suggested in Chapter 8, which enables programming of dialogue
with a terminal user. This might have the interface shown as *ValidInput.def*.

ValidInput.def

```
DEFINITION MODULE ValidInput;

  (* This module enables easy interaction with a terminal user,
     by providing procedures for outputting queries and obtaining
     replies. The replies expected may be Booleans (yes or no),
     integers or cardinals in a prescribed range, or strings.   *)

  PROCEDURE GetBoolean(Question: ARRAY OF CHAR;
                            VAR ReplyIsYes: BOOLEAN);

    (* This procedure gets a yes/no answer to the given question. *)

  PROCEDURE GetCardinal(Prompt: ARRAY OF CHAR;
                            VAR Value: CARDINAL;
                            Lower, Upper: CARDINAL);

    (* This procedure gets a cardinal value in the range Lower .. Upper,
       using the prompt given, which should be of the form:
                 "Input <description of value required>"              *)
```

```
PROCEDURE GetInteger(Prompt: ARRAY OF CHAR;
                     VAR Value: INTEGER;
                     Lower, Upper: INTEGER);
(* This procedure gets an integer value in the range Lower .. Upper,
   using the prompt given, which should be of the form:
      "Input <description of value required>"            *)

PROCEDURE GetString(Prompt: ARRAY OF CHAR;
                    VAR Response: ARRAY OF CHAR;
                    VAR Length: CARDINAL);
(* This procedure gets a string response using the prompt
   given, which should be of the form:
      "Input <description of string required>"
   If the user response is shorter than the array Response,
   the remainder of the array is filled with NUL (0C) chars.
   If the user response is longer than the array Response,
   the response is truncated.  In all cases the actual length
   of the response input is returned as Length.             *)

END ValidInput.
```

Abstract Objects

The WordList module is an example of a module which realizes an abstract object (in this case a list of words and occurrences), whose detailed representation is hidden within the module, with exported procedures providing the only operations applicable to the object. Construction of programs from a set of such abstract objects is an effective design strategy, and we now look at a further example of such an object which might be used in many programs.

A *queue* is a sequence of data items in which all insertions take place at one end (the *rear*), and all removals are from the other end (the *front*), as shown in Figure 12.2. In this case, the item of the sequence which has been in the queue for the longest time is always the next to be removed—hence a queue is described as a first-in, first-out (*FIFO*) or last-in, last-out (*LILO*) data structure.

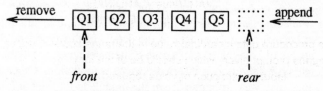

Figure 12.2 A queue

Queues occur frequently in everyday life (at traffic lights, bus stops and supermarket checkouts) but also occur in many computing applications. A computer operating system for example typically organizes the jobs waiting for particular resources of the system into one or more queues—where jobs with different characteristics, e.g., the amount of CPU time required, may enter different queues.

The two main operations associated with a queue are the appending and removal of items. The appending operation adds a new item to the rear of a queue, provided that the queue is not already full. (We assume that some limit may exist on the length of the queue.) The removal operation takes out the item at the front of a queue, provided that such an item exists, i.e., the queue is not empty. Hence, we also need operators to enable us to determine when a queue is empty and when it is full, so that we know when it is safe to apply the removal and appending operators.

We now formulate an *abstract specification* of a queue of items, in the form of a definition-module providing a set of queue operators. In addition to the above operators, we define a *length* function to provide the number of items currently in a queue (this function is sometimes useful in determining how to service queues), a *clear* operator which restores the queue to its empty state, and a *traversal* operator which applies some procedure P to each item in a queue, in the order in which the items joined the queue.

```
DEFINITION MODULE Queue;

  CONST MaxQueueLength = ...;

  TYPE ItemType = ...;
    ItemOperation = PROCEDURE(VAR ItemType);

  PROCEDURE Full(): BOOLEAN;
  PROCEDURE Empty(): BOOLEAN;
  PROCEDURE Length(): CARDINAL;
  PROCEDURE Append(X: ItemType);
  PROCEDURE Remove(VAR X: ItemType);
  PROCEDURE Traverse(P: ItemOperation);
  PROCEDURE Clear;

  END Queue.
```

In this version, the type of items held by the queue is defined as the type Item-Type within the definition module, but in practice the definition and implementation of queue behavior is independent of the details of this type, and the Queue module is capable of being used as a queue of items of any given type, provided the appropriate type definition is inserted prior to compilation. Other aspects of the queue which may vary from one use of the module to the next are

(a) the maximum length permitted for the queue, and

(b) whether or not the procedure P supplied to the traversal operator is permitted to alter the values of items in the queue, i.e., whether P is of type PROCEDURE(VAR ItemType) or of type PROCEDURE(ItemType).

Rather than require that the Queue module itself be edited prior to each use made of it, it is preferable to isolate those attributes that may change in a separate definition module QueueInfo, of the form shown:

QueueInfo.def

```
DEFINITION MODULE QueueInfo;
  CONST MaxQueueLength = ...;
  TYPE ItemType = ...;
       ItemOperation = PROCEDURE (VAR ItemType);
  END QueueInfo.
```

These quantities are then imported as required by the definition- and implementation-modules for Queue. The definition-module is now shown as *Queue.def.*

Queue.def

```
DEFINITION MODULE Queue;
  FROM QueueInfo IMPORT ItemType, ItemOperation;

  (* This module maintains a FIFO queue of items of type ItemType,
     with the maximum queue length also being defined in QueueInfo.
     The queue is initially empty, and its state thereafter may
     be interrogated using the functions Full, Empty and Length.
     Items are added to and removed from the queue via procedures
     Append and Remove. Procedure Traverse applies its procedure
     parameter to each item in the queue in appended order.
     The procedure Clear resets the queue to the empty state.    *)

  PROCEDURE Full(): BOOLEAN;
  PROCEDURE Empty(): BOOLEAN;
  PROCEDURE Length(): CARDINAL;
  PROCEDURE Append(X: ItemType);
  PROCEDURE Remove(VAR X: ItemType);
  PROCEDURE Traverse(P: ItemOperation);
  PROCEDURE Clear;

  END Queue.
```

Defined in this way the Queue module can be used to realize queues of different item types, of different maximum lengths, and with more or less powerful traversal operators, without any need to alter the definition- or implementation-modules for Queue itself. The Queue module is *generic* in the sense that it adapts to the definitions supplied by the QueueInfo module.

How can we represent a queue? The WordList module in the cross-reference program employed a *chained* representation using pointers, and a similar representation could be used for a queue. However, when an upper bound Max-QueueLength on the length of the queue is given, an attractive alternative uses an array of MaxQueueLength elements to hold the items of the queue, as indicated in Figure 12.3. Two variables Front and Rear are required to indicate the limits of the queue.

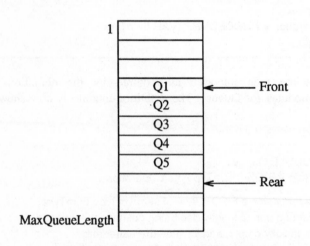

Figure 12.3   Contiguous representation of a queue

The variable Front indexes the array element containing the first item of the queue and Rear indexes the array element in which the next item to be added to the queue will be stored, i.e., it points to the array element immediately following the last item of the queue.

As items are added to and removed from the queue, the values of Front and Rear increase, and the queue migrates down the array. What happens when the rear of the queue reaches the end of the array? One solution is to allow the queue to 'wrap round' the end of the array and let the tail of the queue occupy any empty space at the start of the array as further items are added. The array may then be viewed as circular or cyclic, and this array representation is sometimes known as a *cyclic buffer*.

To initialize such a queue representation, Front and Rear are both assigned the value 1, denoting the empty queue. When the queue subsequently becomes either full or empty, Front and Rear will again have the same value, so an auxiliary length variable is maintained to determine the state of the queue. The complete form of the implementation-module using the cyclic buffer representation is shown as *Queue.mod.*

Queue.mod

```
IMPLEMENTATION MODULE Queue;
  FROM QueueInfo IMPORT MaxQueueLength, ItemType, ItemOperation;

  (* This module implements a FIFO queue as required by the
    corresponding definition module. The queue is represented
    within an array Buffer which is used in cyclic buffer fashion. *)

  VAR Buffer: ARRAY [1..MaxQueueLength] OF ItemType;
    Front, Rear: [1..MaxQueueLength]; CurrentLength: [0..MaxQueueLength];

  PROCEDURE Full(): BOOLEAN;
    BEGIN
      RETURN (CurrentLength = MaxQueueLength)
    END Full;

  PROCEDURE Empty(): BOOLEAN;
    BEGIN
      RETURN (CurrentLength = 0)
    END Empty;

  PROCEDURE Length(): CARDINAL;
    BEGIN
      RETURN CurrentLength
    END Length;

  PROCEDURE Append(X: ItemType);
    BEGIN
      IF CurrentLength < MaxQueueLength THEN
        Buffer[Rear] := X; Rear := Rear MOD MaxQueueLength + 1;
        INC(CurrentLength)
      END
    END Append;

  PROCEDURE Remove(VAR X: ItemType);
    BEGIN
      IF CurrentLength > 0 THEN
        X := Buffer[Front]; Front := Front MOD MaxQueueLength + 1;
        DEC(CurrentLength)
      END
    END Remove;
```

```
PROCEDURE Traverse(P: ItemOperation);
  VAR I, J: [0..MaxQueueLength];
  BEGIN
    J := Front;
    FOR I := 1 TO CurrentLength DO
      P(Buffer[J]); J := J MOD MaxQueueLength + 1
    END
  END Traverse;

PROCEDURE Clear;
  BEGIN
    CurrentLength := 0; Front := 1; Rear := 1
  END Clear;

BEGIN
  Clear
END Queue.
```

Abstract Data Types

One of the drawbacks of the Queue module is that it allows only one queue to be created and manipulated. An alternative approach is that illustrated by the Occurrences module, which defined an exported (opaque) type and a set of operators (expressed as exported procedures and functions) which operate upon variables of the exported type. Such a type, and a set of procedures and functions, which can be understood and used without knowledge of the representation and structure of the type or of the implementation of its operators, is known as an *abstract data type*. In Modula-2 such a type is realized by a module of the following general form:

```
DEFINITION MODULE ADTPackage;

  TYPE ADT;

  PROCEDURE Op1(VAR D: ADT; ...);
  PROCEDURE Op2(VAR D: ADT; ...);
  ...

  END ADTPackage.
```

With such a module the user modules can declare variables using the visible type name ADT and then apply the operators defined by the exported procedures Op1, Op2, etc., passing the appropriate variables as parameters to these procedures as required. Hence we may redefine our Queue module in the form shown as *QueuePackage.def*, again using the module QueueInfo to provide the necessary characteristics of the queues.

QueuePackage.def

```
DEFINITION MODULE QueuePackage;
 FROM QueueInfo IMPORT ItemType, ItemOperation;

 (* This module defines an abstract data type Queue, each value
   of which is a FIFO queue of items of type ItemType,
   with the maximum queue length also being defined in QueueInfo.
   Before being used in any other way, each variable of type
   Queue must be initialized via the procedure Initialize,
   and at the end of its useful lifetime should be finalized
   via the procedure Finalize.

   After initialization a queue is empty, and its state thereafter
   may be tested using the functions Full, Empty and Length.
   Items are added to and removed from a queue via procedures
   Append and Remove. Procedure Traverse applies its procedure
   parameter to each item in a queue in appended order.
   The procedure Clear resets a queue to the empty state.        *)

 TYPE Queue;

 PROCEDURE Initialize(VAR Q: Queue);
 PROCEDURE Full(Q: Queue): BOOLEAN;
 PROCEDURE Empty(Q: Queue): BOOLEAN;
 PROCEDURE Length(Q: Queue): CARDINAL;
 PROCEDURE Append(VAR Q: Queue; X: ItemType);
 PROCEDURE Remove(VAR Q: Queue; VAR X: ItemType);
 PROCEDURE Traverse(VAR Q: Queue; P: ItemOperation);
 PROCEDURE Clear(VAR Q: Queue);
 PROCEDURE Finalize(VAR Q: Queue);

 END QueuePackage.
```

With this module a user program can declare queue variables, as follows:

```
VAR Q1, Q2: Queue;
```

and manipulate these variables by procedure calls such as:

```
Initialize(Q1);
Initialize(Q2);
  ...
Append(Q1, x);
Append(Q2, x);
  ...
```

Note, however, that explicit initialization of the queue variables by use of the procedure Initialize is now required, and that this operation is not identical to the operator Clear used subsequently. In the former case the queue representation is undefined, and must be treated accordingly, while in the latter case the component items of the queue representation have defined values which may or may not require processing, e.g., to dispose of an existing chained representation. For similar reasons, the procedure Finalize is provided, and should be called at the end of the useful lifetime of each queue variable that has been initialized, to dispose of the representation involved. In Modula-2 these problems are accentuated by the restriction of opaque types to pointer types, but in principle the necessity to recognize the distinction between initial, final and intermediate resetting operations on abstract data types is a characteristic of the package approach.

Thus this package approach imposes greater responsibility on the user modules in that initialization and finalization of objects of the abstract data type must be explicitly programmed. However, it does overcome some of the shortcomings of the previous approach. Thus, multiple objects of our packaged Queue type can be declared, perhaps as components of other structures. The approach also allows *polyadic* operators, that is, operators that take more than one object of the exported abstract type as operands or parameters, to be defined within the package itself. Thus QueuePackage might provide a queue union operator, as follows:

PROCEDURE Join(Q1, Q2: Queue): Queue;

The implementation-module *QueuePackage.mod* corresponds to the definition-module for QueuePackage—again it uses a cyclic buffer representation for each queue variable.

QueuePackage.mod

```
IMPLEMENTATION MODULE QueuePackage;

FROM QueueInfo IMPORT MaxQueueLength, ItemType, ItemOperation;
FROM Storage IMPORT ALLOCATE, DEALLOCATE;

(* This module implements the abstract data type Queue defined by
   the corresponding definition module. A queue is represented as
   (a pointer to) a queue record, which comprises an array Buffer
   used in cyclic buffer fashion, and the corresponding auxiliary
   variables indicating the front, rear and length of the queue.   *)
```

```
TYPE Queue = POINTER TO QueueRecord;
   QueueRecord = RECORD
                  Buffer: ARRAY [1..MaxQueueLength] OF ItemType;
                  Front, Rear: [1..MaxQueueLength];
                  CurrentLength: [0..MaxQueueLength];
                END;
PROCEDURE Full(Q: Queue): BOOLEAN;
  BEGIN
    RETURN (Q^.CurrentLength = MaxQueueLength)
  END Full;

PROCEDURE Empty(Q: Queue): BOOLEAN;
  BEGIN
    RETURN (Q^.CurrentLength = 0)
  END Empty;

PROCEDURE Length(Q: Queue): CARDINAL;
  BEGIN
    RETURN Q^.CurrentLength
  END Length;

PROCEDURE Append(VAR Q: Queue; X: ItemType);
  BEGIN
    WITH Q^ DO
      IF CurrentLength < MaxQueueLength THEN
        Buffer[Rear] := X; Rear := Rear MOD MaxQueueLength + 1;
        INC(CurrentLength)   .
      END
    END
  END Append;

PROCEDURE Remove(VAR Q: Queue; VAR X: ItemType);
  BEGIN
    WITH Q^ DO
      IF CurrentLength > 0 THEN
        X := Buffer[Front]; Front := Front MOD MaxQueueLength + 1;
        DEC(CurrentLength)
      END
    END
  END Remove;
```

```
PROCEDURE Traverse(VAR Q: Queue; P: ItemOperation);
VAR I, J: [0..MaxQueueLength];
BEGIN
  WITH Q^ DO
  J := Front;
  FOR I := 1 TO CurrentLength DO
    P(Buffer[J]); J := J MOD MaxQueueLength + 1
  END
  END
END Traverse;

PROCEDURE Clear(VAR Q: Queue);
BEGIN
  WITH Q^ DO
    CurrentLength := 0; Front := 1; Rear := 1
  END
END Clear;

PROCEDURE Initialize(VAR Q: Queue);
BEGIN
  ALLOCATE(Q, SIZE(QueueRecord)); Clear(Q)
END Initialize;

PROCEDURE Finalize(VAR Q: Queue);
BEGIN
  DEALLOCATE(Q, SIZE(QueueRecord))
END Finalize;

END QueuePackage.
```

In Modula-2 the operators assignment and test of equality are applicable to objects of an opaque type, and hence to any abstract data type implemented by the preceding strategy. However, because opaque types are implemented as pointers, the effect of these operations do not in general correspond to the desired operation on objects of the abstract type. Thus, if Q1 and Q2 are variables of the type Queue, the assignment

Q1 := Q2

merely copies the value of the pointer to the queue record for Q2 as the corresponding pointer value for Q1, as shown in Figure 12.4. Immediately thereafter, the values of Q1 and Q2 will be equal as expected since they now share the *same* queue record, but any subsequent modification of Q2 will also affect Q1 and vice versa. Thus, the assignment operator does not have the required effect for the abstract Queue objects and should not be used in this case. Likewise the test Q1 = Q2 would give true if Q1 and Q2 share the same queue

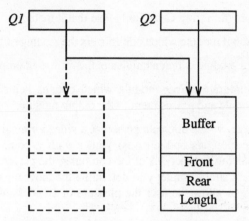

old queue record for Q1   queue record for Q2

Figure 12.4   Result of assignment $Q1 := Q2$

record as in Figure 12.4, but will give false in all normal cases since the pointer value created by Initialize for a given variable of type Queue is distinct from all other pointer values in existence at that time.

Thus the automatic availability of assignment and test of equality as operators on abstract data types is rarely an advantage. In general they can be used only if the user understands the underlying implementation of the abstract data type, and in most cases they should not be used at all. Where copying and equality testing are necessary operators on abstract data types, they should be provided as explicit interface procedures or functions by the module which implements the abstract type.

EXERCISES

12.1 The concordance program developed to date has the following shortcomings:

(a) fixed format printing of each line number within a list is extravagant for short line numbers;

(b) multiple occurrences of the same word on a single line cause the line number to be printed a corresponding number of times in the list of occurrences, which may be unnecessary.

Devise modifications which overcome each of these deficiencies. Consider carefully whether the definition-modules need to be changed before making any changes within the implementation-modules.

12.2 Rewrite the program from Case Study 9 so that it includes:

(a) a word input module which administers the reading of the input file;

(b) an output module which administers the formatted output stream;

(c) a main-program *driver* module which obtains items from the word input module and passes them to the output module.

12.3 Write a program which allows a person at a video terminal to play a series of tic-tac-toe (noughts and crosses) games with a computer. Introduce modules which are abstractions of the computer, the player, and the tic-tactoe grid. Use a simple strategy to determine the moves made by the computer in order to allow the user the pleasure of an occasional victory over the computer.

12.4 An abstract data type is to be defined which provides the concept of a set of values of an ordered base type as defined in Modula-2, i.e., as sets in which each element value can appear at most once. The required set operators are to include:

> insertion and removal of values;
> test of set membership;
> test of set emptiness;
> assignment of ranges of values to a set;
> finding the number of elements present in a set;
> finding the minimum value in a set;
> set union, intersection, difference and relative complement;
> set equality and containment.

Specify this type as an exported type of a package module SetPackage suitable for use as a library module. Implement the module using an array representation and use it to write a program to find all the prime numbers up to some input value N, using the following method (known as the *Sieve of Eratosthenes*):

All the numbers in the range *[2..N]* are initially put on the 'sieve' and the following actions repeated until the sieve is empty:

> select and remove the smallest number in the sieve (necessarily a prime);
> remove all multiples of that number from the sieve.

12.5 Write a definition-module *MatrixPackage* which exports a type *Matrix* whose values are $N \times N$ matrices of real elements. The package should include facilities to enable:

assignment and access to individual elements of a matrix;
addition, subtraction, and multiplication of matrices;
application of a specified operation to each element of a matrix, or of a
specified row or column, in some suitable order;
calculation of the determinant of a matrix.

Write the corresponding implementation-module.

12.6 As buses arrive at a bus depot they join a queue at an inspection point
where each bus is checked. If some mechanical fault has arisen, the bus is
sent to join another queue of buses at a service bay where a team of
mechanics services each bus in turn. Also, at the inspection point, any dirty
buses are sent to a cleaning point where another queue of buses is washed
and cleaned in turn. After any necessary servicing and cleaning, buses join
a ready queue—each time a bus is required to make a journey it is taken
from the front of the ready queue. Sensors at appropriate points send information about the movement of buses to a monitoring program. The arrival
of a bus, internal movement of a bus within the depot, and departure of a
bus on a journey, each cause a single message to be transmitted to the program. When a bus arrives at the inspection point a message A (for arrival)
followed by the four-digit bus number is transmitted. When the inspection
point decides what to do with the bus at the head of its waiting queue it
sends one of three messages:

  IC – sent to be cleaned
  IS – sent to service bay
  IR – sent to the ready queue

It is not necessary to specify the bus involved, since the control program
should always be aware of which bus is currently at the head of any queue.
Each time a bus is cleaned, the message C is transmitted from the cleaning
point and, likewise, completion of servicing causes S to be transmitted.
The dispatcher acquires a bus for the next journey by sending the message:

  D route-number

to the program, which replies with the number of the bus at the head of the
ready queue, which is the bus to be used for the journey. The dispatcher
may also send the message *?*, in which case the program is to output details
of the lengths of the various queues and the buses which are currently waiting in each queue. Implement this program using the QueuePackage
module presented in this chapter, assuming that all messages to the program are input on the standard input stream.

13

Low-level Programming

The features of Modula-2 described in preceding chapters are said to be *high-level* language features, in that they allow the solution to a problem to be expressed in terms which are well-suited to the problem itself, and are largely independent of the particular characteristics of the computer used to execute the resultant program. This high language level is achieved by abstracting away from the computer-oriented notions of bits, bytes, words and machine instructions to the problem-oriented notions of data types and operators.

As a by-product of this abstraction, a high-level language also provides a considerable degree of protection against programming error. By requiring that all data objects are declared to be of specific types, and by checking the consistency of data types with the operators applied, many programming errors are detected at compile-time. For the majority of programming applications, these twin features of problem-oriented concepts and inherent error security are the major advantages of using a high-level language.

However, Modula-2 is also intended for use in writing so-called *system programs*, i.e., programs which require access to particular features of the computer on which they run. Such programs include control programs (such as that controlling the microprocessor imbedded in a washing machine), device driver programs (such as those which control input and output from and to the keyboard and screen of a VDU) and computer operating systems themselves, as well as programs that necessarily manipulate data in terms of the actual machine representation used, rather than any problem-oriented data types involved in its construction.

Modula-2 provides a limited set of facilities which may be used to perform such *low-level* operations. Only a very limited range of programs need to use these facilities, and indeed many programmers may feel no need to read this chapter! Even when they are necessary, the facilities will generally be used in very small parts of each program. Such limited use of these facilities is not only possible, but desirable. Since these low-level features of Modula-2 enable the otherwise-strict type-compatibility rules to be bypassed, the protection against error provided by the type rules is lost in programs which employ these particular facilities. A programmer should only use them whenever the regular language facilities are insufficient for the application. Since the details of many of these low-level features are machine-dependent and implementation-dependent, we shall not discuss them in any great depth here but shall instead confine ourselves to a brief description and an indication of their intended usage.

Most of the low-level facilities provided by Modula-2 are defined as exported data types and procedures of a standard module SYSTEM. By the nature of the facilities it provides, this module cannot be written in Modula-2, so it does not have an actual definition-module or implementation-module like other library modules. Instead its features are built in to the Modula-2 compiler itself, hence it is sometimes described as a *pseudo-module*. However, to the programmer it appears as any other module, with a definition of the following general form:

```
DEFINITION MODULE SYSTEM;

    TYPE WORD;
         ADDRESS = POINTER TO WORD;

    PROCEDURE ADR(VAR V: any type identifier): ADDRESS;

    PROCEDURE TSIZE(any type identifier): CARDINAL;

    PROCEDURE NEWPROCESS(P: PROC;
                         A: ADDRESS; N: CARDINAL;
                         VAR Coroutine: ADDRESS);

    PROCEDURE TRANSFER(VAR CallingCoroutine,
                           CalledCoroutine: ADDRESS);

    ...

    END SYSTEM.
```

As the ellipsis ... implies, individual Modula-2 implementations may provide additional types and procedures within the SYSTEM module. Those shown above are expected to be included by every implementation. In general terms the facilities provided may be classified as

(a) enabling strict checking of data types and operations to be bypassed;
(b) enabling some degree of concurrency or pseudo-concurrency to be introduced; and
(c) enabling access to specific devices or facilities of the computer system involved.

In subsequent sections we consider the facilities provided under each of these headings.

BYPASSING STRICT TYPE-CHECKING

In Modula-2 strict type-checking can be bypassed by using facilities which enable data to be described and accessed in terms of its underlying machine representation, rather than the problem-oriented data types and operators normally applicable. The standard module SYSTEM exports two types WORD and ADDRESS, and two functions ADR, and TSIZE, for this purpose.

A computer's main memory is made up of a sequence of *words*, where each word has a unique address and is itself made up of a fixed number of *bits*. Every data value in Modula-2 is mapped by the compiler onto one or more words. The type WORD represents a single addressable unit of storage in the computer on which the program is to be executed. The only operation applicable to WORD values is that of assignment. However, if a procedure has a formal parameter declared to be of type WORD then the corresponding actual parameter may be of any data type that requires one word for storage of its values on the given Modula-2 implementation (such types normally include CARDINAL, INTEGER, BITSET and all pointer-types).

If the type of a formal parameter is ARRAY OF WORD then the corresponding actual parameter may be of *any* type, including an array- or record-type. Within the procedure, the actual parameter is accessible as the sequence or array of word values involved in its representation.

The type ADDRESS is defined as

TYPE ADDRESS = POINTER TO WORD;

Its values denote the addresses of words in memory. Hence, if a variable is declared thus:

VAR A: ADDRESS

then A^ denotes the word whose address is the value of A. This type is compatible with all pointer-types. It is also compatible with the type CARDINAL, and hence, all integer arithmetic operators can be applied to ADDRESS values. The primary purpose of this type is to enable address computations to be performed, with results which can be considered as either pointer or CARDINAL values.

The definition module for the library module Storage, which was mentioned in Chapter 11, relies on the use of ADDRESS, as shown in *Storage.def*. Since an actual parameter of any pointer type can be passed to formal parameter A, the procedures ALLOCATE and DEALLOCATE can be used as suggested in Chapter 11 for the creation and destruction of pointer values. Within the implementation module for Storage, arithmetic address computation is normally used to manipulate the values involved.

The function

PROCEDURE ADR(VAR V: *any type identifier): ADDRESS;*

Storage.def

DEFINITION MODULE Storage;

FROM SYSTEM IMPORT ADDRESS;

PROCEDURE ALLOCATE(VAR A: ADDRESS; SizeRequired: CARDINAL);

(* This procedure allocates a storage area of the size required,
and returns its address in A. If insufficient storage is available,
the program is terminated.   *)

PROCEDURE DEALLOCATE(VAR A: ADDRESS; Size: CARDINAL);

(* This procedure frees the storage area at address A of the size given *)

PROCEDURE Available(size: CARDINAL): BOOLEAN;

(* This function returns TRUE if an area of the size given can be allocated *)

END Storage.

---

returns as its result the storage address of the first storage location used by the variable V.

The function

PROCEDURE TSIZE(*any type identifier*): CARDINAL;

returns the number of storage units necessary to hold any value of the type denoted by the type-identifier.

There is some confusion in the definition of Modula-2 as to the intended roles of the function TSIZE and of the standard function SIZE, which was added to the language by the third edition of *Programming in Modula-2*. At one point it is implied that SIZE is applicable to variables while TSIZE is applicable to types, but elsewhere the definition of SIZE indicates that it is applicable to both types and variables, in which case the need for the retention of TSIZE is unclear.

It is important to note that the definition given in *Programming in Modula-2* does *not* specify that the unit of storage measurement used by SIZE and TSIZE is the word, i.e., that TSIZE(WORD) = 1. Within the terms of the definition given, it is possible that an implementation on a byte-oriented machine, say, may allocate variable storage in words (where a word is some constant multiple of bytes), measure storage requirements in bytes and express addresses in either word or byte units. Extreme care must therefore be taken to ensure that the assumptions underlying any use of these facilities are consistent with the actual implementation involved.

Another machine-dependent feature of Modula-2 is the facility for using a type-identifier T as a *type transfer function* which converts the value of its operand to a value of type T. Thus, if C is a CARDINAL value, then the expressions

   INTEGER(C)   and   BITSET(C)

enable the bit pattern representing the value C to be interpreted as an INTEGER value, and a BITSET value, respectively.

Such transfer functions do not actually perform any explicit conversion of the value concerned—the stored representation of the operand is simply interpreted as a value of type specified. For reliable use of the facility each Modula-2 implementation must specify the underlying representation used for each data type. In the case of BITSET, for example, the implementation must specify the correspondence between the bits of the word or words used to store a BITSET value and the absence or presence of corresponding member values of the BITSET so represented.

On almost all implementations the representations used for INTEGER and CARDINAL values are identical for the range of values 0 to MAX(INTEGER), so that transfers of the form CARDINAL(I) or INTEGER(C) give expected results. However, a transfer of the form LONGINT(I) is unpredictable, and depends entirely on the implementation—since the amount of storage used by the types INTEGER and LONGINT are usually different, the implementation may even reject such a transfer as invalid. In practice, the use of such type transfer functions normally makes sense only between types such as WORD and BITSET, and the simple types such as INTEGER, CARDINAL, pointer- and enumeration-types, where these are known to map onto the same number of storage units.

COROUTINES

The flow of control in the Modula-2 programs presented so far has been expressed as a hierarchy of procedure calls. A master/slave relationship exists between each procedure and the statement that calls it, in that the procedure is only activated by such a call and can only return control to the same statement, whatever flow of control it may generate during its own execution. Such a procedure or function is sometimes called a *subroutine,* since it is subordinate to the statement that calls it.

In some situations, however, the overall effect of a program is better expressed in terms of a set of two or more control patterns which collaborate by explicit exchange of control. *Coroutines* are program components which interact with each other in this symmetric fashion. They operate at the same level such that any one member of a group of coroutines may be active at a given time while the remainder are passive. At any moment the active coroutine *A* may make itself passive and (re)activate one of the passive coroutines *B* by means of some coroutine-transfer operation. If *B* or some coroutine activated by *B* chooses to reactivate *A,* execution of *A* continues from the point at which it activated *B*.

In any Modula-2 program, the set of coroutines involved in its execution are the main program itself, and any coroutines created via the procedure NEWPROCESS exported by the SYSTEM module. The execution pattern for each coroutine created via NEWPROCESS must be defined as a parameterless global procedure, i.e., a procedure of type PROC. Given such a procedure P, a corresponding coroutine is created by a call of the form:

NEWPROCESS(P, A, N, C)

This coroutine is given as its *execution workspace* (i.e., storage for local variables and other information relevant to its execution) a storage block of size N beginning at memory address A. The coroutine is initialized so that its subsequent activation will cause it to start execution at the first statement of P, and a reference to this initialized coroutine is stored in the ADDRESS variable C, to enable such activation.

Activation of a coroutine is achieved by means of a call to the TRANSFER procedure exported by SYSTEM, thus:

TRANSFER(OldC, NewC)

The calling coroutine (possibly the main program) is suspended and a coroutine reference for its subsequent reactivation is assigned to the ADDRESS variable OldC. The passive coroutine which is referenced by the ADDRESS variable NewC is then activated. Execution of a program terminates when any active coroutine (possibly the main program) either reaches the end of its body or executes the standard procedure HALT.

CASE STUDY 15

The use of coroutines is illustrated by the following example, which is a variation on an early example of coroutines defined by Conway. A program is required to read the contents of an input stream and send them to an output stream with certain editing actions having been performed on the input text. The input text is to be output with 50 characters per line, irrespective of the line structure of the input, and with an extra space inserted to denote the end of an input line. Double asterisks '**' in the input text are to be output as '@'. The end of the input text is denoted by the character '%'. As posed here, the problem is somewhat artificial, but provides a good illustration of the use of coroutines. Many more realistic problems are amenable to a similar solution.

The required program consists of three coroutines Input, Edit and Output, and a main program *driver* which designates the corresponding procedures as coroutines. Input looks after the reading of the input stream, Edit carries out any necessary editing (i.e., replacement of successive asterisks) and Output looks after the production of the output text. Input and Edit communicate by means of a global variable LastInputChar which holds the value of the last character read from the input stream, while Edit and Output communicate via another global variable NextOutputChar which holds the value of the next character to be output.

In Modula-2, the program must define three procedures which are then designated as the required coroutines by means of calls of NEWPROCESS. The editing process is commenced by the main program transferring control to the Input coroutine for production of the first character from the input stream. Hence, the main program must have the following overall form:

```
MODULE TextConversion;
FROM SYSTEM IMPORT ADDRESS, NEWPROCESS, TRANSFER;

VAR Input, Edit, Output, MainProgram: ADDRESS;
    LastInputChar, NextOutputChar: CHAR;

PROCEDURE InputProcedure ; ...;
PROCEDURE EditProcedure  ; ...;
PROCEDURE OutputProcedure; ...;

BEGIN
  NEWPROCESS(InputProcedure, ..., ..., Input);
  NEWPROCESS(EditProcedure,  ..., ..., Edit);
  NEWPROCESS(OutputProcedure, ..., ..., Output);
  TRANSFER(MainProgram, Input);
END TextConversion.
```

where InputProcedure, EditProcedure, and OutputProcedure are the procedures defining the three coroutines required, and the variables Input, Edit, and Output are the reactivation references associated with these coroutines. MainProgram is the reference used for reactivation of the main program when the coroutines have completed the input, editing, and output of the text.

The procedure InputProcedure (which defines the behavior of the coroutine Input) repeatedly reads the next character from the input stream, replaces EOL by blank if necessary, assigns its value to a global variable NextInputChar, and transfers control to the coroutine Edit.

```
PROCEDURE InputProcedure;
VAR Ch: CHAR;
BEGIN
  LOOP
    READ (Ch);
    IF Ch = EOL  THEN LastInputChar := " "
    ELSE LastInputChar := Ch
    END;
```

```
    transfer control to Edit
  END
  END InputProcedure;
```

Note that no terminating condition appears in the input loop—termination of the overall program is taken care of elsewhere.

The Edit coroutine carries out any editing required by the input character (i.e., replacement of successive asterisks by '@'), and assigns each character for output to the global variable NextOutputChar. Each time a character is assigned to NextOutputChar, control is transferred to the Output coroutine. Each time a further input character is required, control is transferred to the Input coroutine. Note that the detection of an asterisk causes two successive activations of Input followed by either one or two successive activations of Output.

```
  PROCEDURE EditProcedure;
  BEGIN
    LOOP
      IF LastInputChar = "*" THEN
        get next character from Input;
        IF LastInputChar = "*" THEN NextOutputChar := "@"
        ELSE
          NextOutputChar := "*";
          transfer control to Output;
          NextOutputChar := LastInputChar
        END
      ELSE NextOutputChar := LastInputChar
      END;
      transfer control to Output;
      get next character from Input
    END
  END EditProcedure;
```

Output repeatedly outputs the value of NextOutputChar (and also outputs a new line every 50 characters) and transfers control to Edit for production of the next character to be output. When Output recognizes the end of text character it causes the program to terminate, by transferring control back to the main program.

```
  PROCEDURE OutputProcedure;
  VAR I: [1..LineLength];
  BEGIN
    LOOP
      FOR I := 1 TO LineLength DO
        IF NextOutputChar = "%" THEN
          IF I <> 1 THEN WriteLn END;
```

```
      transfer control to main program
      END;
      Write (NextOutputChar);
      get next character for output from Edit
    END;
    WriteLn
  END
END OutputProcedure;
```

The various coroutines must all be created with appropriate workspaces. These workspaces are obtained by use of the ALLOCATE procedure provided by the standard Storage module, and are of a size which is dependent on how the particular Modula-2 compiler implements coroutines. The coroutine transfers are all implemented as calls of TRANSFER involving the appropriate ADDRESS variables. The final program is shown as *TextConversion.mod* together with output produced by execution of the program on the following input text:

```
There is no equivalent in Modula-2 of FORTRAN's "**"
i.e., the FORTRAN statement
    X = A**I
is written in Modula-2 (assuming I is  nonnegative) as
    X := 1;
    FOR J := 1 TO I DO X := X*A
%
```

TextConversion.mod

```
MODULE TextConversion;
  FROM SYSTEM IMPORT ADDRESS, NEWPROCESS, TRANSFER;
  FROM InOut IMPORT Read, Write, WriteLn, EOL;
  FROM Storage IMPORT ALLOCATE;

  (* This program converts an input text to an output text as follows:

    (a) line structure in the input text is eliminated, by replacing
        each newline character by an additional space character;
    (b) each adjacent asterisk pair "**" is replaced by a "@";
    (c) the resultant character sequence is output with exactly 50
        characters per line.

  The input text must be terminated by a "%" character.

  The program is implemented as a set of three coroutines, Input,
  Edit and Output, which are responsible for the transformations
  (a), (b), (c) respectively. Characters are communicated between
  these coroutines via the global variables LastInputChar and
  NextOutputChar.                                              *)
```

```
CONST Terminator = "%"; LineLength = 50;
      WorkSpaceSize = 100; (* implementation-dependent *)

VAR Input, Edit, Output, MainProgram: ADDRESS;
    LastInputChar, NextOutputChar: CHAR;
    WorkSpace: ADDRESS;

PROCEDURE InputProcedure;
  VAR Ch: CHAR;
  BEGIN (* coroutine Input *)
   LOOP
     Read(Ch);
     IF Ch = EOL  THEN LastInputChar := " "
     ELSE LastInputChar := Ch
     END;
     TRANSFER(Input, Edit);
   END
  END InputProcedure;

PROCEDURE EditProcedure;
  BEGIN (* coroutine Edit *)
   LOOP
     IF LastInputChar = "*" THEN
       TRANSFER(Edit, Input);
       IF LastInputChar = "*" THEN NextOutputChar := "@"
       ELSE
         NextOutputChar := "*";
         TRANSFER(Edit, Output);
         NextOutputChar := LastInputChar
       END
     ELSE NextOutputChar := LastInputChar
     END;
     TRANSFER(Edit, Output);
     TRANSFER(Edit, Input)
   END
  END EditProcedure;

PROCEDURE OutputProcedure;
  VAR I: [1..LineLength];
  BEGIN (* coroutine Output *)
   LOOP
     FOR I := 1 TO LineLength DO
```

```
        IF NextOutputChar = Terminator THEN
          IF I <> 1 THEN WriteLn END;
          TRANSFER(Output, MainProgram)
        END;
        Write(NextOutputChar);
        TRANSFER(Output, Edit)
      END;
      WriteLn
    END
  END OutputProcedure;

BEGIN
  ALLOCATE(WorkSpace, WorkSpaceSize);
  NEWPROCESS(InputProcedure, WorkSpace, WorkSpaceSize , Input);
  ALLOCATE(WorkSpace, WorkSpaceSize);
  NEWPROCESS(EditProcedure, WorkSpace, WorkSpaceSize, Edit);
  ALLOCATE(WorkSpace, WorkSpaceSize);
  NEWPROCESS(OutputProcedure, WorkSpace, WorkSpaceSize, Output);
  TRANSFER(MainProgram, Input);
END TextConversion.
```

```
There is no equivalent in Modula-2 of FORTRAN's "@
" i.e., the FORTRAN statement    X = A@I is writte
n in Modula-2 (assuming I is   nonnegative) as    X
:= 1;    FOR J := 1 TO I DO X := X*A
```

LOW-LEVEL I/O FACILITIES

As indicated in Chapter 5, Modula-2 does not provide built-in facilities for 'high-level' input and output (I/O) as such. By high-level I/O we mean operations which are directly useful in solving a range of computing problems, such as input or output of numeric values with automatic conversion to character representations, input or output of character strings, and so on. Instead, the language design assumes that such facilities will be made available with each implementation as one or more library modules. In Chapter 5 we looked in detail at the facilities provided by Wirth's InOut module as an illustration of this approach, and elsewhere we have relied on the availability of InOut in the example programs we have produced.

An obvious assumption of the library module approach to high-level I/O is that sufficient 'low-level' facilities are made available by each implementation to enable the programming of the high-level facilities required. However, it is impractical to define within the language the precise form which these low-level facilities must take. A primary reason for adopting the approach is that both the I/O requirements and the I/O capabilities may vary widely between the computers on which Modula-2 is used. At the one extreme Modula-2 may be used to program a dedicated control computer imbedded in a washing machine, while at the other extreme it may be used to program a large multi-user computer for straightforward data-processing applications.

In the case of the washing-machine controller the input operations required involve 'reading' inputs from buttons on the control panel of the washing machine, or from sensors such as temperature gauges within the machine itself. The output operations involve controlling lights and displays on the control panel, sending control signals to the washer mechanisms to activate each phase of the wash-cycle, and so on. The highly variable nature of the I/O devices involved, and the simplicity of the dedicated computers used in such applications, mean that such I/O is normally achieved by direct control of the I/O device itself from within the control program. To enable such programs to be written, the Modula-2 implementation involved must therefore provide facilities for direct I/O device control.

In the case of a multi-user computer, the I/O operations required by its users are typically those provided by high-level modules such as InOut, but the significant characteristic of such computers is that I/O is not normally achieved by direct control of the I/O devices (terminals, disk-drives, printers, etc.) by each user program. Instead, it is undertaken on the program's behalf by the *operating system* which controls overall use of the computer by its various users. I/O requests are therefore expressed in the user program in terms of a range of I/O operations defined by the operating system, usually by invoking a so-called *system call*. Programming of the I/O library modules in Modula-2 implies that such system calls can be made from within the implementation modules involved.

These two extremes indicate the inevitable variation in implementations of Modula-2. In the following subsections we give a brief indication of how such facilities may be provided, by looking briefly at two particular implementations. The subsections are not intended to provide sufficient detail for actual I/O programming on the implementations concerned, only to indicate the overall strategy used. Anyone who needs to program I/O at this level on these or other implementations must study the relevant implementation documentation before beginning.

Direct I/O Device Control

The PDP-11 is typical of computers which use *memory-mapped input and output*. On these, the *device registers* through which an I/O device communicates with a program are allocated to fixed locations in the computer's memory, and I/O operations are effected by operations on these storage locations. On the PDP-11, for example, the keyboard *status register* is allocated to the memory

IM–K*

word with address 777560B, while the keyboard *data register* is allocated to word 777562B. The first problem in writing a Modula-2 program which controls the keyboard through such registers, is how to access them in Modula-2.

In the PDP-11 implementation of Modula-2, a variable-declaration may specify the address of the first location at which it requires the value of a variable to be stored, and the compiler will then arrange for that variable to be allocated the necessary number of storage locations, beginning at the indicated address—such a variable is known as an *absolute-variable*. Using this facility, the status and data registers for the keyboard can be declared as follows:

```
VAR KSR [777560B]: BITSET;  (* PDP-11 keyboard status register *)
    KDR [777562B]: CHAR;    (* PDP-11 keyboard data register  *)
```

Device status registers are normally declared to be of type BITSET (remember that a BITSET occupies one word of storage). Operations involving access to particular bits of a word may be then implemented by means of set operators. For instance, the status of the keyboard of the PDP-11 is represented by the value of bit 7 of word 777562B and the keyboard interrupt disable bit is bit 6 of this word. If we assume that membership of value n in a BITSET is represented by setting bit n to 1, keyboard interrupts may be enabled by, e.g.,

```
EXCL(KSR, 6)
```

and disabled by

```
KSR := BITSET{6}
```

Testing for the presence of input from the keyboard (often called *polling* the device) can be achieved by a statement such as

```
REPEAT (* busy-waiting *) UNTIL 7 IN KSR
```

When the presence of input is indicated by the status register, the input character is obtained simply by accessing the value of the data register KDR, e.g.,

```
NextCh := KDR
```

Equivalent facilities for the declaration of absolute variables may be provided by implementations for other machines. If no such facilities are provided, absolute storage locations may still be accessed by means of auxiliary ADDRESS variables whose values are initialized to the required memory addresses, e.g., a program might declare

```
VAR KSR, KDR: ADDRESS;
```

and initialize them thus

```
KSR := 777560B;
KDR := 777562B
```

The program may subsequently refer to KSR^ and KDR^ (referenced-variables of type WORD, which denote the status and data register respectively) and manipulate these registers by means of suitable transfer functions which enable the WORD values to be treated as the necessary BITSET or CHAR values, e.g.,

    REPEAT (* busy-waiting *) UNTIL 7 IN BITSET(KSR^);
    NextCh := CHAR(KDR^)

The examples so far have suggested a 'busy waiting' approach to I/O operations, in which the program can do no productive work while waiting for, say, keyboard input to arrive. For machines on which an I/O device can *interrupt* the current processing activity, a more effective strategy is possible. In this case the process of looking after, or *handling*, the I/O device, and that of dealing with the data transferred are organized as two coroutines, with automatic transfer of control to the handler coroutine when an interrupt from the corresponding device occurs. Such coroutines can be set up using the Modula-2 facilities described in the preceding section, but the implicit transfer of control which is required when an interrupt occurs must be expressed in some special way. On the PDP-11 implementation of Modula-2, this is provided for by an additional procedure exported from the SYSTEM module, which is used in the device-handling coroutine as follows:

    IOTRANSFER(OldC, NewC, IVA)

The effect of this is to transfer control to the coroutine referenced by NewC, remembering the current device-handling coroutine in variable OldC, as in the case of TRANSFER, but also to note the interrupt vector address IVA. When an interrupt occurs on the device associated with that address, control is implicitly transferred back to the coroutine referenced by OldC, i.e. the device-handling coroutine that executed the IOTRANSFER, and the interrupted coroutine is remembered in NewC. The device-handling coroutine can deal with the device as required, and then resume the interrupted coroutine via IOTRANSFER to continue processing.

A typical means of handling an input device by this method is a local module with the following general form:

MODULE DeviceX [*device priority level*];

IMPORT ADDRESS, NEWPROCESS, TRANSFER, IOTRANSFER;

EXPORT *variables or procedures for transfer of*
  data between handler and user program;

CONST IVA = *interrupt vector address of device*;
  WSSize = *workspace requirement of handler coroutine*;

```
VAR Handler, UserProgram: ADDRESS (* coroutine references *);
    WorkSpace: ADDRESS (* for Handler Coroutine *);

variables or procedures for transfer of
data between handler and user program;

PROCEDURE HandlerProcedure;
  BEGIN
  LOOP
    (* resume user program pending device interrupt: *)
    IOTRANSFER(Handler, UserProgram, IVA);
    service device interrupt, making data available to user program
  END
  END HandlerBody;

BEGIN
  ALLOCATE(WorkSpace, WSSize);
  NEWPROCESS(HandlerProcedure, WorkSpace, WSSize, Handler);
  enable interrupts from device;
  TRANSFER(UserProgram, Handler) (* to initiate handler *)
END DeviceX
```

Note the use of the device priority level in the module heading. The code within any Modula-2 module is executed at the priority level indicated by its heading, and can be interrupted only by signals of higher priority. By associating the priority of each device with its handler module, we ensure that the handler can only be interrupted by devices with a higher priority level.

I/O Under Multi-user Operating Systems

The facilities described in the previous subsection either cannot or should not be used under an operating system which provides general I/O facilities for multiple user programs running under it. Instead I/O by such programs is achieved by invoking some form of system call.

The UNIX† operating system, which is used on many multi-user computers, is typical in this respect. UNIX adopts a simple model for access to data held in file-store files. Named files may be opened and closed as *streams* for read, write or read/write access, with each operation reading or writing a sequence of bytes. A seek operation is also available which resets the current read/write position to a specified byte offset, thus giving effective random access to filed data. Terminal input and output are also accessible as streams when required. The

---

†UNIX is a Trademark of AT&T Bell Laboratories.

operations available are defined as a corresponding set of system calls which are executable by any program running under UNIX.

To enable the programming of library I/O modules, a Modula-2 implementation under UNIX must therefore provide some means of executing system calls.

One means of doing so is demonstrated by the Cambridge University implementation of Modula-2 for Digital VAX computers running UNIX. In this implementation the SYSTEM module exports a procedure UNIXCALL, via which any system call may be invoked, using parameters of type WORD or ADDRESS to transmit the arguments involved.

To read a value of type T from a file opened as stream S to a variable V the following code might be used:

```
BytesNeeded := TSIZE(T);
BytesRead := UNIXCALL(read, S, ADR(V), BytesNeeded);
Success := BytesRead = BytesNeeded;
```

(On the Cambridge implementation, the function TSIZE returns the type's storage requirement in bytes. The UNIX *read* operation returns the number of bytes actually read, so enabling the success of the read operation to be checked.)

Using this basic mechanism, a comprehensive suite of I/O modules can then be provided. In the Cambridge module library these include

(a) a module *Streams* which defines the basic characteristics of an input or output data stream, and basic input and output operations on it, including a seek operation for random access;

(b) a module *FileStream* which enables named file-store files to be opened or closed as data streams;

(c) a module *TermStream* which enables the terminal keyboard and screen to be accessed as a bi-directional data stream;

(d) a module *TextIO* which provides high-level I/O operations such as *ReadIN-TEGER, WriteINTEGER*, etc., which are applicable to any data stream.

Other stream-related modules provide additional I/O facilities for other purposes. The Cambridge suite of I/O modules is typical of those which overcome the inherent limitation of the InOut module, which is that only one input stream and one output stream can be active at any time. Using the Cambridge suite, any number of file-store streams can be active simultaneously, as can the terminal stream. Equivalent multi-stream I/O facilities are provided by library modules available with other implementations.

An alternative to the provision of a specific mechanism for invoking system calls from within Modula-2 modules, is a separate compilation scheme which allows modules compiled from other languages to be combined with modules compiled from Modula-2. The system calls needed for low-level I/O operations can then be programmed in assembler, or a system programming language such as C, and integrated with a Modula-2 module which provides the high-level I/O facilities required. Some Modula-2 implementations achieve the low-level facilities required for I/O programming by this method.

EXERCISES

13.1 Define and implement a module BitCounts which exports

(a) a function Bits1 which can be used to count the number of 1 bits in the representation of a data value of any type which occupies a single word of storage on your implementation of Modula-2;

(b) a function BitsN which can be used to count the number of 1 bits in the representation of a data value of any type on your implementation.

What parts, if any, of the module may have to change to be usable on another implementation?

13.2 An input stream consists of ten-character names, organized as ten names per line. A program is to read these names and output them twelve to a line. After each group of ten names the program is to insert a dummy name consisting of ten asterisks into the output stream. Implement this program using coroutines.

13.3 The input stream to a program consists of a sequence of alphanumeric characters encoded in condensed form. When the contents of the encoded sequence are scanned they are to be interpreted as follows: If the next character is

(a) a space, it is ignored;

(b) a period, then the end of the encoded sequence has been reached;

(c) a digit N, then N repetitions of the following character are denoted;

(d) a non-digit, then the character itself is denoted.

The character sequence represented by this encoding is to be output 120 characters per line in groups of 3 characters with groups separated by single spaces, except for the last group which may contain less than 3 characters. The terminating full stop is not to be output. For example, the encoding

$$A3B4C25F23G.$$

should produce the output

$$ABB\ BCC\ CC5\ 5F3\ 3G$$

Write a program which makes use of two coroutines to carry out this text expansion.

14

Concurrent Programming

CONCURRENT PROCESSES

All of the Modula-2 programs presented so far have been *sequential* programs, i.e., each program described the sequence of actions to be executed in order to carry out a certain activity. In the previous chapter we saw that coroutines enable the sequence of actions to be defined as two or more control patterns which are interleaved at specified points, but the overall effect is still a single sequence of actions. In practice, many programs are more naturally described as a group of activities which, from the programmer's viewpoint, proceed in parallel, or *concurrently*, with one another. In this case, each activity is known as a *process*, and such a program is said to consist of a number of *concurrent processes*. The distinguishing feature of such processes is that, unlike coroutines, overlapping of their execution is not excluded, and their relative rate of progress is not rigidly determined.

Although not strictly synchronized, most concurrent processes are not wholly independent of each other, and generally cooperate in some way to perform the overall task involved. For example, the text conversion program developed in the previous chapter might be formulated as three processes—one which produces the characters from the input text, another which (when necessary) edits the characters, and a third process which sends the characters to the output stream. The input and editing processes communicate by the input process making available to the editing process the characters which it generates. Typically, these characters are stored in some *buffer* data structure which is accessible by both processes, as shown in Figure 14.1. A similar buffer structure is required between the editing and output processes.

If both of the processes Input and Edit have access to the shared buffer InBuffer, this access must be regulated to ensure that both processes do not attempt to access the buffer simultaneously, otherwise an inconsistent situation

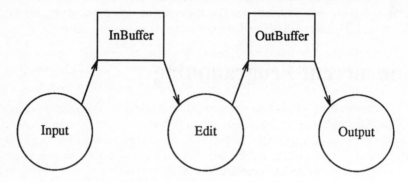

Figure 14.1   Concurrent processes and buffers

could arise. Thus we require this buffer, and likewise OutBuffer, to have the property of *mutual exclusion,* so that only one process at a time may access or change its contents.

Since processes may proceed at different rates, it may also happen that a buffer becomes full or empty at certain times. If a data-producing process, such as Input, when adding a new item to the buffer, finds the buffer to be full then it must wait until a data-consuming process, in this case Edit, enables it to proceed by removing an item from the buffer. Likewise, the Edit process may find InBuffer empty and therefore must wait until the Input process adds an item to the buffer before it tries to remove one. Hence we also require a means of delaying a given process when a required condition does not hold, until such time as the condition holds.

From this analysis of the text conversion example, we see that, to enable concurrent programming, a language such as Modula-2 must provide three additional facilities:

(a)   a means of defining and activating concurrent processes;
(b)   a means of providing mutually exclusive access by processes to shared data structures;
(c)   a means of delaying a particular process until a certain condition holds.

In practice, a number of models exist for the inclusion of such facilities in programming languages, but Modula-2 does not provide any such facilities directly. However, it is possible to define a module which provides such facilities, and in the next section we define a module Processes for this purpose, and illustrate its use by a concurrent version of the text conversion program.

The implementation of concurrent programming facilities may be achieved in two general ways:

(a) by exploiting an underlying machine capacity for truly concurrent execution of processes—this implies that the computer system involved has two or more processors available for simultaneous process execution;

(b) by simulating concurrent execution of processes by some appropriate interleaving of execution of the processes concerned on a single processor. Such an implementation is said to provide *quasi-* or *pseudo-concurrency*.

On a machine which offers two or more processors for execution of processes, the SYSTEM module of an implementation of Modula-2 may provide low-level facilities for processor control. In this case our Processes module might be implemented in terms of these facilities. On a single-processor machine, however, this module can be implemented to provide pseudo-concurrency using the coroutine facilities described in Chapter 13. Such an implementation is demonstrated in the final section of this chapter.

THE MODULE *Processes*

The following definition-module Processes is similar to that presented by Wirth in *Programming in Modula-2*. It differs only in its treatment of process termination, as explained later.

Processes.def

```
DEFINITION MODULE Processes;

   (* This module provides facilities for the activation and termination of
      concurrent processes, and facilities which enable such processes
      to 'wait' on conditions which are 'signaled' by other processes.   *)

   PROCEDURE StartProcess(P: PROC; N: CARDINAL);

      (* activate procedure P as a process which runs concurrently
         with the calling process, using a work space of size N words *)

   PROCEDURE EndProcess;

      (* terminate the calling process *)

   TYPE Condition;

      (* Variables of type Condition enable processes to delay themselves
         pending some required condition, using the procedures defined below: *)

   PROCEDURE Initialize(VAR S: Condition);

      (* each Condition variable must be initialized before use as below *)
```

PROCEDURE Wait(VAR S: Condition);

  (* wait for another process to signal S *)

PROCEDURE Signal(VAR S: Condition);

  (* resume process waiting longest for S *)

PROCEDURE Awaited(S: Condition): BOOLEAN;

  (* is any process awaiting a signal on S *)

END Processes.

The definition and activation of a concurrent process is provided for by the procedure StartProcess. As with coroutines, the pattern of behavior required of a process is represented as a parameterless procedure, e.g.,

```
PROCEDURE Input;
  BEGIN
    ...
  END Input;
```

However, each process defined by such a procedure is created *and activated* by a call of the procedure StartProcess. Hence, the call

```
StartProcess(Input, N)
```

commences execution of the process represented by the procedure Input. As with coroutines, each process requires some workspace in memory to hold information associated with its execution—the size N depends on the local data involved in the process execution and in general its value is implementation-dependent. Unlike coroutines, however, no reference to the process created is required—once created, processes do not refer to one another directly. Their only interaction is through the shared data they access, and any conditions on which they wait from time to time.

The overall structure required for the text conversion program is thus:

```
MODULE TextConversion;
  FROM Processes IMPORT ...;
  FROM InOut IMPORT ...;
```

  declarations of InBuffer and OutBuffer

```
PROCEDURE Input;
  define behavior of input process
  END Input;
```

```
PROCEDURE Edit;
  define behavior of edit process
  END Edit;
```

```
PROCEDURE Output;
  define behavior of output process
END Output;

BEGIN
  initialize buffers;
  StartProcess(Edit, ...);
  StartProcess(Output, ...);
  Input
END TextConversion.
```

The main program itself constitutes a single process. The calls of StartProcess activate Edit and Output as processes which execute concurrently with the main program process, which then calls the procedure Input. Hence Input, Edit and Output all effectively proceed in parallel.

The buffers to which the processes require mutually exclusive access are defined (with suitable access operators Put and Get) as local modules. A module which enforces the mutual exclusion property on the use of its exported procedures is called a *monitor*. Any process calling an exported procedure of such a module while another process is currently executing any exported procedure of the same module is forced to wait until either the other process has completed its execution of the exported procedure concerned, or has relinquished its exclusive access (by executing a *wait* or *signal* operation as explained below). In Modula-2 a module is designated as a monitor by the inclusion of a *priority* in its heading.

$$priority = "[" \ constant\text{-}expression \ "]".$$

The choice of priority value is not of significance in the present context. Hence, the buffer InBuffer might be implemented, as a cyclic buffer of character values, in the following form:

```
MODULE InBuffer [1];
  EXPORT QUALIFIED Put, Get;

  CONST BufferSize = 64; (* say *)

  VAR Buffer: ARRAY [1..BufferSize] OF CHAR;
      Front, Rear: [1..BufferSize]; CurrentLength: [0..BufferSize];
      ...

  PROCEDURE Put(C: CHAR);
    BEGIN
      IF CurrentLength = BufferSize THEN wait until not full END;
      Buffer[Rear] := C; Rear := Rear MOD BufferSize + 1;
      INC(CurrentLength)
    END Put;
```

```
PROCEDURE Get(VAR C: CHAR);
BEGIN
   IF CurrentLength = 0 THEN wait until not empty END;
   C := Buffer [Front]; Front := Front MOD BufferSize + 1;
   DEC (CurrentLength)
END Get;

BEGIN (* InBuffer *)
   CurrentLength := 0; Front := 1; Rear := 1
END InBuffer;
```

OutBuffer will be identical in form. Qualified export of the identifiers Put and Get implies that the buffer involved must be identified in each call, thus:

```
InBuffer.Put(...)      OutBuffer.Put(...)
InBuffer.Get(...)      OutBuffer.Get(...)
```

The monitor property of a module with a priority in its heading ensures that each time a process calls Put or Get of either buffer it is guaranteed to have exclusive access to that buffer until such time as it decides to relinquish this exclusion, either by leaving the monitor, or by *waiting* for some condition within it.

In the case of the input and output buffers, as the outline implies, the buffer being full or empty may require a process to wait. In practice, this is achieved using special queuing variables on which processes can *wait* until *signaled* by other processes that they may continue. These variables are declared to be of the opaque type Condition exported from the Processes module, e.g.,

VAR NotFull, NotEmpty: Condition;

Associated with this type are exported operators Initialize, Wait, Signal and Awaited. Each Condition variable must be initialized within the initialization of its enclosing monitor, e.g., the statement-part of InBuffer must contain statements

Initialize(NotFull); Initialize(NotEmpty)

The step *wait until not full* now becomes

Wait(NotFull)

while *wait until not empty* becomes

Wait(NotEmpty)

How is the condition awaited in each case to be signaled? In principle, a buffer may become non-full as a result of any Get operation, and non-empty as a result of any Put operation. One simple solution, therefore, is to add

Signal(NotEmpty)

at the end of each Put procedure, to indicate to any process waiting for the buffer to become non-empty that it may proceed, and similarly to add

Signal(NotFull)

at the end of each Get procedure, to indicate to any process waiting for the buffer to become non-full that it may proceed.

When a process is delayed by a Wait operation it joins the end of the queue of waiting processes associated with the Condition variable concerned, and exclusion on the use of the monitor is released. A signaling process passes control to the process which has been waiting longest on the particular Condition variable, i.e., the process at the head of the queue, which regains exclusive access to the monitor. The signaling process is itself delayed until the reactivated process has relinquished exclusive access to the buffer. If no process is awaiting the condition concerned, a Signal operation has no effect.

The required behavior when the buffers are empty or full is thus obtained as shown by the following augmented version of the input buffer module:

```
MODULE InBuffer [1];
  EXPORT QUALIFIED Put, Get;
  IMPORT Condition, Initialize, Wait, Signal;

  CONST BufferSize = 64;

  VAR Buffer: ARRAY [1..BufferSize] OF CHAR;
      Front, Rear: [1..BufferSize]; CurrentLength: [0..BufferSize];
      NotFull, NotEmpty: Condition;

  PROCEDURE Put(C: CHAR);
    BEGIN
      IF CurrentLength = BufferSize THEN Wait(NotFull) END;
      Buffer[Rear] := C; Rear := Rear MOD BufferSize + 1;
      INC(CurrentLength);
      Signal(NotEmpty)
    END Put;

  PROCEDURE Get(VAR C: CHAR);
    BEGIN
      IF CurrentLength = 0 THEN Wait(NotEmpty) END;
      C := Buffer [Front]; Front := Front MOD BufferSize + 1;
      DEC(CurrentLength);
      Signal(NotFull)
    END Get;

BEGIN (* InBuffer *)
  CurrentLength := 0; Front := 1; Rear := 1;
  Initialize(NotFull); Initialize(NotEmpty)
END InBuffer;
```

With these buffers, the detailed behavior required of each of the processes Input, Edit and Output is easily programmed, using equivalent logic to that of the corresponding coroutines defined in Chapter 13. For example, the Edit process is defined as follows:

```
PROCEDURE Edit;
  VAR InCh, OutCh: CHAR;
  BEGIN
    LOOP
      InBuffer.Get(InCh);
      IF InCh = "*" THEN
        InBuffer.Get(InCh);
        IF InCh = "*" THEN OutCh := "@"
        ELSE OutBuffer.Put("*"); OutCh := InCh
        END
      ELSE OutCh := InCh
      END;
      OutBuffer.Put(OutCh)
    END
  END Edit;
```

A significant difference does arise, however, when we consider how the processes should terminate. In the coroutine program developed in Chapter 13, termination of the overall sequence of actions implemented by the three coroutines was clearly the responsibility of the Output coroutine, and the other two coroutines had no need to take account of how termination was effected—they were only reactivated if further work had to be done. For concurrent processes, however, the situation is different. In principle the processes may proceed at different rates, and the overall difference in progress at any stage being limited by the size of the buffers used for communication. If buffers of size N are used, then the Input process may be up to N characters ahead of the Edit process, which in turn may be up to N characters ahead of the Output process. Thus, the Input process may finish its useful work when the Output process still has many characters to process.

For a program composed of several concurrent processes, termination of the overall program is deemed to occur when each of its component processes has either terminated or is waiting on some condition. (If all other processes have either terminated or are also waiting, such a condition can never be fulfilled.) To this end, the Processes module exports a procedure EndProcess by which a process may signal its wish to terminate, and program termination is defined to occur when each concurrent process has either executed a call to EndProcess or is waiting on some Condition variable.

For implementation reasons which will become clear in the next section, we exclude a concurrent process from terminating by reaching the end of the procedure which defines it, by executing a RETURN statement in this procedure, by executing a HALT statement, or in the case of the main process by reaching the end of the main program body itself. If a process terminates in any of these ways, execution of the overall concurrent program to completion cannot be guaranteed.

With these decisions on termination, the Output process is now programmed as follows:

```
PROCEDURE Output;
  VAR I: [1..LineLength]; Ch: CHAR;
  BEGIN
    LOOP
      FOR I := 1 TO LineLength DO
        OutBuffer.Get(Ch);
        IF Ch = Terminator THEN WriteLn; EndProcess END;
        Write(Ch)
      END;
      WriteLn
    END
  END Output;
```

In the coroutine solution developed in Chapter 13, the explicit transfer of control between coroutines ensures that the Input coroutine is not reactivated after passing the terminating '%' to the Edit coroutine, but with concurrent processes this is not so. The Input process may now get significantly ahead of the Edit and Output processes, so it must guard against exhausting the input stream, as follows:

```
PROCEDURE Input;
  VAR Ch: CHAR;
  BEGIN
    LOOP
      Read(Ch);
      IF NOT Done THEN EndProcess END;
      IF Ch = EOL THEN Ch := " " END;
      InBuffer.Put(Ch)
    END
  END Input;
```

Termination as such is not an issue for the Edit process. Assuming that the Input process terminates, or at least stops putting characters in InBuffer, the Edit process, programmed as above, will eventually exhaust InBuffer, and then wait forever on the NotEmpty condition in its next call to InBuffer.Get. Overall program termination, therefore, involves termination of the Input and Output processes, with the Edit process in a permanent waiting state.

The final concurrent form of the text conversion program is shown as *TextConversion.mod*.

TextConversion.mod

```
MODULE TextConversion;

FROM Processes IMPORT
  StartProcess, EndProcess, Condition, Initialize, Wait, Signal;
FROM InOut IMPORT Read, EOL, Done, Write, WriteLn;

(* This program converts an input text to an output text as follows:

  (a) line structure in the input text is eliminated, by replacing
      each newline character by an additional space character;
  (b) each adjacent asterisk pair "**" is replaced by a "@";
  (c) the resultant character sequence is output with exactly 50
      characters per line.
  The input text must be terminated by a "%" character.

  The program is implemented as three concurrent processes, Input,
  Edit and Output, which are responsible for the transformations
  (a), (b), (c) respectively. Characters are communicated between
  these processes via the monitor modules InBuffer and OutBuffer.    *)

CONST Terminator = "%"; LineLength = 50; WorkSpaceSize = 1000;

MODULE InBuffer [1];

  IMPORT Condition, Initialize, Wait, Signal;
  EXPORT QUALIFIED Put, Get;

  CONST BufferSize = 64;

  VAR Buffer: ARRAY [1..BufferSize] OF CHAR;
      Front, Rear: [1..BufferSize]; CurrentLength: [0..BufferSize];
      NotFull, NotEmpty: Condition;

  PROCEDURE Put(C: CHAR);
    BEGIN
      IF CurrentLength = BufferSize THEN Wait(NotFull) END;
      Buffer[Rear] := C; Rear := Rear MOD BufferSize + 1;
      INC(CurrentLength);
      Signal(NotEmpty)
    END Put;
```

```
PROCEDURE Get(VAR C: CHAR);
BEGIN
  IF CurrentLength = 0 THEN Wait(NotEmpty) END;
  C := Buffer [Front]; Front := Front MOD BufferSize + 1;
  DEC(CurrentLength);
  Signal(NotFull)
END Get;

BEGIN (* InBuffer *)
  CurrentLength := 0; Front := 1; Rear := 1;
  Initialize(NotFull); Initialize(NotEmpty)
END InBuffer;

MODULE OutBuffer [1];
... identical to InBuffer ...
END OutBuffer;

PROCEDURE Input;
 VAR Ch: CHAR;
 BEGIN
  LOOP
    Read(Ch);
    IF NOT Done THEN EndProcess END;
    IF Ch = EOL THEN Ch := " " END;
    InBuffer.Put(Ch)
  END
 END Input;

PROCEDURE Edit;
 VAR InCh, OutCh: CHAR;
 BEGIN
  LOOP
    InBuffer.Get(InCh);
    IF InCh = "*" THEN
      InBuffer.Get(InCh);
      IF InCh = "*" THEN OutCh := "@"
      ELSE OutBuffer.Put("*"); OutCh := InCh
      END
    ELSE OutCh := InCh
    END;
    OutBuffer.Put(OutCh)
  END
 END Edit;
```

```
PROCEDURE Output;
  VAR I: [1..LineLength]; Ch: CHAR;
  BEGIN
    LOOP
      FOR I := 1 TO LineLength DO
        OutBuffer.Get(Ch);
        IF Ch = Terminator THEN WriteLn; EndProcess END;
        Write(Ch)
      END;
      WriteLn
    END
  END Output;

BEGIN
  StartProcess(Edit, WorkSpaceSize);
  StartProcess (Output, WorkSpaceSize);
  Input
END TextConversion.
```

The TextConversion example shows an inherent weakness in the way in which Modula-2 provides mutual exclusion—by associating each region of mutual exclusion with a module. When two or more identical objects with separate mutual exclusion requirements are involved, as in the case of InBuffer and OutBuffer, two or more modules must be used, with considerable duplication of program text in many cases. Creating multiple buffers as instances of an abstract data type exported by a single module is not a satisfactory alternative. In this case all buffers so created would be subject to a single exclusion, i.e., one process could not operate on one buffer while another process operated on another.

AN IMPLEMENTATION OF *Processes*

The implementation presented in this section is based on that given by Wirth and assumes that the computer on which the program is to be executed has a *single* central processing unit. It uses coroutines to achieve *quasi*-concurrent execution of processes, and takes the form of a *scheduler* which is responsible for sharing the processor's time fairly among the various processes in a program. Calls of Wait and Signal are translated by the module into coroutine TRANSFER operations which identify the transfer destination, i.e., the process which is to be reactivated.

The Processes module associates with each concurrent process in the program a *process descriptor* which maintains information about the current state of the process.

```
TYPE DescriptorPointer = POINTER TO ProcessDescriptor;

ProcessDescriptor = RECORD
                      Next,
                      NextWaiting: DescriptorPointer;
                      Coroutine: PROCESS;
                      Runnable: BOOLEAN
                    END;
```

These process descriptors are connected in a circular list, or *ring*, chained together by means of the Next field. A variable

```
VAR RunningProcess: ProcessDescriptor;
```

is used to indicate the descriptor of the process which is being executed at any time. The NextWaiting field is used to order the descriptors of processes currently waiting on particular conditions (a process may be in at most one such waiting queue at any time). The processes are actually implemented as coroutines, and hence the Coroutine field is used to hold the reactivation address of the associated suspended coroutine. The field Runnable denotes whether a process is currently a candidate for use of the processor, i.e., it is not either delayed awaiting a signal on some Condition variable, or terminated.

Figure 14.2 shows the ring of process descriptors *p1, p2, p3, p4* and associated variables for a system of four concurrent processes which make use of a single Condition variable C.

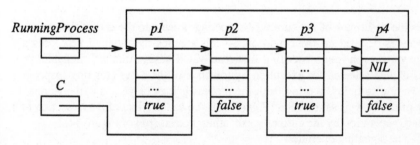

Figure 14.2   Process descriptor ring

The process with descriptor *p1* is currently executing, *p2* is currently delayed on the Condition variable C, *p3* is capable of execution when the processor becomes available, and *p4* is also delayed on C. A call of Signal(C) will reactivate *p2* since it is the process whose descriptor is at the head of the queue associated with C.

To generate this structure, the procedure

```
PROCEDURE StartProcess(P: PROC; N: CARDINAL);
```

constructs a new process descriptor and inserts it into the process descriptor ring as the currently executing process. A workspace of size N words for its associated coroutine is also allocated and then the procedure NEWPROCESS (exported from the SYSTEM module) is called to designate the procedure P as a coroutine. A call of TRANSFER then causes execution of that coroutine to commence. Since the process that called NEWPROCESS must have been 'runnable', it remains a candidate for subsequent execution simply by leaving its Runnable flag true.

The descriptor ring is initialized by the body of the Processes module with a single descriptor which represents the main program itself as the currently running process.

As indicated in Figure 14.2 a Condition variable is represented simply as a pointer to the descriptor of the process at the head of the queue of processes delayed on the associated condition. The descriptors of the delayed processes are chained via their NextWaiting pointer fields. Hence the opaque type Condition is defined as follows:

TYPE Condition = DescriptorPointer;

and the condition variable initialization procedure

PROCEDURE Initialize(VAR S: Condition);

simply assigns NIL to its variable parameter S.

The procedure

PROCEDURE Wait(VAR S: Condition);

adds the descriptor of the currently executing process to the end of the queue of processes delayed on the condition S—this ensures that waiting processes are reactivated on a longest-waiting first-reactivated basis. Another, runnable, process is then selected for execution by traversal of the descriptor ring inspecting the Runnable fields, starting from the process being delayed. and the Runnable flag of the latter is set to false. Figure 14.3 shows the effect of the execution of a Wait(C) operation by the currently executing process (p1) of Figure 14.2.

The signaling operation

PROCEDURE Signal(VAR S: Condition);

takes the process descriptor (if any) at the head of the queue of processes delayed on the condition S and transfers control to the associated coroutine from the running process (which remains runnable). Figure 14.4 shows the effect of the currently executing process (p3) in Figure 14.3 performing a Signal(C) operation. The Awaited operation merely involves inspection of the associated Condition variable.

The procedure EndProcess simply sets the Runnable flag of the currently executing process to false, and traverses the process descriptor ring to find

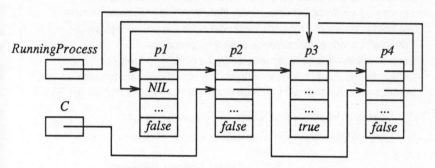

Figure 14.3 Process descriptor ring after *Wait(C)*

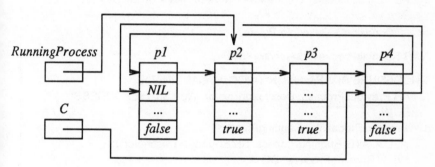

Figure 14.4 Process descriptor ring after *Signal(C)*

another process to execute. Since the terminating process is not on any condition queue, there is no way in which it can ever become runnable again.

If no runnable process can be found when executing either a Wait or an EndProcess operation, then all processes are either terminated or delayed on various conditions and the concurrent program is deemed to have terminated.

The full implementation-module for Processes is thus as follows:

Processes.mod

IMPLEMENTATION MODULE Processes [1];

FROM SYSTEM IMPORT ADDRESS, TSIZE, NEWPROCESS, TRANSFER;
FROM Storage IMPORT ALLOCATE;

(* This module implements the concurrent processing facilities defined
in the corresponding definition module, in quasi-concurrent mode.
Each process is implemented as a coroutine, with control transfers

between coroutines being effected within the StartProcess, Wait,
Signal and EndProcess operations. Details of the processes involved
are held in a ring of process descriptors, with the pointer Running-
Process indicating the currently executing process.
Each condition queue is represented as a pointer to the descriptor
for the first process, if any, waiting on the condition, with queued
processes being chained in queue order via the field NextWaiting.   *)

```
TYPE DescriptorPointer = POINTER TO ProcessDescriptor;

     ProcessDescriptor = RECORD
                         Next,
                         NextWaiting: DescriptorPointer;
                         Runnable: BOOLEAN;
                         Coroutine: ADDRESS
                         END;

     Condition = DescriptorPointer;

VAR RunningProcess: DescriptorPointer;

PROCEDURE StartProcess(P: PROC; N: CARDINAL);
  VAR PreviousProcess: DescriptorPointer; WorkSpace: ADDRESS;
  BEGIN
    PreviousProcess := RunningProcess;
    ALLOCATE(RunningProcess, SIZE(ProcessDescriptor));
    WITH RunningProcess^ DO
      Next := PreviousProcess^.Next;
      PreviousProcess^.Next := RunningProcess;
      ALLOCATE(WorkSpace, N);
      NEWPROCESS(P, WorkSpace, N, Coroutine);
      Runnable := TRUE
    END;
    TRANSFER(PreviousProcess^.Coroutine, RunningProcess^.Coroutine)
  END StartProcess;

PROCEDURE EndProcess;
  VAR TerminatingProcess: DescriptorPointer;
  BEGIN
    TerminatingProcess := RunningProcess;
    FindNextRunnable;
    TerminatingProcess^.Runnable := FALSE;
    TRANSFER(TerminatingProcess^.Coroutine, RunningProcess^.Coroutine)
  END EndProcess;
```

```
PROCEDURE FindNextRunnable;
  VAR SuspendingProcess: DescriptorPointer;
  BEGIN
    SuspendingProcess := RunningProcess;
    REPEAT
      RunningProcess := RunningProcess^.Next
    UNTIL RunningProcess^.Runnable;
    IF RunningProcess = SuspendingProcess
    THEN (* all processes waiting or terminated *) HALT
    END;
  END FindNextRunnable;

PROCEDURE Initialize(VAR S: Condition);
  BEGIN
    S := NIL
  END Initialize;

PROCEDURE Wait(VAR S: Condition);
  VAR WaitingProcess: DescriptorPointer;
  BEGIN
    WaitingProcess := RunningProcess;
    Append(S, WaitingProcess);
    FindNextRunnable;
    WaitingProcess^.Runnable := FALSE;
    TRANSFER(WaitingProcess^.Coroutine, RunningProcess^.Coroutine)
  END Wait;

PROCEDURE Signal(VAR S: Condition);
  VAR SignalingProcess: DescriptorPointer;
  BEGIN
    IF S <> NIL THEN
      SignalingProcess := RunningProcess;
      Remove(S, RunningProcess);
      RunningProcess^.Runnable := TRUE;
      TRANSFER(SignalingProcess^.Coroutine, RunningProcess^.Coroutine)
    END
  END Signal;

PROCEDURE Awaited(S: Condition): BOOLEAN;
  BEGIN
    RETURN (S <> NIL)
  END Awaited;
```

```
PROCEDURE Append(VAR S: Condition; JoiningProcess: DescriptorPointer);
VAR PreviousProcess, ThisProcess: DescriptorPointer;
BEGIN
  IF S = NIL THEN S := JoiningProcess
  ELSE (* add to end of queue *)
    PreviousProcess := S;
    ThisProcess := PreviousProcess^.NextWaiting;
    WHILE ThisProcess <> NIL DO
      PreviousProcess := ThisProcess;
      ThisProcess := PreviousProcess^.NextWaiting
    END;
    PreviousProcess^.NextWaiting := JoiningProcess
  END;
  JoiningProcess^.NextWaiting := NIL
END Append;

PROCEDURE Remove(VAR S: Condition;
                     VAR LeavingProcess: DescriptorPointer);
BEGIN
  LeavingProcess := S; S := S^.NextWaiting
END Append;

BEGIN
  (* create a process descriptor for the main program
     as the running process on a one-descriptor ring *);
  ALLOCATE(RunningProcess, SIZE(ProcessDescriptor));
  WITH RunningProcess^ DO
    Next := RunningProcess; Runnable := TRUE
  END
END Processes.
```

The mutual exclusion implied by monitor modules needs no consideration in such an implementation. Since the implementation is for a single-processor computer, it is impossible for processes to access any shared data structure simultaneously. Since execution of a Wait or Signal operation implies that the executing process relinquishes any exclusive access that it has, the restriction of control transfers between processes to Wait and Signal operations is sufficient to maintain the required mutual exclusion property.

When the number of processes involved is small, and the length of each condition queue is equally small, the use of a single ring of processor descriptors, with a secondary pointer chain for each condition queue, can be an effective approach to the implementation of pseudo-concurrency.

Under other conditions, however, this simple strategy can cause significant overheads:

(a) If the number of processes created becomes large, and most of them spend most of their time on condition queues, the round-robin strategy for locating a runnable process to execute may become a significant overhead. This problem is accentuated if a large number of quick-terminating processes are involved, since the implementation shown leaves terminated processes on the ring with no prospect of them ever becoming runnable.

(b) The representation of each condition as a single pointer to the first process waiting on it is also a source of potential inefficiency, since it forces the wait operation to traverse the queue to find the tail each time a new process waits on that condition. In applications where long queues build up, this overhead could also be significant.

The problems of terminated processes and of long queues can each be overcome by minor modifications to the existing strategy—in one case by eliminating terminated processes from the ring, in the other by representing each condition queue by head and tail pointers. The latter is a direct trade-off between the storage used for each condition and the potential inefficiency of the wait operation.

A more radical alteration is to replace the process ring by a set of disjoint queues, one for each condition and one for runnable processes. At any moment every process other than the currently executing process must be on exactly one of these queues, terminating processes being immediately and easily discarded. With head and tail pointers for each queue there is then no variable overhead in any rescheduling operation. In addition, the storage cost of head and tail pointers for each queue may be more than offset by the fact that each process descriptor now needs no Runnable flag, and only one pointer—to link it to its successor in whichever queue it occupies. Implementation of this alternative strategy is left as an exercise for the reader.

Appendix 1

MODULA-2 SYNTAX DIAGRAMS

The syntax of Modula-2 may be described by means of syntax diagrams. The sequences of symbols allowed for a language construct may be described by a syntax diagram, which is a directed graph with one entry and one exit. Each path through the graph defines an allowable sequence of symbols.

For example, the structure of a complete Modula-2 *compilation-unit* is defined by Figure A1. The occurrence of the name of another diagram, such as *definition-module* and *program-module* in Figure A1, indicates that any sequence of symbols defined by the other diagram may occur at that point. Diagram names are always represented as italicized words; all other symbols occurring are symbols of the language itself.

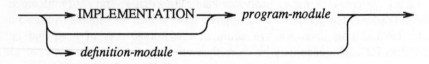

Figure A1 *compilation-unit*

Alternative or repetitive sequences of symbols are indicated by forks or loops in the corresponding syntax diagram. For example, an identifier is defined by Figure A2. The names *letter*, *digit*, *octal-digit* and *hexadecimal-digit* are used to denote any of the 52 upper- and lower-case letters, the 10 decimal digits, the 8 octal digits and the 16 hexadecimal digits respectively.

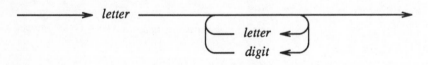

Fig A2 *identifier*

The diagrams in Figures A3-34 define the complete syntax of Modula-2. All names that end with *-identifier*, such as *procedure-identifier*, *variable-identifier*, etc., are syntactically equivalent to *qualified-identifier*, and merely indicate the class of declared identifiers that may occur at that point.

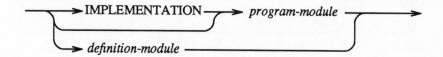

Figure A3 *compilation-unit*

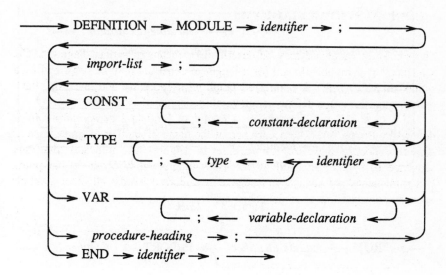

Figure A4 *definition-module*

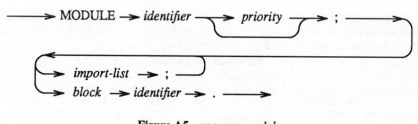

Figure A5 *program-module*

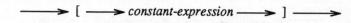

Figure A6 *priority*

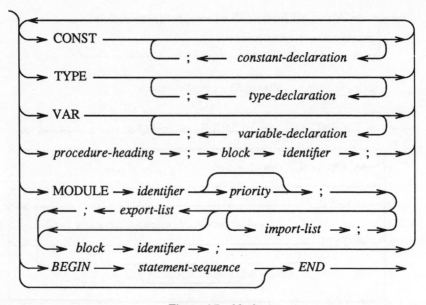

Figure A7 *block*

FROM → *module-identifier* → IMPORT → *identifier-list* →

Figure A8 *import-list*

EXPORT → QUALIFIED → *identifier-list* →

Figure A9 *export-list*

→ *identifier* → = → *constant-expression* →

Figure A10 *constant-declaration*

→ *identifier* → = → *type* →

Figure A11 *type-declaration*

Figure A12 *variable-declaration*

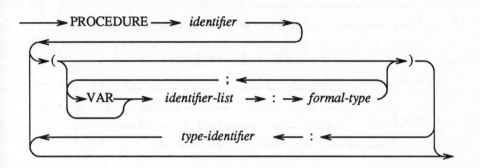

Figure A13 *procedure-heading*

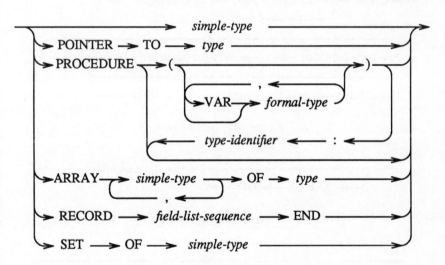

Figure A14 *type*

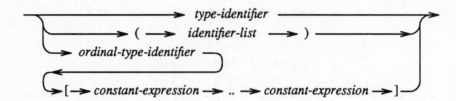

Figure A15   *simple-type*

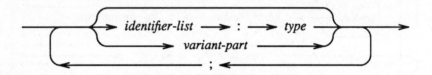

Figure A16   *field-list-sequence*

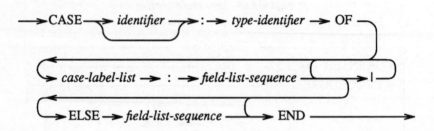

Figure A17   *variant-part*

Figure A18   *formal-type*

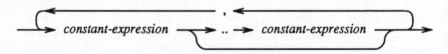

Figure A19   *case-label-list*

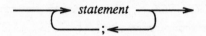

Figure A20 *statement-sequence*

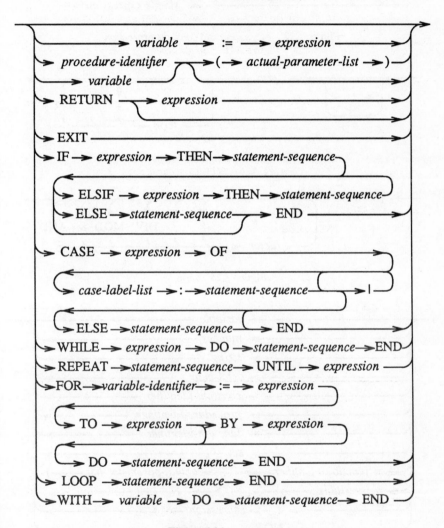

Figure A21 *statement*

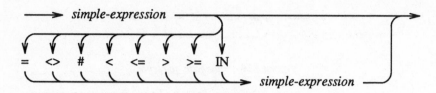

Figure A22 *expression* and *constant-expression*

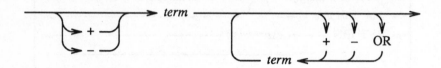

Figure A23 *simple-expression*

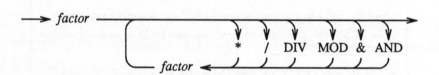

Figure A24 *term*

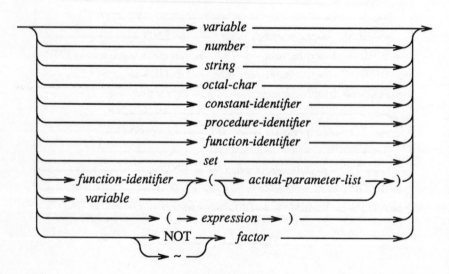

Figure A25 *factor*

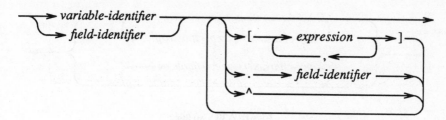

Figure A26 *variable*

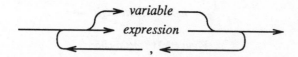

Figure A27 *actual-parameter-list*

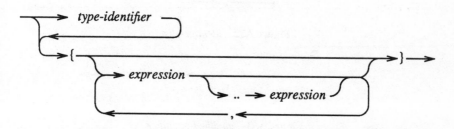

Figure A28 *set*

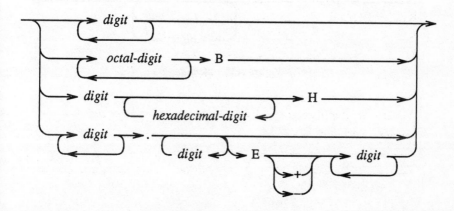

Figure A29 *number*

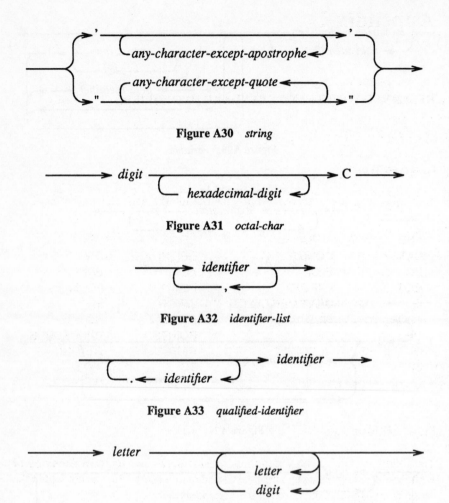

Figure A30 *string*

Figure A31 *octal-char*

Figure A32 *identifier-list*

Figure A33 *qualified-identifier*

Figure A34 *identifier*

Appendix 2

Reserved Words

The following are reserved words in Modula-2, and cannot be used as identifiers:

AND	ARRAY	BEGIN	BY
CASE	CONST	DEFINITION	DIV
DO	ELSE	ELSIF	END
EXIT	EXPORT	FOR	FROM
IF	IMPLEMENTATION	IMPORT	IN
LOOP	MOD	MODULE	NOT
OF	OR	POINTER	PROCEDURE
QUALIFIED	RECORD	REPEAT	RETURN
SET	THEN	TO	TYPE
UNTIL	VAR	WHILE	WITH

Standard Identifiers

The following are standard identifiers in Modula-2—the standard definition of each is said to be pervasive, and can be used at any point which is not within the scope of an explicit declaration of the same identifier:

Identifier	Usage	Identifier	Usage
ABS	*function*	INTEGER	*type*
BITSET	*type*	LONGINT	*type*
BOOLEAN	*type*	LONGREAL	*type*
CAP	*function*	MAX	*function*
CARDINAL	*type*	MIN	*function*
CHAR	*type*	NIL	*constant*
CHR	*function*	ODD	*function*
DEC	*procedure*	ORD	*function*
EXCL	*procedure*	PROC	*type*
FALSE	*constant*	REAL	*type*

FLOAT	*function*	SIZE	*function*
HALT	*procedure*	TRUE	*constant*
HIGH	*function*	TRUNC	*function*
INC	*procedure*	VAL	*function*
INCL	*procedure*		

On implementations which conform to the second or earlier editions of *Programming in Modula-2*, the identifiers LONGINT, LONGREAL, MAX, MIN and SIZE are not standard, but the identifiers NEW and DISPOSE are standard procedure-identifiers on such implementations.

Appendix 3

This Appendix contains definitions of modules which are provided in an (almost) standard form in most Modula-2 implementations. The actual facilities provided may vary slightly among implementations—the definitions given here are based upon those given in the third edition of *Programming in Modula-2*, but comments indicate where significant variations may occur.

MathLib0

```
DEFINITION MODULE MathLib0;

    (* This module provides a range of basic REAL mathematical functions *)

    PROCEDURE Sqrt(R: REAL): REAL;
        (* if R >= 0.0 then result is square root of R *)

    PROCEDURE Exp(R: REAL): REAL;
        (* result is e to the power R *)

    PROCEDURE Ln(R: REAL): REAL;
        (* if R >= 0.0 then result is natural logarithm of R *)

    PROCEDURE Sin(R: REAL): REAL;
        (* result is sin R where R is in radians *)

    PROCEDURE Cos(R: REAL): REAL;
        (* result is cos R where R is in radians *)

    PROCEDURE ArcTan(R: REAL): REAL;
        (* Result is tan^{-1} R in radians, in range -π/2 .. π/2 *)

    PROCEDURE Real(I: INTEGER): REAL;
        (* Result is the REAL representation of I *)

    PROCEDURE Entier(R: REAL): INTEGER;
        (* Result is greatest INTEGER value <= R *)

END MathLib0.
```

InOut

DEFINITION MODULE InOut;

(* This module enables single-stream text I/O between the program and
either the terminal (by default) or files named by the terminal user.   *)

CONST EOL = 15C;   (* end of line character - of type CHAR;
                                            value is implementation-dependent   *)

VAR Done: BOOLEAN;   (* success of calls of InOut procedures *)

   termCH: CHAR;   (* terminating character of ReadInt,
                                         ReadCard, and ReadString   *)

PROCEDURE OpenInput(DefaultExtension: ARRAY OF CHAR);

   (* Requests file name from user—if name ends with "."
      then DefaultExtension is appended to file name;
      Done := 'named file opened successfully';
      if Done then named file becomes the current input stream *)

PROCEDURE OpenOutput(DefaultExtension: ARRAY OF CHAR);

   (* Requests file name from user—if name ends with "."
      then DefaultExtension is appended to file name;
      Done := 'named file opened successfully';
      if Done then named file becomes the current output stream. *)

PROCEDURE CloseInput;

   (* If current input stream is a named file
      then file is closed and subsequent input is taken from the terminal
      else effect is implementation-defined.   *)

PROCEDURE CloseOutput;

   (* If current output stream is a named file
      then file is closed and subsequent output is sent to the terminal
      else effect is implementation-defined.   *)

PROCEDURE Read(VAR Ch: CHAR);

   (* Done := not at end of input stream;
      if Done then Ch := next character in input stream *)

PROCEDURE ReadString(VAR S: ARRAY OF CHAR);
(* Skip over leading blanks in input stream;
   Assign to S the sequence of characters up to, but not including,
   the next blank or control character (other than DEL);
   assign this terminating character to termCH.

   DEL is used for backspacing when input is from terminal.

   Effect when string read is longer than S is implementation-dependent. *)

PROCEDURE ReadInt(VAR I: INTEGER);
(* Read a string and convert to Modula-2 INTEGER;
   Done := 'valid integer was read';
   if Done then I := value read in.   *)

PROCEDURE ReadCard(VAR I: CARDINAL);
(* Read a string and convert to Modula-2 CARDINAL;
   Done := 'valid cardinal was read';
   if Done then I := value read in.   *)

PROCEDURE Write(Ch: CHAR);
(* Output the character value Ch *)

PROCEDURE WriteLn;
(* Terminate output line—usually equivalent to Write(EOL) *)

PROCEDURE WriteString(S: ARRAY OF CHAR);
(* Output the string S—effect of NULs in S is implementation-defined *)

PROCEDURE WriteInt(I: INTEGER; FieldWidth: CARDINAL);
(* Output I using at least FieldWidth characters—
   if FieldWidth > number of characters required by I
   then leading blanks are inserted as required.   *)

PROCEDURE WriteCard(I, FieldWidth: CARDINAL);
(* Output I using at least FieldWidth characters—
   if FieldWidth > number of characters required by I
   then leading blanks are inserted as required.   *)

PROCEDURE WriteOct(I, FieldWidth: CARDINAL);
(* Output I as above but in octal rather than decimal form. *)

PROCEDURE WriteHex(I, FieldWidth: CARDINAL);
(* Output I as above but in hexadecimal rather than decimal form. *)

END InOut.

RealInOut

```
DEFINITION MODULE RealInOut;

(* This module enables input and output of real values
   via the text streams currently in use by the module InOut. *)

VAR Done: BOOLEAN;

PROCEDURE ReadReal(VAR R: REAL);
   (* Read a string and convert to Modula-2 REAL;
   Done := 'valid real was read';
   if Done then R := value read in.
   (The string is usually read via InOut.ReadString,
   in which case InOut.termCH gives the terminating character.) *)

PROCEDURE WriteReal(R: REAL; FieldWidth: CARDINAL);
   (* Output R using at least FieldWidth characters.
   If FieldWidth > number of characters required
   then leading blanks are inserted as required.
   Representation used includes a decimal point and possibly
   an exponent, but precise format varies among implementations *)

END RealInOut.
```

SYSTEM

The module SYSTEM is a *pseudo-module* whose facilities are determined by
each Modula-2 compiler. The following 'definition module' indicates the facilities which should be common to all implementations.

```
DEFINITION MODULE SYSTEM;

TYPE WORD; (* smallest allocatable storage unit *)
     ADDRESS = POINTER TO WORD;

PROCEDURE ADR(VAR V: any type identifier): ADDRESS;
   (* Returns address of first word of storage used by variable V;
   address units are implementation-dependent.              *)
```

```
PROCEDURE TSIZE(any type identifier): CARDINAL;

  (* Returns number of storage units occupied by each value of the
     type specified; storage units are implementation-dependent—
     TSIZE(WORD) is not necessarily 1!                              *)

PROCEDURE NEWPROCESS(P: PROC;
                          A: ADDRESS; N: CARDINAL;
                          VAR Descriptor: ADDRESS);

  (* Creates a coroutine defined by P with workspace
     of size N beginning at storage address A,
     and returns an initial reference to it as Descriptor.    *)

PROCEDURE TRANSFER(VAR CallingCoroutine,
                        CalledCoroutine: ADDRESS);

  (* Transfers control to the coroutine with reference CalledRoutine,
     leaving a current reference to the calling coroutine in CallingCoroutine *)

END SYSTEM.
```

Storage

```
DEFINITION MODULE Storage;

  FROM SYSTEM IMPORT ADDRESS;

  (* This module enables allocation and deallocation of storage *)

  PROCEDURE ALLOCATE(VAR A: ADDRESS; Size: CARDINAL);

    (* Tries to allocate Size units of free storage;
       if sufficient space available then A := address of allocated area
       else effect is implementation-defined—some implementations
       set A to NIL, others abort execution but provide an additional
       function which enables storage availability to be tested first.    *)

  PROCEDURE DEALLOCATE(VAR A: ADDRESS; Size: CARDINAL);

    (* Releases Size units of storage beginning at address A *)

END Storage.
```

Appendix 4

THE ASCII CHARACTER SET

	0C	1C	2C	3C	4C	5C	6C	7C
00C	NUL	SOH	STX	ETX	EOT	ENQ	ACK	BEL
01C	BS	HT	LF	VT	FF	CR	SO	SI
02C	DLE	DC1	DC2	DC3	DC4	NAK	SYN	ETB
03C	CAN	EM	SUB	ESC	FS	GS	RS	US
04C		!	"	#	$	%	&	'
05C	(	)	*	+	,	−	.	/
06C	0	1	2	3	4	5	6	7
07C	8	9	:	;	<	=	>	?
10C	@	A	B	C	D	E	F	G
11C	H	I	J	K	L	M	N	O
12C	P	Q	R	S	T	U	V	W
13C	X	Y	Z	[	\	]	^	_
14C	'	a	b	c	d	e	f	g
15C	h	i	j	k	l	m	n	o
16C	p	q	r	s	t	u	v	w
17C	x	y	z	{			}	~	DEL

In the above table the ordinal value of any character is obtained by prefixing its column index with the row index shown in the leftmost column. Hence, ORD(*CR*)=015C. The character with ordinal value 40C is the blank character; the character with ordinal value 137C is the underlined space.

The control characters are those with ordinal values 0C to 37C (*NUL..US*), inclusive, and 177C (*DEL*). The following control characters are frequently used and usually have the indicated meanings in Modula-2 programs:

NUL	- often used as a string terminator
BEL	- rings the terminal 'bell' when output
BS	- backspace
LF	- vertical line feed
FF	- form feed (take a new page or clear the screen)
CR	- carriage return: take a new line starting at left margin
DEL	- delete (used for erasing input characters)

Appendix 5

SOLUTIONS TO SELECTED EXERCISES

Exercise 2.1

Valid integer-numbers in Modula-2:

   127   6000   27365892   0

Valid real-numbers in Modula-2:

7.4	275.0	0.0001	0.074E3
0.1E999	275.	0.0620	

Invalid numbers in Modula-2:

3,475	contains a comma
.1475	no digits before the decimal point
6E3	scale factor not preceded by a real number
10E-4	scale factor not preceded by a real number

The following numbers denote the same value:

   275.0   275.

The following numbers are unacceptable to many implementations:

27365892	integer value is too large
0.1E999	real value is too large

Exercise 2.2

Decimal	Octal	Hexadecimal
9	11B	9H
10	12B	AH
11	13B	BH
12	14B	CH
13	15B	DH
14	16B	EH
15	17B	FH
16	20B	10H
17	21B	11H
18	22B	12H
19	23B	13H

Exercise 2.3

Valid identifiers in Modula-2:

H2SO4	alphabetic	ALPHABETIC	ALPHA	McDougall
ALPHABETICAL	omega	X99999	trunc	NEW

Exercise 2.4

The line

   'HIS WIFE'S DOG'

is not a valid string.

The other lines contain valid strings which denote the character sequences:

   SPRATT'S WIFE
   JACK SPRATT
   six + one = ninety seven
   SPRATT'S WIFE
   """"

Exercise 3.1

67 DIV 8	valid	– value 8
12*2.75	invalid	– operands are of different types
		(INTEGER and REAL)

67 MOD 8	valid	– value 3
(–3) DIV 8	valid	– value 0
ABS (–2.5)	valid	– value 2.5
"A" < "Z"	valid	– value TRUE
67/8	invalid	– operands must be real values
6.7 DIV 8	invalid	– first operand is a real value
1001*1001	valid	– value 10000200001
67 MOD (–8)	invalid	– second operand is negative
CAP("a")	valid	– value "A"
10.0E4*10.0E4	valid	– value 100.0E8
CHR(62)	valid	– value ">"
ORD ("A")	valid	– value 65
FLOAT(–7)	valid	– value 7.0

The value of 1001*1001 may lie outside the implemented range of INTEGER values in many implementations.

Exercise 3.2

constant-identifiers:	LineMax	PrintWanted	TRUE
	Single	Double	Treble
type-identifiers:	LinePosition	Spacing	CHAR
variable-identifiers:	ThisChar	LastChar	ThisPosition
	SpacingNow		

Exercise 3.3

```
CONST InchesPerMeter = 39.37;
      CurrencySymbol = "$";
      DegreesPerRadian = 180.0/3.142;
      SpeedLimit = 60 (* miles per hour *);
```

Exercise 3.4

```
TYPE Age = [0..120];
     Sex = (Male, Female);
     Height = REAL;
     Weight = [0..500] (* pounds *);
     MaritalStatus = (Single, Married, Widowed, Separated, Divorced);
```

Exercise 3.5

```
VAR Bedrooms, ReceptionRooms: [0..10];
    Heating: (None, OilFired, GasFired, SolidFuel, Electric);
    Garage: BOOLEAN;
```

Exercise 4.1

Expression with brackets	*Value*
6.75 − (12.3/3.0)	2.65
(6*11) − (42 DIV 5)	58
((175 MOD 15) DIV 3) * 65	195
13 + (7*5) − ((4*5) DIV 2)	38
((11 MOD 4) DIV 2) <> 0	TRUE
("A"<="Z") OR (("9">="8") AND ("A"<"I"))	TRUE

Exercise 4.2

The final values of X, Y and Z are 17, 217 and 218 respectively.

Exercise 4.3

(a) (1<=I) AND (I<=100)
(b) (J MOD K = 0) OR (K MOD J = 0)
(c) (Y <> 1900) AND (Y MOD 4 = 0)

Exercise 4.4

Assuming an auxiliary variable:

    VAR Temporary: REAL;

the required statements are:

    Temporary := X; X := Y; Y := Temporary;

Exercise 4.5

Assuming variables:

    VAR Sum, Product: INTEGER; Average: REAL;

the required statements are:

```
Sum := X + Y + Z;
Product := X * Y * Z;
Average := FLOAT(Sum) / 3.0;
```

Exercise 4.6

The required statement is:

```
I := 100*(ORD(H)–ORD("0")) + 10*(ORD(T)–ORD("0")) + (ORD(U)–ORD("0"))
```

Exercise 5.2

Assuming an import-list:

```
FROM InOut IMPORT WriteString, Write, WriteLn, WriteCard;
```

and additional declarations

```
VAR WholePart: CARDINAL; FractionalPart: REAL;
```

the following statements should have the desired effect on any implementation which supports InOut:

```
WriteString(" NUMBER    RANGE    MEAN"); WriteLn;
WriteCard(Count, 5); WriteCard(Min, 9);
WriteString(".."); WriteCard(Max, 2);
(* correct Mean to first decimal place *)
Mean := Mean + 0.05;
(* output as cardinal.cardinal to get required format *)
WholePart := TRUNC(Mean);
WriteCard(WholePart, 8); Write(".");
FractionalPart := Mean – FLOAT(WholePart);
WriteCard(TRUNC(FractionalPart*10.0), 1);
```

Outputting the value of Mean is very much easier on implementations which provide a procedure to write real numbers in a specified fixed-point format. Check if your implementation of Modula-2 has such a facility. (Similar problems arise with the real number output required in Exercises 5.3 and 5.4.)

Exercise 6.5

```
MODULE Exercise65;
  FROM InOut IMPORT Write, WriteLn;

  (* This program outputs a digit pyramid *)

  TYPE Digit = ["0".."9"];

  VAR CentralDigit, NextDigit: CHAR; J: INTEGER;

  BEGIN
    FOR CentralDigit := "1" TO "9" DO
      (* print next line of pyramid *)
      FOR J := 1 TO 20 – ORD(CentralDigit) + ORD("0") DO Write(" ") END;
      FOR NextDigit := "1" TO CentralDigit DO Write(NextDigit) END;
      NextDigit := CentralDigit;
      WHILE NextDigit <> "1" DO DEC(NextDigit); Write(NextDigit) END;
      WriteLn
    END
  END Exercise65.
```

Exercise 6.6

```
MODULE Exercise66;
  FROM InOut IMPORT
    OpenInput, CloseInput, Read, Done, EOL,
    Write, WriteLn, WriteString, WriteCard;

  (* This program reads and outputs lines of text from an input file, determ-
    ining the numbers of lines, words and sentences in the text. It assumes
    that the filed text is well-formed, with an EOL at the end of every line. *)

  VAR NumberOfSentences, NumberOfLines, NumberOfWords: CARDINAL;
      Character: CHAR;

  BEGIN
    OpenInput("");
    IF Done THEN
      WriteLn; WriteLn;
      NumberOfSentences := 0; NumberOfLines := 0; NumberOfWords := 0;
      LOOP
        Read(Character);
        IF NOT Done THEN EXIT END;
```

```
        (* scan a line *)
        INC(NumberOfLines);
        LOOP
          IF Character = EOL THEN EXIT END;
          IF (Character >= "a") AND (Character <= "z") OR
             (Character >= "A") AND (Character <= "Z") THEN
            (* scan a word *)
            INC(NumberOfWords);
            REPEAT
              Write(Character); Read(Character)
            UNTIL ((Character < "a") OR (Character > "z")) AND
                  ((Character < "A") OR (Character > "Z"))
          ELSE
            (* scan a character *)
            IF Character = "." THEN INC(NumberOfSentences) END;
            Write(Character); Read(Character)
          END
        END;
        WriteLn
      END;
      WriteLn; WriteLn;
      WriteString("Text consists of :"); WriteLn;
      WriteCard(NumberOfLines, 4); WriteString(" lines"); WriteLn;
      WriteCard(NumberOfSentences, 4); WriteString(" sentences"); WriteLn;
      WriteCard(NumberOfWords, 4); WriteString(" words"); WriteLn;
      CloseInput
    END
  END Exercise66.
```

Exercise 7.5

```
MODULE Exercise75;
  FROM InOut IMPORT EOL, Read, Write, WriteCard, WriteString, WriteLn;

  (* This program inputs a digit and outputs all numbers in the range [1..100]
     such that the decimal representation of the number, its square and its cube
     all contain the specified digit. It assumes MAX(CARDINAL) > 1000000 *)

  CONST MaximumNumber = 100;

  TYPE Digit = [0..9]; TestRange = [1..MaximumNumber];
```

```
PROCEDURE GetDigit(VAR D: Digit);
  VAR Ch: CHAR; OK: BOOLEAN;
  BEGIN
    REPEAT
      WriteString("Enter your chosen digit :"); Read(Ch);
      IF (Ch >= "0") AND (Ch <= "9") THEN
        OK := TRUE; D := ORD(Ch) – ORD("0")
      ELSE
        OK := FALSE; WriteString(" – not a digit, try again"); WriteLn;
        WHILE Ch <> EOL DO Read(Ch) END
      END
    UNTIL OK
  END GetDigit;

PROCEDURE Present(D: Digit; I: CARDINAL): BOOLEAN;
  VAR NextDigit: Digit;
  BEGIN
    REPEAT
      NextDigit := I MOD 10; I := I DIV 10
    UNTIL (NextDigit = D) OR (I = 0);
    RETURN (NextDigit = D)
  END Present;

VAR TestDigit: Digit; TestNumber: [1..MaximumNumber];
    Square, Cube: CARDINAL;

BEGIN
  GetDigit(TestDigit); WriteLn;
  WriteString("NUMBER    SQUARE      CUBE"); WriteLn;
  FOR TestNumber := 1 TO MaximumNumber DO
    IF Present(TestDigit, TestNumber) THEN
      Square := TestNumber*TestNumber;
      IF Present(TestDigit, Square) THEN
        Cube := Square*TestNumber;
        IF Present(TestDigit, Cube) THEN
          WriteCard(TestNumber, 6); WriteCard(Square, 11);
          WriteCard(Cube, 11); WriteLn
        END
      END
    END
  END
END Exercise75.
```

Exercise 8.3

```
MODULE Exercise83;
  FROM InOut IMPORT
  OpenInput, CloseInput, Read, Done, Write, WriteLn, WriteString, WriteCard;

  (* This program reads a text and outputs the number of occurrences
   of each adjacent letter pair appearing within the text. Upper- and
   lower-case occurrences are not distinguished.              *)

  TYPE UpperCaseLetter = ["A".."Z"];

  VAR ThisCharacter, LastCharacter: CHAR; LastWasLetter: BOOLEAN;
      Count: ARRAY UpperCaseLetter, UpperCaseLetter OF CARDINAL;
      FirstLetter, SecondLetter: UpperCaseLetter;

  PROCEDURE IsLetter(Ch: CHAR): BOOLEAN;
    BEGIN
      RETURN (Ch >= "A") AND (Ch <= "Z") OR
             (Ch >= "a") AND (Ch <= "z")
    END IsLetter;

BEGIN
  OpenInput("");
  IF Done THEN
    FOR FirstLetter := "A" TO "Z" DO
      FOR SecondLetter := "A" TO "Z" DO
        Count[FirstLetter, SecondLetter] := 0
      END
    END;
  LastWasLetter := FALSE;
  LOOP
    Read(ThisCharacter);
    IF NOT Done THEN EXIT END;
    IF IsLetter(ThisCharacter) THEN
      IF LastWasLetter THEN
        INC(Count[CAP(LastCharacter), CAP(ThisCharacter)]);
      ELSE LastWasLetter := TRUE
      END;
    ELSE LastWasLetter := FALSE
    END;
    LastCharacter := ThisCharacter
  END;
```

```
    WriteLn; WriteLn;
    WriteString("Occurrences of letter pairs"); WriteLn; WriteLn;
    FOR FirstLetter := "A" TO "Z" DO
      FOR SecondLetter := "A" TO "Z" DO
        IF Count[FirstLetter, SecondLetter] <> 0 THEN
          Write(FirstLetter); Write(SecondLetter); WriteString(": ");
          WriteCard(Count[FirstLetter, SecondLetter], 3); WriteLn;
        END
      END
    END;
    CloseInput
  END
END Exercise83.
```

Exercise 9.2

```
MODULE Exercise92;

  FROM InOut IMPORT Write, WriteString, WriteCard, WriteInt, WriteLn;
  FROM ValidInput IMPORT GetCardinal, GetBoolean;

  (* This program repeatedly reads four pairs of values which represent the
     vertices of a quadrilateral on a cardinal grid, and determines whether
     it is a square, a rectangle, or otherwise.                          *)

  CONST XLimit = 100; YLimit = 100;

  TYPE Coordinates = RECORD X: [0..XLimit]; Y: [0..YLimit] END;
       Point = (A, B, C, D);

  VAR Vertex: ARRAY Point OF Coordinates;
      ThisPoint: Point; UserFinished: BOOLEAN; I: CARDINAL;

  PROCEDURE SquareOfLength(P1, P2: Point): CARDINAL;

    VAR XStep: [-XLimit..XLimit]; YStep: [-YLimit..YLimit];

    BEGIN
      XStep := INTEGER(Vertex[P1].X) - INTEGER(Vertex[P2].X);
      YStep := INTEGER(Vertex[P1].Y) - INTEGER(Vertex[P2].Y);
      RETURN XStep*XStep + YStep*YStep
    END SquareOfLength;
```

```
BEGIN
  REPEAT
    WriteLn;
    WriteString("Enter details of the 4 points");
    WriteString(" - terminate each number with <RETURN>"); WriteLn;
    FOR ThisPoint := A TO D DO
      WITH Vertex[ThisPoint] DO
        GetCardinal("Enter x coordinate", I, 0, XLimit); X := I;
        GetCardinal("Enter y coordinate", I, 0, YLimit); Y := I
      END
    END;
    WriteString("The points");
    FOR ThisPoint := A TO D DO
      WITH Vertex[ThisPoint] DO
        WriteString(" ("); WriteCard(X, 1); Write(",");
        WriteCard(Y, 1); Write(")")
      END
    END;
    WriteString(" represent a ");
    IF (SquareOfLength(A, B) = SquareOfLength(C, D)) AND
      (SquareOfLength(B, C) = SquareOfLength(D, A)) AND
      (SquareOfLength(A, C) = SquareOfLength(B, D)) THEN
      (* opposite sides and diagonals are equal *)
      IF SquareOfLength(A, B) = SquareOfLength(B, C) THEN
        WriteString("square")
      ELSE WriteString("rectangle")
      END
    ELSE WriteString("quadrilateral")
    END;
    WriteLn;
    GetBoolean("Are you finished ?", UserFinished)
  UNTIL UserFinished
END Exercise92.
```

Exercise 10.4

```
MODULE Exercise104;
  FROM InOut IMPORT WriteString, WriteCard, WriteLn;
  FROM ValidInput IMPORT GetCardinal, GetBoolean;
  (* This program reads a bar length and a list of outstanding orders for
    lengths to be cut from such bars, and chooses (by recursive trial and
    error) the set of ordered lengths to be cut to minimize bar wastage.  *)
  CONST MaximumNumberOfOrders = 15;

  TYPE OrderNumber = [1..MaximumNumberOfOrders];
       OrderSet = SET OF OrderNumber;

  VAR SizeOfOrderList: [0..MaximumNumberOfOrders];
      Length: ARRAY OrderNumber OF CARDINAL;
      BestSet: OrderSet; ActualBarLength, BestLength: CARDINAL;

  (* Sets of order numbers are used to describe the trial solution, the
    best solution so far, and potential components of the solution.
    BestSet—the orders making up the best solution found so far.
    BestLength—the total length of the orders in BestSet              *)
  PROCEDURE GetOrderList;
    VAR InputComplete: BOOLEAN;
    BEGIN
      WriteString("Now input the current order list"); WriteLn;
      SizeOfOrderList := 0;
      REPEAT
        INC(SizeOfOrderList);
        GetCardinal("Enter next order length",
                    Length[SizeOfOrderList], 1, MAX(CARDINAL));
        GetBoolean("Is the order list complete ?", InputComplete)
      UNTIL InputComplete OR (SizeOfOrderList = MaximumNumberOfOrders);
    END GetOrderList;

  PROCEDURE OutputSet(Set: OrderSet);
    VAR ThisOrderNumber: OrderNumber;
    BEGIN
    FOR ThisOrderNumber := 1 TO SizeOfOrderList DO
      IF ThisOrderNumber IN Set THEN
        WriteCard(Length[ThisOrderNumber], 4); WriteString(" mm"); WriteLn
      END
    END;
    END OutputSet;
```

```
PROCEDURE TrySolution(TrialLength: CARDINAL;
                      TrialOrders, OrdersRemaining: OrderSet);
  (* TrialLength—the total length of orders in TrialOrders.
  TrialOrders—orders in the current trial solution.
  OrdersRemaining—orders available for inclusion in the trial solution *)
  VAR NextOrder: [0..MaximumNumberOfOrders];
BEGIN
  IF TrialLength <= ActualBarLength THEN
    (* this is an acceptable solution *)
    IF TrialLength > BestLength THEN
      (* best solution so far, so record it *)
      BestSet := TrialOrders; BestLength := TrialLength
    END;
    NextOrder := 0;
    WHILE OrdersRemaining <> OrderSet {} DO
      (* find an available order number *)
      REPEAT INC(NextOrder) UNTIL NextOrder IN OrdersRemaining;
      (* remove it from OrdersRemaining *)
      EXCL(OrdersRemaining, NextOrder);
      (* does it improve the solution? *)
      TrySolution(TrialLength + Length[NextOrder],
                  TrialOrders + OrderSet{NextOrder},
                  OrdersRemaining)
    END
  END
END TrySolution;

BEGIN
  GetCardinal("Give the manufactured bar length",
              ActualBarLength, 1, MAX(CARDINAL));
  WriteString("The manufactured bar length is ");
  WriteCard(ActualBarLength, 5); WriteLn; WriteLn;
  GetOrderList;
  WriteString("Order List"); WriteLn;
  OutputSet(OrderSet {1..SizeOfOrderList}); WriteLn; WriteLn;
  BestLength := 0; BestSet := OrderSet {};
  TrySolution(0, OrderSet {}, OrderSet {1..SizeOfOrderList});
  WriteString("Optimal order set"); WriteLn; OutputSet(BestSet); WriteLn;
  WriteString("Wastage in cutting = ");
  WriteCard(ActualBarLength - BestLength, 4); WriteString(" mm"); WriteLn
END Exercise104.
```

Exercise 11.2

```
MODULE Exercise112;
  FROM InOut IMPORT
    OpenInput, CloseInput, OpenOutput, CloseOutput, EOL,
    Read, ReadCard, termCH, Done, WriteLn, WriteString, WriteCard;
  FROM Storage IMPORT ALLOCATE, DEALLOCATE;
  (* This program reads a file of employee name/telephone number records,
    and outputs a list of telephone numbers and associated employees     *)
  CONST NameLength = 16;
  TYPE NameRange = [1..NameLength];
       Spelling = ARRAY NameRange OF CHAR;
       PhoneNumber = CARDINAL;
       Employee = RECORD Name: Spelling; Number: PhoneNumber END;
       ListPointer = POINTER TO Occupant;
       Occupant = RECORD Name: Spelling; NextOccupant: ListPointer END;
       ListOfOccupants = RECORD First, Last: ListPointer END;
       RoomPointer = POINTER TO RoomRecord;
       RoomRecord = RECORD
                        Number: PhoneNumber;
                        Occupants: ListOfOccupants;
                        NextRoom: RoomPointer
                    END;
  VAR FirstRoom: RoomPointer;
  PROCEDURE GetEmployeeRecord(VAR ThisEmployee: Employee;
                              VAR EndOfFile: BOOLEAN);
    (* read next employee record, if any *)
    VAR I: NameRange; Ch: CHAR;
    BEGIN
      WITH ThisEmployee DO
        Read(Name[1]);
        IF Done THEN
          EndOfFile := FALSE;
          FOR I := 2 TO NameLength DO Read(Name[I]) END;
          ReadCard(Number);
          Ch := termCH; WHILE Ch <> EOL DO Read(Ch) END
        ELSE EndOfFile := TRUE
        END
      END
    END GetEmployeeRecord;
```

```
PROCEDURE LocateRoom(NumberSought: PhoneNumber;
                     VAR RoomFound: RoomPointer);
  (* create new room record on room list for NumberSought, if
     necessary, and return pointer to room record in either case *)
  VAR ThisRoom, PreviousRoom: RoomPointer; PositionFound: BOOLEAN;
  PROCEDURE InsertNewRoomRecord;
    (* insert a record for NumberSought between Previous- and ThisRoom *)
    VAR NewRoom: RoomPointer;
    BEGIN
      ALLOCATE(NewRoom, SIZE(RoomRecord));
      WITH NewRoom^ DO
        Number := NumberSought;
        WITH Occupants DO First := NIL; Last := NIL END;
        NextRoom := ThisRoom
      END;
      IF PreviousRoom = NIL THEN FirstRoom := NewRoom
      ELSE PreviousRoom^.NextRoom := NewRoom
      END;
      RoomFound := NewRoom
    END InsertNewRoomRecord;
  BEGIN
    ThisRoom := FirstRoom; PreviousRoom := NIL;
    PositionFound := FALSE;
    WHILE NOT PositionFound AND (ThisRoom <> NIL) DO
      IF ThisRoom^.Number >= NumberSought THEN
        PositionFound := TRUE
      ELSE
        PreviousRoom := ThisRoom;
        ThisRoom := ThisRoom^.NextRoom
      END
    END;
    IF PositionFound THEN
      IF ThisRoom^.Number = NumberSought THEN
        RoomFound := ThisRoom
      ELSE InsertNewRoomRecord
      END
    ELSE InsertNewRoomRecord
    END
  END LocateRoom;
```

```
PROCEDURE Include(ThisEmployee: Employee; VAR List: ListOfOccupants);
   (* add ThisEmployee to list of occupants List *)
   VAR ThisOccupant: ListPointer;
   BEGIN
      ALLOCATE(ThisOccupant, SIZE(Occupant));
      WITH ThisOccupant^ DO
         Name := ThisEmployee.Name; NextOccupant := NIL
      END;
      WITH List DO
         IF First = NIL THEN First := ThisOccupant
         ELSE Last^.NextOccupant := ThisOccupant
         END;
         Last := ThisOccupant
      END
   END Include;

PROCEDURE OutputDirectory;

   (* output directory as list of phone numbers with users *)

   PROCEDURE OutputOccupants(Number: PhoneNumber;
                                     Occupants: ListOfOccupants);
      (* output phone number Number with list of users Occupants *)
      VAR ThisOccupant, NextOccupantOfRoom: ListPointer;
            FirstLine: BOOLEAN;
      BEGIN
         WriteLn;
         FirstLine := TRUE; NextOccupantOfRoom := Occupants.First;
         REPEAT
            ThisOccupant := NextOccupantOfRoom;
            IF FirstLine THEN
               WriteCard(Number, 6); WriteString(" "); FirstLine := FALSE
            ELSE WriteString("        ")
            END;
            WriteString(ThisOccupant^.Name); WriteLn;
            NextOccupantOfRoom := ThisOccupant^.NextOccupant;
            DEALLOCATE(ThisOccupant, SIZE(Occupant))
         UNTIL NextOccupantOfRoom = NIL
      END OutputOccupants;

   VAR ThisRoom, NextRoomInList: RoomPointer;
   BEGIN
      OpenOutput("");
      IF Done THEN
```

```
        WriteString("ROOM LIST"); WriteLn; WriteLn;
        NextRoomInList := FirstRoom;
        REPEAT
          ThisRoom := NextRoomInList;
          WITH ThisRoom^ DO OutputOccupants(Number, Occupants) END;
          NextRoomInList := ThisRoom^.NextRoom;
          DEALLOCATE(ThisRoom, SIZE(RoomRecord))
        UNTIL NextRoomInList = NIL;
        CloseOutput
      END
    END OutputDirectory;

  VAR RoomOccupied: RoomPointer; ThisEmployee: Employee;
      EndOfEmployeeFile: BOOLEAN;
  BEGIN
    OpenInput("");
    IF Done THEN
      FirstRoom := NIL;
      LOOP
        GetEmployeeRecord(ThisEmployee, EndOfEmployeeFile);
        IF EndOfEmployeeFile THEN EXIT END;
        LocateRoom(ThisEmployee.Number, RoomOccupied);
        Include(ThisEmployee, RoomOccupied^.Occupants)
      END;
      CloseInput;
      OutputDirectory
    END
  END Exercise112.
```

Exercise 12.4

The definition module for the required set package might be as follows:

```
DEFINITION MODULE SetPackage;
  FROM SetInfo IMPORT BaseType;

  (* This module defines an abstract data type Set which represents sets of the
     unbounded ordinal type BaseType. Variables of type Set must be init-
     ialized and finalized using the procedures InitSet and FinalizeSet.
     Direct assignment and test of equality must not be used on variables
     of type Set. The set operators provided are defined below largely in
     terms of the corresponding Modula-2 operations on bounded sets.      *)
```

```
TYPE Set;

PROCEDURE InitSet(VAR S: Set);
PROCEDURE FinalizeSet(VAR S: Set);

PROCEDURE Clear(VAR S: Set); (* S := Set{} *)
PROCEDURE Range(VAR S: Set; L, U: BaseType); (* S := Set{L..U} *)
PROCEDURE Insert(VAR S: Set; I: BaseType); (* INCL(S, I) *)
PROCEDURE Remove(VAR S: Set; I: BaseType); (* EXCL(S, I) *)

PROCEDURE Contains(VAR S: Set; I: BaseType): BOOLEAN; (* I IN S *)
PROCEDURE Empty(VAR S: Set): BOOLEAN; (* S = Set {} *)
PROCEDURE Size(VAR S: Set): CARDINAL; (* cardinality of S *)
PROCEDURE Min(VAR S: Set): BaseType; (* min value in non-empty S *)

PROCEDURE Union(VAR S1, S2, Result: Set);  (* Result := S1 + S2 *)
PROCEDURE Intersection(VAR S1, S2, Result: Set);  (* Result := S1 * S2 *)
PROCEDURE Difference(VAR S1, S2, Result: Set);  (* Result := S1 - S2 *)

PROCEDURE Equals(VAR S1, S2: Set): BOOLEAN; (* S1 = S2 *)
PROCEDURE Subset(VAR S1, S2: Set): BOOLEAN; (* S1 <= S2 *)
END SetPackage.
```

and the corresponding implementation module as follows:

```
IMPLEMENTATION MODULE SetPackage;
  FROM SetInfo IMPORT BaseType;
  FROM InOut IMPORT WriteLn, WriteString;
  FROM Storage IMPORT ALLOCATE, DEALLOCATE;

  (* This module implements the abstract data type Set, as defined in the
     corresponding definition module, using a Boolean array representation. *)

  TYPE Set = POINTER TO SetRecord;
  TYPE SetRecord = RECORD
                     Member: ARRAY BaseType OF BOOLEAN;
                     Size: CARDINAL
                   END;

  PROCEDURE InitSet(VAR S: Set);
    BEGIN
      ALLOCATE(S, SIZE(SetRecord))
    END InitSet;
```

```
PROCEDURE FinalizeSet(VAR S: Set);
 BEGIN
   DEALLOCATE(S, SIZE(SetRecord))
 END FinalizeSet;

PROCEDURE Clear(VAR S: Set);
 VAR B: BaseType;
 BEGIN
   WITH S^ DO
     FOR B := MIN(BaseType) TO MAX(BaseType) DO
       Member[B] := FALSE
     END;
     Size := 0
   END
 END Clear;

PROCEDURE Range(VAR S: Set; L, U: BaseType);
 VAR B: BaseType;
 BEGIN
   Clear(S);
   WITH S^ DO
     FOR B := L TO U DO Member[B] := TRUE END;
     Size := ORD(U)–ORD(L)+1
   END
 END Range;

PROCEDURE Insert(VAR S: Set; I: BaseType);
 BEGIN
   WITH S^ DO
     IF NOT Member[I] THEN Member[I] := TRUE; INC(Size) END
   END
 END Insert;

PROCEDURE Remove(VAR S: Set; I: BaseType);
 BEGIN
   WITH S^ DO
     IF Member[I] THEN Member[I] := FALSE; DEC(Size) END
   END
 END Remove;

PROCEDURE Contains(VAR S: Set; I: BaseType): BOOLEAN;
 BEGIN
   RETURN S^.Member[I]
 END Contains;
```

```
PROCEDURE Empty(VAR S: Set): BOOLEAN;
  BEGIN
    RETURN (S^.Size = 0)
  END Empty;

PROCEDURE Size(VAR S: Set): CARDINAL;
  BEGIN
    RETURN S^.Size
  END Size;

PROCEDURE Min(VAR S: Set): BaseType;
  VAR B: BaseType;
  BEGIN
    WITH S^ DO
      IF Size = 0 THEN (* error - result is undefined *)
      ELSE
        B := MIN(BaseType);
        LOOP
          IF Member[B] THEN RETURN B ELSE INC(B) END
        END
      END
    END
  END Min;

PROCEDURE Union(VAR S1, S2, Result: Set);
  VAR B: BaseType;
  BEGIN
    WITH Result^ DO
      Size := 0;
      FOR B := MIN(BaseType) TO MAX(BaseType) DO
        IF S1^.Member[B] OR S2^.Member[B] THEN
          Member[B] := TRUE; INC(Size)
        ELSE Member[B] := FALSE
        END
      END
    END
  END Union;

PROCEDURE Intersection(VAR S1, S2, Result: Set);
  VAR B: BaseType;
  BEGIN
    WITH Result^ DO
      Size := 0;
```

```
          FOR B := MIN(BaseType) TO MAX(BaseType) DO
            IF S1^.Member[B] AND S2^.Member[B] THEN
              Member[B] := TRUE; INC(Size)
            ELSE Member[B] := FALSE
            END
          END
        END
      END Intersection;

    PROCEDURE Difference(VAR S1, S2, Result: Set);
      VAR B: BaseType;
      BEGIN
        WITH Result^ DO
          Size := 0;
          FOR B := MIN(BaseType) TO MAX(BaseType) DO
            IF S1^.Member[B] AND NOT S2^.Member[B] THEN
              Member[B] := TRUE; INC(Size)
            ELSE Member[B] := FALSE
            END
          END
        END
      END Difference;

    PROCEDURE Equals(VAR S1, S2: Set): BOOLEAN;
      VAR B: BaseType;
      BEGIN
        FOR B := MIN(BaseType) TO MAX(BaseType) DO
          IF S1^.Member[B] <> S2^.Member[B] THEN RETURN FALSE END
        END;
        RETURN TRUE
      END Equals;

    PROCEDURE Subset(VAR S1, S2: Set): BOOLEAN;
      VAR B: BaseType;
      BEGIN
        FOR B := MIN(BaseType) TO MAX(BaseType) DO
          IF S1^.Member[B] AND NOT S2^.Member[B] THEN
            RETURN FALSE
          END
        END;
        RETURN TRUE
      END Subset;
    END SetPackage.
```

To use this package in implementing the sieve of Eratosthenes, the definition module SetInfo might be defined as follows:

```
DEFINITION MODULE SetInfo;
  TYPE BaseType = [2..100];
  END SetInfo.
```

with the sieve program itself taking the following form:

```
MODULE Eratosthenes;
  FROM SetInfo IMPORT BaseType;
  FROM SetPackage IMPORT Set, InitSet, FinalizeSet, Range, Clear,
                                Contains, Min, Insert, Remove, Empty;
  FROM ValidInput IMPORT GetCardinal;
  FROM InOut IMPORT WriteString, WriteLn, WriteCard;

  (* This program outputs the prime numbers up to an input bound N *)

  TYPE PrimeRange = BaseType;

  VAR Sieve, Primes: Set; N, Multiple: CARDINAL; NextPrime, I: PrimeRange;
  BEGIN
    GetCardinal("Enter upper prime limit", N, 2, MAX(BaseType));

    (* find primes by sieve method *)
    InitSet(Sieve); Range(Sieve, 2, N);
    InitSet(Primes); Clear(Primes);
    REPEAT
      (* extract next prime from sieve *)
      NextPrime := Min(Sieve); Insert(Primes, NextPrime);
      (* remove NextPrime and all multiples from sieve *)
      Multiple := NextPrime;
      REPEAT
        Remove(Sieve, Multiple); Multiple := Multiple + NextPrime
      UNTIL Multiple > N
    UNTIL Empty(Sieve);

    (* output primes found *)
    WriteString("Primes between 2 and "); WriteCard(N, 1); WriteLn;
    FOR I := 2 TO N DO
      IF Contains(Primes, I) THEN WriteCard(I, 1); WriteLn END
    END;
    FinalizeSet(Sieve); FinalizeSet(Primes)
  END Eratosthenes.
```

Exercise 13.3

```
MODULE Exercise133;
  FROM SYSTEM IMPORT ADDRESS, NEWPROCESS, TRANSFER;
  FROM InOut IMPORT
    OpenInput, CloseInput, Done, Read, Write, WriteString, WriteLn;
  FROM Storage IMPORT ALLOCATE;

  (* This program reads an encoded character string from an input file
    and outputs a translation which is defined as follows:

    (a) input spaces are ignored;
    (b) an input digit N causes the next character to be replicated N times;
    (c) other characters are output without translation.

    The input string is terminated by the first period, which is not output.

    The translated string is output as 60-character lines, with a space
    between each group of 3 characters.

    The program is implemented as two coroutines:
    coroutine Input which handles input spaces and replication, and
    coroutine Output which handles output formatting and termination.    *)

  CONST WorkSpaceSize = 25; (* implementation-dependent *)
        Terminator = "."; MaximumNumberInGroup = 3; LineLength = 60;

  VAR Input, Output, MainProgram: ADDRESS; WorkSpace: ADDRESS;
      CharacterToOutput: CHAR;

  PROCEDURE InputControl;

    (* This procedure defines the Input coroutine *)

    VAR NextChar: CHAR; Digit, J: [0..9];
    BEGIN
      LOOP
        REPEAT Read(NextChar) UNTIL Ch <> " ";
        IF (NextChar >= "0") AND (NextChar <= "9") THEN
          Digit := ORD(NextChar) - ORD("0");
          Read(CharacterToOutput);
          FOR J := 1 TO Digit DO TRANSFER(Input, Output) END
        ELSE
          CharacterToOutput := NextChar; TRANSFER(Input, Output)
        END
      END
    END InputControl;
```

```
PROCEDURE OutputControl;
  (* This procedure defines the Output coroutine *)
  VAR GroupSize: [0..MaximumNumberInGroup];
      NumberOfGroups: CARDINAL;
  BEGIN
    GroupSize := 0; NumberOfGroups := 0;
    LOOP
      IF CharacterToOutput = Terminator THEN
        WriteLn; TRANSFER(Output, MainProgram)
      ELSE
        Write(CharacterToOutput);
        INC(GroupSize);
        IF GroupSize = MaximumNumberInGroup THEN
          Write(" "); INC(NumberOfGroups);
          IF NumberOfGroups =
            LineLength DIV (MaximumNumberInGroup+1) THEN
            WriteLn; NumberOfGroups := 0
          END;
          GroupSize := 0
        END;
        TRANSFER(Output, Input)
      END
    END
  END OutputControl;

BEGIN
  OpenInput("");
  IF Done THEN
    ALLOCATE(WorkSpace, WorkSpaceSize);
    NEWPROCESS(InputControl, WorkSpace, WorkSpaceSize, Input);
    ALLOCATE(WorkSpace, WorkSpaceSize);
    NEWPROCESS(OutputControl, WorkSpace, WorkSpaceSize, Output);
    TRANSFER(MainProgram, Input);
    CloseInput
  END
END Exercise133.
```

Index

This index provides a comprehensive list of the words and terms used throughout the book. Those shown in *italics* are standard terms used in the definition of Modula-2. The page number of a defining occurrence of a word or term is shown in **heavy** type, with other significant occurrences in normal type.

ABS 24 26
absolute variable 318
abstract data types 298
actual-parameter **114**
actual-parameter-list 100 113 **114** 124
actual-value **114**
actual-variable **114**
addition-operator **45**
ADDRESS 308 356
ADR 308 356
ALLOCATE 232 357
AND 29
arithmetic operators 23 26
array-type **146** 177
array-variable **147**
assignment compatible 47 160
assignment-statement 42 **46**

backtracking 221
base-type **209**
binary tree 251
BITSET 226 308 310
block **19** 101 123 261 272
block structure 107
BOOLEAN 29

CAP 28
CARDINAL 25
cardinality 32 170 209
case-label-list **74** 195
case-labels **74**
case-limb **74**
case-statement 68 **74** 196
CHAR 27
CHR 28
CloseInput 63
CloseOutput 64
comments 17
compilation-unit **272**
component-variable 46 **177**
concurrent processes 323
Condition 325 328
conditional-statement 66 **68**
constant-declaration **34** 272
constant-declaration-part 19 **34**
constant-expression 32 **35** 74
constant-identifier **35** 46
constant-set **211**
control characters 17
control variable 84
coroutines 310
cyclic buffer 296

data types 22
DEALLOCATE 234 357
DEC 48
decimal-digit **13** 14
declaration **19**
declaration-part **19** 101
definition **272**
definition-module **272**
digit **12** 15
digit-sequence **14**
DISPOSE 235
DIV 23
Done 57 354

EBNF 10
element **210**
element-list **210**
element-type **146**
empty-statement 42 67
entire-variable 46 **177**
enumerated-type **31** 36
equivalence operator 31
EXCL 213
exclusive or operator 31
exit-statement 42 **94**
export-list **261** 269 274
expression 42 **45**
expression-list **147**
Extended Backus–Naur Form 10

factor **45** 124
FALSE 29 35
field-designator 177 **181**
field-identifier 46 **180** 181
field-list **179** 195
field-list-sequence **179** 195
field-width 53
final-expression **84**
fixed-part **180**
FLOAT 27

formal-parameter-list 101 **113** 123
formal-parameter-section **114**
formal-procedure 132
formal-specification **131**
formal-type **114** 131
formal-type-list **131**
for-statement 80 **84** 147
function-body **123**
function-call 45 **124**
function-heading **123**
function-identifier 45 **123**
function-procedure-declaration **123**

hexadecimal-digit **13**
HIGH 170
host-type-identifier **32**

identifier **14**
identifier-list **19** 31 38 180
if-statement **68**
implementation-module **272**
implication operator 31
import-list 19 58 **261** 270 272
IN 212
INC 48
INCL 213
increment-expression **84**
indexed-variable **147** 177
index-type **146**
initial-expression **84**
InOut 52 354
input parameter 116
input stream 51
INTEGER 23
integer-number **13**
intersection 213

letter **12**
library modules 52 353
lifetime 111 136 262 288

LONGINT 25
LONGREAL 27
loop-statement 80 **93**
lower-bound 32

MathLib0 291 353
MAX 37
MIN 37
MOD 23
module-declaration 19 **261**
monitors 327
multiplication-operator 45 **45**
mutual exclusion 323

NEW 232
NEWPROCESS 307 311 357
NIL 35 233
NOT 29
number **13** 45

octal-digit **13** 17
ODD 31
opaque types 282
open array parameters 169
open-array-schema 114 131 **170** 172
OpenInput 63 354
OpenOutput 64 354
operator precedence 42
OR 29
ORD 28 30 32
ordinal types 24 29 30 32 37
output parameter 115
output stream 51
overflow 24 26

pointer-type 36 39 **230**
pointer-variable 229 **232**
predecessor 24 48
priority 261 272 **327**

procedure-body **101**
procedure-declaration 19 **101**
procedure-heading **101** 272
procedure-identifier 45 **101**
procedure-statement 42 **100**
procedure-type 36 **131**
procedure variable 132
process 323
Processes 325 331
program-heading 10 **19**
program-module **19** 272

qualified-identifier **16** 269 287
Queue 294
QueuePackage 299

Read 56 354
ReadCard 56 355
ReadInt 56 355
ReadReal 56 356
ReadString 58 161 171 355
REAL 26
RealInOut 52 58 356
real-number 13 **14**
record-type 177 **179**
record-variable **181** 182
recursion 110 135
referenced-variable 46 177 **232**
relational-operator **45** 211
relative complement 213
repeat-statement 80 **83**
repetitive-statement 66 **80**
reserved words 12 351
result-type **123** 131
return-statement 42 **105**

scale-factor **14**
scope 39 107 109 286
selective updating 181
selector 74

separate compilation 272 281
set 45 **210**
set-type 177 **209**
side effects 126
sign **11**
signed-digit-sequence **11**
simple-expression **45**
simple-statement **42**
simple-type **36**
SIZE 232 309
special-symbol **12**
stack 235
standard functions 24–31 37 170 232
standard identifiers 16 351
statement **42** 66
statement-part 19 **41** 101 262 278 288
statement-procedure-declaration **101**
statement-sequence **41** 66
stepwise refinement 59
Storage 232 235 357
string **17** 45 159
structurally compatible 133
structured-statement 42 **66**
structured-type **36** 177
subrange-type **32** 36
subscripting 147
successor 24 48
symmetric difference 213
SYSTEM 307 356

tag-field **195**
term **45**
termCH 57 161 354
TRANSFER 307 311 357
transput parameter 115
TRUE 29 35
TRUNC 27

TSIZE 307 309 357
type **36** 38 177
type-declaration **36**
type-declaration-part 19 **36**
type-identifier **36**
type transfer functions 25 309

union 213
unsigned-digit-sequence **11**
unstructured types 23
upper-bound **32**

VAL 37 49
value parameters 114 116 172
value-parameter-section **114**
variable 37 **46** 177
variable-declaration **37** 272
variable-declaration-part 19 **37**
variable-identifier **38** 46
variable parameters 114 172
variable-parameter-section **114**
variant **195**
variant-part 179 **195** 199
variant records 195

while-statement 80 **81**
with-statement 66 **182** 196
WORD 307 308 356
Write 53 355
WriteCard 53 355
WriteInt 53 355
WriteLn 53 355
WriteReal 53 356
WriteString 53 160 171 355